# NEW WRITING 5

*New Writing 5* is the fifth volume of an annual anthology which promotes the best in contemporary literature. It brings together some of our most formidable talent, placing new names alongside more established ones, and includes poetry, essays, short stories and extracts from novels in progress. Distinctive, innovative and entertaining, it is essential reading for all those interested in British writing today. *New Writing 5* is published by Vintage, in association with the British Council.

**Christopher Hope** was born in Johannesburg. His novels include *A Separate Development* (winner of the 1981 David Higham Prize for Fiction), *Kruger's Alp* (1985 Whitbread Prize for Fiction), *The Hottentot Room*, *My Chocolate Redeemer* and *Serenity House* (short-listed for the 1992 Booker Prize). His new novel, *Darkest England*, will be published in 1996. Other books include *The Love Songs of Nathan J. Swirsky* and *Moscow! Moscow!*

**Peter Porter** was born in Australia in 1929 and has lived in London since 1951. He has published thirteen collections of poetry and collaborated with the painter, Arthur Boyd, on four books of poems and pictures. He is also a reviewer of literature and music in journals and for the BBC. After his *Collected Poems* (Oxford University Press, 1983), his recent publications include *The Automatic Oracle* (1987), *Possible Worlds* (1989) and *The Chair of Babel* (1992).

*Also available from Vintage*

*New Writing 4*
edited by A. S. Byatt and Alan Hollinghurst

# Praise for *New Writing 4*

'Who has time to read everything even all-time favourites write, let alone keep up with the brilliant new talent that squeezes into the literary limelight each year? Now you can catch up with the known and catch on to the new with this terrific anthology of short stories, extracts from novels-to-come, essays and poetry. *New Writing* is the publisher's equivalent of a first-class pudding trolley'

*Cosmopolitan*

'Abundant with good and even daring contributions'

*Guardian*

'A strong, varied collection . . . It is a pleasure, at the cusp of the millennium, to find British writing so outward looking. *New Writing 4* is a reassuring outpost on the path ahead'

*The Times*

'*New Writing 4* is one of the rare catch-all anthologies to offer a truly appetizing buffet of poetry, essays, short stories and excerpts of novels-in-progress'

*Scotland on Sunday*

'The good thing about *New Writing* is its unpredictability. It is a fascinating mix of established authors and new writers – a must for anyone interested in where writing is going'

*Daily Mirror*

'With one Booker Prize-winner and another short-listed candidate as editors, this annual selection should be seriously top-hole stuff; and so it is. Some of the finest Scots of old and new generations are here ... amid a judiciously chosen host of starry and lesser known British fiction-writers, poets and essayists ... Over 400 pages of the liveliest new writing at an affordable price'

*Scotsman*

'Excellent ... The anthology succeeds admirably, marshalling an eclectic rattlebag of literary gems into a forceful argument for the burgeoning strength of British writing'

*Independent on Sunday*

# New
# Writing
# 5

edited by

## CHRISTOPHER HOPE
### and
## PETER PORTER

*V*

VINTAGE

in association with
The British Council

Published by Vintage 1996

2 4 6 8 10 9 7 5 3 1

Collection copyright © The British Council 1996
edited by Christopher Hope and Peter Porter
For copyright of contributors see pages xii–xiii

Vintage
Random House, 20 Vauxhall Bridge Road, London SW1V 2SA

Random House Australia (Pty) Limited
20 Alfred Street, Milsons Point, Sydney
New South Wales 2061, Australia

Random House New Zealand Limited
18 Poland Road, Glenfield,
Auckland 10, New Zealand

Random House South Africa (Pty) Limited
PO Box 337, Bergvlei, South Africa

Random House UK Limited Reg. No. 954009

A CIP catalogue record for this book
is available from the British Library

ISBN 0099545411

Papers used by Random House UK Ltd are natural,
recyclable products made from wood grown in
sustainable forests. The manufacturing processes
conform to the environmental regulations of the
country of origin

Phototypeset by Intype, London
Printed and bound in Great Britain by
The Guernsey Press Co. Ltd., Guernsey, Channel Islands

# PREFACE

*New Writing 5* is the fifth volume of an annual anthology founded in 1992 to provide an outlet for new short stories, work in progress, poetry and essays by established and new writers working in Britain or in the English language. The book is designed primarily as a forum for British writers, and the main object is to present a multi-faceted picture of modern Britain; contributions from English-language writers of non-British nationality will occasionally be accepted if they further this aim. *New Writing* was initiated by the British Council's Literature Department, who hoped through it to respond to the strong interest in the latest British writing not only within Britain but overseas, where access to fresh developments is often difficult. The intention is that, over the years, and through changing editorships, it will provide a stimulating, variegated, useful and reasonably reliable guide to the cultural and especially the literary scene in Britain during the 1990s.

*New Writing 6*, edited by A. S. Byatt and Peter Porter, will appear in March 1997. Though work is commissioned, submissions of unpublished material for consideration (stories, poetry, essays, literary interviews and sections from forthcoming works of fiction) are welcome. Two copies of submissions should be sent: they should be *double-spaced*, with page numbers (*no* staples), and accompanied by a stamped addressed envelope for the return of the material, if it cannot be used. They should be sent to

> *New Writing*
> Literature Department
> The British Council
> 11 Portland Place
> London W1N 4EJ

The annual deadline is 30 April.

# CONTENTS

CONTENTS

**Extracts from novels in progress**

**Poetry**

# CONTENTS

# CONTENTS

# INTRODUCTION

WHAT MAKES WRITING 'new'? Little is ever really new and when it is, that fact often emerges later. If a piece of writing is any good, you are too busy reading it to say how new it is. This strikes me not so much as a problem but as part of the solution. Since editors are also people, they wish for the moment when professional judgement falters and falls silent, something catches fire and you turn into that lucky being, the beguiled reader.

Where the spark showed we celebrated the fact – though choosing was never easy. The energy that goes into the solitary, sedentary, alarming occupation of putting words on paper was overwhelming. *New Writing 5*, when packed between covers, is a capacious, broad anthology. But it did not start like that. It began tall, with a Manhattan of submissions: flurries of poems and stories which, if laid one on another, would have towered like skyscrapers.

Our choices have been eclectic; running order arbitrary. We lay story, poem, libretto, essay, autobiography beside each other. The voices at play, like the lands from which the contributors come, are very diverse. The sad, the sly, the shocking, the unexpected and the impudent take their places and speak for themselves. Here is new writing from Britain, Ireland, China, India, Africa and Eastern Europe.

The result is not so much a series of snapshots as a photomontage of some five dozen writers at work. If we have a prejudice, and editors are a bundle of prejudices, it is for the vigorous and unexpected. But is this new? I invite the reader to share our happy confusion.

Christopher Hope

# A. S. Byatt

## A LAMIA IN THE CEVENNES

IN THE MID-1980s, Bernard Lycett-Kean decided that Thatcher's Britain was uninhabitable, a land of dog eat dog, lung-corroding ozone and floating money, of which there was at once far too much and far too little. He sold his West Hampstead flat and bought a small stone house on a Cevenol hillside. He had three rooms, and a large barn, which he weatherproofed, using it as a studio in winter and a storehouse in summer. He did not know how he would take to solitude, and laid in a large quantity of red wine, of which he drank a good deal at first, and afterwards much less. He discovered that the effect of the air and the light and the extremes of heat and cold were enough, indeed too much, without alcohol. He stood on the terrace in front of his house and battled with these things, with mistral and tramontane and thunderbolts and howling clouds. The Cevennes is a place of extreme weather. There were also days of white heat, and days of yellow heat, and days of burning blue heat. He produced some paintings of heat and light, with very little else in them, and some other paintings of the small river which ran along the foot of the steep, terraced hill on which his house stood; these were dark green and dotted with the bright blue of the kingfisher and the electric blue of the dragonflies.

These paintings he packed in his van and took to London and sold for largish sums of the despised money. He went to his own Private View and found he had lost the habit of conversation. He stared and snorted. He was a big man, a

1

burly man, his stare seemed aggressive when it was largely baffled. His old friends were annoyed. He himself found London just as rushing and evil-smelling and unreal as he had been imagining it. He hurried back to the Cevennes. With his earnings, he built himself a swimming-pool, where once there had been a patch of baked mud and a few bushes.

It is not quite right to say he built it. It was built by the Jardinerie Emeraude, two enterprising young men, who dug and lined and carried mud and monstrous stones, and built a humming power-house full of taps and pipes and a swirling cauldron of filter-sand. The pool was blue, a swimming-pool blue, lined with a glittering tile mosaic, and with a mosaic dolphin cavorting amiably in its depths, a dark blue dolphin with a pale blue eye. It was not a boring rectangular pool, but an irregular oval triangle, hugging the contour of the terrace on which it lay. It had a white stone rim, moulded to the hand, delightful to touch when it was hot in the sun.

The two young men were surprised that Bernard wanted it blue. Blue was a little *moche*, they thought. People now were making pools steel-grey or emerald-green, or even dark wine-red. But Bernard's mind was full of the blue dots now visible across the southern mountains when you travelled from Paris to Montpellier by air. It was a recalcitrant blue, a blue that asked to be painted by David Hockney and only by David Hockney. He felt something else could and must be done with that blue. It was a blue he needed to know and fight. His painting was combative painting. That blue, that amiable, non-natural aquamarine was different in the uncompromising mountains from what it was in Hollywood. There were no naked male backsides by his pool, no umbrellas, no tennis-courts. The river-water was sombre and weedy, full of little shoals of needle-fishes and their shadows, of curling water-snakes and the triangular divisions of flow around pebbles and boulders. This mild blue, here, was to be seen in *that* terrain.

He swam more and more, trying to understand the blue, which was different when it was under the nose, ahead of the eyes, over and around the sweeping hands and the flick-

ering toes and the groin and the armpits and the hairs of his
chest, which held bubbles of air for a time. His shadow in
the blue moved over a pale egg-shell mosaic, a darker blue,
with huge paddle-shaped hands. The light changed, and with
it, everything. The best days were under racing cloud, when
the aquamarine took on a cool grey tone, which was then
chased back, or rolled away, by the flickering gold-in-blue of
yellow light in liquid. In front of his prow or chin in the
brightest lights moved a mesh of hexagonal threads, flashing
rainbow colours, flashing liquid silver-gilt, with a hint of
molten glass; on such days lines of liquid fire, rosy and yellow
and clear, ran across the dolphin, who lent them a thread of
intense blue. But the surface could be a reflective plane, with
the trees hanging in it, with two white diagonals where the
aluminium steps entered. The shadows of the sides were a
deeper blue but not a deep blue, a blue not reflective and yet
lying flatly *under* reflections. The pool was deep, for the
Emeraude young men envisaged much diving. The wind
changed the surface, frilled and furred it, flecked it with
diamond drops, shirred it and made a witless patchwork of
its plane. His own motion changed the surface – the longer
he swam, the faster he swam, the more the glassy hills and
valleys chopped and changed and ran back on each other.

Swimming was *volupté* – he used the French word, because
of Matisse. *Luxe, calme et volupté.* Swimming was a strenu-
ous battle with immense problems, of geometry, of chemistry,
of apprehension, of style, of other colours. He put pots of
petunias and geraniums near the pool. The bright hot pinks
and purples were dangerous. They did something to that
blue.

The stone was easy. Almost too blandly easy. He could
paint chalky white and creamy sand and cool grey and para-
doxical hot grey; he could understand the shadows in the
high rough wall of monstrous cobble-stones that bounded
his land.

The problem was the sky. Swimming in one direction, he
was headed towards a great rounded green mountain, thick
with the bright yellow-green of dense chestnut-trees, making

a slightly innocent, simple arc against the sky. Whereas the other way, he swam towards crags, towards a bowl of bald crags, with a few pines and lines of dark shale. And against the green hump the blue sky was one blue, and against the bald stone another, even when for a few brief hours it was uniformly blue overhead, that rich blue, that cobalt, deep washed blue of the South, which fought all the blues of the pool, all the green-tinged, duck-egg tinged blues of the shifting water. But the sky has also its greenish days, and its powdery-hazed days, and its theatrical louring days, and none of these blues and whites and golds and ultramarines and faded washes harmonised in any way with the pool blues, though they all went through their changes and splendours in the same world, in which he and his shadow swam, in which he and his shadow stood in the sun and struggled to record them.

He muttered to himself. Why bother. Why does this *matter* so much. *What difference does it make to anything if I solve this blue* and just start again. I could just sit down and drink wine. I could go and be useful in a cholera-camp in Colombia or Ethiopia. *Why bother to render the transparency in solid paint or air on a bit of board?* I could *just stop*.

He could not.

He tried oil paint and acrylic, water-colour and gouache, large designs and small plain planes and complicated juxtaposed planes. He tried trapping light on thick impasto and tried also glazing his surfaces flat and glossy, like seventeenth-century Dutch or Spanish paintings of silk. One of these almost pleased him, done at night, with the lights under the water and the dark round the stone, on an oval bit of board. But then he thought it was sentimental. He tried veils of watery blues on white in water-colour, he tried Matisse-like patches of blue and petunia – pool blue, sky blue, petunia – he tried Bonnard's mixtures of pastel and gouache.

His brain hurt, and his eyes stared, and he felt whipped by winds and dried by suns.

4

He was happy, in one of the ways human beings have found in which to be happy.

One day he got up as usual and as usual flung himself naked into the water to watch the dawn in the sky and the blue come out of the black and grey in the water.

There was a hissing in his ears, and a stench in his nostrils, perhaps a sulphurous stench, he was not sure; his eyes were sharp but his profession, with spirits and turpentine, had dulled his nostrils. As he moved through the sluggish surface he stirred up bubbles, which broke, foamed, frothed and crusted. He began to leave a trail of white, which reminded him of polluted rivers, of the waste-pipes of tanneries, of deserted mines. He came out rapidly and showered. He sent a fax to the Jardinerie Emeraude. What was Paradise is become the Infernal Pit. Where once I smelled lavender and salt, now I have a mephitic stench. What have you done to my water? Undo it, undo it. I cannot co-exist with these exhalations. His French was more florid than his English. I am polluted, my work is polluted, *I cannot go on.* How could the two young men be brought to recognise the extent of the insult? He paced the terrace like an angry panther. The sickly smell crept like marsh-gas over the flower-pots, through the lavender-bushes. An emerald-green van drew up, with a painted swimming-pool and a painted palm-tree. Every time he saw the van, he was pleased and irritated that this commercial emerald-and-blue had found an exact balance for the difficult aquamarine without admitting any difficulty.

The young men ran along the edge of the pool, peering in, their muscular legs brown under their shorts, their plimsolls padding. The sun came up over the green hill and showed the plague-stricken water-skin, ashy and suppurating. It is all OK, said the young man, this is a product we put in to fight algae, not because you *have* algae, M. Bernard, but in case algae might appear, as a precaution. It will all be exhaled in a week or two, the mousse will go, the water will clear.

'Empty the pool,' said Bernard. '*Now.* Empty it now. I will not co-exist for two weeks with this vapour. Give me back my clean salty water. *This water is my life-work.* Empty it *now.*'

'It will take days to fill,' said one young man, with a French acceptance of Bernard's desperation. 'Also there is the question of the allocation of water, of how much you are permitted to take.'

'We could fetch it up from the river,' said the other. In French this is literally, we could draw it *in* the river, *puiser dans le ruisseau*, like fishing. 'It will be cold, ice-cold from the source, up in the mountain,' said the Emeraude young men.

'Do it,' said Bernard. 'Fill it from the river. I am an Englishman, I swim in the North Sea, I like cold water. Do it. *Now.*'

The young men ran up and down. They turned huge taps in the grey plastic pipes that debouched in the side of the mountain. The swimming-pool soughed and sighed and began still sighing to sink, whilst down below, on the hillside, a frothing flood spread and laughed and pranced and curled and divided and swept into the river. Bernard stalked behind the young men, admonishing them. 'Look at the froth. We are polluting the river.'

'It is only two litres. It is perfectly safe. Everyone has it in his pool, M. Bernard. It is tried and tested, it is a product for *purifying water.*' It is only you, his pleasant voice implied, who is pigheaded enough to insist on voiding it.

The pool became a pit. The mosaic sparkled a little in the sun, but it was a sad sight. It was a deep blue pit of an entirely unproblematic dull texture. Almost like a bathroom floor. The dolphin lost his movement and his fire, and his curvetting ripples, and became a stolid fish in two dimensions. Bernard peered in from the deep end and from the shallow end, and looked over the terrace wall at the hillside where froth was expiring on nettles and brambles. It took almost all day to empty and began to make sounds like a gigantic version of the bath-plug terrors of Bernard's infant dreams.

The two young men appeared carrying an immense boa-constrictor of heavy black plastic pipe, and an implement that looked like a torpedo, or a diver's oxygen pack. The mountainside was steep, and the river ran green and chuckling at its foot. Bernard stood and watched. The coil of pipe was uncoiled, the electricity was connected in his humming pumphouse, and a strange sound began, a regular boum-boum, like the beat of a giant heart, echoing off the green mountain. Water began to gush from the mouth of the pipe into the sad dry depths of his pool-pit. Where it trickled upwards, the mosaic took on a little life again, like crystals glinting.

'It will take all night to fill,' said the young men. 'But do not be afraid, even if the pool overflows, it will not come in your house, the slope is too steep, it will run away back to the river. And tomorrow we will come and regulate it and filter it and you may swim. But it will be very cold.'

'*Tant pis*,' said Bernard.

All night the black tube on the hillside wailed like a monstrous bullfrog, boum-boum, boum-boum. All night the water rose, silent and powerful. Bernard could not sleep; he paced his terrace and watched the silver line creep up the sides of the pit, watched the greenish water sway. Finally he slept, and in the morning his world was awash with river-water, and the heart-beat machine was still howling on the river-bank, boum-boum, boum-boum. He watched a small fish skid and slide across his terrace, flow over the edge and slip in a stream of water down the hillside and back into the river. Everything smelled wet and lively, with no hint of sulphur and no clear smell of purified water. His friend Raymond Potter telephoned from London to say he might come on a visit; Bernard, who could not cope with visitors, was non-committal, and tried to describe his delicious flood as a minor disaster.

'You don't want river-water,' said Raymond Potter. 'What about liver-flukes and things, and bilharzia?'

'They don't have bilharzia in the Cevennes,' said Bernard.

*

The Emeraude young men came and turned off the machine, which groaned, made a sipping sound and relapsed into silence. The water in the pool had a grassy depth it hadn't had. It was a lovely colour, a natural colour, a colour that harmonised with the hills, and it was not the problem Bernard was preoccupied with. It would clear, the young men assured him, once the filtration was working again.

Bernard went swimming in the green water. His body slipped into its usual movements. He looked down for his shadow and thought he saw out of the corner of his eye a swirling movement in the depths, a shadowy coiling. It would be strange, he said to himself, if there were a big snake down there, moving around. The dolphin was blue in green gloom. Bernard spread his arms and legs and floated. He heard a rippling sound of movement, turned his head, and found he was swimming alongside a yellow-green frog, a frog with a salmon patch on its cheek and another on its butt, the colour of the roes of scallops. It made vigorous thrusts with its hind legs, and vanished into the skimmer, from the mouth of which it peered out at Bernard. The underside of its throat beat, beat, cream-coloured. When it emerged, Bernard cupped his hands under its cool wet body and lifted it over the edge: it clung to his fingers with its own tiny fingers, and then went away, in long hops. Bernard went on swimming. There was still a kind of movement in the depths that was not his own.

This persisted for some days, although the young men set the filter in motion, tipped in sacks of white salt, and did indeed restore the aquamarine transparency, as promised. Now and then he saw a shadow that was not his, now and then something moved behind him; he felt the water swirl and tug. This did not alarm him, because he both believed and disbelieved his senses. He liked to imagine a snake. Bernard liked snakes. He liked the darting river-snakes, and the long silver-brown grass-snakes who travelled through the grasses beside the river.

Sometimes he swam at night, and it was at night that he first definitely saw the snake, only for a few moments, after he had switched on the underwater lights, which made the water look like turquoise milk. And there under the milk was something very large, something coiled in two intertwined figures of eight and like no snake he had ever seen, a velvety-black, it seemed, with long bars of crimson and peacock-eyed spots, gold, green, blue, mixed with silver moonshapes, all of which appeared to dim and brighten and breathe under the deep water. Bernard did not try to touch; he sat down cautiously and stared. He could see neither head nor tail; the form appeared to be a continuous coil like a Mobius strip. And the colours changed as he watched them; the gold and silver lit up and went out, like lamps, the eyes expanded and contracted, the bars and stripes flamed with electric vermilion and crimson and then changed to purple, to blue, to green, moving through the rainbow. He tried professionally to commit the forms and the colours to memory. He looked up for a moment at the night sky. The Plough hung very low, and the stars glittered white-gold in Orion's belt on thick midnight velvet. When he looked back, there was the pearly water, vacant.

Many men might have run roaring in terror; the courageous might have prodded with a pool-net, the extravagant might have reached for a shot-gun. What Bernard saw was a solution to his professional problem, at least a nocturnal solution. Between the night sky and the breathing, dissolving eyes and moons in the depths, the colour of the water was solved, dissolved, it became a medium to contain a darkness spangled with living colours. He went in and took notes in water-colour and gouache. He went out and stared and the pool was empty.

For several days he neither saw nor felt the snake. He tried to remember it, and to trace its markings into his pool-paintings, which became very tentative and watery. He swam even more than usual, invoking the creature from time to time. 'Come back,' he said to the pleasant blue depths, to the twisting coiling lines of rainbow light, 'Come back, I need you.'

And then, one day, when a thunderstorm was gathering behind the crest of the mountains, when the sky loured and the pool was unreflective, he felt the alien tug of the other current again, and looked round quick, quick, to catch it. And there was a head, urging itself sinuously through the water beside his own, and there below his body coiled the miraculous black velvet rope or tube, with its shimmering moons and stars, its peacock eyes, its crimson bands.

The head was a snake-head, diamond-shaped, half the size of his own head, swarthy and scaled, with a strange little crown of pale lights hanging above it like its own rainbow. He turned cautiously to look at it and saw that it had large eyes with fringed eyelashes, human eyes, very lustrous, very liquid, very black. He opened his mouth, swallowed water by accident, coughed. The creature watched him, and then opened its mouth, in turn, which was full of small, even, pearly human teeth. Between these protruded a flickering forked tongue, entirely serpentine. Bernard felt a prick of recognition. The creature sighed. It spoke. It spoke in Cevenol French, very sibilant, but comprehensible.

'I am so unhappy,' it said.

'I am sorry,' said Bernard stupidly, treading water. He felt the black coils slide against his naked legs, a tail-tip across his private parts.

'You are a very beautiful man,' said the snake in a languishing voice.

'You are a very beautiful snake,' replied Bernard courteously, watching the absurd eyelashes dip and lift.

'I am not entirely a snake. I am an enchanted spirit, a Lamia. If you will kiss my mouth, I will become a most beautiful woman, and if you will marry me, I will be eternally faithful and gain an immortal soul. I will also bring you power, and riches, and knowledge you never dreamed of. But you must have faith in me.'

Bernard turned over on his side, and floated, disentangling

his brown legs from the twining coloured coils. The snake sighed.

'You do not believe me. You find my present form too loathsome to touch. I love you. I have watched you for months and I love and worship your every movement, your powerful body, your formidable brow, the movements of your hands when you paint. Never in all my thousands of years have I seen so perfect a male being. I will do *anything* for you –'

'Anything?'

'Oh, *anything*. Ask. Do not reject me.'

'What I want,' said Bernard, swimming towards the craggy end of the pool, with the snake stretched out behind him, 'what I want, is to be able to paint your portrait, *as you are*, for certain reasons of my own, and because I find you very beautiful – if you would consent to remain here for a little time, as a snake – with all these amazing colours and lights – if I could paint you *in my pool* – just for a little time –'

'And then you will kiss me, and we will be married, and I shall have an immortal soul?'

'Nobody nowadays believes in immortal souls,' said Bernard.

'It does not matter if you believe in them or not,' said the snake. 'You have one and it will be horribly tormented if you break your pact with me.'

Bernard did not point out that he had not made a pact, not having answered her request yes or no. He wanted quite desperately that she should remain in his pool, in her present form, until he had solved the colours, and was almost prepared for a Faustian damnation.

There followed a few weeks of hectic activity. The Lamia lingered agreeably in the pool, disposing herself wherever she was asked, under or on the water, in figures of three or six or eight or O, in spirals and tight coils. Bernard painted and swam and painted and swam. He swam less since he found the Lamia's wreathing flirtatiousness oppressive, though occasionally to encourage her, he stroked her sleek sides, or

11

wound her tail round his arm or his arm round her tail. He
never painted her head, which he found hideous and repulsive.
Bernard liked snakes but he did not like women. The Lamia
with female intuition began to sense his lack of enthusiasm
for this aspect of her. 'My teeth,' she told him, 'will be lovely
in rosy lips, my eyes will be melting and mysterious in a
human face. Kiss me, Bernard, and you will see.'

'Not yet, not yet,' said Bernard.

'I will not wait for ever,' said the Lamia.

Bernard remembered where he had, so to speak, seen her
before. He looked her up one evening in Keats, and there she
was, teeth, eyelashes, frecklings, streaks and bars, sapphires,
greens, amethyst and rubious-argent. He had always found the
teeth and eyelashes repulsive and had supposed Keats was as
usual piling excess on excess. Now he decided Keats must have
seen one himself, or read someone who had, and felt the same
mixture of aesthetic frenzy and repulsion. Mary Douglas, the
anthropologist, says that *mixed* things, neither flesh nor fowl,
so to speak, always excite repulsion and prohibition. The
poor Lamia was a mess, as far as her head went. Her beseeching eyes were horrible. He looked up from his reading and
saw her snake-face peering sadly in at the window, her halo
shimmering, her teeth shining like pearls. He saw to his locks:
he was not about to be accidentally kissed in his sleep. They
were each other's prisoners, he and she. He would paint his
painting and think how to escape.

The painting was getting somewhere. The snake-colours
were a fourth term in the equation pool>sky>mountains-
trees>paint. Their movement in the aquamarines linked and
divided delectably, firing the neurones in Bernard's brain to
greater and greater activity, and thus causing the Lamia
to become sulkier and eventually duller and less brilliant.

'I am so *sad*, Bernard. I want to be a woman.'

'You've had thousands of years already. Give me a few
more days.'

'You see how kind I am, when I am in pain.'

*

12

What would have happened if Raymond Potter had not kept his word will never be known. Bernard had quite forgotten the liver-fluke conversation and Raymond's promised, or threatened visit. But one day he heard wheels on his track, and saw Potter's dark red BMW creeping up its slope.

'Hide,' he said to the Lamia. 'Keep still. It's a dreadful Englishman of the fee-fi-fo-fum sort; he has a shouting voice, he *makes jokes*, he smokes cigars, he's bad news, *hide*.'

The Lamia slipped under water in a flurry of bubbles like the Milky Way.

Raymond Potter came out of the car smiling and carried in a leg of wild boar and the ingredients of a ratatouille, a crate of red wine, and several bottles of *eau de vie Poire William*.

'Brought my own provisions. Show me the stove.'

He cooked. They ate on the terrace, in the evening. Bernard did not switch on the lights in the pool and did not suggest that Raymond might swim. Raymond in fact did not like swimming; he was too fat to wish to be seen, and preferred eating and smoking. Both men drank rather a lot of red wine and then rather a lot of *eau de vie*. The smell of the mountain was laced with the smells of pork crackling and cigar smoke. Raymond peered drunkenly at Bernard's current painting. He pronounced it rather sinister, very striking, a bit weird, not quite usual, funny-coloured, a bit over the top? Looking at Bernard each time for a response and getting none, as Bernard, exhausted and a little drunk, was largely asleep. They went to bed, and Bernard woke once in the night to realise he had not shut his bedroom window as he usually did; a shutter was banging. But he was unkissed and solitary; he slid back into unconsciousness.

The next morning Bernard was up first. He made coffee, he cycled to the village and bought croissants, bread and peaches, he laid the table on the terrace and poured heated milk into a blue and white jug. The pool lay flat and still, quietly and incompatibly shining at the quiet sky.

Raymond made rather a noise coming downstairs. This

was because his arm was round a young woman with a great deal of hennaed black hair, who wore a garment of that see-through cheesecloth from India which is sold in every southern French market. The garment was calf-length, clinging, with little shoulder-straps and dyed in a rather musty brownish-black, scattered with little round green spots like peas. It could have been a sundress or a nightdress; it was only too easy to see that the woman wore nothing at all underneath it. The black triangle of her pubic hair swayed with her hips. Her breasts were large and thrusting, that was the word that sprang to Bernard's mind. The nipples stood out in the cheesecloth.

'This is Melanie,' Raymond announced, pulling out a chair for her. She flung back her hair with an actressy gesture of her hands and sat down gracefully, pulling the cheesecloth round her knees and staring down at her ankles. She had long pale hairless legs with very pretty feet. Her toenails were varnished with a pink pearly varnish. She turned them this way and that, admiring them. She wore rather a lot of very pink lipstick and smiled in a satisfied way at her own toes.

'Do you want coffee?' said Bernard to Melanie.

'She doesn't speak English,' said Raymond. He leaned over and made a guzzling, kissing noise in the hollow of her collarbone. 'Do you, darling?'

He was obviously going to make no attempt to explain her presence. It was not even quite clear that he knew that Bernard had a right to an explanation, or that he had himself any idea where she had come from. He was simply obsessed. His fingers were pulled towards her hair like needles to a magnet: he kept standing up and kissing her breasts, her shoulders, her ears. With considerable distaste Bernard watched Raymond's fat tongue explore the coil of Melanie's ear.

'Will you have coffee?' he said to Melanie in French. He indicated the coffee pot. She bent her head towards it with a quick curving movement, sniffed it, and then hovered briefly over the milk jug.

'This,' she said, indicating the hot milk. 'I will drink this.'

14

She looked at Bernard with huge black eyes under long lashes.

'I wish you joy,' said Bernard in Cevenol French, 'of your immortal soul.'

'Hey,' said Raymond, 'don't flirt with my girl in foreign languages.'

'I don't flirt,' said Bernard. 'I paint.'

'And we'll be off after breakfast and leave you to your painting,' said Raymond. 'Won't we, my sweet darling? Melanie wants – Melanie hasn't got – she didn't exactly bring – you understand – all her clothes and things. We're going to Cannes to buy some real clothes. Melanie wants to see the film festival and the stars. You won't mind, old friend, you didn't want me in the first place. I don't want to interrupt your *painting*. *Chacun à sa boue*, as we used to say in the army, I know that much French.'

Melanie held out her pretty fat hands and turned them over and over with considerable satisfaction. They were pinkly pale and also ornamented with pearly nail-varnish. She did not look at Raymond, simply twisted her head about with what could have been pleasure at his little sallies of physical affection, or could have been irritation. She did not speak. She smiled a little, over her milk, like a satisfied cat, displaying two rows of sweet little pearly teeth between her glossy pink lips.

Raymond's packing did not take long. Melanie turned out to have one piece of luggage – a large green leather bag full of rattling coins, by the sound. Raymond saw her into the car like a princess, and came back to say goodbye to his friend.

'Have a good time,' said Bernard. 'Beware of philosophers.'

'Where would I find any philosophers?' asked Raymond, who had done theatre design at art school with Bernard and now designed sets for a successful children's TV programme called *The A-Mazing Maze of Monsters*. 'Philosophers are extinct. I think your wits are turning, old friend, with stomping around on your own. You need a girl-friend.'

'I don't,' said Bernard. 'Have a good holiday.'

'We're going to be married,' said Raymond, looking surprised, as though he himself had not known this until he said it. The face of Melanie swam at the car window, the pearly teeth visible inside the soft lips, the dark eyes staring. 'I must go,' said Raymond. 'Melanie's waiting.'

Left to himself, Bernard settled back into the bliss of solitude. He looked at his latest work and saw that it was good. Encouraged, he looked at his earlier work and saw that that was good, too. All those blues, all those curious questions, all those almost-answers. The only problem was, where to go now. He walked up and down, he remembered the philosopher and laughed. He got out his Keats. He reread the dreadful moment in *Lamia* where the bride vanished away under the coldly malevolent eye of the philosopher.

> *do not all charms fly*
> *At the mere touch of cold philosophy?*
> *There was an awful rainbow once in heaven:*
> *We know her woof, her texture; she is given*
> *In the dull catalogue of common things.*
> *Philosophy will clip an Angel's wings,*
> *Conquer all mysteries by rule and line,*
> *Empty the haunted air and gnomed mine –*
> *Unweave a rainbow, as it erstwhile made*
> *The tender-personed Lamia melt into a shade.*

Personally, Bernard said to himself, he had never gone along with Keats about all that stuff. By philosophy Keats seemed to mean natural science, and personally he, Bernard, would rather have the optical mysteries of waves and particles in the water and light of the rainbow than any old gnome or fay. He had been at least as interested in the problems of reflection and refraction when he had had the lovely snake in his pool as he had been in its oddity – in its *otherness* – as snakes went. He hoped no natural scientist would come along and find Melanie's blood group to be that of some sort of Herpes, or do an X-ray and see something odd in her spine. She made a very good blowzy sort of a woman, just right for Raymond. He wondered what sort of a woman she would have become for him, and dismissed the problem. He didn't want a woman. He wanted another visual idea. A mystery to be explained by rule and line. He looked around his breakfast table. A rather nondescript orange-brown butterfly was sipping the juice of the rejected peaches. It had a golden eye at the base of its wings and a rather lovely white streak, shaped like a tiny dragon-wing. It stood on the glistening rich yellow peach-flesh and manoeuvred its body to sip the sugary juices and suddenly it was not orange-brown at all, it was a rich, gleaming intense purple. And then it was both at once, orange-gold and purple-veiled, and then it was purple again, and then it folded its wings and the undersides had a purple eye and a soft green streak, and tan, and white edged with charcoal . . .

When he came back with his paintbox it was still turning and sipping. He mixed purple, he mixed orange, he made browns. It was done with a dusting of scales, with refractions of rays. The pigments were discovered and measured, the scales on the wings were noted and *seen*, everything was a mystery, serpents and water and light. He was off again. Exact study would not clip this creature's wings, it would dazzle his eyes with its brightness. Don't go, he begged it, watching and learning, don't go. Purple and orange is a terrible and violent fate. There is months of work in it. Bernard attacked it. He was happy, in one of the ways in which human beings are happy.

# Michael Donaghy

## IRENA OF ALEXANDRIA

Creator, thank You for humbling me.
Creator, who twice empowered me to change
a jackal to a saucer of milk,
a cloud of gnats into a chandelier,
and once, before the emperor's astrologers,
a nice distinction into an accordion,
and back again, thank You
for choosing Irena to eclipse me.

She changed a loaf of bread into a loaf of bread,
caused a river to flow downstream,
left the leper to limp home grinning and leprous,
because, the bishops say, Your will burns
bright about her as a flame about a wick.

Thank You, Creator, for taking the crowds away.
Not even the blind come here now.
I have one bowl, a stream too cold to squat in,
and the patience of a saint. Peace be,
in the meantime, upon her. And youth.
May sparrows continue to litter her shoulders,
children carpet her steps in lavender,
and may her martyrdom be beautiful and slow.

# CALIBAN'S BOOKS

*Hair oil, boiled sweets, chalk dust, squid's ink ...*
Bear with me. I'm trying to conjure my father,
age fourteen, as Caliban – picked by Mr Quinn
for the role he was born to play because
'I was the handsomest boy at school'
he'll say, straight-faced, at fifty.
This isn't easy. I've only half the spell,
and I won't be born for twenty years.
I'm trying for rainlight on Belfast Lough
and listening for a small blunt accent barking
over the hiss of a stove getting louder like surf.
But how can I read when the schoolroom's gone
black as the hold of a ship? Start again.

*Hair oil, boiled sweets ...*
But his paperbacks are crumbling in my hands,
seachanged bouquets, each brown page
scribbled on, underlined, memorised,
forgotten like used pornography:
*The Pocket Treasury of English Verse*
*How to Win Friends and Influence People*
*30 Days to a More Powerful Vocabulary*

*Fish stink, pitch stink, seaspray, cedarwood ...*
I seem to have brought us to the port of Naples,
midnight, to a shadow below deck
dreaming of a distant island.
So many years, so many ports ago!
The moment comes. It slips from the hold
and knucklewalks across the dark piazza
sobbing *maestro! maestro!* But the duke's long dead
and all his magic books are drowned.

# OUR LIFE STORIES

What did they call that ball in *Citizen Kane*?
That crystal blizzardball forecasting his past?
Surely I know the name. Your mum's souvenir
Of Blackpool underwater in winter –
Say we dropped it. What would we say we broke?
And see what it says when you turn it over . . .

I dreamt the little Christmas dome I owned
Slipped my soapy fingers and exploded.
Baby Jesus and the Virgin Mother
Twitching on the lino like dying guppies.
Let's shake this up and change the weather.

Catch! This marvellous drop, like its own tear,
Has leaked for years. The tiny ferris wheel has surfaced
In an oval bubble where it never snows
And little by little all is forgotten. Shhh!
Let's hold the sad toy storms in which we're held,
Let's hold them gingerly above the bed,
Bubbles gulping contentedly, as we rock them to sleep,
Flurries aswim by our gentle skill,
Their names on the tips of our tongues.


# THE BREAK

Like freak Texan sisters joined at the hip
playing saxophone duets in vaudeville,
we slept leaning, back to back.
When, more and more, our silences deepened,
a new perfume, a phone bill in her padlocked journal,
were props on a stage inside my head
where I woke sweat-drenched, alone.
Now she's gone, I seem to crowd myself because
it takes a second soul to hear the soul,

a third to hear the second . . . they keep coming:
angels many-armed, heraldic chimeras,
two-headed monsters at the map's edge screaming.

Inseparable sisters, I watch you every night
from my half-world, my single mattress.
You are smoking out back between shows
wearing the teal silk double cocktail dress.
You never speak. You pass the smoke
and the silence between you is a lake on the moon.
Daisy, Violet, you are a girl at a dance
resting, for a moment, against a mirror.

# Sean O'Brien

## RIDING ON *THE CITY OF NEW ORLEANS*

From the Crescent City slowly
Over stormy Pontchartrain,
Through Louisiana dusk
And into Mississippi night,
To Tennessee and Illinois,
Which are impossible,
From rémoulade and sin towards
A Klieg-lit German paradise,
The train goes, crying *Train, train.*
We are travelling so slowly,
Two-four on the joints, two-four,
The journey could be proof, almost,
That home, or hope, or what you need,
Is only now departing: run
And you could board it still
Beneath the cover of that cry.
That voice is returned from the walls
Of graves in the permanent lockdowns,
Over sweating antebellum lawns
Beneath the levee. Or it stirs
A snaredrum sat tight in its kit
On the stage of the Wild Kingdom Bar,
A concrete expression of popular will
Where music and murder take place
Every night of the long week of Sundays.
*Train,* the voice whispers,
And breath clouds a saxophone's bell.

*Train*, down the tarpaper length
Of a shotgun slavehouse
Beside a reactor. *Train*,
And the poor are once more reinvented,
Sleeping in the slowly rocking coach.
To name the states that lie
On either hand from sea to sea
Is neither here nor there. To dismount
At the edge of a field, or a road, or a river,
And watch the train depart, becoming
Swaying lights and then the dark
In which its very name recedes,
Could make a man forget his own
Or stay repeating it for ever.

# Douglas Livingstone

## GIOVANNI JACOPO MEDITATES
### (on *Supping with the Vegans*)

Staring disbelievingly at my Plate
Flanked by Cutlery cunningly designed
Of Wood (to negate the Negative Magnetics in Metals),
I counted discrete Curls of Sprouting Beans
– Each limp as a discarded Mapping-Pin.
On the half-empty Platter long resigned
To bearing slim Pickings, lurked Fowl-Run Stains,
Six brown Stems of strange wilted Greens,
One fallen Leaf & three Rose Petals.
There being little Else to challenge her Jaws,
Our Hostess proved a relentless Talker.
What finally resolved my Fate
Was upsetting the Jar of unrefined Malt
As I wrestled with the Log of Mahogany Bread.

Forewarned is Forearmed, they do say.
Gasping, panting, Eyes rolling about,
I stood up coughing, knuckling my Brains.
Muttering: 'My Tablets. Must have Air',
I seized my Manuscript Case & ran out.
The Night in the Garden saved my Day.
I peaceably downed a Sandwich spread
With Roast Beef, Mustard, Pepper & Salt,
Chopped green Chillies, a plump halved Pair
Of Pickled Onions & an Airline Nip of Johnny Walker.
I belched; had a Smoke; wiped the Smile off my Face,

& returned contritely, dabbing my Chin.
I quietly waded back to my Place
Through the Monologue flowing with never a Pause.

# Don Paterson

## HOMESICK PATERSON, LIVE AT THE BLUE BANNOCK, THURSO

So there was me and Lafayette NcNab
the month before we tore up the West Coast.
They'd warned us, mind: this cunt had tried to roast
every button-box that played the club –

a five-row dude, they said. Wis he fuck:
jist a half-a-dozen early Shand licks
and the same Scott Skinner riff if he got stuck.
His Ma had pit his shed in wi an axe

and he'd the sort o puss ye'd never tire o hittin,
but sharp threads, man. Mohair minikilt, wee brogues
wi leather tassles. 'Mind if I sit in?'
I looks over at McNab. He shrugs.

Six numbers later, he's on his fifteenth chorus
o 'Kailyard Blues', gien it *genius is pain*,
eyes screwed shut, pretendin tae ignore us.
So Eh'm gaun tartan cuin' the head back in

when Lafayette stands up, leans over, flashes
this big neep gully fae his jacket, slashes
the boy's bellows up the middle – chiv posed,
erse on stool before his hi-hat's closed.

Meanwhile, he's still dyin o constipation
but that's soon sorted – cos next big squeeze
his box is futterin like a coo's erse, wi the soon-
effects tae match. The hoose is on its knees.

Some axe, mind: a JS Custom Thunderbass,
the '62, with triple reeds and rhinestones.
White as a sheet, he pits it in his furry case
and marches oot. They huvnae seen him since.

High Fives, 'Take the A-Road', then a break.
So here's me heading for the Vladimir
when I gets this waft o Consulate. 'Hey . . .
    Hameseek . . .'
Sure enough, jist the wey Ah'd left her,

nursin a hauf o Irn Bru and Tequila,
fannin hersel doon wi the *People's Friend*.
'Lang time.' No sae lang's Eh dinna mind.
'Cat got yer tongue? Ye were aye a queer-like fella . . .

but wee man, dye ken, you were the best?'
'Sorry doll,' says I. 'Nae requests.'

**Glossary:** button-box = button accordion; shed = hair parting; gully = knife; head = theme; axe = any musical instrument; posed = hidden; Vladimir = musician's rhyming slang for lavatory

# Simon Burt

## FIFTY/FIFTY ORANGE JUICE AND OXTAIL SOUP

THE STATE OF being in love is an alternative state of being. There is normal life, and there is being in love. Rarely, fingers of one hand rarely, the state of being in love modulates further into love itself, and the two states of being meld. More often, most often, they are parallel lines between which, like excited electrons, we move. At certain times, in certain places, under certain circumstances on the line of normal life, there is a moment that feels like a moment of awakening, and we are on the other line. We stay on the other line for as long as it takes. It can take seconds. It can take years. Until there is a second moment of awakening, and we dissolve back on to the first line. These moments of awakening themselves are of startling clarity. They remain in the mind like the last moments of a dream. Also, as with dreams, there is room for argument about which is the state of sleep and which the state of wakefulness. In both states we feel awake, until we wake.

### JEAN-PASCAL

He has a garden flat, and a snake, a plump green boa the size of a draught excluder, which he feeds live white mice which he buys in a pet shop in Streatham, and calls Hopkins. Opkeens. Naked from his bath, over his shoulder a view of stone steps leading up to a garden, and a statue, a Silenus with grapes, overlooking the steps, he winds Hopkins round his neck like a scarf, holds his head up to his face, and tickles him under the chin.

'Are you 'appy, 'Opkins?' he says. ''Opkins. 'Opkins.'

We are in a bar. Banquettes and Windsor chairs. Velvet and a cast-iron fireplace with artificial coals. I put a cigarette, a Gitane, into my mouth, and he takes out his Zippo and strikes it for me.

'Je t'allume?' he says.

## PINO

He has gone back to Naples for June, and every week he has sent me a card. Only two have arrived. The first, he tells me when he gets back, and the third. The first is a reproduction of 'Perseus Turning Phineas and His Companions to Stone', by Luca Giordano. Its text consists, apart from my address, of the letter I. The third is a Californian postcard, an LA skyscape with clouds, the setting sun, and the crests of palm trees. Closer examination shows that the clouds form words: Sit On My Face. On it he has written the word You. The pictures on the second and fourth, he tells me, he cannot remember, but the text of the fourth, mailed last week so it may still arrive, was my name, and of that of the second, mailed three weeks ago so it must be lost, was the word Love.

A crowded bus-stop at Notting Hill. I am going to visit a friend who lives on Brook Green. We have been waiting, the queue and I, for over half an hour. A solidarity has grown up between us. Buses are not frequent. A bus of the number we need has passed, too full to stop. Eventually our bus arrives and we turn immediately from fellow-sufferers to competitors. As I push on to the bus I see Pino, across the road, hiding behind a tree.

## TADDEO

He is American, he tells me. His name is accented on the second syllable, Tadayo. We have met on the Old Brompton Road, and it is late at night, nearer two o'clock than one.

'I have a lover,' he says.

'Me too,' I say.

'He is waiting for me,' he says.

'Mine too,' I say.

'I can picture him,' he says. 'Sitting up in bed, wearing glasses, reading and waiting.'

'My lover doesn't wear glasses,' I say.

'I meant mine,' he says.

'Ah,' I say.

'Shall we go?' he says.

'Where?' I say.

'We'll find a place,' he says.

It is New Year's Eve. A hi-tech bedroom in Shepherd's Bush. Blue and green with metal shelves and rubber flooring. On the floor a scatter of wine bottles and clothes. On floor and bed, ditto of naked bodies. Someone called Eric, I notice, a friend of one of the bodies, up for the night from Cambridge, a rangy man in his early thirties, with a line of dark hair down his stomach, receding curls and a cock-ring, has just spilled a glass of red wine on the grey pullover which was one of my mother's Christmas presents. It is four o'clock in the morning and we are tired. We are playing charades, miming the titles of films, and it is Taddeo's turn. He lies naked and still on the bed.

'This is it,' he says. 'I'm doing it.'

'Go on,' he says. 'Guess. I'm doing it. Can't you guess?'

'*The Big Sleep*,' he says.

## LANCE

He is a rock singer out of Vancouver. He is tall, rake-thin, with down-at-heel cowboy boots and spiked hair. He has been shopping. He is sitting on the floor of his kitchen unpacking bag after bag of kitchen implements, colanders, jugs, sieves, funnels, bottles, spoons, all in brightly coloured plastic. Red, yellow, blue.

The idea is, he says, to get this sort of hoop and hang it from the ceiling. And then hang all this from the hoop. Good, huh?

He has a wife, he says, back in Vancouver. They married when they were very young, eighteen, nineteen. His wife is schizophrenic. It's no joke, he says, being married to a schizophrenic. For him the language of lust and the language of love are the same. 'Fill me with your love,' he says. 'Fuck me up the ass.' He likes to interrupt sex with talk. 'You know,' he says. 'Hey, you know. I've always had this fantasy of getting it on with my dad.'

## LUIS

We are standing in a wide white street in Kensington. The street is lined with cherry trees in white blossom. It is windy. Gusts of wind blow my hair forward round my face and his back from his. The air is full of windblown blossom. The top of his head is as high as my sternum. I have not shaved in five days.

We are watching television. My mind is wandering. I glance round the room. A bed-sitting room. A rosary hung on a nail above the bed, a single bed, the bedstead iron. Shirts hanging from the picture rail. A sheepskin rug in front of the gas fire. Suddenly there, on the news, is the King of Spain.

'Mira, mira,' he says. 'Su Majestad.'

31

## ALAN

It is morning and I am in a hurry. I have to meet someone in the King's Road at eleven o'clock. I've just woken up in Mount Street at half past ten. I am running round his flat collecting my clothes from where he threw them last night. I can't find them all.

'My socks,' I say. 'Shit, where are my socks? Shit, Alan, I can't find my socks.'

'I burned them,' he says. 'They stank. God but they stank. I burned them.'

The Connaught Hotel. I have taken the train up from Wiltshire and a taxi to the hotel. He won't be in, he has said. He has to go to a party. But he has left his key at the desk for me to collect. Be careful, he has said. They are snotty in there. They won't even let you in if you're not wearing a tie. And don't wear jeans. They haven't yet grasped the ultimate chic of blue denim. Carefully suited and tied I get out of the taxi and go to ask for his key at the desk. As I go through the foyer I hear him call my name. He is wearing a red polo shirt and red Newman's jeans. He is holding his key.

## FELIX

A night-club, black lacquer and chrome, somewhere off Regent Street. It is my birthday. I am sitting on a high stool at the bar. Felix is leaning against me. He has opened my thighs on the stool and is leaning back between them. He has taken my hands and put them in his pockets. He is writing his name and address on a card for someone he has met at the bar.

SAS, le Prince Félix de Luxembourg, he writes. The RAC Club, London W1.

His name, I know, is Julian Spong. He has a small flat in Orme Square.

*

Maggie, his flatmate, and I are sharing the last glass of wine in the sitting-room. She is telling me how to get stains out of leather trousers. Felix is in the kitchen, boiling the kettle for coffee. We have been to a late-night film at the Electric cinema, leaving Felix's mother, who has come to stay for a day or two, to spend an evening at the Bingo in Shepherd's Bush. She likes Bingo, and often comes back with a bottle of vodka or two which she has bought with her winnings.

'What you do,' Maggie says, 'is rub the spot with a mixture of milk and methylated spirits, let it dry, and polish it.'

There is a crash from the kitchen. Maggie and I run to investigate, and in the corridor we see Felix's mother going upstairs. Felix, in the kitchen, has slammed the china cupboard door, and is beating it with his fists.


## MAN-CHIH


He is sitting on my bed. He has unwrapped a green Marks and Spencer's bag and taken out a new pair of yellow and grey Argyll socks. He holds the socks up to his nose, and sniffs them.

'My socks,' he says.

He is lying on my chest, his face close to mine. He has, I see, a slight strabismus. His left eye floats, independent of his right. He sees from my eyes that I have noticed this, and he looks away.


## TONY


An attic bedroom in his parents' house in St John's Wood. It is early morning and I am reading John Wain, listening to a noise on the stairs. The attic bedroom is above his parents' room and the stairs creak. Would I please, his parents have asked me, make sure that I climb the stairs very slowly and quietly so as not to make them creak. They pass directly behind their bed, and they don't like to be woken up. There is a way, I have found, of climbing the stairs without making them creak. If you tread on the extreme edge of each stair it doesn't creak. Tony does not know this. I hear him slowly, quietly and very slowly, climbing the stairs.

We are at school. In his room. I am sitting at his desk. He is sitting on the bed. The walls are hung with blue cotton, Madras print, pinned to the wall. We are drinking coffee and talking. I have brought some apples, Granny Smiths, and put them in a bowl on the desk. The room is full of the fragrance of apples.

## ALEXANDER

He is sitting on a corduroy-covered Adeptus armchair. It is midnight. We have been watching television. We have watched *The Spider's Stratagem* by Bertolucci. Now we are drinking coffee. I watch him as he spoons one, two, three, four spoonfuls of sugar into his coffee.

The day after the Notting Hill Carnival. Outside my flat is a wind trap. Refuse from the Portobello Road round the corner blows into my street and into my area, and piles up against my door. We have just swept this up. We have swept up two black plastic binbags full of beer cans, chip paper, Kentucky Fried Chicken boxes with their debris of chicken bones and grease, cigarette butts and packets empty and full, several condoms, a single running shoe, a green cable-knit polo-neck pullover gone at the elbows, a syringe, and twenty pounds – two fivers and a tenner – from the area, and are celebrating with a cup of coffee. I watch him as he spoons one, two, three, four spoonfuls of sugar into his coffee.

## ZACKER

'Look at those cushions,' he says.

I look at the cushions.

'How would you arrange them?' he says. 'Show me how you would arrange them. Take them from the sofa and show me how you would arrange them.'

I take the cushions and arrange them on the sofa. There are five of them, made from various materials – gold brocade, black silk, pink corduroy, a blue and white floral chintz, and a black and white striped mattress ticking –'and of various sizes. I arrange them, more or less at random, on each end of the sofa.

'Ah,' he says. 'I see. Of course, I would do it like this.'

He arranges them, again more or less at random, but all at one end of the sofa.


'It doesn't matter how hard you try,' he says. 'It doesn't matter how hard you work out. Have you noticed? It doesn't matter how pumped up you are. There are always two parts of your body you can't stop looking vulnerable. The bit of your arm where it joins the shoulder, seen from behind. And the soles of your feet.'


## JAMES

He has a key to my flat. He comes, every now and again, to see to the cats my first lover left behind him when he went to Japan, rank, dust-clouded creatures whom I long to lose, and when he leaves he almost invariably takes my keys with him. Our keyrings are similar. He reaches for something familiar, takes it and leaves, never mind that his own are in his pocket. This leaves me without my keys. I have to go round to his flat, where he is not on the phone, and collect them. To do this I have to shut my flat door without the keys to get back in again. This does not do a whole lot for my temper. One day, back from his flat with my keys, I find a note from him pushed through my letterbox.

'Why,' the note reads, 'is there never anyone here when I need them? I'm in the pub. Come for a drink.'

He is training to be a chef. He feeds me the dishes he is learning how to cook. Sometimes he invents one of his own and tries it out on me. This evening it's a soup. He gives me the recipe.

'You take a can of Campbell's Condensed Oxtail Soup,' he says, 'and you mix it fifty/fifty with pure orange juice. You heat it and serve it with segments of fresh orange and fine shreds of orange zest.'


## KATE

I wake to the bang of a door. I am alone in bed and the room is full of moonlight. I did not expect to be alone. Against my alarm clock is a note.

'It's late,' the note reads. 'The moon shines right in the window, right into my eyes. If I turn over the moon is reflected in the mirror, and also shines right into my eyes. So, *début de nuit blanche*, I'm afraid. I'm going home. I'll call you.'

Barefoot on the beach at Sandycove. The incoming tide ripples up to the sea-wall and back again over our toes. She is laughing. We are laughing. It is early on a cold morning, and we are drunk. We have been up all night. She shivers. I take off my coat and hang it over her shoulders.

'There are too many words,' she says. 'Don't you think? Don't you think there are too many words?'

## DAVID

He is writing a treatise on William Faulkner. He talks about the sense you get in Faulkner's sentences, the same sense you get in Walker Evans' photographs, the sense of a stark choice between starvation and grinding daily toil. He talks of a similar sense in Joseph Conrad, and James Purdy, and Henry James. Writers, he says, the real hero of whose work is the act of narration itself.

It is morning. I wake up and turn over in his bed. He is still asleep. Suddenly the curtains are drawn back and I see a young boy, nine, maybe ten years old, standing by the window.

'Hello,' the boy says. 'Is my dad awake? I need my lunch money.'

## GABRIEL

He is standing by the open fridge. It is night and the only source of light is the light from the fridge. He is thirsty and has got up to get a drink of orange juice. He stands in the fridge light and drinks the orange juice. His body is one long line from the upraised carton of juice to his heels on the kitchen floor. I can see the shadows in his throat move as he swallows.

He wants to be an air steward, he says. We are standing in Portobello Road by the Sun in Splendour. He is looking up at the vapour trail left by an aeroplane across the sky.

'My life,' he says.

## SCOTT

It is Saturday evening. We are sitting on his sofa watching television. *Jim'll Fix It*, a programme he likes greatly. He is telling me how he washes his hair. He always uses Johnson's Baby Shampoo, he says. It is the only shampoo that really gets his hair clean. And then Alberto Balsam Conditioner. He has soft and flyaway hair, and this is the only conditioner that will control it.

'He has been and gone,' my flatmate says. 'He came and smoked a cigarette or two, and we chatted, and then he had to go. He says he'll call. He's trying to give up smoking, he says. He cleaned the ashtrays anyway. It was all I could do to stop him doing the washing up.' The kitchen, I find, has been tidied. The washing up from breakfast, if not done, is stacked neatly on the draining board, the cutlery soaking in the sink. I do the washing up, and as I open the bin to scrape in a bacon rind, I find that it is full of smoke from his unextinguished cigarette.

## RICHARD/TONY

A bar in Dublin. It is light outside, but the bar is dark. As I come in I hear my name shouted from a booth, where a group of people are sitting round a middle-aged American in a fur coat. I join the group and Richard/Tony offers me a glass of champagne.

'This is Maurice,' he says of the American. 'He's from Chicago. He wants to buy us all champagne. He wants us all to be happy. He wants to buy me a motorbike, too, don't you, Maurice? A motorbike would make me happy.'

A club, also in Dublin. We are leaving the dance floor. As he is stepping down from the floor, another man is stepping up. He steps to the left to avoid us and we step to the right into his way. And vice versa. And again. Richard/Tony takes the man's hand and puts it to his chest, under his shirt, where, I know, there is a tattoo of a mouse between his nipples.

'All right,' he says. 'Next dance. I promise.'

## HUGH

A bedroom floor in Glasgow. A mattress on the floor. Five of us have been to see a play at the Citizens' Theatre, and have been to a party afterwards at the Assembly Rooms in the Town Hall. Now we are all piled on to the mattress on the floor of one of the cast's flat where we are to sleep. I am lying next to Hugh, who may or may not be asleep. From next door come the cooings and flutings of our host and his girlfriend, as one or both of them approach orgasm.

He holds his hands strangely. He is holding his thumbs in his fingers. I ask him why, and he blushes. It's his nails, he says. He bites his nails. He doesn't like anyone to see. I ask him to show me and he opens his fingers for me to see. Each thumb-nail has been bitten down, allowed to grow, and bitten down again. So often that each thumb now is spatulate, each nail a series of corrugations from base to tip.

## SOPHIE

We are on a train. She is sitting opposite me. We are going to spend the weekend at her parents' house outside Arundel. It is her birthday, and I have just given her a parcel. A record, Joni Mitchell's 'Mingus', wrapped and ribboned. In a single movement, she sloughs her shoes and draws her legs up under her to sit cross-legged on the seat. The light cotton of her dress, almost transparent, a flower-printed blue, floats down over her feet as she unwraps her present.

We are walking up the avenue to Golders Hill Park, a long avenue shaded with overarching trees. The day is very hot, but it is cool under the trees, the entrance to the park bright at the end of the tunnel. We are walking slowly, slowly up the avenue, talking. What we are saying engrosses us, and we walk more and more slowly until, half-way along the avenue maybe, we stop.

## SELIM

He is a student of film. His favourite film is *Breakfast at Tiffany's*, which he knows by heart. He has just fascinated his tutor, he tells me, with his theory of the edible mother.

'The edible mother?' I say.

'Yes,' he said. 'That's what my tutor said too. I didn't have the heart to tell him he hadn't heard me right. I meant the Oedipal mother. I had to make up a whole myth on the spur of the moment about eating your mother.'

The stairs of a club in Kensington. I have just passed out on the stairs. It happens sometimes. There is something wrong with my heart. I get a spurt of tachycardia and I pass out. Everyone in the club thinks I'm drunk, and the manager orders me curtly off the stairs. Selim snaps at him that I'm ill and he is to call a taxi. We take the taxi back to his place, and I lie, cold and sweating, a veil of blood over my vision, while Selim makes love to me, sitting on me, and pressing the palm of my hand hard, hard against his face.

## EMMETT

He wears his hair in a thousand slim, shoulder-length plaits, each plait tipped with a blue glass bead. He is wearing black jeans and black suede cowboy boots, a Nehru-collared cotton jacket in browns, yellows and reds, and round his neck is a small silver bell on a leather thong. On the thumb and forefinger of his left hand he wears two tiny brass cymbals which he sometimes clashes together in time to the music.

We have had lunch in a pub, and spent the afternoon in a drinking club in Covent Garden. We have spent the evening in the bars, have gone on to a club, and are now drinking coffee in an all-night restaurant in Soho.

It is possible, I suggest, to have enough of all this.

'Oh no,' he says. 'Oh, no way, no. Not if you come from Arkansas.'

As he moves his head the beads on his plaits rub together with the noise of waves against shingle.

He is in England to study music. It is his ambition to write a musical on the sinking of the *Titanic*: 'Could you move a little faster, Mrs Astor?' We are in his flat, and he is playing for me 'Rejoice in the Lamb', by Benjamin Britten. It is just coming up to my favourite bit:

> For the officers of the peace are at variance with me,
>     and the watchman smites me with his staff.
> For Silly Fellow! Silly Fellow! is against me, and belong-
>     eth neither to me nor to my family.

'This bit,' he says. 'This is the bit. Don't you just love that bit? Doesn't that just say everything?'


## AMAR

We are crossing the Pont des Arts. It is windy. A flock of starlings is mobbing a buzzard above the river. The buzzards are moving back, he says, into the towers of Notre Dame. The buzzard wheels this way and that in a smoke of starlings.

'I don't believe in symbolism,' he says. 'Do you? I think that a spade is more beautiful if you call it a spade.'

And then:

'Look,' he says. 'Look. There. Up behind the Louvre. A balloon.'

It is the hour between dog and wolf. In the streets it is darkening towards twilight. In the houses the lights are going on. In his room and mine the lights are on. He lives with his parents in the flat opposite mine. I am working at my desk at the window of my room, and his bedroom is immediately opposite me. He is standing in his window looking at me across the street. He is naked. His body is very hairy. His chest, his shoulders, his groin, his legs are covered in a thick pelt of glossy black hair. At first glance you might think he is wearing a pair of dungarees. I look up from my work and see him looking at me. He stands to attention, very still. Then he reaches up, takes off his glasses, and stands to attention again.

Certainly I can't help you to distinguish between them. Either between sleep and wakefulness, or between one moment and the other. All I can do is remember the moments. Which is which I no longer know. One of them, I know, is the moment of awakening into, the other – call it the second if you wish, you are free to do so; although I would advise against it; if I don't know, how should you? – the other the moment of awakening out of, love. The people were very dissimilar. Some were old, some were young. Some were witty, some were dull. Some were rich, some clever, some dim, some poor. Some were beautiful, some not. All that they had in common was that, for as long as it took, I was in love with them. Of the time I spent with them, either in or out of love with them, I remember all but nothing. All that remains of them – all, all that remains of them; they are all dead – is the luminous moment of transition.

# Carmen Callil

## LEBANESE WASHING STORIES

IT WASN'T UNTIL I came to live in London, in 1960, that I began to think of myself as anything other than a usual Australian. My childhood and youth were passed in a seaside suburb of Melbourne, at convents and then at Melbourne University. My family name did not mark me out from anyone else: Callils were thick upon the ground in Melbourne, disturbing the peace generally. I was a Melbourne Catholic with an excessive number of rather eccentric relations, and that was that.

To British people, however, Australians are of British descent, and the little they know about the so-near Middle East is never connected with the equally little they know about so-distant Australia. It was only through living in England and constantly having to explain the source of my name, that I started to wonder about the Lebanon, my Lebanese grandparents and the Lebanese uncles who formed the fortress walls of my childhood and youth.

My particular world was entirely Austral-Irish. We were taught the 3Rs, English literature and grammar, European history, the Catholic religion and Australian sport. British history came with a dash of Irish persecution in it and I knew a great deal more about the Star Chamber, the Troubles, the Potato Famine and the evils of Cromwell than I did of the Ottoman Empire or the Maronite religion. Of that religion which was, in one way, the sole reason my mother and father came to marry, I knew nothing at all.

Now I know that the Maronite religion is an eastern rite

of the Roman Catholic Church. It was founded by St John Maroun in the fifth century and persecution and the advent of Islam caused his followers, in the tenth century, to hole up on the highest mountain peak in Lebanon, above their sacred Qadisha Valley. Mount Lebanon, and its topmost village, Bsharri, the home of my grandparents, was thus a bastion of Christianity in an Islamic sea.

There are various peculiarities about the Maronite sect. First its history is extremely warlike – 'generous in their martyrdom' is the Maronite wording for this. To the rest of us more habituated to ten Hail Marys or a bit of flagellation at most, the complexity of this violent history is beyond human understanding. Most of the people of the Mountain and the Biblical lands surrounding it have spent two thousand years dividing into sects, like amoebas, and then using such divisions as an excuse to assassinate their nearest neighbours. They argued about everything to do with God: was he divine only? – Monophysites; or God *and* Man? – Chalcedonians. These then divided into Jacobites, Copts, Abyssinians, Syriac Orthodox, Armenian Gregorians, Maronites, Melkites, Greek Orthodox. This partial list includes neither all the Christian sects nor the equally numerous subdivisions within the Syrian and Lebanese Muslim world.

The Maronite mass is celebrated in Aramaic Arabic and is much longer than the Latin mass. This second disadvantage was the reason given to me by my mother for the instant disappearance of a strangely garbed Maronite priest who turned up in Melbourne in the 1940s, or it might have been the 1950s. My practical mother said, 'Who is to cook the Sunday lunch if mass is as long as that?' However, it is only recently that the true reason for the seamless absorption of the Maronite Catholic Lebanese into Australia became clear to me. Maronite priests marry. (In fact other Eastern Catholic sects have married priests, not that the Pope ever admits this in public.) The thought of Catholic priests *and their wives* mixing and mingling with the Jansenist Irish Catholics of my local parish church cannot be imagined: I am sure my grandfather shovelled the poor priest back to Bsharri with a one-way ticket. In 1995 I went to the Lebanon for the first time, with the writer David Malouf. I saw a priest flirting on the porch of the Maronite church of St Jean Baptiste in Byblos, before mass on Palm Sunday. It was like seeing Nixon dictating his tapes.

These Mountain Christians first came up for breath from wallowing in the liquidation of heretical neighbours when they encountered the Crusades in the eleventh century and many fought with the Christians against their Arab brethren, for which they were not forgiven. This, together with nine centuries of connection with the Papacy in Rome and the consistent attention of France, who first placed the Lebanon under her wing in the thirteenth century, meant that Maronites were always a people who felt they could afford to be different, and who would fight to the death to continue to be so. What this meant in the 1870s when it is said that my grandfather arrived first in Australia, was that he was not considered an Arab, he was seen as a Christian. And so he was allowed entry, went to mass at the Catholic church and from then on entered Australian life with no trouble at all. Muslims were not treated thus.

Most of my grandparents came to Australia for religious reasons. According to my mother, my Irish great-grandparents James Keane and Johanna O'Leary left Cork and Tipperary in 1850 because Catholics could not own land there. When I checked this with the Irish historian, Roy Foster, he pointed out that this was untrue. Nevertheless, in that quintessentially Irish way, it was true to *them*, because they handed this fact down from generation to generation. I have a tape recording of my 89-year-old mother telling me: 'My mother (Theresa Keane) told me her mother Johanna Keane hated the English, because her father, Peter O'Leary, could never own the land although he was a prosperous man. Absentee English landlord. She used to say that if she had had a rifle and seen the absentee landlord she'd have shot him. That was the temper of my grandmother.'

Anecdotes of this kind are common enough among Australians: there were hundreds of reasons for resentment against the English, not least from those English who'd left the old country as convicts, or under a cloud of one sort or another, but religious resentment from the Irish population was a particularly firm thread in the fabric of Australian politics and literature. A central portion of the Australian character has my Irish great-grandmother's temper.

My Lebanese grandfather, Butros Kahlil Fakhry, arrived in Australia, according to some records, in 1876, the first Lebanese person to go there. Other records say he arrived in 1881. As he was born in 1863 and thirteen seems a bit young to have sailed in the bottom of a boat to the other side of the world, 1881 seems right, but who knows? He left a tiny country of two million people, only 125 miles long, and was dumped in Melbourne, then a city of half a million inhabitants, speaking no English and thinking he was elsewhere anyway. My grandfather had no intention of going to Australia. He wanted to go to America – the United States – where all emigrants wanted to go, or to South America where there were already others from Bsharri. He was taken to Melbourne, willy-nilly: my Last Uncle told me that these unscrupulous sea captains would dump the migrant in Lisbon, or some miscellaneous port: 'Here you are, this is America.' Another trick was to take the hapless migrant to the farthest and costliest place: this was Australia or New Zealand, where many more of the clan settled in the 1890s. There are accounts of Lebanese living in Australia for years before they realised they were not in 'Al-Na-Yurk' (New York).

Lebanon then was not a separate state: it was – as now again – subsumed into Syria; and all of that was part of the Ottoman Empire. It is said that my grandfather left because of religious persecution. Research into this reveals that the Christian Maronite massacres took place in 1860, and that they were perpetrated by the Druze, the schismatic Muslims with whom the Maronites shared Mount Lebanon. However, further delving suggests that the Turks put the Druze up to it.

There is a fixed truth about Lebanese history: no explanations for anything are at all clear and most people who

46

recount it lie – so this reason for his emigration does not explain why he waited nearly twenty years after the massacres to get a move on. A more Marxist interpretation says that in the 1860s the economy of the Mountain was under siege. The silk industry, which constituted a considerable part of Maronite income, began to collapse under competition from industrialised nations and the invention of artificial silk; and the ancient Phoenician trading ports – Tyre, Sidon, Beirut, Tripoli – fell into decline with the opening of the Suez Canal in 1869.

I was also told that Maronites on the Mountain felt persecuted because when they encountered a Muslim Lebanese or Turk in the villages and towns of the Mountain, they were required to bow low to them and cross the road in order to get out of the way of the ruling panjandrum. My grandfather and his kin hated this.

The reason which brought all my ancestors to Australia – religious difference – continued to boil and bubble in both Ireland and the Lebanon a hundred years after they got away. During the Lebanese Civil War of 1975–90 Ian Paisley could have popped over to the Lebanon at any time and merged into a happy throng of raving bigots, and the IRA and the Maronite Phalange both speak with that familiar Catholic righteousness that sounds so akin to madness.

However much my grandfather must have suffered as an illiterate Arabic-speaking mountain peasant arriving in Australia with nothing to his name, not one echo of pain, suffering, misery or anguish has been handed down from his mouth to ours. He worked hard, of course, and so did my grandmother, but they prospered and seem to have slithered into Australian life with ease and gusto. He contradicts all sociological accounts of emigration at this time. He arrived twenty years before the White Australian policy was thought of – under this policy he would be classified as Asian and, if a new emigrant, would be unlikely to manage the language tests required to gain entry to the country. But even earlier, in 1880, as a subject of the Turkish Empire, he should have been designated non-white and refused citizenship.

None of this happened to him. By 1884, four years after his arrival, he had a large building at No. 274 Exhibition Street, in the centre of the city of Melbourne, with the words *Latoof & Callil 1884* inscribed at its height – the building was still there until a year or two ago. He had brought over his brother Latoof, had returned to the Lebanon to bring back my grandmother Henineh (Anna) Yazbeck and had brought more cousins to extend the clan. By 1895 he was a naturalised citizen and had beautifully embossed business paper describing his company as 'Importers of Fancy Goods'.

As to his name, whoever let him in at Port Melbourne wrote down in English his first two names and that seems to have been that. Butros is Arabic for Peter, and Callil is a good Irish version of Kahlil, though Mr Kelly, which my Number One Uncle was often called, might have been easier.

Most Australian literature of the 1880s and 1890s is bush literature: tales and stories about conquering the outback, settling the country, the loneliness and the heartbreak of working the unforgiving land. In those bush tales you often come across stories of the Syrian pedlars, and sometimes illustrations of them: dark-jawed, beaknosed, carrying cottons and laces and news from homestead to homestead. This must be what my grandfather did, though my Last Uncle swore that all he did was have a good time wandering around Australia as a rouseabout. But then, much as I loved him, my Last Uncle was not too keen on humble beginnings.

To Australians of that time, in the 1880s, the Lebanese didn't exist. The 'Syrians' and Syrian pedlars who appear in early Australian writing are almost all Lebanese, for something like four thousand Lebanese migrated to Australia in the years before the First World War, and many more since, the number in Australia now, according to some, being in the region of half a million. Syrians rarely came, generally because most of them were Muslim, but also because Syrians were less adventurous than the Lebanese who set off in shoals, to South America, the USA, Africa, the Caribbean, Canada, Australia and New Zealand in formidable numbers, bringing family and most important of all, to them, bringing

their food with them. I was told that my grandmother travelled from Bsharri to Australia nursing her *laban* (yoghurt)
which was to become the source of all future Callil yoghurt,
to be found bubbling and squeaking in every family heating
cupboard. My mother always swore she could tell the difference between a Syrian and a Lebanese (I still can), which
gave me my first childish understanding that these were two
peoples who should not be shackled together, and that should
they be so shackled, the Lebanese were infinitely superior.

So, when my grandfather became an Australian citizen
on 28 November 1894, he was described portentously as a
merchant. But one of the brothers he brought to Australia,
Selim (I knew him as Uncle Sam), reveals more. The Melbourne police describe Uncle Sam in 1896: 'He has been
engaged in business with his two brothers who are importers
of fancy goods and he has had a hawker's licence and made
a living by hawking fancy goods through the country districts
with a horse and cart.' A cousin, Michael Fakhry, is also
described as working for them and 'having a hawker's
licence'. So it seems that my grandfather did indeed start out
as a pedlar, then graduated to sending his brothers and
cousins out in a horse and cart with the 'fancy goods' he
supplied for them and for other pedlars. He then went on to
become a considerable clothing manufacturer with factories
in three cities, buying and selling all over the world. He made
enough money to provide in varying ways for a vast family,
for battalions of grandchildren and great-grandchildren and
often for those unrelated to himself.

Every one of my grandparents had large families and came
from large families. My Irish grandmother was the youngest
of nine, my grandfather, her husband, one of eight, not counting those who died of diphtheria, drowning or mischance.
As a child, I loved to hear their names recounted; wonderful
names they were to me: Norberts and Ernests; Alfreds and
Walters, Doras and Lilys and Sissys. In these voluminous
families disgrace or death came in unexpected ways: Great
Uncle Alfred ate poisoned mushrooms, Great Uncle Joe went
to Valparaiso and edited the *Valparaiso Times* and wrote

shocking poetry. Great Uncle Frank walked into the sea and was never seen again.

It seems to be the first generation offspring of hardy immigrants who pay the price for their parents' insouciance, for the stories of my Lebanese aunts and uncles were in every way more fractured, more tragic and more hilarious than those of their parents, as though they had a harder time containing their Mountain temperaments in the calmer waters of Australian suburban life.

My grandmother Anna had nine children. Far less is known about her than about my grandfather for the usual Arab reasons. Typically, my Last Uncle said to me, 'If only you had been a boy', but in fact it was much easier to be a girl than a boy in my family, as we girls could never disappoint. The Lebanese writer, Hanan Al Shaykh, tells me that Bsharri is famous for the ferocious strength of its women. Of the seven clans of Bsharri, my grandmother came from one which was far more warlike than that of my grandfather and her force of personality erupted from the kitchen, where I would see her pounding *kibbe* and creating eternal family feasts: she was a stern Mountain matriarch, and her children knew it. As my mother and father lived across the road from this large family I saw them constantly throughout my childhood. They furnished my theatre of life with generosity, eccentricity and vigour, and I hated, feared and loved them in equal measure. This overabundant parade of Callils provided me with the standards by which I would lead my life, for good or ill.

They were tremendously argumentative. Even those words don't seem sufficiently strong for the decibel level of their narrative and conversation. They truly liked a nice row. The greatest challenge of life was to get out exactly what you thought about a subject *immediately*, before anyone else could get a word in. Secondly they were both unspeakable to, and prodigiously loyal and generous to each other. Anyone with the family blood was included in this exhausting attention. They kept their eye on you, even if you were the fourth child of the fifth brother. 'Do you need anything?'

Each conversation would end with this question. The ritual reply was 'No thank you, Uncle'. 'Are you *sure* you don't need anything? All right then . . .'

Full brothers and sisters were to be trusted. There was a problem with the next generation, because other blood had mixed with the sacred stream. Wives were viewed with suspicion, but husbands of sisters were treated like hell. Money was given in abundance to nephews and nieces, but as soon as nephews and nieces married the question always came: 'What are you going to do with it?' When daughters, nieces or nephews died, and left their money to spouses, this caused true agony in the family. No one could understand why what was theirs now belonged to a perfect stranger whom they had viewed with considerable suspicion right from the beginning.

Two other matters loomed large in the lives of these brothers and sisters: religion and gambling. Some took up only the one, some only the other, some dabbled in both. The Catholic Church, and horse and dog racing, cards, backgammon, casinos and sport played a major part in Callil daily life. In that way the Lebanese took to Australia like Arab ducks to water.

Everyday life was completely Australian, but most of them spoke French and Arabic, though I only heard the latter when the men let out Arabic swear-words in their all-night gambling sessions. They were always surrounded by hordes of dazed friends, generally attending a table groaning with Lebanese food, French wine and the occasional pavlova, bread-and-butter pudding or other favoured piece of Oz-English cuisine. Most Sundays of my childhood I used to have to go to their house to pay my respects first to my grandparents, and later to my uncles and aunts. When I came to England in 1960, I continued to lunch with my uncles every Sunday when they were in London, until the family flat in Mayfair was finally disbanded when my Last Uncle became too old to travel. But that was only in the 1980s. The price they paid as first generation immigrants was most apparent in their marriages: it cannot have been only bad luck that caused most of them to live alone for most of their lives. Death played a part too but the crippling question was: who could match up to the family, in blood or in anything else?

The first of the nine was Joseph, who was born and died almost instantaneously. Next came Mary. The trials of being the first girl child in a new land are all too apparent in the story of her life. Mary was about five feet tall and seriously ugly. She certainly had a moustache, but she seemed also to have a beard. She looked exactly like her brother George, but what is acceptable in a plump Lebanese male looks alienating, to say the least, in a woman. She was peculiar, perhaps mad? But then, perhaps they drove her mad. When I knew her, she had been married off to a favourite uncle-by-marriage, the Spanish one, Uncle Eloi, who later disappeared, sensible man. This hapless refugee from Franco was verbally abused and despised by all members of the family. His Spanish-Australian English was incomprehensible beyond imagining. He used to visit my mother, and would sit mournfully recounting some new tale of persecution. 'Garmin,' he would say to me, 'your fam'ly. Dey are all MENTALLY RETAR', and would soulfully tap the side of his head to demonstrate insanity.

I first realised Aunt Mary *was* mad when I was sent to stay with her after the death of my father, when I was nine. We would kneel down after supper, which would consist of some extremely dubious form of Lebanese food, and say the rosary for him. For Aunt Mary the rosary was whatever she wanted to dish out: not for her ten Hail Marys five times over. Being a good convent girl, this was agonising to me, so I would try to intersperse a quick Hail Mary or two, under my breath, to bring the numbers up to the required level. This led inevitably to silence on my part as I was careering through additional Hail Marys at times when she expected me to reply to some incantation she had stuck in *ad hoc*. 'Can't you even pray for your poor dead father?' she would scream.

Most members of the family lived near my Lebanese grandparents. This was because my grandparents and their children wanted it like this, but also because my grandparents bought their children houses within shouting distance of the family home. In Mary's case though, it was a measure of her lack of favour that she lived at least two suburbs away. I often encountered her on the tram home from school or university and I learned to hide to avoid the embarrassment of exchanges with her tempestuous person. And too, she was top of the Callil shouting league. Often she would spot me hiding and would shriek through the packed tram: 'There she is, my dead brother's child and she won't say hello to her Aunty.'

Aunt Mary was a rich source of Lebanese washing stories. (Lebanese women seem to be obsessed with cleaning.) One day I was passing by her house and saw her munchkin body in the front garden fiercely directing a hose at a fully pegged out rotary line of sodden washing, which also seemed, on closer inspection, to be ramrod stiff with some mysterious substance. She bustled me off to the new washing machine my Number One Uncle had bought for her that day. She had poured the entire contents of three giant packets of Persil into the machine (my family always bought everything in bulk). Lebanese women like to see *suds*, lots of suds. The clothes were rigid with soap, the machine destroyed.

My other Aunt Mary, wife to my third uncle, was equally washing orientated. I used to do the family washing on Mondays, in the years when I was at Melbourne University. I hated doing it, and what I didn't bury in the garden I would peg out lickety split on the rotary line and then retire to my books. This Aunt Mary would sometimes turn up and re-peg the whole thing: all *socks* together, all *red socks* together, all *red socks* pegged in *the same direction*, and so on through every colour and item until perfect symmetry was achieved. There are lots of Lebanese washing stories. David Malouf tells of a female relative of his who, whenever he went to stay, woke him up early in the morning by gently rocking him to and fro to ease out the sheet beneath his sleeping body in order to get it into the wash before the day began. Lebanese women are particularly fixated on sheets.

After Mary came the first George, who was run over by a milk truck at the age of one. He was followed by Jim who, according to my Last Uncle, went to fight in Gallipoli, was gassed and died a war hero at the age of thirty-one, in Sydney – always a suspicious place for any member of my family to visit, least of all to die in. Others report that he died of the booze. Then came Rose, the sourest Rose you could come across, the most pious of all the uncles and aunts, who looked after her brothers' children when wives died or disappeared and who was known as 'Tante'. Tante had a cold heart but a hard life. Madness or the Catholic Church was the lot of women of the first generation and the happiest of them chose the former.

After Rose came the second George, the head of the family, and my Number One Uncle. George was the Godfather responsible for the brothers, sisters and cousins of his generation and the nephews, nieces, first, second and third cousins who constituted the clan by the time he took over as head of the family, when my grandfather died in 1943. George's jobs as Capo were onerous. If there was no father around he was involved in decisions about schools and careers; he provided money, food, clothing, Christmas presents to all and sundry, and miscellaneous gifts at all times. When the time came for the fatherless girls to marry he squired them down the aisle. George was a gambling Callil: horses, casinos, you name it. He was a great cash man, in fact all my uncles carried wads of cash to peel off for those who might need it, and their suspicious view of banks I honour religiously to this day. As he was dying in London in 1969 he tried to tell me where he'd left sums stashed away in various European hotspots, but I couldn't make out what he was talking about. I'll bet somewhere in the gardens outside the Beaulieu Casino, in the South of France – the family's favourite gambling den – are one or two of Uncle George's disaster funds buried for a rainy day.

He had in quintuplicate the Callil habit of buying in bulk. By the time he took over the family business, half his time was spent living in London. His favourite part of London life was Covent Garden market where he would go at the crack of dawn every morning and buy crates of anything that caught his eye. His entire acquaintance, and the family in London, which consisted of his daughter, the hovering Tante, and myself, would wake up in the morning to boxes of avocados, tomatoes, cauliflower, whatever he decided upon. I hate avocados to this day. It was the men at old Covent Garden who used to call him Mr Kelly. Everyone else in London called him Poppa.

My Number One Uncle had a large heart and he was clever, particularly at business. He shot around the world doing deals behind the Iron Curtain, in China, in Manchester – where he kept a permanent bar at the Midland Hotel – spreading largesse and losing and making money as he went. A widower, he followed his daughter Lilette around like an anxious St Bernard. In his daughter his bullying generosity transformed itself into a contagious relish for life which would have made a snail dance. A giver of light, I sometimes think she invented sixties London, and enjoyed every single moment of it until she died of heart disease when she was thirty-three.

My Number One Uncle nevertheless kept an eye on everything to do with the family, wherever he was. In the early sixties I was in the Middlesex Hospital in London about to have an abortion on the National Health. In those days abortions were illegal. To have one on the National Health you had to be certified insane, or somesuch. By the time I got through the interview system at the Middlesex I was insane, so that was OK. I slunk anonymously into the hospital, put on my nightie and wished I was dead. I heard a familiar voice rushing towards me – my uncle, with a vast box of chocolates, his monkey face screwed up in the nearest he could ever get to distress, puffing anxiously, 'I know what you're up to,' and dishing me out tenners in the usual way. I'd told no one where I was going, or what my trouble was.

Next came the gentle uncle, my Uncle Phil, put upon by his towering brothers, notable though for siring the best and brightest of the next generation, in the shape – shape being the relevant word – of my enormous cousin John, who died of Hodgkin's disease in his thirties, and who looked like a Lebanese mountain gorilla. A comic genius, his way of talking was a combination of the best Australian argot with a Lebanese lack of belief in, or respect for, everything except God (and even He . . . ). In my family there is a lot of death: his was the biggest waste.

The next child was my father, Frederick, who died of Hodgkin's disease when he was forty-eight. He was the only brother not to go into the family business but became a barrister instead and a lecturer in French at Melbourne University. All the boys except my Last Uncle were sent back to the Lebanon to be educated, generally in pairs, and there they stayed until their education was over, looked after by an aunt, or cousin, or priest. Born in 1899, my father would have been about five or six when he went because my mother says he was so small he could not tie his shoelaces for himself. The sons had their photographs taken before they went off on the long, long journey to St Joseph's School and University in Beirut. Sad little photographs, poor little boys: they look stricken. All were back from exile by the outbreak of the First World War.

Of all the sons my father was the most dedicated gambler. When he died he left my mother racehorses, an overflowing library and a good part of the greyhound coursing club in Melbourne. Horses, cards, backgammon, combined with a passion for books – the purchase and reading thereof – caused him to stay in bed until the middle of the afternoon and pupils of his later told me that if he had a tutorial in the morning, he would sometimes turn up in his pyjamas.

My Last Uncle, Alex, the baby of the family, was a man of enormous grit and self-confidence. He knew exactly what he thought about everything, and he knew he was right. A practising Catholic of the most vociferous kind, he shared with Tante a fanatical devotion to the Catholic Church. I can't think of one opinion he and I shared but there is no question that he's the one I loved the best of all. It's not as though we didn't know we disagreed with each other, although, well trained, I would rarely air my opinions in the middle of his diatribes: it was just that in a combustible sort of way we both put up with each other for being exactly the same but entirely different. He was utterly black and white; grey was a colour he couldn't even spell. Sin was sin, and hell was hell, where you went if you sinned. The sort of politician he liked was Margaret Thatcher or Franco, the latter being a particular favourite.

He didn't mind the opinions of other people as long as they did not expect him to be swayed by them for one minute. In fact he expected others to hold as tightly to their version of the truth as he did to his. Unmerciful to all minorities, he could nevertheless take it on the chin if chance disturbed his airtight Catholic Puritanism. Every summer he would return to London to the flat in Park Street, Mayfair, which he loved, and once a week I would accompany him to the theatre. His favourite dictum was that he went to the theatre to be entertained thank you very much and didn't want anything else, no messages, no problems and no incomprehensible prose. For my sins I saw every British farce in the West End over the years but the worst moment of our theatrical adventures came when he insisted on going to see Ian McKellen in *Bent*, which tells of the persecution of homosexuals under Hitler, and portrays harrowing scenes in the concentration camps. At one point Ian McKellen simulated masturbation on stage, and I thought my Uncle would collapse with fury – he was a cripple and had a dicky heart. I wheeled him out at the end of it all, stuffing him with heart pills to keep him conscious. Homosexuality was absolutely beyond the pale, and yet . . . there was something sad and innocent about his intolerance. The other brothers used gambling to see the day through; Catholic prejudices were far harder to live with and his marriage and much else – the family business – disappeared under the force of his rigidity.

For the family at large my Last Uncle was in no way the Capo that my Number One Uncle had been, he lacked his older brother's generous heart. But he was vigorous and strong and a fighter, and he loved adventures. Typical of his life were the two-week flights he took to London in the 1920s on those grand seaplanes built like the Savoy with wings. They had to stop every day to reload with petrol. No matter how bizarre the staging post, each night they would dine magnificently – in the jungles of Borneo or the deserts of the Gulf – in white tie and tails, on beautifully decorated tables. He thought being alive was the best, best thing. In that way he *was* the last of the Mohicans.

In 1993 I flew to Australia for his funeral. He died at the age of ninety-one, and almost everyone with a drop of clan blood was there for the funeral. What struck me, looking round the church, was that everything my grandfather and grandmother set out to do had now been achieved. All the great-grandchildren and cousins, by this time two, three, and four times removed, had bits and pieces of them and of the uncles and aunts bestowed about their persons. There was the curly hair again, there the familiar balding spot; there were the two or three regulation Callil noses, the wheezy chests and always, for the women, those thunderthigh Mount Lebanon legs. But it was all mixed up with injections from Australians of Irish, Scottish, English, Italian and more various stock. For those who left the Mountain a hundred years before, everything was just as it should be.

But I miss waking up to find a pig's head on a case of cauliflowers outside my front door. I miss hearing the bellicose opinions and their feeling that life is about caring and making things happen and about insisting on putting up with as little as possible under all circumstances. And I truly miss the calls, 'Do you need anything? Are you absolutely sure you're all right?'

# Miroslav Holub

## IT COULD BE A LOT WORSE:
## CZECH LITERATURE IN THE NINETIES

*Translated from the Czech*
*by Ewald Osers*

THE BEST INDICATOR of the state of culture under European conditions is literature. The best indicator of the state of literature, more accurately of the relation between authors and reader interest, is the publication and purchase of books. There is a general impression in the Czech Republic that 'a lot' of books are being published, that it was not only the floodgates of free opinion that opened, but, rather more so, those of commercial interest, and that the people are being dulled rather than enlightened by the unleashed flood of printed paper.

That impression, I believe, is more or less correct.

The problem is that we are dealing with impressions rather than solid facts, since solid facts went out with the Russian-style autocracy, where solid facts were provided by solid controls.

The chaotic market-place of Czech literature today contains four thousand registered publishing firms (compared with thirty publishing houses licensed by the communist state in the 1980s). Of that total some 250 to 300 exhibit some activity beyond mere registration; about fifty are surviving economically without resorting to trash, which in its Czech form is even worse as a result of being translated by certain semi-literate people with only a nodding acquaintance with the English and Czech languages.

Each week some 200 books are published, with fiction accounting for over 40 per cent. A bookseller refusing to stock trash receives each week about a hundred titles, i.e. forty to fifty fiction titles, including some ten slim volumes of poetry, among which the percentage of titles published 'at the author's expense' is growing significantly. Best-sellers of the Umberto Eco or Milan Kundera type are published in print runs of over 40,000; poetry is published in fewer than 1,000 copies, even though, in my experience, it is possible to sell 2,000 copies of a volume of poetry within four months. (Under the communists this number of copies by not-too-dissident authors would have sold within four hours.)

I don't think that, in a nation of ten million, this is a disastrous situation, even though, according to one estimate, a good 15 per cent are socially and culturally deprived – which, by comparison with other European countries, is entirely within the norm.

According to a survey by sociologists from the Charles University in Prague, 86.4 per cent of the 1,200 respondents described themselves as regular readers and 44 per cent stated that they had more than 1,000 books in their homes. As for *genre*, the readers of non-fiction are on the increase, while fiction generally takes second place, and poetry is of interest only to an insignificant number of respondents, most of them with personal poetic aspirations.

If the owners of these domestic libraries and regular readers were by definition good people, then – despite rampant commercialisation – we'd be a nation of angels. But no such correlation exists. We only have readers and non-readers, and the only positive sociological parameter of a reader is that while he is reading he isn't doing anything worse.

The situation of our literature is generally complicated by the fact that – quite apart from the chaotic market – the catalytic link author–author–reader–author, i.e. the phenomenon of the literary periodical in the strict sense, has disappeared. It is not just that the old literary reviews have folded up or that there is a shortage of money. Some cultural periodicals receive more or less substantial subsidies from the state or private sponsors. But the editorial offices of cultural journals, and more especially of literary ones, suffer from the syndrome of theory-diarrhoea. Literature, prose (mostly memoirs) and poetry (mostly avant-garde), occupies only some 12 per cent of the contents of literary journals. The rest are political, philosophical, historical and meta-literary reflections, a small proportion of them reviews and a large proportion abstract 'thoughts' which, by their sheer quantity, ensure that no reader can find the time to think. This is partly due to the Czech urge to catch up with the 'post-modernist' West and partly to the uncertainty of where precisely the lower threshold of 'literature' lies in a liberated atmosphere (i.e. one that has gone wild).

Except for plays, literature has totally vanished from television (under communist rule it was featured, often with disastrous flops but sometimes successfully), and on radio it has been pushed into the late-night schedules, when only insomniacs or alcoholics are listening.

The lack of communication through journals results in an isolation of creative individuals. In human terms, writers tend to know each other from the pub rather than from their work. This means that no one really knows what the state of Czech literature is or what its trends have been in the past five years since the factor of opposition to those in power disappeared. The situation is further complicated by the fact that the clear majority of editors and critics have adopted the bold plan of comparing and judging four streams of pre-November-1989 literature – the official regime literature, the literature of the grey (i.e. tolerated) zone, the literature of political dissent, and exile literature. Even though most editors made the task easier for themselves by simply eliminating all former official literature, the situation in the three remaining spheres is unclear. It is not only a case of different contexts and personal attitudes, but mainly one of generation gaps between people who experienced at least the Soviet occupation of 1968 and those who only knew the decay of the communist system and its censorship. The journals have brought to the readers a large number of previously unknown authors, whose principal merit was the fact that they were unknown or suppressed under the communist regime. It turned out that some of them were unknown not because of the logic of the communist censor, but because their work was no good. Moreover, some authors from the beginning of the century are being dug up, authors who had fallen into oblivion even in their own time. Thus the context is becoming even more complex – we are faced with a mixture of several generations, several styles and a colourful assortment of old junk.

On the one hand we are learning what was silenced or suppressed. On the other we have a climate that exercises a formative pressure. New authors – and especially poets panting for air – notice carefully what is being published and what is in vogue, and, as far as their nature permits, are guided by it, to ensure they are themselves published and their apparel is up to date. Individual types of authors, as they first appeared towards the end of the 1960s, now turn into processions, individual mutants into types. This process, a kind of literary 'polymerase chain reaction', takes place in the stages author–editor–author–an army of debutants–editor. This PCR functions chiefly thanks to the restricted publication opportunities mentioned above. Thus when in one and the same issue of a literary journal we encounter a single poet and two prose writers, we are sometimes faced not with artistic necessity but with anxious imitation.

If you publish more and more post-decadent pranks spiced with new possibilities of scatology and liberated by sexual technologies and deviations, you will, by a positive feedback, create a new literary generation of the voluntarily damned fraternising with antiquarian demons and copulating on graves, in more serious cases *with* graves. If you publish several authentic Young Werthers, you'll be supplying artificial nutriment to a poetry of disillusionment, exclusivity and painful Take-what-you-can, including drugs (if only because it's something 'from the West'). It is just like the 1960s, when, after a memorable visit by Allen Ginsberg, many young men here concluded that you had to be a homosexual and later began to crowd the waiting-rooms of psychiatric clinics with complaints that they wanted to do it but didn't like it. If here and there you publish a Marian litany as a novelty, you'll be creating something like an awed rhymed Christian-confessional poetry over which will sough the Czech lyrical spirit defined by Seifert. If you embark on an increasingly frequent publication of French poetry, from which the Czech mainstream clearly retreated after 1945, you'll get a flowering of the poetry of silence, abstraction and hermetic spirituality. If you publish something as contagious for a post-modern anarchistic intellectual as Boris Vian (seven books since 1989) you'll get a clone of well-intentioned literary bums.

At the same time the publishing policy of the existing literary media and of the more serious publishing houses also produces the phenomenon of a higher standard of discourse and a higher intellectual level – provided that amidst the gentle howling of the writers, like frustrated puppies, there is room for these. So long as we know what to say and how to say it, we present it in a form that had no parallel in the old days.

Those frustrated canine beasts of prey moreover regard themselves as independent intellectuals in the meaning of Timothy Garton Ash – a concept defended at the International PEN Congress in Prague and frequently published (e.g. in the *New York Review of Books*, January 1995) – mainly because Ash's opponent was the Czech prime minister Václav Klaus. An independent intellectual, of course, is independent of premiers and their political moves, because he is dependent on his fundamental opposition to premiers and political or economic moves, even indispensable ones. An independent intellectual believes that the human intellect exists to seek the truth independently, even though it is equally probable that it may exist for the justification of his own emotional urges and ties.

The fact that over the past five years the Czech economy (thanks also to Klaus's team) has achieved considerably more than Czech literature, including poetry, is a source of further frustration and other negative emotions to any literary worker loyal to his craft – provided, of course, he admits this to himself and isn't living in some mouldering literary nest from where the transition from totalitarianism to an open society must seem a bitter awakening from the dream of one's own importance.

But intellect itself is a word to argue over, and reason, for modish philosophers and certain natural literary talents, is a source of deviation from 'natural' man and the 'natural' world. That's why it's wise to bracket out reason altogether. From the bold statement of the philosopher Václav Bělohradský, 'The intoxicating flight of philosophy has gone on for more than two thousand years. The time has come for us to feel like morons', many natural talents have taken on board only the second sentence. And so they have become the champions of their own and of observed oddity. The authenticity of psychiatric or sociological deviation is higher than the authenticity of axiomatic thought; the authenticity of verbal vomiting is, in principle, more valuable than the foundation stones of secondary school education.

Ranged against the debased taste of 'popular' strata, stimulated by the offer of bloodthirsty, erotic and sentimental literature, are the new-style transcendentalists who are offering blood, sex and spirituality in a dozen other, if possibly less readily comprehensible, ways. This is an interesting antithesis, but unfortunately not a very constructive one.

The basic statement of Czech literature during the five years of freedom and human dignity is strikingly egocentric. Any indication of a 'we' has disappeared, as have any indications of solidarity with the ordinary person (who is evidently a willing victim of slightly dotty advertisements and publicity), and even any indication of communication. The nest syndrome is holding sway, along with the droppings from the nest. While the mainstream of so-called East European poetry under the communist regime was characterised by a hidden energy, by inventiveness, by a synchronisation with the human movements of the entire national community and, indeed, by a certain optimism, we now face the flabby spirit of permanent disillusionment of one's ego, a disillusionment which ultimately doesn't give a damn in what way we were disappointed by sex and in what way by Klaus – so long as we were disappointed by someone. The basic attitude of those slight (let's call them) poems in prose which the new authors are producing on the conveyor belt is the attitude of a corpse cowering in its grave, of an embryo in the womb and of a convict on his bed or in some other confined space where surrealist transubstantiations take place, an invasion by spiritual jurassic monsters and the degradation of Enlightenment values, among which the Hofrat Goethe appears especially obsolescent.

It is as if the suddenly opened space were suspiciously large and empty, as if we were afraid of the draught for which we collectively thirsted for fifty years. We close our shutters to prevent our domestic demons from catching cold and the delicate gear wheels of our magic realism from being damaged – that magic realism which unites the categories of poetry and prose to such an extent that the difference between them is, as it were, washed away and we get some hybrid forms between an absurdist story and a poem in prose. These products are sometimes interesting in the original, but in translation, as a rule, fall into the category of the *déjà vu*. Larger forms of prose also fall apart into facets and microsnapshots, into a personal mythology which conceals the personal ideas, horizon and goal to such a degree that Kundera's novel-essay differs from the Czech meta-novel rather like cosmology from insect collecting.

There's nothing against insect collecting in literature, at least so long as the insects are interesting, touching, or even a new species. But if this collecting acquires the character of the mainstream, in which a novel is the work of a hand drawing a hand which is itself being drawn, in which Borges and Marques are peeping out of every other sleeve, a mainstream in which Bukowski (peeping out of a trouser leg) is about the most concrete stereotype, then unconventional and *épatant* authenticity becomes a paper poisoning, where all are the same to the extent that they are divertingly diverse.

In the context of literary criticism, which suffers from the faint syndrome of the new opportunism, the overall state of literature is best defined by the young film director Filip Renč: You can't make a generation film in a period which – unlike the 1960s – has no style.

All I can say by way of an excuse is that if you thrash about in turbulent water for fifty years, now and again calling for help, you won't produce many style-creating ideas. And if in the 1960s you discern a style of calling for help, then this is no use to you anyway in the 1990s when it appears as literary decline.

It is too early to judge the state of our literature; the water is stirred up from the very bottom and it carries a multitude of pollutants, mud snails and water fleas. But slowly it is calming down.

However, I would already venture to discern the outlines of a new literary constitution – irony, self-irony, mild sorrow on your face, deep laughter in your heart, as Jaroslav Seifert put it. Even the Czech meta-novel, even Czech neo-decadent poetry, even orthodox Czech post-modernism all bear the traits of inner humour and of a sceptical smile. Even in the fragmentation of experience and in the self-centred attitude of a poem it is sometimes possible to discover a grain of the Czech salt of understatement and wit.

Even if liberated Czech literature were to create something like a new concept of man, it would still contain something like: 'So sorry, but it could be a lot worse.'

# Fleur Adcock

## BED AND BREAKFAST

They thought he looked like Gregory Peck, of course;
and they thought I looked like Anne somebody –
a name I vaguely recognised: no one special,
not Greer Garson or Vivien Leigh.
What they really must have thought I looked like
was young. But they were being kind;
and anyway, we'd asked for separate rooms.

When it was late enough, Gregory Peck
came into mine – or did I go into his?
Which of us tiptoed along the passage
in our pyjamas? And to do what?
                                        Not sex,
but what you did when you weren't quite doing sex.
It made you a bit sticky and sweaty,
but it didn't make you pregnant,
and you didn't actually have to know anything.
You didn't even take off your pyjamas.

Unfortunately since it never got anywhere
it went on most of the night. No sleep.
At breakfast, though, I can't have looked too haggard:
Gregory Peck was not put off.
For that I could thank the resilience of youth –
one of the very few advantages,
as far as I could see, of that hateful condition.

Anne Whatsit might have looked worse;
but then I suppose she'd have had makeup.

# Moniza Alvi

## DELHI CHRISTMAS

In hotel lobbies skinny Christmas trees
rest on beds of egg-white satin

hold blunt finger-strips of cotton wool.
Santa gestures like a tour leader

next to log cabin, jewelled caravan.
Piano and cello send incessant *Jingle Bells*

into the costly international atmosphere.
And *The Times of India* hosts recipes

for 'ginger hut' and marzipan.
Inhabitants of silent corridors – the workers

murmur Merry Christmas, nod and smile.
Fierce air-conditioning creates a winter chill.

Sunbathers, indolent, line the swimming pool,
while England floats contained, so far away

like a glass-domed scene with shaken snow.
Cliff-like in the cool night air

Eastern hotels tap lightly into Christmas.
English couples talk of cats in Abingdon.

# Alison Brackenbury

## CLEARING UP

The house tonight is unkempt as my hair,
there are people I love who no longer write,
it is midnight, and everywhere, small bags of apples.
Wax apples for children, for school, then for horses:
the small and scuffled ones nursing green cores.

God, I ate none of them! Look, they become
wild trees again, a tunnel of flower,
in the bag of your eyes they dance but bring
no orchards now. Wooden floors hold your sleep,
perfectly dry as a winter apple.

## ON THE ROAD

The rag is the squirrel. Grey screamer at magpies,
tree-flyer, tail-snapper, he's gone.
His airy bounds met the final car.
He could have stepped safely, lived long,
but he left the soft air for the dangerous earth,
I do not say he was wrong.

# POSTCARD

Another meeting that we never had
was in the South resort where we
both went, separately, to work,
where wedding-cake hotels and sea
are not the hot glint of its name:
Brighton, with Sandra's crumpled card
in the first newsagent's you meet,
where tongues touch icecream, in a Sunday fog
still roughened by the cooling sheets.
There never was a better place
not to see you, as your face
quieter, younger, stared across
the pebbles' sleek collapsing cliff
past shaking dogs, red blowing coats,
where the waves' long shine and lift
praise to me, in their shameless stir
all that you are, and never were.

# Maura Dooley

## 1847

Ma's face is black with hair
her hands are paws.
She does not know me any more.

Nights toss us cruelly.
Afraid I'll no more wake
I sit stony.

What knots my belly now's
not hunger. Anger.

In Liverpool ships gob us up.
We rot, we scatter.
The quays are maggoty with us.
We do not matter.

## UP ON THE ROOF

You wonder why it is they write of it, sing of it,
till suddenly you're there, nearest you can get
to flying or jumping and you're alone, at last,
the air bright. Remembering this, I go
with my too-light jacket up to the sixth floor,
out on to the roof and I freeze under the stars
till he comes with my too-heavy jacket, heavier

and heavier, as he tries to muffle my foolishness.
*A blanket on a fire* (he says) and it's true
I am left black, bruised a little, smouldering.

You can sit with a book up there and reel in
life with someone else's bait. You can let your eyes
skim the river, bridges, banks, a seagull's parabola.
At night, you can watch the sky, those strange galaxies
like so many cracks in the ceiling spilling secrets
from the flat above. You can breathe. You can dream.

But he turns to me, as you'd coax a child
in the back of a stuffy car: *we could play I-Spy?*
I look at the black and blue above and the only
letter I find is 'S'. I cannot name
the dust of starlight, the pinheaded planets,
but I can join the dots to make a farming tool,
the belt of a god: all any of us needs is work,
mystery, a little time alone up on the roof.

# MAKING TEA IN THE CORRIDORS OF POWER

We all knew that disease idled in the water tank
but only she could say who favoured a Hobnob
and from whom the Nice biscuits were hidden.

Turner's was black with very little sugar
but Bates wanted lightener *swirled like a cloud*.
No sweeteners. No sweeteners of any kind.

Bailey's came in a china cup
the spoon's *tinkle, tinkle* pleasured him,
the vibration, the promise.

After late meetings there was a shuffle, a scuttle
over stale crumbs and in the mornings she could
smell them. Once, she even glimpsed a scaly tail.

# FREIGHT

I am the ship in which you sail,
little dancing bones,
your passage between the dream
and the waking dream,
your sieve, your pea-green boat.
I'll pay whatever toll your ferry needs.
And you, whose history's already charted
in a rope of cells, be tender to
those other unnamed vessels
who will surprise you one day,
tug-tugging, irresistible,
and float you out beyond your depth,
where you'll look down, puzzled, amazed.

# BITING POINT

In a borrowed car I am following instruction.
*Reverse the car around this corner and pull up
safely.* It is uphill, uneven, blind,
the road is busy. I look back. I move slowly.
I look back. Under my baggy shirt
another person stirs, shrugging my skin
like too many bedclothes, impatient.

*In a moment I am going to say* **stop**
*and I want you to stop, under full control,
as if in emergency.* My feet stamp the floor.
My daughter bangs crossly. *Stop.*
I have stopped. I have looked back.

I have looked hard in the mirror.
The car hasn't even stirred the gravel.

*Good*, says my examiner, *I shan't ask you to do that again.*
Outside a birch lets go of leaves,
I think of my girl and me, each in our carriage,
like Russian dolls. *Drive on*,
the stranger's voice commands. And we do.

# Paul Bailey

## KITTY AND VIRGIL

*Prologue to a novel to be published by Fourth Estate, 1996*

### A COMICAL HERO

WHEN SHE LEARNED that Virgil Florescu was gone from her life, Kitty Crozier remembered their first, silent encounter. She had opened her eyes after a long, drug-induced sleep to find a stranger sitting by the side of her hospital bed. He'd risen as soon as she looked at him. She had noticed there was a glint of something like silver in his smile.

Then he took his smile out of the ward, and she surprised and amused herself by thinking, 'I can't have your baby now, even if I wanted to.' Months would pass before she spoke the thought aloud, to the very same man who was its inspiration that October morning.

'I am not easy in English,' said Dinu Psatta, who had come from Paris to bring her the news. 'Not like Virgil.'

She assured him there was no need to apologise. The only Romanian words she understood were the ones Virgil had taught her – about a hundred, if that, in all.

'You might solve a mystery for me, Mr Psatta. If you can.'

'Mystery? Which mystery?'

'Virgil never told me how he escaped from Romania. Do you know how?'

'Yes. The Dunârea. You say the Danube. He crossed the river Danube.'

'In a boat?'

'No, no. With body.'

'He swam?' She pretended to swim – her arms beating a way through imaginary water. 'Virgil swam across the Danube?'

'Yes, yes. From Turnu Severin. God was with him. Many others were shot. Many were caught and shot. Virgil survive.'

He had crawled into the country that once was Yugoslavia, Kitty heard. Somehow – it was quite a miracle, in Dinu Psatta's view – he had got from Kladovo, near the border, to Split, and from there to Ancona in Italy. He had slept in fields, washed in streams, hidden himself in forests, in the manner of the gypsy.

'He had dollars, in a leather bag, for food.'

She tried to picture a heroic Virgil, a man of daring, of extraordinary physical prowess, and could not see him in her stooped, shambling lover.

'It is natural you are distressed, Mrs Kitty. I am not embarrassed. Cry, as you please.'

What was causing her to weep, she wanted to explain, was the fact that she found it almost impossible to believe in Virgil's courageous swim to freedom, and felt ashamed at doubting his bravery. Yet it was the God-attended atheist, the miracle-worker, who even now was responsible for her being so sceptical, as she recalled his constant references to his puniness ('I am more bone than flesh, Kitty') and his distaste for sport.

'The idea of an athletic Virgil is – '

She choked on the word she had in mind.

'Comical, perhaps?' Dinu Psatta offered.

'Yes, comical. Ludicrous. Terribly funny.'

'It is the truth, Mrs Kitty, the comical truth, that Virgil swam, with body, the Dunârea.'

She had no alternative but to answer, 'Of course it is,' such was the conviction in his voice. 'I'm sure it is,' she added, more emphatically. 'I'm sure it is, Mr Psatta.'

'He talked of his escaping just one time, and he laughed.'

'Did he?'

'Yes, yes. He mocked himself. He mocked what he did

with his body. For him, as for you, it was funny. Not so serious, not so important, as his poems.'

'That one time, Mr Psatta – when was it?'

'Seven, eight years past. Before he was in England, in London. We met in Rome.'

'Then you escaped, too?'

'No, no. I was lawful, if that is the exact term. I had a post in the embassy. I feared I would be ordered back to Bucharest every day and night. I am a coward.'

'I'm sure you aren't.'

'You cannot be sure, Mrs Kitty, of what you do not know.' It was the gentlest of rebukes, delivered with a smile. 'I truly am a coward.'

'If you insist, Mr Psatta.'

'Please,' he said, and nodded. 'I am one of millions upon millions, all frightened. I am no one unique.'

'Oh, but you are': the phrase came to her spontaneously, but she did not say it. She offered him a drink instead. 'I have nothing stronger than wine.'

'I shall take wine with you. I shall be happy.'

He took most of the bottle, while she lingered over the small amount she had poured for herself. Dinu Psatta regretted he was not so easy in languages as Virgil. He was forced to stumble in English, the words like stones in his path – 'On bad days they are boulders, Mrs Kitty' – but in French he had less trouble. Now that he was living in Paris, his French path was clearer than it had been for him in Romania, with no big stones left to stop him. He could make his way without falling, now that he was the owner of an apartment on rue de Dunkerque.

'Is there a word for small stones, tiny stones, Mrs Kitty?'

'We call them pebbles.'

'Then I have just pebbles to worry me. On my French path.'

She suspected that he might have Italian and German paths, and waited numbly for reports of his progress along them. But he stayed silent.

'Virgil – ' he began, and stopped.

'Virgil? What of him?'

'There are papers, Mrs Kitty, and some books. There is a letter. They are for you.'

'Where are they? Have you brought them?'

'Yes and no. They are in the hotel, in the hotel's safe. I didn't bring them with me today – here I am stumbling, and at your mercy – because of etiquette. I thought it would be discreet to bring first the news, and after the news to bring the books and papers and letter. I did not want you to have a too great shock at once.'

Although she was irritated by his perverse thoughtfulness, she thanked him for showing her consideration.

'I am in London until Wednesday. I can visit you at any hour tomorrow. You will be at home?'

'In the early evening.'

'With your permission, Mrs Kitty, I shall come with the books, the papers and the letter from Virgil.'

'Of course you have my permission,' she almost snapped.

'You will not need to offer me your beautiful wine and delectable biscuits. I shall come and be gone in moments.'

He kissed her hands and bowed his farewell.

'Is one of the books *Miorița*, Mr Psatta?'

'Yes.'

'And is another the *Meditations* of Marcus Aurelius?'

'It is.'

'His old, old copies?'

'So old, Mrs Kitty, they are *infirm*.' He smiled at his choice of word, which amounted, he realised, to a conceit. She smiled, too, in appreciation. He could have observed that they were battered or used or much read, but 'infirm' nicely described the look of them, if not their substance.

'And they were with him when he crossed the Danube?'

'In his leather bag, yes.'

He kissed her hands again. 'Dear Mrs Kitty, they were only made a little wet. He dried them in the sun, with his dollars, in a field near Kladovo.'

Kitty Crozier did not sleep that night. She lay with closed

eyes on the bed she had often shared with Virgil Florescu, aching for his bony embrace. She longed to hear him insist that he had to leave before morning, while it was dark outside, with his familiar joke: 'I have no home to go to.' He sometimes added, as bleak decoration, '. . . I must see if it's still there' or '. . . and it's where my heart is.'

She dozed once, briefly, and in those seconds or perhaps minutes she saw her lover wearing the kind of clothes her father wore in his modelling days in America – a bright green blazer, a yellow shirt, a floral tie; trousers with perfect creases, polished brogues. He seemed comfortable, happy even, in this implausible outfit, for he was smiling the wide smile that revealed his communist tooth, which glinted like silver.

Soon after his arrival, 'on the dot of the nineteenth hour', Dinu Psatta urged Kitty Crozier to address him by his first name: 'You were the friend of Virgil, and I was also his friend.'

'That's a good enough reason, Dinu.'

'Exactly, Mrs Kitty.'

'No, not "Mrs". Relieve me of "Mrs". Let me be Kitty.'

She wondered if she should tell Virgil's plump ambassador, his bearer of bad tidings, that she did not merit the title, having been rescued from marriage with Freddy by Freddy's sudden defection to Ethiopia. 'I prefer to be Kitty,' she simply said.

All that Virgil had left her was contained in a bag from Galeries Lafayette. 'I bought him a pullover there,' Dinu Psatta explained. 'For his birthday. It was two sizes too small. I had to drag him to the shop to change it.'

'I didn't know he had a birthday,' she said, and then apologised for sounding ridiculous. 'Virgil kept the day of his birth a secret from me.'

'It was the five of May.'

'And the year? It was 1946, wasn't it?'

'The same as myself, yes. I am a month behind, in June.'

She took the bag from him and remarked that she wasn't surprised to find it so light.

'It holds his books and his poems, but nothing more, Kitty. His letter for you is also inside.'

'Have you read it?'

'Virgil's letter? No, no, most certainly not. It is private. It is for yourself alone. It is sealed. It is not opened.'

'Forgive me.'

'You must not imagine, Kitty, that because I worked in an embassy I have the habit of reading always the letters of others. I am away from diplomacy for ever. You will trust a music publisher, which I am today, I hope.'

'I trust you, Dinu.'

'You should.'

She persuaded him to break his promise to come and be gone in moments and to share a simple dinner of fish and salad. She assumed that he understood why Virgil had had an abhorrence of meat, and made no reference to it. Nevertheless she asked him, casually, if he was a vegetarian.

'I regret no. I enjoy lamb, Kitty. Lamb is my ultimate weakness in food. But I shall be most happy tonight with your trout.' He hummed the opening bars of Schubert's Piano Quintet in A, and laughed. 'Whichever way it is cooked.'

'Plainly, Dinu. Under the grill.'

Dinu Psatta ate everything she set before him with obvious pleasure. Food, for Virgil, had rarely been more than a necessity, except on those occasions – she recalled to herself – when his delight in the world encompassed it. Then, an oatcake or a handful of raisins would be ambrosia; whisky or water, nectar. Then, a glistening dollop of jam on his breakfast plate would be the cause of inexpressible joy.

'I see why you live in Paris, Dinu.'

'I see what you see.' He patted his stomach. 'Yes, alas, yes. I cannot resist the place. I cannot resist this cheese also.'

She took *Miorița* out of the bag, and Marcus Aurelius, and a pocket edition of George Herbert – stained with tea or coffee and annotated with innumerable pencilled comments – that he must have added recently to his portable library.

Virgil had added to each of his poems his own rendering into English prose.

She opened the letter, cautiously, with a paper knife. It ran to twelve pages, of which she only managed to read the first before the most terrible dismay possessed her. She let out a howl of misery, and listened to the silence that followed it.

# Murray Bail

## OBLIQUA

*Extract from* Eucalyptus, *a novel in progress*

WE COULD BEGIN with *desertorum*, common name Hooked Mallee. Its leaf tapers into a slender hook, and it is normally found in semi-arid parts of the interior.

But *desertorum* (to begin with) is only one of several hundred eucalypts; there is no precise number. And anyway the very word *desert-orum* harks back to a stale version of the national landscape and from there in a more or less straight line to the national character, all those linings of the soul and the larynx, which have their origins in the *bush*, so it is said, the poetic virtues (can you believe it?) of being belted about by droughts, bushfires, smelly sheep and so on; and don't let's forget the isolation, the exhausted shapeless women, the crude language, the always wide horizon, and the flies.

It is these circumstances which have been responsible for all those extremely dry (dun-coloured – can we say that?) hardluck stories which have been told around fires and on the page. All that was once upon a time, interesting for a while, but largely irrelevant here.

Besides, there is something unattractive, unhealthy even, about *desertorum*. It's more like a bush than a tree; has hardly a trunk at all: just several stems sprouting at ground level, stunted and *itchy*-looking.

We might as well turn to the rarely sighted *Eucalyptus pulverulenta*, which has curious heart-shaped leaves, found only on two narrow ledges of the Blue Mountains. What about *diversifolia* or *transcontalia*? At least they imply breadth and richness of purpose. Same too with *E. globulus*. Normally employed as a windbreak, a solitary specimen could be seen from Holland's front veranda at two o'clock, a filigree pin, greyish-green, stuck stylishly in a woman's felt hat, giving stability to the bleached and swaying vista.

Each and every eucalypt is interesting for its own reasons. Some eucalypts imply a distinctly feminine world (Yellow Jacket, Rose-of-the-West, Weeping Gum). *E. maideni* has given photogenic shade to the Hollywood stars. Jarrah is the timber everyone professes to love. *Eucalyptus camaldulensis*? We call it River Red Gum. Too masculine, too overbearingly masculine; covered in grandfatherly warts and carbuncles, as well. As for the Ghost Gum (*E. papuana*), there are those who maintain with a lump in their throats that it is the most beautiful tree on earth, which would probably explain why it's been done to death on our nation's calendars, postage stamps and tea towels. Holland had one marking the north-eastern corner, towards town, waving its arms in the dark, a surveyor's peg gone mad.

We could go on for ever holding up favourites or returning to botanical names which possess almost the right resonance or offer summation, if such a thing were possible, or others which are hopelessly wide of the mark but catch the eye for their sheer linguistic strangeness – *platypodus* – whereas all that's needed, aside from a beginning itself, is a eucalpyt independent of, yet one which is . . . it doesn't really matter.

Once upon a time there was a man – what's wrong with that? Not the most original way to begin, but tried and proven over time, which suggests something of value, some deep impulse beginning to be answered, a range of possibilities about to be set down.

There was once a man on a property outside a one-horse town, in New South Wales, who couldn't come to a decision about his daughter. He then made an unexpected decision. Incredible! For a while people talked and dreamed about little else until they realised it was entirely in keeping with him; they shouldn't have been surprised. To this day it's still talked about, its effects still felt, in the town and surrounding districts.

His name was Holland. With his one and only daughter Holland lived on a property, bordered along one side by a khaki river.

It was west of Sydney, over the ranges and into the sun – about three hours in a Japanese car.

All around the earth had a geological camel-look; slowly rearing brown, callused and blotched with shadows, which appeared to sway in the heat, and an overwhelming air of patience.

Some people say they remember the day he arrived.

It was stinking hot, a scorcher. He stepped off the train alone, not accompanied by a woman, not then. Without pausing in the town, not even for a glass of water, he went out to his newly acquired property, a deceased estate, and began going over it on foot.

With each step the landscape unfolded and named itself. The man's voice could be heard singing out-of-tune songs. It all belonged to him.

There were dams the colour of milky tea, corrugated sheds at the trapezoid tilt, yards of split timber, rust. And solitary fat eucalypts lorded it over hot paddocks, trunks glowing like aluminium at dusk.

A man and his three sons had been the original settlers. A local dirt road is named after them. In the beginning they slept in their clothes, a kelpie or wheat bags for warmth, no time for the complications of women – hairy men with pinched faces. They never married. They were secretive. In business they liked to keep their real intentions hidden. They lived in order to acquire: to add, to amass. At every opportunity they kept adding, a paddock here and there, acres and acres, going into hock to do it, even poxy land around the other side of the hill, sloping and perpetually drenched in shadow and infected with the burr, until the original plot on stony ground had completely disappeared into the long undulating spread, the shape of a wishbone or a broken pelvis.

These four men had gone mad with the ring-barking. Steel traps, fire, and all manner of poisons and chains were used. On the curvaceous back paddocks great gums slowly bleached and curled against the curve like trimmings of fingernails. Here and there bare straight trunks lay scattered and angled like a catastrophe of derailed carriages. The men had already turned their backs and concentrated on the next acquisition.

When at last it came to building a proper homestead they built it in pessimistic grey stone, ludicrously called 'bluestone', quarried in a foggy and distinctly dripping part of Victoria. At a later date one of the brothers was seen painting a wandering white line between the brick courses, up and along, concentrating so hard his tongue protruded. As with their land, bits were always being tacked on – verandas, outhouses. To commemorate dominance of a kind they added in 1923 a tower where the four of them could sit drinking at dusk and take pot-shots at anything that moved – kangaroos, emus, eagles. By the time the father died the property had become one of the district's largest and potentially the finest (all that river-frontage); but the three remaining sons began fighting among themselves, and some of the paddocks were sold off.

Late one afternoon – in the 1940s – the last of the bachelor brothers fell in the river. No one could remember a word he had said during his life. He was known for having the slowest walk in the district. He was the one responsible for the infuriating system of paddock gates and their clumsy phallic-fitting latchbolts. And it was he who built with his bare hands the suspension bridge across the river, partly as a rickety memorial to the faraway World War he had missed against all the odds, but more to allow the merinos with their ridiculous permed parted heads to cross without getting their feet wet, when every seven years floodwaters turned the gentle bend below the house into a sodden anabranch. For a while it had been the talk of the district, its motif, until the next generation saw it as an embarrassment. Now it appears in glossy books produced in the distant city to illustrate the ingenious, utilitarian nature of folk art: four cables slung across two trees, floored with cypress, laced with fencing wire.

In the beginning he didn't look like a countryman, not to the men. Without looking down at his perforated shoes they could tell at once he was from Sydney. It was not one thing; it was everything.

To those who crossed the street and introduced themselves Holland offered a soft indifferent hand, the proverbial fish ready to slip out under the slightest pressure. The men walking about either had a loose smile, or faces like grains of wheat. And every other one had a fingertip missing, a rip in the ear, the broken nose, one eye in a flutter from the flick of the fencing wire. As soon as talk moved to the solid ground of old machinery, or pet stories about bank managers or the power of certain weeds, it was noticed that although Holland looked thoughtful he took no part.

Early on some children had surprised Holland with pegs in his mouth while he was hanging the washing, and the row of pegs dangling like camel-teeth gave him a grinning illiterate look. Actually he was shrewd and interested in many things. The word soon was he didn't know which way a gate opened. His ideas on paddock rotation had them grinning and scratching their necks too. It made them wonder how he'd ever managed to buy the place. As for the perpetually pissing bull which had every man and his dog steering clear of the square back-paddock he solved that problem by shooting it.

It would take years of random appearances in all weather, at arm's length and across the street, before he and his face settled into place.

He told the butcher's wife, 'I expect to live here for seven years. Who knows after that?' Catching the pursing of her Presbyterian lips he added, 'It's nice country you've got here.'

It was a very small town. As with any new arrival the

women discussed him in clusters, turning to each other quite solemnly. Vague suggestions of melancholy showed in the fold of their arms.

They decided there had to be a woman hidden away in a part of his life somewhere. It was the way he spoke, and the assumptions settled in his face. And to see him always in his black coat without a hat walking along the street or at the Greek's having breakfast alone, where nobody in their right mind took a pew and ate, was enough to produce in these dreaming women elongated vistas of the dark-stone home-stead, its many bare rooms, the absence of flowers, all those broad acres and stock untended – with this man, half lost in its empty dimensions. He appeared then as a figure demand-ing all kinds of attention, correction even.

A certain widow with florid hands made a move. It didn't come to much. What did she expect? Every morning she polished the front of her house with a rag. In quick succession she was followed by the mothers of sturdy daughters from properties surrounding Holland's, inviting him to their home-steads facing north, where heaps of mutton were served. These were kitchen meals on pine scrubbed to a lung colour, kitchens dominated by the black horizontality of the stove; other houses employed the papered dining-room, the oakish-looking table, pieces of silver, crystal and Spode – a purple husband looking like death at the head. And the mothers and daughters watched with interest as this complete stranger in their midst took in the food by his exceptionally wide mouth, mopped up with his hunk of white bread.

He nodded in appreciation. He dropped his aitches, which was a relief.

Afterwards he took out his handkerchief and wiped his hands, so to these women it was like a magician offering one of his khaki paddocks as an example, before whipping it away, leaving nothing.

Almost five months had passed; on a Monday morning Hol-land was seen at the railway station. The others standing about gave the country-nod, assuming he was like them there to collect machinery parts ordered from Sydney.

Holland lit a cigarette.

The heavy rails went away parallel to the platform, on the regularly spaced sleepers darkened by shadow and grease, and darkened further as they went away into the sunlight, the rails converging with a silver wobble in bushes, bend and mid-morning haze.

The train was late.

Those darkened sleepers which cushioned the tremendous travelling weight of trains: they had been axed from the forests of Grey Ironbark (*E. paniculata*) around hilly Bunyah, a few hours to the east. The same dark eucalypts felled by the same axemen filled export contracts for the expansion of steam across China, India, British India. Most of the sleepers for the Trans-Siberian railway were cut from the forests around Bunyah, and so – here's poetic injustice – carried the weight of thousands of Russians transported to isolation and far worse. Truly, Ironbark is one of the hardest woods available to man.

Faint whistle and smoke. The rails began their knuckle-cracking. The train appeared, grew, and eventually came to rest alongside the platform, letting out a series of sighs like an exhausted black dog, dribbling, its paws outstretched.

For a moment people were too occupied to follow Holland.

Holland had tilted his bare head down to a small girl in a blue dress. As they left the station Holland was seen taking her small wicker case and doing his best to talk. She was looking up to him.

Soon after women came out in the sunlight on the street and appeared to bump into each other, joined by others. Normally the days were still and slow in their part of the world. The news quickly jumped the long distances out of town, and from there spread in different directions, entering the houses Holland had sat down and eaten in, the way a fire leaps over fences, roads, bare paddocks and rivers, depositing smaller, always slightly different, versions of itself.

She was his daughter; he could do anything he liked with

her. Yes; but weeks passed before he brought her into town. 'Acclimatising' was very much on his mind.

The women wanted to see her. They wanted to see the two of them together. Some wondered if he'd be stern with her; the various degrees of. Instead Holland appeared unusually stiff, at the same time, casual.

Traces of him showed around the child's eyes and jaws. There was the same two-stage smile, and when answering a question she frowned. To the town-women she was perfectly polite.

She was called Emily.

Holland had met and married a river-woman from outside Waikerie, on the Murray, in South Australia. Emily never tired of hearing the story. Her father had placed one of those matrimonial advertisements.

'What's wrong with that? It has a high curiosity value for both parties. You never know what's going to come up. That's what I'm going to do when you're old enough. I'll write the advertisement myself. I'll try to list your most attractive features, if I can think of any. We'll probably have to advertise in Scotland and Venezuela.'

It is still the custom for certain rural newspapers to run these advertisements, handy for the man who simply hasn't got around to finding himself a suitable wife, or one who's been on the move, doing seasonal work. It's a custom well and truly established in other places, such as Nigeria, where men are given the names of flowers, and in India, one newspaper especially, published in New Delhi, is read avidly just for these advertisements artfully penned and placed from all corners of the sub-continent. There it's a convenient service for marriages arranged by others, when it becomes necessary to cast the net wider.

Worth mentioning in this context: in circular New Delhi, wherever the eye turns, even as a bride tilts her cloudy mirror-ring to glimpse for the first time the face with pencil moustache of her arranged husband, it invariably picks up a Blue Gum (*E. globulus*) – they're everywhere: just as the tall fast-growing *E. kirtoni*, common name Half Mahogany, has virtually taken over the dusty city of Lucknow.

Of the three replies to Holland's one-liner clearly the most promising was the one printed in soft pencil from a fresh widow: here was another man who'd ended up headfirst in the river, still in his boots.

She was the eldest of seven or eight. Holland saw pale bodies draped everywhere, mostly sisters, transfixed by lines of piercing light, as if the tin shack had been shot up with bullet holes.

'I introduced myself,' Holland explained. 'And your mother went very quiet. She hardly opened her mouth, as if she realised just what she'd let herself in for. To answer the ad was one thing. Now there I was, standing in front of her. Maybe she took one look at my mug and wanted to run a mile?' (Daughter smiled.) 'A very, very nice woman. I had a lot of time for your mother.'

Sometimes a sister sat alongside and without a word began brushing her elder sister's hair. It was straw blonde; the others were dark. The kitchen table had its legs standing in jam-tins of kero. The father would come in and go out. He hardly registered Holland's presence. No sign of the mother. Holland presented an axe and a blanket as if they were Red Indians.

At last he carried her back to Sydney.

There in his rooms which was more or less within his world she appeared plump, or (put it this way) softer than he imagined, and glowed, as if dusted with flour. And she busied herself. Casually she introduced a different order. Unpinned, her hair fell like a sudden dumping of sand and rhythmically she brushed it, a religious habit, in front of the mirror. Amazing was her faith in him: how she allowed him to enter. His hands felt clumsy and coarse, as did sometimes his words. Here was someone who listened to him.

What happened next began as a joke. On the spur of the moment he took out, with some difficulty, insurance against his river-woman delivering twins. He was challenging Nature. It was also his way of celebrating. The actuaries calculated tremendous odds; Holland had immediately increased the policy. He waved ye olde world certificate with its phoney red seal in front of his friends. Those were the days he was drinking.

'I'd emptied my pockets, every spare zac I had.'

Emily showed no interest in the money subject.

'You were the first born,' he nodded. 'We named you Emily. I mean, that was your mother's preference – Emily. Your brother lived just a few days. Something broke in your mother. No one has ever seen anyone cry as much, I'm willing to bet. The top of your head, here, was always wet. And blood, a lot of blood. She just lay there crying, you know, softly. She couldn't stop. She grew weak with it. As I watched, her life seemed to leak away. There was nothing I could do. I'd hardly even got to know her. I don't know how it happened.

'And you, the picture of health and the fat cheque arriving soon afterwards. I should have been throwing my hat up in the air. I'd never seen so much money, so many noughts. I had all this money on a piece of paper in the back of my trousers for a month or more before I marched into a bank with it. And so, here we are. There's a fine view from the veranda. At least I've got some say in that. And look at you. Already you're the prettiest doll for a hundred miles.'

And Emily never tired of hearing the story, and asking questions, often the same questions, about her mother.

Often in the re-telling Holland would stop and say, 'Come over here and give your father a big kiss.'

# Philip Hensher

## WHITE GOODS
### *For Shefali Malhoutra*

SO VERA SAID to me, 'Oh, oh, oh. You English. You have
no idea. You young. You have everything. You have no idea.
No notion –' she often produced these English words she
was so proud of knowing – 'no notion of what it is to fly
your country with terrible fear of death, with nothing. I have
nothing, still, and you young, you have everything. You
have no notion.'

I looked around me at Vera's red and purple drawing-
room, with its teapots and seven little tables, each draped
with three table-cloths, and the china dogs elbowing each
other out of the way on the mantelpiece, and the curtain,
and the under-curtain, and the net curtain, pulled across, and
the second net curtain underneath it, for privacy. It was a
room impossible to walk across. It was a room a Tsar could
have lived in, if he had had to live in a two-bedroomed house
on the outskirts of Cambridge. There was one beautiful thing
in it, a tiny portrait of a fierce, bearded man propped up like
a Christmas card, and everything else was plush and velvet
and unspeakable but somehow nice. 'No,' I said. 'I don't
suppose I have.'

'Ha,' she said. 'You English.'

For Vera, all foreigners were English. But I was English,
actually.

I suppose I ought to say how I ended up in Vera's house.
I don't know. I was a painter once, although this seems to
surprise most people. I don't paint any more; I stopped after

I left Cambridge. I started because I thought for a while I was good at it. My teachers at school told me I should carry on after I got an A level, and I did. Like most painters, I had no money, but like most people, I needed a place to live. My parents were poor, or poor by the standards I now have; although they did not seem especially poor to me then, they certainly could not have supported me in my romantic ideas. One of my romantic ideas was that I would live in someone's house for nothing, someone who adored the way I painted, and felt privileged I was their lodger. Or – a still more romantic idea – that I would live in someone's house and, instead of rent, paint a picture each month for them. After a year, they would be no richer, but they would have twelve marvellous paintings, and they'd be glad of it. Where I got the notion – as Vera would say – that there were such patient people in the world I do not know. But there are not.

Instead, there was Vera; and I would say how she ended up in her house; except that I have no idea. She did not tell me her autobiography as she interviewed me for her room. I supposed, wrongly, that once I had moved in she would tell me how she fled from the communist hordes clutching a suitcase and leaving her diamonds behind. I was wrong to think that she would tell me all this, and she certainly did not tell me as I sat in her over-filled, over-red drawing-room.

'Twenty pounds only,' she said, instead, stirring the teapot. 'Very cheap, very clean.'

'I am clean myself,' I said, sitting on the edge of my chair in a clean shirt and pair of trousers.

'I did not suggest you were not. I have to think about it.'

She poured herself a cup of tea. On the tray in front of her was a pot of raspberry jam – not a very delicious sort, but a sort that was pink with chemicals and not fruit. She took a spoonful of the jam, and stirred it into her tea. She did not offer me anything, and I was to come to learn that the raspberry jam was kept by Vera for Vera's sole use.

'Very well,' she said after a time. 'You may live here. Would you witness my will and testament, please?'

'Your will?' I said.

'Yes,' Vera said. 'I have just changed it, and my signature needs to be witnessed, if you please.'

She pushed the piece of paper over the table to me. It was written in an improbably beautiful copperplate hand.

'You may write this address as your address after your signature,' she said. 'I do not think it matters a great deal. I will tell you where you can find the will, once I have decided on a safe hiding place.'

Over the next year, I witnessed Vera's signature half a dozen times. She was very well up on the law about wills, which she always called 'will and testament' – and was for ever changing her tiny legacies. When I got to know her better, I understood that what she fantasised about was everyone turning up after the funeral, to claim their prize, old friends and lovers and enemies, all in an embarrassing huddle. I don't think she quite understood she wouldn't be there. Her great obsession – what she was constantly concerned with – was the idea that her last will might be lost and a previous, discredited one adhered to.

It was quite a nice room, Vera's spare room, although the bed sagged in a hummocky way, and the violently flowery wallpaper, crawling over the ceiling and even the panels of the door, was immediately oppressive, and there was no view of anything whatsoever. Which suited me. The only problem, in fact, was Vera, who was incapable of having someone in her house without having them in her life.

'Young man,' she said a day or two after I moved in, 'when I die, you will find my last will and testament under the bed. The most recent will, the one you witnessed so kindly for me. Do not forget. Or Stalin's daughter will come to take the lot.'

'Stalin's daughter?' I said, laughing. 'Who is Stalin's daughter?'

'Stalin's daughter? Stalin's daughter?' Vera said. 'Have you never heard of Stalin?'

'Yes, of course,' I said.

'Well, Stalin's daughter is the daughter of Stalin,' Vera

said. 'I am glad you think it funny. You have strange notions of amusingness, young man.'

'Do you know her?' I said, marginally astounded.

'Yes,' Vera said. She immediately got up and left the room, dramatically.

The next day, curiously, Stalin's daughter came to the house.

'I am Svetlana,' the very firmly dressed woman on the doorstep said. 'I wish to see Vera.'

'I am not here,' a muffled shout came from upstairs.

'I wish to see Vera,' Svetlana said pointedly.

'She isn't here,' I said, hopelessly.

Svetlana turned and went.

'She gave me a refrigerator, you see,' Vera said, coming downstairs. 'She thinks I am poor. And I am poor, and I took the refrigerator. But that does not mean she can insult me and expect me to go on being grateful to her.'

It was characteristic of Vera that she had taken to referring to the refrigerator itself as 'Stalin's daughter'. It was an enormous white humming affair, into which she put, without discrimination, every item of food she ever bought. I wonder now what I put into the fridge; and, indeed, what I ate then. When I compare how I shop now, our immense trips to the immense supermarkets we drive to, tossing tiny expensive bottles and curious breakfast cereals into the wheeled cage until we have spent enough money, to the way I tried to buy food then, I wonder. I remember going to the supermarket after five in order to buy bread which had been reduced in price, because it was stale; I know that I ate so much tinned tuna and so many tinned chickpeas that for years afterwards I felt sick at the smell of them. I think I was effectively a vegetarian, because meat is expensive. I only ate meat if it was very poor offal, or if Vera took pity on me and cooked something for me. Which, now I think of it, she did not. A week after I had first done so, I asked Vera again how she knew Stalin's daughter. She corrected me.

'I did know her once,' she said, her eyes closed as if to envisage her. 'I do not know her any more. This is the letter

96

I have written to her.' She whisked out a piece of blue lined paper from underneath the cushions on the sofa.

'Stalin's daughter,' the letter began, 'you are a brute, a murderer and a KGB agent.' Above KGB, in pencil, giving way to the flood of her inspiration, Vera had written 'Triple' with three exclamation marks after it.

'You cannot know,' Vera said, chuckling, 'what Stalin's daughter has done to me.'

Taken some jam without asking, probably, I thought, but said nothing.

'I detested her when I first saw her, when we were both children, and I was right to detest her. I was mad to agree to meet her in Cambridge. She is here to destroy my life. She has always worked and planned against me in her money-making schemes.'

'I didn't know you knew her before you came here,' I said. 'Odd that you should end up in the same place.'

'Ha ha ha,' Vera said mirthlessly. 'Odd, he says, that Stalin's daughter should follow me here. Strange, he thinks, that Stalin should send his daughter to follow me. The strange thing is – you want to know the strangest thing, young man? You want to know? The strange thing is that I, Vera, am here, and have nothing, and accept the gifts of a daughter of a man like Stalin.'

'Extraordinary,' I said, since I didn't know what she meant.

'I whose lands once stretched to the horizon and beyond,' Vera started. I concentrated on my tea. Once Vera hit on a White Russian vein in her monologue, there was no point in listening.

'And a woman like that,' she wound up, 'a woman with the blood of nobody in her body, gives me a refrigerator. Bloody, bloody thing.'

She went into the kitchen and kicked Stalin's Daughter. I could hear it whinnying slightly.

Vera's campaigns against Svetlana once got as far as her standing, stout-booted, in the market square with a petition against Svetlana, Daughter of Stalin and Her Deeds. Too angry and shy to accost anyone, her petition went unsigned until the lady with the CND petition and the gentleman with the anti-apartheid petition took her for a cup of tea in the cellar coffee shop in the market-place and wrote their names on the crumpled sheet. Vera, who grew quickly merry with tea and toast, found the signatures of two petitioners against Svetlana, Daughter of Stalin, too much of a temptation, and forged a third signature in a cunningly backward-slanting hand. She never quite got the hang of English names, and what she wrote was Miss Susan Michael Selection, out of what Russian name I could not guess. Absent-mindedly, however, or not trusting to her powers of invention, the address she added was her own.

'You see?' she said. 'Three people feel the same as I do. And,' she added mysteriously, 'I did not ask everyone.'

'Oh good,' I said.

The next day Svetlana came to tea, and after that it was quite all right. What I had thought of as a serious breach turned out to be a tiny annual feud, which needed almost no reason to set it off. I dare say Svetlana – a woman I was allowed to answer the door to, but almost never allowed to talk to – herself needed a break from Vera from time to time. I thought of her, though I did not meet her, as a woman of quite un-Stalin-like patience. I used sometimes to pass the red crowded sitting-room when they were there together, and listen to the effortful English they strangely used to talk to each other.

I had few friends in Cambridge, and, while I lived at Vera's house, I relished the few a great deal. I have never had the knack of making friends, which I heard once defined as the art of being a good listener. I ought to be a good listener, since I am not talkative, and people sometimes think me shy. That does not seem to be the answer. I knew three boys in Cambridge whom I had known at school, but I liked them no better in Cambridge than I had at school, and after two or three months they had amassed enough friends, from their faculties and their colleges and their weekly inter-collegiate societies, not to trouble me any more.

The only people I thought I knew were the people I shared

a studio with at the art school. The art school had too many
students in it, and too few rooms, so I shared a studio with
two other painters and a sculptor. There were two girls who
came in very early, who both had black bobs and wore black
thick tights and black miniskirts and lived on black coffee
and no lunch. They both painted enormous blank or scribbled canvases in little time, and they were both short and
pale. I told them apart because one smoked and the other
didn't, but that was all the difference I could see. They looked
at my little pointlessly detailed canvases, and did not bother
to criticise my foolish attempts to make a bit of cloth look
like something it wasn't. Perhaps they were right not to say
anything.

The sculptor was a pink-faced boy with a shock of blond
hair, called James, who came in late in the morning or early
in the afternoon. By then, the piles of scrap metal and bits
of rubber and packing cases which he found on the street
and turned into huge sculptures, of a sort, had often been
pushed into a corner by one of the diligent painters. This
was a great cause for complaint, and, though I did not exactly
like him, we often went out for a drink together in the early
evening so that he could complain about the two girls in the
studio. Once, I told him about a play by Sartre I had once
seen called *Les Putains Respectueuses*. I immediately regretted it, since he laughed thoroughly for almost five minutes
in an insufficiently empty pub, and afterwards would never
stop referring to the two perfectly nice, hard-working girls
as the *putains respectueuses*, and getting up lurid fantasies
of their sex lives for my entertainment and, worse, seeming
to regard the matter as a joke between the two of us. If he
ever said, 'Come out for a drink and meet this girl I know,'
on the other hand, I usually would. I only remember one girl
I met like this, because I married her.

'Where do you come from?' my wife said.

She was not my wife then. She was a girl I had met five
minutes before, and we were sitting together in a pub over a
glass of beer each while James went to buy some cigarettes.

'I come from Nottingham,' I said.

'Nottingham?' she said. 'The Nottingham painter.'

'I am a painter, and I do come from Nottingham,' I said. 'Yes.'

'Are you always going to paint,' she said. 'Or are you going to get a job?'

'Don't say that,' James said, coming back. 'He's a bloody good painter. A bloody genius. Can draw anything. Ask him.'

'Do your paintings sell?' she said.

'I bought one,' James said. 'And I'd buy it again. Bloody brilliant. Not like those old *putains* with their bloody old wank.'

'Draw me, then,' she said.

'All right,' I said. I liked the way she had of looking at me as if she were making a joke out of me; I liked the way she was supposed to be a friend of James, and paid no attention to him, which of course was the way to treat him. There was an old envelope in the plastic bag I carried things around in. I fished it out and began to draw her.

'Who are the old *putains*?' she said to me. 'Anyway.'

'These horrible old tarts we have to share a bloody studio with, who get in at six o'clock every morning and are sour as bloody old lemons,' James said. 'I was telling you about them. This old bugger calls them the *putains respectueuses*.'

I handed over what I had done. My wife looked at it for a while.

'Is that me?' she said.

'Yes,' I said.

'I don't think I look like that at all,' she said. 'My nose isn't as big as that and my eyes aren't like that. Look, he's made my eyes too close together.'

'Just a sketch,' I said.

'Come on,' James said loyally, 'it looks just like you.'

'I don't think so,' she said.

'I've drawn,' I said, 'what you look like inside, I've drawn your character.'

She looked at the little sketch for a while, and then up at me, her mouth slightly open, and then, without warning, she began to laugh violently. It seemed as involuntary and solitary as a fit of hiccoughs, and James and I neither ignored it nor joined in with it. We simply sat and looked at her until she had finished.

'You're wonderful, you are,' she said. 'Has my character got a big nose?'

'I think so,' I said.

'Where did you find this one?' she said to James.

'Behind the shopping centre,' he said. 'I rescue him once a day from the foul clutches of his landlady, who used to be a Russian Grand Duchess and has a million pounds' worth of roubles inside the stuffed corpse of a serf in the attic.'

'Oh yes,' she said, not laughing. 'I ought to be off.'

Once, Svetlana asked Vera to supper at her house.

'I shall not be home a week on Tuesday,' Vera said casually, bustling through the kitchen like a small rhinoceros.

'Why not?' I said.

'None of your business, young man,' she said, making a show of her astonishment. But the news that she had been invited out was too much to keep quiet, and on her way back through the kitchen, she paused. 'I have been invited to a dinner.'

'A dinner party?' I said.

'That is what I said,' Vera said. 'A week on Tuesday.' She refused to tell me who had invited her. Perhaps she felt the fact it was only Svetlana – and it could hardly be anyone else, since Vera knew no one else – would somehow diminish the glamour.

A week on Sunday, Vera called me into her room.

'I should like your advice,' she said. 'I wondered which dress you thought I should wear.'

On the bed she had laid out five dresses. It was impossible to imagine Vera in any of them. Four were chiffon flowery numbers – intimidatingly flowery, actually – and sweetly dated. One was ribboned and boned and lacy and stood up on its own; the sort of cream dress I think Evelyn Waugh describes as manufactured solely for the younger daughters of duchesses. It could only have been Vera's mother's.

'That's rather nice,' I said. 'Isn't it a bit grand?'

'Grand?' Vera said, as if she didn't know the meaning of the word – hadn't invented it, indeed.

'In any case,' I said, poking a bit at it, 'it looks as if the moths have been at it.'

'I see no holes,' Vera said, like Nelson. 'Which do you prefer, of my dresses?'

I chose the least flowery of the chiffon dresses.

'I knew it,' Vera said triumphantly. 'You have no taste whatever. You, a painter? That is a dress I could never wear.'

'Well, the others are dresses you should never wear,' I said in my room.

On Tuesday I dreaded telling Vera how nice she looked in her cream and lace dress. I would have gone to my studio, but I couldn't face that either. Instead, I went out very early and went to the town library, where I sat all day, looking at the tall books of the works of the great painters. I read not a word. I just looked at the pictures, until I had looked at every painting in every book about painting. I thought about how bad the reproductions of the colours were, and how nice it would be to paint a picture in precisely those muddy reds and muddy blues which merged into each other. This was what I called work. Much of the day I spent going up and down to the little café underground in the market-place for cups of tea.

At seven, the library closed, and I trudged out into the rain, hoping that Vera would have gone out. Hoping against hope. I was passing her room when a dim wail came out of it.

'Oh, young man,' her voice cried.

I ignored her, since I was dripping with rain, the soles of my shoes sucking at the soles of my feet.

Ten minutes later she called me again, more querulously, and this time I went in. As I foresaw, she had put on the cream dress, which, frayed out here and there by moths nibbling at it, looked like a slow-motion photograph of an explosion in a dairy. She had succeeded in half-hooking herself into it, but the middle hooks were just too much for her stiff old arms; I don't suppose the makers of the dress thought that anyone would ever wear it who didn't have a maid to stitch her into it.

'I am so sorry, young man,' she said, and in fact she sounded sorry, her voice not just apologetic, but trembling, and perhaps even tearful. 'I wish there was someone else I could ask.'

'Well, all right,' I said meanly. 'I don't like doing it, but I will.'

I noted clinically that she wasn't wearing a bra or a corset, and her brown old flesh squeezed out as I tugged at the dress. It was monstrously tight – she couldn't have worn it for ten years – and when it was done she could not lower her arms from the horizontal.

'How is it?' she asked when I had finished.

'What is that on the bed?' I asked. There was a small plastic bag with what looked like a piece of bloody meat inside it.

'It is a present for Stalin's daughter,' Vera said. 'I was always brought up to take a present, a small one, to dinner parties. I am taking her a very nice joint of pork I saw in the butcher's this morning, who the butcher recommended to me very much.'

'Which the butcher recommended to you,' I said absently. 'I think some flowers would have done.'

'Ha,' Vera said. 'You young people, what do you know?'

'You look quite nice,' I said, in the end.

She had that knack of wearing you down. When she had gone out, in a rare and significant taxi, I telephoned my wife, on a whim, to ask her out for a drink.

'Where do you live?' I said.

'Why, where do *you* live?' she said.

'In a house just over there,' I said. 'I've got an eccentric Russian landlady called Vera. She's got a fridge called Stalin's Daughter.'

'Oh yes,' she said. 'Why is it called Stalin's Daughter?'

'Because Stalin's daughter gave it to her,' I said. 'She lives here, you know, Stalin's daughter.'

'In Cambridge?'

'Yes,' I said. 'They are always having some kind of feud.'

'How interesting,' she said. 'Are you really a painter?'

'Yes,' I said.

'Did you keep that drawing you did of me?'

'No,' I said. 'I could always do another one, a better one, not on the back of an envelope or anything.'

'That would be nice,' she said. 'I'm afraid I was a bit horrible to you that time. It's James really. He just annoys me so much.'

'Me too,' I said. Sometimes people say fateful things, and this was one of those times. If she hadn't said she was annoyed by James, I wonder if I would have seen her again.

'Are you going to carry on being a painter?'

'I don't know,' I said. 'I'll probably get a job.'

'Isn't that a bit sad?' she said.

'Not really,' I said. 'There are worse things. Like being a painter whose paintings nobody wants to buy.'

'Don't your paintings sell? I thought someone bought one?'

'James bought one,' I said. 'Other than that. I would try to give my landlady one instead of a month's rent, if I had the nerve.'

'I would buy one,' she said. She seemed quite different, and I liked her again, and in a different way.

All afternoon the next day, Vera sat in the drawing-room with a great pile of photographs on the sofa, out of shoe-boxes, sorting them. I went in around tea-time and sat down. She said nothing.

'How was Svetlana's dinner?' I said.

'Good,' she said.

'What did she cook?'

Vera carried on sorting. She clearly did not want to talk about it.

'Who was there?'

'Oh, oh, Svetlana was there, and I was there, and there were other people there as well. You want some tea, young man.'

She got up and left the room. I sat there for a moment in the dark room, alone. I do not pretend to be able to explain what I now did. On the table next to me there was the portrait I had often admired, of a middle-aged man, or perhaps only seeming middle-aged because of his beard, perhaps quite young. It was not a large portrait; five inches by three and a half. But the work was exquisitely fine, with an untouched hard sheen of glaze which seemed almost enamelled, as if no brush had ever touched the surface. The artist in this tiny space had included so much of the man, the slight slyness of his gaze, the gingery beard which was not thick, but a lacy veil over his starched, uncomfortable shirt front. I often wore baggy corduroy trousers with big pockets. It went in easily.

Vera came back with the tea and the pot of raspberry jam, and we chatted for a while about nothing in particular, before I went up to my room to write a letter and read a book I had read before. I put the picture in a drawer; I did not especially want to look at it. It wasn't, in fact, until the day after the day after that that Vera asked me for the picture back, and then asked me to find somewhere else to live after the end of the month. Sometimes I think that it was because of my wife that I gave up painting and became a lawyer, but I know I am just indulging myself. It was nothing to do with her. I always knew I would have to stop sooner or later, just as I knew that sooner or later I would have to find somewhere else to live. But we need people to blame for the way our lives go. Vera knew that. And it is nobody's fault but our own, and the things that happen to us are because of how we are.

When I left Vera's house, I felt that her feud with me wouldn't last long. After all, I'd watched her feuds with Svetlana run their course and exhaust themselves. It was easy to anticipate turning up at Vera's house with a large bunch of flowers and letting myself be embraced by her. Or perhaps with a joint of pork. Anyway, it didn't happen. I don't know why. Once I did go and see her, six months or a year after I had moved out. When I rang the doorbell, she inspected me from the window, pulling aside the net curtain. I pretended not to have seen her. I heard her shuffling to the door and peering at me, first through the little fish-eye lens, and then, strangely, through the letterbox. I stood there ringing the doorbell a little longer, but she never answered. And three years after I had left Cambridge for a different sort of a life, I decided on a whim to go back there.

This time she answered the door, in her old floral dress. But she didn't know me, or said she didn't, and wouldn't let me in. 'Go away,' she said. 'I am too old.' She didn't say for what. 'You remember me, Vera,' I said, humouring her. I wasn't at all sure that she did. 'I have my own life,' she said. 'I'm not here to entertain you.' In the end I produced my business card, with my address on it, and pressed it on her. She looked at it for a while, but took it, shutting the door without saying goodbye.

Years later, one December, I had to be in Cambridge one day. The business I was there for finished early, and I was on my own. I could have gone back to the office, or home, but instead I went for a walk among the tall colleges with their backs to the narrow streets. I used to see the same faces in the streets every day, and some of them were still here, still walking the streets, a little greyer, a little more crumpled. I walked about like a tourist until it was too cold and beginning to be too dark, and then went to a tea-shop I used sometimes to go into. There she was.

'Ah,' Stalin's daughter said. 'The shy lodger.' She was sitting at a small table on her own, with a formidable pile of cakes in front of her. I looked at her, as I did before, for signs of a resemblance to her father – a walrus moustache, perhaps, or a murderous glint in the eye. There was none. She was entirely unchanged.

'I didn't know I was shy,' I said, meaning that I didn't know they had a name for me.

'There were three,' she said. 'The shy one, the drunken one and the short one. I can't remember what order they came in. Come and sit by me, young man.'

'She never mentioned any of the others,' I said, sitting down.

'Well, she was never very interested in them,' she said. 'At least she said she wasn't. She often seemed to end up talking about you, and your doings.'

'She talked to me about you,' I said. 'And Russia.'

'I imagine so,' she said. She took a cake – one of those knotted glazed doughy ones which break off in soft strips – and began to tear it absently. 'And her husband, I suppose.'

'No,' I said. 'I never knew she was married.'

'It was after he left her for the last time she took in lodgers.'

'She never mentioned it.'

'Now I see why you were shy. How you were shy. You never talked to her if she never mentioned anything.' She laughed raucously, head back. 'Ask that man for some more cakes.'

I did so, slightly admiring her servanted ease.

'I suppose she left you something in her will,' Svetlana said. 'Strange, that she remembered almost everyone she'd ever known. What was it?'

'Five hundred pounds,' I said. I was surprised, too, and had wondered why when the solicitor had got in touch. Perhaps she had changed her mind about me, perhaps she had been changing her will and testament one day, and the card I had left had been to hand, and she had temporarily forgotten who I was. Or, as Svetlana said, she just left something to everyone she had ever known. My wife had speculated in a slightly tiresome way about what Vera might have left me. I think, in our little house conveniently close to the centre of London, and inconveniently full of rooms ten feet by twelve, my wife might have imagined Vera leaving me half of Georgia.

'Five hundred pounds,' Svetlana said. 'Useful, but boring.'

'Yes, rather boring,' I said. 'Not very characteristic, somehow. Was she rich?'

'Oh, no,' Svetlana said. 'Not very.'

'Still,' I said. 'It will be useful. My wife's just had a baby, and we've got to redecorate the spare bedroom. I'm a lawyer now.' I wondered why I had said that.

'The chocolate one,' Svetlana said to the waiter, 'and the other chocolate one, thank you. I thought you were a painter, not a lawyer.'

'I was,' I said. 'I gave it up.'

'Mmm,' Svetlana said. 'A good profession, law. People will always need lawyers.'

'I know,' I said, since this was always what everyone had said to me, and I needed no reminding that what people needed was more lawyers. 'What did she leave you?'

'A little picture,' she said. 'Very pretty, a man with a beard. I never saw it before. Perhaps it was in her room. Perhaps it is you who has painted it?'

'No,' I said. 'Not me.'

'Well, this has been nice,' Svetlana said, getting up. I suddenly saw that I had been sitting with Stalin's daughter for half an hour, and I would never see her again, and in a second I would miss my chance.

'Tell me something about your father,' I said, taking her arm.

She hardly blinked, and I realised this must happen to her twice a day.

'This has been nice,' she said, with a great flash of charm. 'Buy something special with Vera's money, to remember her with. Now, what will you buy?'

We bought an electrical appliance with it – a fridge, of course. We had an immense argument about it in the white goods department, in the well-lit Saturday basement of the department store, about whether we had room for a double-doored one, and if we did, whether we needed one. Among all the white boxes, among all the other young marrieds arguing about their needs. I can't remember which of us wanted a double-doored fridge now, or why. Sometimes I look at my single-doored fridge and think what I would call it, if it had a name. Sometimes people, when they come to dinner, ask me to draw them, and sometimes I do, and sometimes they recognise themselves in what I have drawn. Not often. I was a painter once, although this seems to surprise most people. Not any more. I am a lawyer now. I stopped painting after I left Vera's house. That's everything I remember. I thought it was important to write it down before it was all forgotten.

# Martin Bax

## VIOLENCE IN THE FAMILY

*Extract from* Consummation on Offa's Dyke, *a novel in progress*

THE GOOD THING about Craig was that now you were no longer lovers you could talk to him about your affairs. Perhaps it was after all possible to have intimacies with a man, a thing you had previously regarded as impossible. Any rate you could talk to Craig about Rupert and his demands and Craig thought it was funny which was a curious relief. The mismatch between Rupert and Jonathan amused him, the Black African knight, he said, with the White English bishop. They held each other in check and he said seriously, 'They held you in check. It was good you got out of them.' 'There was nothing wrong with Jonathan.' 'But he wasn't right for you.'

Knighton took little exploring in the morning although they paid a visit to the old school which was the headquarters of the Offa's Dyke Society and paced around the exhibition. They each bought society badges. Craig was keen to walk on the dyke and Celestine encouraged him to climb Panpunton Hill from which Celestine had descended yesterday. The opening of the Southern Route which she would take today was wooded and she thought she would not find the magnificent views which she had had the evening before. Craig walked her through the back streets of the town and watched her set off up through the trees as she headed south to the Newcastle Rings, Burfa Camp (both of which earthworks Offa ignored) and Kington.

In any event, it was time to let Craig go. He had been a lifeline and a comfort while she had been accepting that she had let Jonathan go. Before she went to Zimbabwe, after she had told him she was going, she had 'cracked up'. She supposed that was the only way to describe it. She had found herself constantly weeping, waking Jonathan at night saying, 'I do love you, I do love you. I'm sorry about Rupert, I was wrong, wrong, wrong.' Jonathan had not been very good at that. There seemed to him to be nothing to say.

Joan was sharing a flat at this point with Sylvia. Joan had explained that Sylvia was butch and 'that's good, puts men off' and 'I have some time to myself'. Sylvia was a tall, strong girl, she did weight lifting to keep herself in shape and she worked in that most male of environments, a garage, where she was a fully trained mechanic. But her presence made Joan less available as a comforter and adviser.

Celestine even went once or twice to a church. Her father had been a non-believer and had bred into Celestine a good deal of cynicism about church and church-going while sending his daughter off to schools where a 'Christian upbringing' was part of the agenda. That famed biology teacher at Easthurst had also influenced her by never attending chapel, commenting airily to Celestine once: 'I could never believe that beetles or any other animal for that matter had souls and I can't conceive that man is anything but an animal. It seems there will be nothing left of me to go to heaven or hell and I remain therefore essentially uninterested in the landlords of such establishments.'

But Celestine went into a church one Sunday thinking, maybe I'll talk to the parson afterwards. But he seemed to Celestine a fool with his text for the day and there was such a lot of bowing and scraping to various religious objects (she had walked into a High Anglican service) that the whole performance disgusted her and she slid out before the service ended to avoid the embarrassment of having to meet the man. So she had left for Zimbabwe tearful about Jonathan but unresolved. He had written to her formal little letters

110

enclosing mail, finding himself unable to write about their relationship.

So, thought Celestine, what did I do? I really bitched him. She sent him a postcard on which she wrote: 'I am having an affair. Do you mind?' To which Jonathan had not replied. He forwarded her mail without comment.

She didn't tell him when she was getting back and went straight to her father's flat in Victoria. But on the first Saturday she went over to their apartment: Jonathan's and her apartment. She stood outside the door for some time and then, greatly daring, got out her key and went in. It was about half-past three in the afternoon and there was no one there now, but there had been recently. They had eaten some pasta for lunch and drunk two-thirds of a bottle of Spanish Rioja. The glasses on the table were her glasses, some she'd seen in a shop in the Loire valley long ago and her father had given them to her. She went to the bedroom. Two people had clearly slept there; indeed there were a skirt and blouse tossed on the bed, a dirty bra and pants mixed in with a pile of dirty shorts of Jonathan's.

On Monday she went to the post office and put in a re-direct for the mail of *Mrs* Celestine Woodwood as well as the mail of Celestine Quareine. She was tempted but did not take the glasses. A month later she sent Jonathan another postcard simply saying she was back in London and 'I can be contacted at the Victoria address'. She did not expect a reply and got none. Finis. Was that why this ten years or so later she was walking the dyke?

Walking, travelling, moving, those were all activities she liked. She didn't really like to be stationary for long. She liked her own long legs, liked to use them to walk. She walked fast, she always had, taking those long paces, and here she was climbing as ever up Frydd Hill between the Great and Little Frydd wood. The dyke, constructed on a grand scale in Knighton, is scarcely more than a hedge bank in the wood but at the south corner of field 40 the dyke is a little larger, and the improved scale continues in fields 41 and 42. On the boundary between these fields the dyke is irregular and spoil holes are seen on the west side. The end of this is a crest line and is marked by pine trees.

On passing it the dyke presents a completely altered character, both bank and ditch being on the grand scale. The contrast is dramatic; a patch of scrub separates a bank and ditch so small that it might easily escape notice from a high rampart and deep west ditch sixty feet overall and twenty-eight feet on the scarp. That this change – both of scale and character – takes place on a crest line, a spot as easily recognised as the col at Hergan, is significant; and it is most fortunate that the junction has escaped serious damage. The stretch from the valley to this point was undoubtedly the work of the Cwmsancham-Panpunton Hill gang as the east ditch shows.

Turning again to detail, the dyke and west ditch are well preserved on the margin of field 47; the earthwork is on the normal Offan scale, not the tremendous structure we have lately studied. The dyke now traverses open moorland. Crossing the shallow embankment the dyke rises on to the forward (W) slope of Hawthorn Hill. The scale is normal, scarp twenty feet in slope, breadth about fifty feet; there is a well-marked east ditch but no trace of one on the west. There never was one here; the corn crop is scanty along the field edge, indicating lack of soil over the rock.

Craig had been curious about her trip; unlike the others who had thought only of themselves, Craig had wanted to know what she was up to. He had questioned her about the books she was carrying. 'Travelling light, I know, Celestine, but you never go anywhere without a book. What are you carrying?' And Celestine had to confess to her two slim volumes, *Pride and Prejudice* and *The Hunting of the Snark*. 'An ill-assorted pair,' had been Craig's comment. 'They are both travelling somewhere: one eminently sensible and one absurdly insane. *The Snark* is the first truly modern poem, people talk about Hopkins with all his technical skills but the content, the content; *The Snark* is about the future.'

There were dangers on the trip for all members of the crew. Not only external dangers from the Bellman's incompetent navigation but dangers within the crew themselves. In particular there was the situation that involved the Beaver and the Butcher. What was the Beaver aboard for anyway? The Bellman said that the Beaver had often saved them from wreck though none of the sailors knew how, but the Beaver paced on the deck or sat making lace in the bow. In the end the lace was the only product from the whole trip. Indeed initially the Beaver went on making lace when the others had actively started to seek for the Snark. The Barrister was shocked by this and tried to appeal to the Beaver's pride and vainly proceeded to cite a number of cases in which making lace had been proved an infringement of right.

In addition to the incompetent Baker who was unable to bake them any useful provision, the Bellman had engaged another provider who was to prove incompetent and who needs especial remark: he looked an incredible dunce – he had just one idea – but, that one being 'Snark', the good Bellman engaged him at once.

> He came as a Butcher: but gravely declared,
>     When the ship had been sailing a week,
> He could only kill Beavers. The Bellman looked scared,
>     And was almost too frightened to speak:
>
> But at length he explained, in a tremulous tone,
>     There was only one Beaver on board;
> And that was a tame one he had of his own,
>     Whose death would be deeply deplored.
>
> The Beaver, who happened to hear the remark,
>     Protested, with tears in its eyes,
> That not even the rapture of hunting the Snark
>     Could atone for that dismal surprise!

The Beaver advised that the Butcher should be conveyed in a separate ship; the Bellman refused this proposal. The Baker suggested the Beaver should procure a second-hand dagger-proof coat while the Banker offered for hire excellent policies, one against fire and one against damage from hail. However, whenever the Butcher was by, the Beaver kept looking the opposite way and appeared unaccountably shy.

The Beaver, Celestine had always noted, was referred to as 'it', another example of Carroll's avoidance of anything sexual in his work. She had even laboured through *Sylvie and Bruno* (and *Sylvie and Bruno (Concluded)*). The childish couple were half fantasies of an adult couple who did indeed marry but their courtship was conducted as if they were children and their bodies didn't intrude into the relationship in any way. Celestine thought she would like to add ten women to the crew that hunted the Snark. All the names of the crew began with B and the girls' names would begin with C. Joan used a four-letter C word pretty freely though it was a word that some feminists would not use. Celestine liked it as a term of abuse, liked it as a term for part of her body.

Ralph had called her cunt all the time and she had loved it and he had meant it too – partly to imply that she was simply his sexual object and for a time that had been what she wanted. Nothing more. She had been for him the truly compliant lover feeding the ego-trip he was continuously pursuing. She couldn't conceive now how she had behaved in the way she had. Well, she would meet him tonight and maybe he would explain himself. She feared what he would do.

It was difficult sometimes to appreciate the dyke when her mind became occupied with her life. Sometimes she looked later at the guidebook and saw she should have seen 'magnificent views again' and yet in the evening she couldn't remember if she had. The walking itself, of course, held one's attention; the placement of the foot avoiding muddy places, searching the next field hedge for the stile; sometimes it would be an accompanying post with the Offa's Dyke mark on it. Her binoculars, a present that year from her father, were invaluable in this, helping to distinguish a farm post which looked like the OD post or a doubled piece of fencing which might be a stile.

There was a tendency too to spend a lot of time at each

pause studying the guidebook, the Offa's Dyke Society route notes, the strip maps the society provided and of course the Ordnance Survey map. There was the constant calculation of how many miles you had done and how many more there were to do. Would she get to her destination in time?

There were interruptions. As here today, in the middle section of the dyke, suddenly she had heard that strange cat-like sound, the mewling of buzzards. She swung her glasses and soon located the pair gliding, as ever, so high up that they didn't look the big birds she knew them to be. There were buzzards all up and down the dyke, great sentinels of the air, patrolling this boundary, seeming not to be the hunters they were, and Celestine had never seen one dive for prey, but thought rather they had some custodial role, watching to see that no one damaged the property – the dyke – which lay below them.

And apart from the views there was her constant need to understand what the dyke was doing. Changes from major mounds to what seemed even originally to have been quite a slight mound needed explanation, as did the variation between straightness and irregularity. There was no doubt that these changes had a physiological character. It was in this area that the dyke was first built, but in heavily forested areas, and much of this area was heavily forested, the engineer essentially threw up a mere boundary bank made from a succession of spoil holes. In his maturity further north he cast off these defects and even in forest he built a dyke, although in places on the steeper hills it was more like a platform or berm. But the berm was a sign of his maturity.

The Easthurst brochure which her father had shown her emphasised that the school aimed to turn out mature young women. When, thought Celestine, did she become mature? One wasn't mature ever but there was a time when you were grown-up. You couldn't be grown-up unless you knew about who your mother was or at least something about her. Over and over again during the last years at school Celestine had conversations in her head with her father when she said 'I must know about my mother,' but over and over again when the holidays came she couldn't bring herself to mention the subject which she knew he didn't want to talk about.

The nearest she ever came was to say to him one evening, 'I would like to see a photo of my mother.' He said nothing for perhaps five minutes, sat there having allowed the paper he was reading to drop to his lap. Then he went over to his desk which was in their sitting-room and took a key out of the top drawer and got out a framed photo and gave it to Celestine.

'Put it back and lock the drawer,' he said, leaving the room. Celestine thought he had left her to look at the picture alone but in a moment he was back carrying a jewel case. 'These are your mother's jewels. They are for you. Don't wear them in my presence. I'm going to bed.' And then he did leave her alone.

Celestine stared at the photo, trying to get some feeling, response from the mute photo. It was a young woman, twenty-three, twenty-four, she guessed, with her hair cut short with a fringe. The photo was black and white of course but Celestine judged the hair to be a darker brown than her own. Otherwise she simply stared straight at the camera not quite smiling but with her lips looking as if they could easily move. She stared back at Celestine giving her no message. The jewel case contained a good string of pearls, a gold chain with a cross, two or three quite nice brooches, some thin silver bracelets; Celestine thought they might be English and she slipped one on and liked it. It was curious to think that the last person to have worn it must have been her dead mother. She was struck by the fact that there were no rings in the box.

The only other person she could enquire from was her aunt. She was her mother's older sister but there had been a big gap between them – ten years had separated Celestine's grandparents' only two children. Her grandmother had been over forty when Hazel – Celestine's mother – had been born. Celestine had no memories of her grandmother, who was dead by the time Celestine first came to England.

Her aunt had talked about her childhood and her little

sister, but at eighteen her aunt left home to become a nurse and had married when she was twenty-three and become immersed in the 'practice'. Later she had her own children to worry about and she could tell Celestine very little about Hazel as a young woman. 'She trained as a secretary and worked for a law firm, that was how she met your father, I think.' The summer she was eighteen, Celestine said to her, 'You must tell me how my mother died.' But her aunt didn't really know. 'Your father would never tell me the details. She was killed, murdered I think, in some sort of robbery.'

That summer Aunt was busy. Gilly was getting married. It seemed to Celestine that this was the first of a rush of summer marriages. Old school friends, college friends, new work friends, there was this scene on English lawns in what always seemed to be the Home Counties. Driving in a car with new clothes and wearing a hat – that last item seemed to be *de rigueur* – to an English country church.

Then there was the quaintness of the English vicar delivering a homily to bride and groom. Some of the sermons were truly awful with arch remarks about going forth and prospering and bringing forth the good seed. The services lacked all passion and commitment. Afterwards there was the photographic scene which as the years passed got longer and longer with video to add to flashing still cameras. Celestine sometimes wondered if the young couples spent all their married life examining these mementoes which they had collected in such volume.

But Gilly's wedding was the first of these occasions and it had a strange sequel for her. She and her father had stayed on in Bournemouth for a week after the wedding and were there to see the local paper's report of the marriage. 'Prominent Bournemouth GP's daughter married' and lists of misspelt guests followed. But Celestine suddenly thought that newspapers covered not only marriages and births but also deaths. She made a casual enquiry of her father about Indian newspapers, were they in English? 'The Times of India,' he said, 'modelled on *The Times* but a very good copy.' Then from her aunt, the date of her mother's death: early March, she remembered.

Where in London did you find *The Times of India* for eighteen years ago? She thought of the Indian Embassy but went and asked first the local library and they told her: 'Colindale, they keep every paper there.' So out to Colindale she went. There was some resistance from the librarians there at first. What research was she doing that required her to have access to the paper? So she told them: 'My mother died and I'm sure that there was a report of it in the paper because she was killed and I want to know about it.' That last remark she forced out, almost crying as she said it. Then they helped her.

She was sat down in a little room and brought what she asked for, *The Times of India* for February and March. She didn't know whether there would be a headline or whether she would have to look in the death columns, but if she was killed there must surely have been a news report.

It had been a leap year. February, the twenty-ninth. 'Young British lawyer's wife missing.' Fears for her safety. Mrs Quareine had formed the most unwise habit of walking by herself after dark in parts of old Delhi. She had left her house in her car at nine o'clock. The car was found near the Red Fort but Mrs Quareine was not in it. A distraught Mr Quareine said, 'I begged her not to go out by herself. I was working. Midnight I found I was alone. The bearer told me her car had gone.'

Then nothing for four days. Monday, 4 March, *The Times of India*: 'Lawyer's Wife's Mutilated Body Found'. Celestine didn't know whether she wanted more detail or less. The naked body of a white woman found in a ditch. Police believe she had been held prisoner for three days and killed Sunday night. Sexually mutilated and repeatedly stabbed. No clues as to the killers. Two weeks later there was a report of the inquest but again no details and verdict of 'Unlawful Killing by Persons Unknown'.

That night she did ask her father a direct question. 'Did they ever find the people who killed my mother?' Startled, he replied, 'No, nothing was ever found out about them.' Celestine said, 'I read the pieces in *The Times of India*.' 'Ah,' he said. 'I had asked her not to go out. I had to work in the evening.' And he very deliberately picked up the book he had been reading, adjusted his glasses and turned his head and the book away from Celestine. So Celestine was left with the horror of her mother's death and the question mark over that comment of her father's. Why did her mother go out at night, leaving her father and a six-month baby, Celestine herself, alone?

It was not exactly crowded but the further south one got, it seemed to Celestine the number of walkers on the dyke increased. Today she had met one group of six who were on their last day, they were doing the southern part of the path but finishing at Knighton. The dyke too, which in its northern part passed through barely a village, now in the south passed through major towns. Her stops for the next few nights were in towns, Kington, Hay-on-Wye, Monmouth. Visitors to these towns walked out of them along the dyke to sample it. Celestine and the long-distance walkers rather despised them. 'Transients', one serious-minded rambler had called them.

It had also occurred to Celestine that apart from her China-man on the first day, 'ethnics' had been absent, the walkers were Saxons in general. She hadn't even met many Welsh, perhaps they took their border for granted. But here now coming towards her was a little family, who were transients in a way but they attracted Celestine's admiration because they had two young children. One child, who she guessed might just be walking, was in a carrier on his father's back while a scrap of three or four had been half-carried, Celestine guessed, all the way up Rushock Hill. She stopped for a chat, and to congratulate the little boy. The couple too interested her because they were of mixed race . . . the father a Saxon clearly but the mother an invader new to the dyke, Celestine guessed she was West Indian. They seemed very relaxed and glad, as was Celestine, to sit and chat for a bit. They were driving up the dyke, stopping here and there to walk bits depending on how much they could manage with their kids.

Soon Celestine felt relaxed enough to ask the girl whether she'd been born in England: 'Yes, my parents came from Jamaica though, although I'm supposed to have a Scottish great-grandfather,' she laughed. 'No Welsh background though.' 'You're an invader, like me,' said Celestine. 'I come from India but my name is Welsh.'

The new way/wave of migrations/movements of people drawn not as with the old migrations with an expulsion or a shortness of food but because they were attracted to a new world by the promise of work, money, fortune, life like *Dallas*. Celestine wondered how the dyke would deal with this new group of borderers. They were, she realised, the re-entrants entering not the place they had come from but the place they thought was their Motherland.

Woman 1   I'm going to England because my mother sent for me. I'm staying five years.

Woman 2   I'm going to England because I hear that other people are doing good. I'm going to stay about three years.

Woman 3   I'm going to England because there's no employment here. I'm staying two years.

Woman 4   I'm going to England because my fiancé is there. I'm staying five years.

Woman 5   I'm going to England to do nurse training. I'm staying three years.

Woman 6   I'm going to England because it is my mother country.

Woman 7   I'm going to England to make money. I'm staying one year.

Woman 8   I'm going to England to join my husband. I'm staying four years.

Woman 9   I'm going to England because they said they needed me; I'm not sure how long I'm staying.

Woman 10   I'm going to England to ensure a better future for my children. I'm staying for as long as it takes.

We used to sing songs about England, the West Indian woman said. You know like: (she sings) 'Rule Britannia, Britannia rules the waves' and we used to chant 'Red, white and blue, what does it mean to you? Shout it aloud, Britain's awake. These are the chains that nothing can break.' Those are the songs we grew up with and we had to dress up in blue skirt and white blouse when they having these coronations, or when they crowning Queen Elizabeth and King George. Yes we felt very much involved and we had to sing: (she sings) 'There'll always be an England and England shall be free, if England mean so much to you as England mean to me.'

It was a cold, cold November day. People were so cold. I wanted to turn around and go back; it had all been a horrible mistake. I don't want to do nursing, I don't want to be here. I didn't realise it would be that cold and it was misty. Now I can look back and say it was misty; at the time it was dense fog. One of the things that shocked me was looking around and seeing English people doing manual work. It seemed so depressing, the picture that I had built up in me mind. It wasn't that I thought it was the golden land but the streets, the space, the accent, the strange accent . . . There were curious onlookers standing around looking; anxious black people and curious white people . . .

I fear the prolonged wandering of the displaced. About three years later one of the most painful episodes of my childhood took place. This time it was inside a classroom. Mr Thompson, an English literature teacher, decided to demonstrate his knowledge of all things by explaining the origins of our surnames. So Greenberg was Jewish, Morley originally came from the small Yorkshire town of the same name, and McKenzie was a Scot. I felt a hot flush of embarrassment long before he turned towards my desk. 'Phillips,' he mused, 'you must be from Wales.' The whole class laughed, while I stared back at him stony-faced, knowing full well that I was not from Wales. The truth was I had no idea where I was from as I had been told that I was born in the Caribbean but came from England. I could not participate in a joke which made my identity a source of humour. Even those I considered my friends were laughing.


The West Indian girl on the dyke laughed. Scottish blood – same as Welsh – maybe I'm a bit of a Celt.

Celestine left the friendly family and pressed on to the top of the hill. Just here were the famous three yew trees, the Three Shepherds, on the dyke itself. They were called this as they were thought to represent the souls or bodies of three shepherds who died in a winter blizzard. Above them, on the shoulder of Rushock Hill, there is a definite lower ditch and upper spoil ditch. The dyke is following up to its head a small re-entrant. Here too are the last views of the Welsh mountains, for now the Herefordshire plain opens out widely east and west. At the yew trees the plateau begins to narrow and the hill to have a definite ridge. The yew trees are visible from all parts of Radnorshire. Yews are frequently seen on earthworks in southern England but Fox had not yet seen them in Wales. Perhaps for this reason he ended his 1930 season of work here. At these secular trees his survey was suspended until 1931. Celestine had a further two miles to walk in her season down to Kington, with Ralph awaiting her, no doubt, at the Burton Hotel.

As she became a more senior editor in publishing she became aware of the powers behind the industry. Until the mid-1970s publishing still had something of a gentlemanly (or womanly?) flavour to it but then the moguls moved in thinking there was money to be made. One thing they though of as potential money was ESL publishing, so Celestine was in a protected bit of the business. But she also began to meet the managing directors, chairmen, people who actually spoke to Robert Maxwell, or had connections with senior civil servants in the Department of Education. She would go off to talk to prominent politicians, or back-bench whips. Name-dropping began to be part of her life and she found that meeting these people gave her a curious frisson. She wanted to be seen in their company. Why, she couldn't say, but she wanted to know famous people. She never saw herself as becoming famous but she wanted to be associated with these gods.

Buy-outs, mergers, suddenly the old managing editor of their trade division was gone. We're getting Ralph Edgehorn out of Random House. He's coming. Ralph had started in broadcasting, started publishing books of the series, made a swift move to a senior post with Penguin, at thirty-five had suddenly been head-hunted to New York. Now, at forty-three, head-hunted to do many things but one was 'to turn the trade division around'. He'll do it in two years, everybody said. *Publisher's Weekly* gave him a whole-page profile. But there was more than publishing. They were linked to a video-tape and CD company, all run together by Ralph. Got to get publishing as part of the whole entertainment business. Wish there was equipment we could sell to record with. Our video-recorders are having a good year. I make sure they do! And the aim – where the big money is – satellite TV. Then we'll make real money. 'The sky's the limit.' Gaffawing laughs. And he was off to the main board of directors with Lord Haram, 'but Jeffers, you know, the US division head, really runs us'.

So here he was suddenly in the lift, 'Hullo, hullo, good to meet', and although education was part of the technical division it was also part of trade. Celestine represented education at trade sales meetings, trying to push a book of theirs over to the trade representative. There was Ralph. 'Volume is too small, we have to double it this year, we must scavenge titles, titles that sell. We'll try to buy from outside.' Then suddenly, 'Education, some of those teach-yourself style language books, we've got some good ones. Why don't we develop something? Cut some of our old texts down to something simpler. Digest them, that can be done quietly in house.'

Celestine was soon running this teach-yourself list. 'We

want twenty titles by next spring, Celestine.' Ralph would pour into her office, sit on her desk, ruffle through typescripts she was reading. Stir things up. He was always in the office hours after everyone else. People started staying later to catch his eye. If you didn't catch his eye, you might find yourself fired over a weekend. 'New wood,' he said, 'prune, prune.'

'You're here late, Celestine. I'll take you to eat. Hurry while I call the White Tower, they can usually fit me two downstairs.' Personal names of most of the staff and other diners. 'Excuse me, Celestine, here's Brendan. These High Anglican bishops, they do themselves well.' Someone else did things well.

'I'm still living in Claridge's, haven't had time to get anything sorted out. Must get an apartment – flat, of course, here – soon. Come round.' Claridge's rooms – or at least the one Ralph had – seemed to Celestine like an apartment already. There was a little ante-room and a separate sitting-room with a bedroom beyond. 'Take a brandy.' Ralph disappeared into his bedroom to re-appear five minutes later wearing just a slight robe through which his erection was clearly visible. He embraced her and kissed her hard then said, 'Go into the bedroom and come back naked.' Celestine did as she was told.

There began a strange period of her life. Her phone would ring at the office or at home with not invitations but instructions. 'We're having dinner with Lady Anscombe,' or 'We're taking Jeffers out tonight,' or 'We're going to the opera. I've got the Arts Council box.' There was some generosity, like a gift of a diamond-studded brooch. 'I picked it up at the airport.' And once when she said, 'I've nothing to wear, I haven't had time to do any laundry,' he reached into his pocket and gave her five hundred pounds in notes and said, 'Buy yourself some new clothes.'

The demands to join him in bed were as peremptory too. 'Hi, cunt, there's a car on its way for you.' She got used to walking through the lobby of the hotel and up to his suite watched by the eyes of the night staff. Celestine went, saying, 'I'm exhausted, Ralph. You never really sleep.' Whatever time he got in, Ralph was up every morning at six o'clock. When he went to the States for a long weekend she stayed in her own flat and slept the whole weekend away.

She told him that she was dining with Joan and Sylvia on Thursday. But mid-morning there was a call, 'Dinner with Jeffers: important, you must come.' But she had to resist. 'No, Ralph, I can't, won't come.' She could feel the fury down the phone. On Friday night, the car was sent for her around ten. She found Ralph in his robe awaiting her, and she was ordered straight to bed. 'Lie on your belly, Celestine, you are going to be whipped. When I say come to dinner, you come.'

Once she had submitted to this humility, it began to happen that she would fail him on a regular basis: she realised he would plan her failures. Afterwards she realised that although he published, promoted apparently, the Arts, said various opera stars he knew were marvellous, she never really heard him enthuse about anything unless it was people: they were important people. It was manipulation, it was possessions, it was money. It was owning people like her. It was months before she remembered that she had not given Ralph a word: and by this time she knew what the word was, 'nasty'.

Nasty: gnastie, naustie: origin obscure, what language would want to claim the word? Of five meanings, the nicest related to the weather. Others: foul, filthy, dirty, indecent, obscene. Or offensive in some respect, disagreeable, unpleasant, objectionable, annoying, ill-natured. Difficult to deal with, dangerous, bad. Johnson added a curiously more modern word: polluted.

# D. J. Taylor

## A YOUNG PERSON'S GUIDE TO THE MODERN ENGLISH NOVEL

SOMEWHERE IN LONDON – in fact in a room in a flat high above a Bayswater square – a writer is putting the finishing touches to a novel. What sort of a writer? And what kind of a novel? The writer – let us call him Max Doubtfire – is a young man of twenty-eight or twenty-nine, white, the possessor of a minor public school education and an upper second-class degree in English literature from the University of Cambridge (it was supposed to be a first, but, alas, Max was having an emotional crisis in the week of finals). By day he reads manuscripts for a literary agency whose office is a couple of miles down the road in Notting Hill. At night he returns to his room – the flat is owned by an old college friend who works for a merchant bank – to get on with *Imbroglio*. This, it should be said, is not Max's first novel. There are another three lying in cardboard folders under the bed, solid integuments and a dusty tomb: the Cambridge comedy he wrote one summer vacation; the 400-page imitation of *The Magus*; the spiky experimental one (entitled *Gasps from the Abyss*, and done entirely in dialogue). This, however, is the first that is likely to be published. What is it about? As it happens, *Imbroglio* is about a man in his late twenties who lives in west London and works for a literary agency. There is also a lot about drugs (Max has never taken anything stronger than a Pro-plus tablet) and a graphic description of an old lady's cat being eviscerated by a teen-aged hoodlum. All in all it is a fairly typical first novel, and

126

Max (white, male, public school, vague literary connections, Martin Amis fixation) is a fairly typical first novelist.

What happens? Max's employers specialise in glitzy commercial thrillers and celebrity autobiographies, several of which Max has found himself rewriting from time to time, and this stab at high art would be rather beyond them. But Max has a friend, another old college chum, recently promoted to the post of editorial director at the firm of Rosencrantz & Guildenstern, once a legendarily fastidious independent, now a single imprint in a vast porn-mags-to-CD-Rom-Anglo-American empire. Happily the friend quite likes it, and – there being a gap in the next Spring List caused by an eminent lady novelist going off in a huff to a rival firm – resolves to publish it. The advance, Max is informed, will be £6,000: a third on signature, another third on hardback publication, a final third on the book's appearance in softcover. Gratified and astounded at the fulfilment of a decade-long dream, Max accepts, treats himself to a new typewriter and takes his girlfriend (a rather severe young woman who works in the High Street Kensington branch of Messrs Waterstone) off for a fortnight's holiday in the Dordogne.

A year passes. Snug in his Notting Hill office, at a desk covered with the illiterate reminiscences of film actors and former associates of the Kray twins, Max consoles himself with the thought that he at any rate is a *writer*. The note of asperity that creeps into some of his reader's reports does not go unnoticed by his employers. Eventually, several months after its original publication date (the delay explained by 'scheduling difficulties'), *Imbroglio* appears, in a hardback edition of 1,500 copies, priced at £15.99. Max, seeing a pile – a very small pile – in the Charing Cross Road branch of Books Etc, is transfixed by a glow of serenity he had not previously thought possible, and spends several minutes surreptitiously shifting it to a position of prominence on the central display table. Meanwhile, reviews have begun to emerge. The *Daily Telegraph*, noticing it fourth in a column devoted to six first novels, says that it shows 'considerable promise, while remaining in thrall to the worst kind of

Amisian stylistic excess'. The *Sunday Times*, summarising it in 150 words, thinks that 'Max Doubtfire is undoubtedly a writer to watch' (Max photocopies this encomium and sends it to every college friend with whom he is still in touch). Other criticism is less inspiring. The *Swindon Evening Advertiser* – all the cuttings are forwarded by Rosencrantz & Guildenstern's publicity department – reproduces the jacket copy, misspells the names of the two principal characters and laments the author's 'impenetrable cleverness'. Worst of all is a piece in the *Guardian* by a rising young critic Max vaguely remembers from Cambridge (they both wanted the editorship of the same student magazine, and Max won) suggesting that 'readers of *Imbroglio* – if such there be – will be pleased to learn that the business of writing a novel and getting it accepted for publication is, on this evidence, a good deal easier than they might suppose.'

On balance, though, Max is not discouraged. On the strength of *Imbroglio* he is invited to review a life of Cyril Connolly for the *Spectator*; the piece ('The Great Procrastinator') is well received by the magazine's literary editor. A royalty statement, despatched some months later by Rosencrantz & Guildenstern, advises him that *Imbroglio* has sold 654 copies in the UK (20 to Max himself at author discount) and 189 copies in various parts of the Commonwealth. Brought out in softcover at £5.99 by the paperback arm of Rosencrantz & Guildenstern's parent company nine months later, in an edition of 5,000 copies, it sells a further 3,000, prompting the accountants to write off 25 per cent of the advance. Meanwhile, Max is experiencing something of a revolution in his personal life, specifically the relocation of himself and his girl-friend to a two-bedroom flat in Fulham, and the acquisition of an Abbey National mortgage. The payments are £500 a month (Max gets £12,000 a year from his job in the agency, his girl-friend a touch less), but there is another novel three quarters written by this time, *Astride the Grave* (Max has been reading Beckett), and within a couple of months this, too, is winging its way off to Rosencrantz & Guildenstern's Lubyanka-like offices in Chelsea, or rather to the cramped half of the top floor on which the 'literary' end of the parent company's business hangs out. Here, however, change is in the air. Max's friend the editorial director has resigned to write a novel of his own or become an agent. The new boss is a serious young Yale-reared feminist with a brief from on high to reshape, radically, a list that has lately been looking 'rather tired', to use the CEO's expression, and the upshot is that a fortnight later *Astride the Grave* is returned to Max's trim new premises in the Fulham Road with a polite but regretful note in an unknown hand. Max's only subsequent communication from Rosencrantz & Guildenstern is a letter, six months later, inviting him to buy paperback copies of *Imbroglio* at a knockdown price of 49p prior to the remaindering of the stock (the 650 hardbacks were pulped a year ago).

Why write novels? In the age of the Information Superhighway and ever-proliferating media channels, it is commonly assumed that the urge to write fiction is in decline, that no 25-year-old with an idea about human motivation and the means of expressing it would ever think twice about pursuing a career that was so patently arduous, uncertain and profitless (while exact comparisons are unhelpful, it should be pointed out that the starting salary for a London-based trainee in a Big Six accountancy firm is around £15,000 – more than the advance on at least half the books you see in an average bookshop). Two or three years ago a sad young man took up nearly a page of the *Guardian* to suggest that no one (least of all his circle of intellectual friends) aspired to write fiction any more, that the bright boys became stockbrokers, or film producers, or magazine journalists. This struck me then, and strikes me now, as nonsense. Everybody writes novels. My wife, who works at one of the big London publishing houses, brings a bag of them home every night: fat white typescripts written by retired postmistresses in Aberdeen, model agency proprietors, bright thirtysomething journalists keen to expand their horizons. Once, just after I left university, I worked, like Max, for a literary agent, an enlightened old gentleman who had made the fatal mistake of suggesting in his *Writers' and Artists' Yearbook* entry that he 'encouraged' new writers. For quite a long time after the paragraph's publication (he changed it for the next edition, but the *Writers' and Artists'* had a long underground shelf-life), the average contents of his daily postal delivery was sixty parcels. For years after leaving his employment I used to think of the dozens of manuscripts I wrote reports on (and for the record I think I recommended that four be sent to publishers and of these one actually appeared in print) and shudder at the vision of fruitless endeavour it conjured up.

But why write novels? Leaving aside the go-getters who write for money or vanity, the typical educated person who picks up a pen one day and decides to write a book of the kind it is possible to respect is motivated by a variety of promptings. Chief among them, perhaps, is a simple wish to emulate whichever literary hero suggested to him or her that the business of novel-writing was a worthy aesthetic endeavour: most first novels, and quite a few second or third novels, are simply acts of homage, a rather public paying off of old debts to Martin or Muriel or whoever. Then there are the old stirrings of aesthetic and ideological purpose. I happen to believe, along with Orwell, that all art is propaganda of a sort, if not in quite the absolute terms that Orwell maintained, and it is unquestionably true that most books can be broken down until they reveal some kind of political bedrock. Similarly, every novel has a self-evident aesthetic purpose, if only to convince the reader that the particular style by which it proceeds is a rewarding one. But perhaps even more important than this is that writing a novel is one of the few modern activities that has any kind of intellectual glamour attached to it. Inevitably, this notion has become slightly debased given the large number of celebrities, politicians and what-not who have gravitated towards the profession, but the fact remains that to the average English graduate who has spent three years having it dinned into his or her head that reading Dickens and Shakespeare is the only civilised way to spend your time, most traditional career paths seem simply degrading. No one *wants* to be a chartered accountant, or a stockbroker, or a loss adjuster. No one *wants* to sit in a cheerless office block in EC2 sweating his or her guts out for a collection of self-satisfied halfwits who use *impact* as a verb and whose corporate hand-outs talk about 'envisioning the future'. In these circumstances, writing a novel is a delightful way of getting your own back at the wider throng of smug, grey-suited humanity (anyone who doubts this, by the way, should take a look at Jeanette Winterson's musings on the subject of 'artists', in which the contempt for what might be called the processes of ordinary life verges on the hysterical).

All this might give the impression that novel-writing is a kind of dilettante-ish sub-occupation, practised by an exclusive group of unemployables and social misfits. In fact, the pressures on the average young novelist are quite as profound, if not more so, as those experienced by the average pen-pusher in Bishopsgate or Leadenhall Street. Something of their nature may be gauged by a look at the career of a real novelist, as opposed to the fictitious travails of Max Doubtfire. Richard Burns died by his own hand on 31 August 1992, the day before his thirty-fourth birthday and a fortnight before the publication of his fourth novel, *Sandro and Simonetta*. According to the *Guardian*, whose Ian Katz provided a sympathetic account of the case, Burns – alone in the house he shared with his wife and children, and sedated with alcohol – destroyed himself by stepping off a chair while suspended by a noose from the banisters. I knew Richard Burns very slightly, to the extent of chatting to him at parties given by the *Independent* (for whom we both reviewed) or by the Flamingo paperback imprint of HarperCollins (by whom we were both at one time or another published). In conversation, he came across as a shy, diffident man whose diffidence concealed, or failed to conceal, a burning assurance of his own abilities.

Before his death and the posthumous publication of *Sandro and Simonetta*, Burns wrote three novels (there were also a couple of fantasies, a thriller and some poetry): *A Dance to the Moon*, *The Panda Hunt* and *Fond and Foolish Lovers*.

Each of them gives notice of a prodigious talent that is rather uncertain about the best means of unravelling itself, and *Fond and Foolish Lovers*, in particular, is a grand panorama of artifice, mingling quantum physics, scholarly pastiche and faked subtexts with a well-observed love story trying to get out from underneath. Burns called it 'South Yorkshire's own *Middlemarch*, and I don't care a toss that everyone else will argue that I can't do it: I'm quite capable of proving that on my own.' Trying to construct a picture of this quiet, reserved and likeable man, one stumbles up against a single, grinding resentment: against a publishing world and a literary establishment which, he believed, ignored his talents while wasting money on rubbish. In a letter to his agent, reflecting on the £6,000 he had earned in the four years she had represented him, he observed that 'This may not be your fault, but it is an unbearable situation, particularly when every other writer I know – some perhaps better than me, but many who are not – earns much more . . . I cannot assess my market value but if it is really so low then I ought not to be writing at all.'

What was Richard Burns's market value? The average sale of a 'serious' literary novel, published in hardback at £15.99 and reviewed in the broadsheets, is around a thousand copies. Certainly none of his books sold much more than this. And yet in the context of fiction publishing over the past ten years, Burns's career is a triumph of a sort. Around the time of *A Dance to the Moon*'s publication, its publishers, Jonathan Cape, made great play of the fact that they were issuing the work of no fewer than ten first novelists that Spring. Only two, of whom Burns was one, went on to make any kind of reputation. Despite this success – which most members of a provincial writers' group would give a limb for – Burns spent much of his time merely scraping a living. His income during the last year of his life, so far as one can make out, was put together out of *Independent* reviews, freelance teaching and hand-outs. Three weeks before his death the bank had frozen all his cash and payment cards. It would be fatally easy to mark Richard Burns down as a ghastly symbol of the modern literary life. As his agent pointed out, though, if everyone in his financial position committed suicide there would be no novelists left. The equation is complicated, too, by the fact that Burns was about to take a full-time job as head of Lancaster University's creative writing department at a salary of £20,000 a year, and it seems plausible to speculate that the insecurities that led him to kill himself would probably have shown through whatever his choice of career. All the same, the story of Richard Burns – whom I believe to have been a genuinely underrated writer, if not quite as underrated as he imagined – cannot help but shed light on some of the pressures to which the average literary life is subject. These can be summarised under four headings: *economic*, *occupational*, *political* and *aesthetic*.

*Economic*. Most first novels get written when the writer is in his or her late twenties, usually as a respite from part- or full-time occupations. The money, consequently, is a pleasant little fillip to the salary allowed one by Messrs Slow & Bideawhile, literary agents, the *Daily Telegraph* or whoever. Moreover, it comes at a time when general living expenses are low. As an example, when my first novel was accepted for publication in 1984, I was working for a Covent Garden public relations agency, living in a room in somebody's flat in Pimlico, and was able to regard Secker & Warburg's £750 advance as a gratifying dollop of pocket money. However, by the time the writer has moved a book or two into his career, reached his mid-thirties, say, and is trying to write the solid third novel that will establish his reputation ('With this novel Mr X confirms his position as one of our most . . .' *Times Literary Supplement*) he is quite likely to have acquired a wife and a family, not to mention a mortgage or at least a fairly hefty rent. How to maintain them? Estimates vary, but it is difficult to conduct any kind of decent *familial* middle-class life in London on much less than £25,000 a year. Where is the money to come from? Let us say that X has a wife and two children under five. X's wife has a part-time job, synchronised with the children's visits to a childminder, that brings in £8,000 a year. This leaves X with £17,000 a year to find from his writing. As it happens, X's publishers are particularly supportive, and prepared to pay him £10,000 for a novel that only realises two thirds of its advance, but X, who belongs to the Flaubert school of revisers, can only produce one every two years. Fortunately, he has already made a minor name for himself as a reviewer: occasional pieces for the *Sunday Times* (£300 a throw), the *Spectator* (£90 but prestigious) and the *Literary Review* (nominal, but it pays to keep in with Bron). This brings in, let us say, £5,000 a year. Infrequent one-off commissions such as appearances at literary festivals, TV (less likely now that the *Late Show* has gone bust), short stories on the radio (a crowded market) might realise another thousand or two. In a good year X, one of our most promising younger novelists, remember, whose first book *Breathless Statues* was short-listed for the John Llewellyn Rhys award, might make £12,000 out of his writing – gratifying, because money earned by one's pen somehow seems more real than that earned in an office, but insufficient to meet the expenses of a family of four living in a three-bedroom flat in Barnes. Plainly, X is going to have to get a job. But what sort of job? And here X, who spent three years a decade ago trying and failing to become a chartered accountant, turns horribly fastidious. The BBC would be nice, or two days a week on the books page of a daily newspaper. Eventually he gets a post teaching English part-time to one of the American universities with what are called 'London semesters': oner-ous, in that it involves giving lectures on books he hasn't read for fifteen years, and unsatisfactory in that the students are gum-chewing USAF servicemen's children from Arkansas whose sole concern is their grade-point average. The result of this disruption to cherished routines is that X's next book, the one that will definitely establish him as our leading etc., etc., is not quite as good as the last, gets mixed reviews and loses his publishers even more money than usual. Amid all this discouragement, X cannot help but notice that Mrs X, who once used to cut his reviews admiringly out of the newspapers but has now turned thirty-five and wants another baby, has grown decidedly cool.

*Occupational.* Every profession has its professional association. Accountants send their subs to the Institute of Chartered Accountants in England and Wales at Moorgate Place; solicitors are gathered together under the wing of the Law Society; and no branch of the life assurance or marine underwriting trades is so obscure that it lacks its institute or round table with a president in a silver collar. For the corporation of the goosequill, to borrow Thackeray's phrase, there is a bread-and-butter trade organisation, the Society of Authors, which exposes crook agents and protests about publishers' agreements, and one or two more exalted redoubts such as the Royal Society of Literature. The real business of the literary world, however, the genuine tourneying and reputation-brokering takes place at literary parties, and ultimately in the books pages of daily and weekly newspapers. The part played by reviews and reviewers in the literary world is a curious one. On the one hand it is an article of faith among publishers that reviews don't sell books. On the other hand, among 'serious' writers whose books don't sell they are taken very seriously indeed. Who writes them? Apart from a handful of grand panjandrums – academics glancing down from Parnassus to nod at the scurrying traffic of the foothills, assorted pillars of the literary establishment – most books get reviewed by a handful of young men and women in their late twenties and early thirties, all of whom have written or (more likely) are intending to write novels. Keeping in with these people consequently remains the literary novelist's most pressing occupational duty.

Rather too much has been written in the past few years about the incestuousness of the literary world – inevitable in any case, given the tiny size of the books industry – but its effect can be seen in the treatment meted out to nearly every serious novelist who offers his work up for public inspection. Generally speaking, any young author in this country is likely to have served an apprenticeship as a reviewer – in the *Guardian*, say, or the *Independent*, both of which (to their credit) make a point of encouraging new blood. His (or her) novel, when it appears, is seized upon by his three or four close friends in the trade and acclaimed as a work of startling promise, while simultaneously disparaged by his enemies (people whom he has been unwise enough to criticise, old rivals from university) as an example of the depths to which modern publishing has sunk. This is an exaggeration, perhaps, but not much of one. Two years ago, for example, the writer Philip Hensher published his first novel. Now Mr Hensher is a forceful reviewer and no respecter of reputations. The result was (to anyone not in the know) a bewildering divergence of opinion: half the papers thought it was a thoroughly worthy début; the other half thought it should have been sent straight to the remainder bin. This kind of reaction, it must be said, is not helped by papers such as the *Guardian*, which used until recently to take a curious delight in sending books to the reviewer least likely to appreciate them, first novels to people writing first novels and so on. Again, not long ago, Jonathan Coe published a long and hugely satirical novel about Britain in the 1980s (*What a Carve Up!*, 1994). It received almost uniformly excellent reviews. The *Independent on Sunday*, though, sent it to a writer named Hugh Barnes who just happened to be about to publish a hugely satirical novel about Britain in the 1980s. It seems scarcely necessary to add that Mr Barnes, doubtless for excellent aesthetic reasons, didn't like it. A general rule in the reviewing game is that any slight will be repaid with interest. The consequence of this – apart from bringing about a precipitous decline in standards of reviewing – is that most young novelists spend half their time looking over their shoulder and make a virtue of never offending anyone, praying all the while that the literary editor of the *Spectator* won't send their new one to B the demon reviewer, whose violent dislike some overheard party conversation suggests they have enflamed.

*Political*. Most serious writers unhesitatingly subscribe to the old Left/liberal orthodoxy. In the 1980s and early 1990s this allegiance manifested itself in a variety of mass-signature letters to the *Guardian* (most amusingly the one complaining about the abortive *coup* against Gorbachev), in the public

rebuke of Ian McEwan by the *Sunday Times*, in Salman
Rushdie's 'Mrs Torture' and so forth. It is fair to say that
'Thatcherism' inspired a degree of unanimity in the literary
establishment that had not been seen since the heady days of
the 1930s. Unquestionably this kind of mass orthodoxy had a
profound effect on the literary climate. One of the depressing
features of literary life in the 1980s was the complete refusal
of writers – I speak as a member of the Labour Party by the
way – to begin to appreciate or understand the depth of Mrs
Thatcher's appeal to a very large proportion of the electorate.
Only the other week, opening some magazine questionnaire
to find Julian Barnes marking down Lady Thatcher as the
person he most disliked or something of the kind, one felt
like saying: look, Julian, isn't it about time you found something else to bang on about; isn't it about time you acknowledged the political void out of which she emerged, and the
aspirations – decent aspirations, for the most part – of
the millions of people for whom she featured as a personal
saviour? The consequences for the writer of this habitual
liberal disdain are, perhaps, threefold. First, it has produced
critical double standards of the kind that appeared to lambast
– say – the late Kingsley Amis on aesthetic grounds while
actually knocking him for being a cross-grained old Tory.
Second, it has reinforced the well-deserved reputation for
Hampstead élitism worn by so many of the literary world's
finest. Third, it has encouraged large numbers of writers to
write a kind of novel that is rather beyond their ingenuity
to fabricate. If the 'political' novels of the late 1980s and
early 1990s demonstrate anything, it is the difficulty of writing a political novel in the present age. Thus Ian McEwan's
*The Child in Time* (1987), a grim projection of the post-
Thatcher era, showed itself unable to imagine political life in
anything but the most rudimentary stereotypes. Such was
the uncertainty of approach, or perhaps the elusiveness of the
quarry, that the clutch of recent books professing to satirise
Mrs Thatcher – Michael Dibdin's *Dirty Tricks* (1991), for
example, or Tim Parks' *Goodness* (1991) – often ended up
uncomfortably close to celebration. But the pressure on the

writer to line up on the right – or rather the left – side of the political equation remains, and is nearly always likely to have a vitiating effect on his or her work.

*Aesthetic.* However idiosyncratic or outwardly detached, the majority of young novelists are part of a wider aesthetic tendency, caught up in a pattern of cause and response of which they may only be dimly aware. Broadly speaking the guiding influence of the past fifteen years has been the kind of writing massed under the banner of 'post-modernism': tricksy, playful, parodic, Bradbury-blessed. The approaching dominance of this type of fiction was advertised, perhaps, by the award of the 1981 Booker Prize to Salman Rushdie's *Midnight's Children*, and confirmed by the subsequent appearance of Graham Swift's *Waterland* (1983) and Martin Amis's *Money* (1984). Even now, over a decade later, I can still recall the effect that each of these three books had on me – Rushdie's unthought-of deployment of language, Swift's reinvention of the regional novel, Amis's construction of a kind of transatlantic pontoon bridge. Ten years on it is hard not to conclude that this promising shift in the alignment of the British novel has frittered itself away in self-indulgence and inertia. The three most written about novels of early 1995 – Kazuo Ishiguro's *The Unconsoled*, Adam Thorpe's *Still* and Amis's *The Information*, dazzling exercises in post-modernism all – were so ruinously overblown as to be almost unfinishable. For the modern English writer at the start of his career, the question of influence generally reduces itself to a single name. It is a statement of fact to say that to anyone under the age of thirty-five in this country the most influential living writer is Martin Amis. It is also a statement of fact to say that this influence has been almost entirely malign. Amis has had an odd career: three sharp early novels (the second, *Dead Babies*, a furious dystopian morality play), a curious fourth book (*Other People*) which doesn't quite come off, followed by *Money* (1984), which still seems to me to be *the* English novel of the 1980s. Then *London Fields* (1989), in which a quite funny book about darts and low-life seemed to be cancelled out by throat-clearing about the

Bomb. Then *Time's Arrow* (1991), a conceit pushed to dangerously extravagant lengths, and finally *The Information* (1995), in which a great many elderly themes and locations are pressed into service to illuminate the not very enticing topic of literary jealousy. If there is a complaint to make about the later Amis it is that the moral determinism is entirely stifling, the cipher characters impossible to care about, and the language beginning to fall into the Updike trap of seeming to bring the reader nearer to the object described but in fact carrying him or her further away. Meanwhile, Amis's status has reached such a peak that influence is frequently detected where none exists, with the result that merely to attempt a novel about criminal dead-beats from the back streets is to have yourself written down as one of Mart's lads.

Finally, let us go back to the two-bedroom flat in the Fulham Road. Beset on all sides by pressures of this sort – lack of money, inadequate connections, the wrong political views, a fatal addiction to formulations like *Jimmy was badly fucked. Fucked. Badly. He felt like an old, tired ghost, shagged out from too much haunting* – what will happen to Max Doubtfire? In a year or so the literary agency he devils for will give him a discreet hint that it is time to be moving on (agencies have high turnover rates, and in any case Max is growing snooty about the work). Max's girl-friend, meantime, wants a house and a baby. Clearly, something will have to be done. Whatever it is will almost certainly not involve fiction. In the end, using what connections he has, and a letter of reference from an actor represented by his employers, Max gets a job as the administrator of an arts centre in the West Country, and his salary enables them to live in comparative comfort in a three-bedroom terraced house on the outskirts of Bath. Sometimes, in the intervals of commissioning pottery exhibitions and sitting in on the auditions for the feminist theatre week, Max tells himself that he will write another book. After all, he has all the time in the world. Meanwhile, he keeps up his Public Lending Right registration for *Imbroglio* (1994/5 receipts £5.07).

# Peter Redgrove

## CHRISTIAN THOUGHTS

Yesterday walking through the tunnel of branches
Up to Budock Church I found there were
Unpleasant though Christian thoughts left over
From last Sunday hanging about the path
And dangling from the branches
Like the sloughs of gigantic Eden snakes
Resembling large coherent dandruff as though you scratched
Your puzzling head and the whole lot came off
In a head-and-body mask. These mists

Hanging about on the Christian pathway.
What were these castoff foggy skins but scales
Fallen from the eyes? On Sunday in church
The parson in black droning like a fly laid his verbal eggs
Under your skin, where they hatched and they irritated,
So you scratched, the whole congregation scratched,
Until by next Sunday the masks came off on the way to
    church,
Until the whole skin came off and like the snake
Newly-born they glide along their Christian paths leaving
    their skins
Perplexing the fruit-trees of the small orchards and oaks by
    the way.

# BETWEEN SHOWERS

## I

Spring thunder
At the dentist's –
Glittering
In all his instruments
He looked like lightning
In that white coat –
Dropped my false teeth
With an oath they grinned at.

## II

A small spider at centre, basking
In the sun, considering the whole
As unity –
No beginner in this all-round arena.

## III

The seven-year-old girl
Walking through the downpour
Does the thing most acceptable to her
By strolling with her tongue poked out,
Tasting the rain to its roots.

## IV

After the heavy spring shower
The bird calls out
'Still here! still here!'

# HERDING CALLS

The weather is spitting, there is
An inversion layer over the creek,
It is a radar anomaly, and the great

Beams of the Inspector Dish Aerials cannot find
The missiles if any in this Cornish weather now. Accordingly
I listen to the mist and fog programmes on Radio 3, my heart

Stopping when the twinings of our atmosphere
Sever the broadcast in a jet of static, for this same sound
Would precede the shock-wave if London were

Vaporised; but so far thank God it's the subdued
Low-browed Neanderthal lightning of Cornwall
Bowing its music on my radio-set; I hear the broken

Currents that surround Mendelssohn like crackling thorns.
Under the mist, the water is mildly archaic
With static charge, three men row a coracle

With long oars dipping, and there glides
An energumen out of the speaker, which is
An air-born cylinder of coracle, rain and great composer

Sliding into my ears like herding-calls.

# Penelope Shuttle

## ARTIST IN INK

The octopus, artist in ink,
impulsively draws eight pictures at once,
but none are portraits of dry land,
as the scuba-diving critic remarks . . .

There are so many ways of painting,
especially with eight arms . . .
Why, the octopus uses only one colour,
notes the shark, that devourer of art,
circling, never sleeping, gnawing
the leg of the diver-cum-critic . . .

But the octopus just inks in his seascapes,
juicily uninfluenced,
his ocean floor abstracts
endlessly octaving . . .

# OLD CITY

## 1

Old City sailing by,
lost in its emotions,

playing the piano in its sleep,
lowering boats full of mazurkas

into the murky siesta plazas,
yes, if you want afternoons like this,

Old City has plenty,
cloudy and deserving praise . . .

## 2

Most mornings in Old City
Captain Virginia-Water takes his wife

on horseback to Marks and Spencers
where she works all day . . . smiling . . .

She never tells him of her hopeless love
for the Inspector of Sacred Pictures,

for her husband wishes her at all costs
to avoid first person narration . . .

He never tells her that he wants
to ride alone across an immense empty prairie,

where not even one wagon
of an early emigrant family lurches . . .

But Old City of fog and crystal
just drones – God-dammit Krishna!

For Old City still has yins within its yangs . . .
Old City shows everyone pictures of his children asleep,

Old City tells everyone how to forget
what they want to forget,

Old City of frozen rubble:
better houses for the dead than for the living . . .

Yet one man here
sees his seed swimming fast under bold magnification,

he has achieved otherness, clearly,
here in tempting Old City . . .

# Jon Silkin

## ORION

*Orion, a giant slain on account of his ego, was restored to life, given vision and light, and put with the stars.*

Lilac's congregating flowers perk, ignorant
of death, but my body is without fragrance.
I did not nurse the crushed miner, nor was I one
to a havering woman, helping her shit.
Nor with faded-blue breast, a parent
having the moisture and smell of authority.
I want to use my childhood, not derange
a river's migrant track, or crush
the tree-lined current's milky-green undertow.
A softer radiance would be OK. But I would become
Orion I was designed for, my vision
of light with intent eyes.

Here's summer, its solstice, people
raging in happiness, red currant, feeding the season
a trickling viscid juice. I am lonely.
Look, the iris's flimsy visage,
and the common lily, ours; it goes on,
dies, comes to, from deathly pale to papery incensed life.
I, too, if you please. I strike through woods
making the leaves volatile.
Dabbing and laying my light on your cheek
I disclose your dark skin, with mutual delight.
And you touch me unawares. I believe, humans,
you have survived yourselves. It is the gift.

# N. S. Thompson

## ODYSSEUS AFTER THE SIRENS

A Bloomian world. A lost patrol that kept
Him sifting warm deserted dunes of sand,
But nothing came of them. And he was left
There, standing in the Wakes, below the tides
Of scaffolding which stretched beyond the ends
Of empty avenues, until he launched
His epic cycle down towards the main
Road's bubbling tarmac, ploughing roadside silt
And dust, no roar of passing trades to curb
Him pedalling furiously to shop for troops.

A traffic island beacon flashed above
A zebra crossing; by a red eye, he
Watched as a baker's wasp scaled icing. But
Where were the model ranks of Empire kept
Preserved in amber cellophane? No sign
Of them. Pounded by waves of traffic on
A girder bridge, he sweated on, till lost
In depths of streets, he heard the sirens scream
Swirling towards bleak warehouse cliffs, and came
To grief beside a bombsite left in weeds.

# THE LIFE WITHIN

The weight of doors swings, hinged on memory
In vestibules of leaded glass, where milk
Wrapped in a cool white uniform stood guard
On dreams of butter curled in dappled light,
Before the warmth of waiting rooms gave signs
Of life within. A pint-size, I could clasp

The cut-glass doorknobs, press brass plates, to try
My hands at contact, but thick lenses viewed
Me dimly, brown wallpaper hanging there
As high tea rattled on the slack of life
Picked up. I wove word-skeins in tapestries
To camouflage the emptiness. Left with

An album of familiar stamp-size prints,
Cut off below a standard lamp from small
Talk, cards and life dealt out, I passed and dreamed
Another life within each life, lodged in
The cool and promise of a vestibule,
Where first impressions never lose their grip.

# Charles Tomlinson

## DRAWING DOWN THE MOON

I place on the sill a saucer
that I fill with water:
it rocks with a tidal motion,
as if that porcelain round
contained a small sea:
this threshold ocean
throws into confusion
the image that it seizes
out of the sky – the moon
just risen, and now in pieces
beneath the window: the glass
takes in the image at its source,
a clear shard of newness,
and lets it into the house
from pane to pane
riding slowly past:
when I look again
towards the sill, its dish
of moonlight is recomposing:
it lies still, from side to side
of the ceramic circle
curving across the water,
a sleeping bride:
for the moon's sake
do not wake her,
do not shake the saucer.

# THE FIRST DEATH

*in memoriam*
*Bruce Chatwin*

The hand that reached out from a painted sleeve
   When you sensed that you were dying, gathered you
Into the picture: clothes, furs, pearls,
   Bronze of a vessel, silver of a dish
From which the grapes were overflowing. Tangible
   The minute whiteness of those pearls, the galaxies
They strung; the velvets, sleeves, the welcome
   Among convivial company; the offered hand,
All those glistening appearances that now
   Were to declare the secret of their surfaces –
Surfaces deep as roots. You told
   How you were led at that first death
Through the Venetian plenitude of a room
   Across which a glance confirmed the presence there
Of windows spilling light on this festivity,
   And running beyond them, a silhouette –
The columns of a balustrade – then sky.
   You were let into the anteroom of your heaven
By the eye, moving and attending, finding good
   Those textures it had grazed on like a food.
The second time you died without remission,
   Leaving no report on the lie of the land
Beyond that parapet's stone sill, beyond the gloss
   On all surfaces, rich and indecipherable.

# Rose Tremain

## THE BEAUTY OF THE DAWN SHIFT

WHEN HECTOR S set out on his journey to Russia, he was wearing his uniform. It was his winter uniform, made of woollen serge, because this was December in East Berlin. While packing his knapsack, Hector S had told himself that he would have to travel in his uniform, that he had no choice; he didn't possess any other really warm clothes and where he was going, it would be as cold as death.

He was a man with a narrow frame, not tall, with pale, anxious eyes. Women thought him beautiful, but found him frigid. He was twenty-eight and he'd slept with only one girl. This one girl was his sister, Ute.

Ute kept a pet swan in a lean-to hutch on the apartment estate. She'd named it Karl and fed it on sunflower seeds. Morning and evening, she'd let it out to peck the grass and it allowed her to stroke its neck. There were no lakes or rivers in Prenzlauer Berg, the suburb of East Berlin where they lived, and when Hector informed Ute that he was leaving for Russia, she asked him to take her and Karl with him. But he told her it was impossible, that he had to go alone with almost nothing, just his bicycle and a bag of tinned food and his rifle. He told her he couldn't travel across Poland with a swan.

Ute took this badly. She clutched at Hector's arm. She was already imagining the beautiful Russian lake where Karl would remember the lost art of swimming.

'Hecti,' she said, 'don't leave us behind!'

Hector S disliked emotional scenes. When their mother,

Elvira, had died in 1980 Hector had basked in the wonderful quiet that descended suddenly upon the apartment. He told Ute that it was different for her, that she would be able to fit in to the New Germany and that she had nothing to be afraid of. She began to cry in exactly the same way Elvira used to cry, grabbing two hunks of her hair and saying she hated being alive. Hector walked away from her. One part of him wanted to say: 'When I get there, Ute, I promise I will send for you,' but another part of him wanted to remain as silent as the tomb, and on this occasion it was the tomb that prevailed.

Hector's father, Erich, on the other hand, didn't try to persuade his son to take him with him; neither did he try to persuade him not to leave. All he said was: 'A frog in a well says that the sky is no bigger than the mouth of the well, but now you have to become something else, Hector, and see the whole fucking sky. In the old imperial fairy-tales, frogs turn into princes, eh?' And he slapped his knee.

Hector replied that he had no intention whatsoever of turning into a prince.

'So,' said Erich, 'what are you going to become?'

'I don't know,' said Hector. 'Don't ask me yet.'

'All right,' said Erich, 'but remember, when you walk away from one place, you are inevitably walking towards another.'

'I know that,' said Hector. 'That's why I'm going east.'

What should Hector take with him? This question troubled him more than many others. His knapsack wasn't large. It was the bag in which he carried his lunch or his supper, depending on which shift he was working. He would make more room in it by attaching his water bottle to the outside of it. Then there were the two saddle bags on his bicycle, but this was all. He decided, eventually, to line the saddle bags with underwear and socks. Then he put in jars of dill pickles and some plastic cutlery. He tucked these in with maps of Poland and the Brandenburg Marshes. He added a compass made in Dresden and five boxes of matches. The knapsack he filled almost entirely with tinned meat, wrapped in a woollen sweater. There was room for a torch and two spare batteries, a notebook and a pen. He put in a solitary lemon. He packed no books, only a small photograph album, filled with pictures of Ute, including one of her naked, developed privately by a colleague of Hector's who had dreams of becoming a professional photographer. In the naked photograph, Ute was leaning on a stool with her back to the camera and her bottom was very pale in the bleached light of early morning. Her legs looked skinny and her soft blonde hair parted at the back and hung forward, revealing her narrow white shoulders.

Hector didn't tell Ute or Erich when he was going to leave, because he thought farewells were futile and also because he didn't really know. He had to set off before the lemon in his knapsack went rotten, that was all. He knew he would recognise the moment when it came – and he did. It was the morning of 9 December 1989, one month exactly after the Wall had started to come down. He was alone in the apartment. He had exchanged all the money he possessed for D-Marks at the humiliating rate of 10–1. It amounted to DM143 and he laid it out on the kitchen table and looked at the blue and pink notes, then gathered them up, stuffed them into his wallet and put on his greatcoat and his hat. It was a fine morning, cold and clear. He walked to the window and looked out at the blocks of flats and the scuffed grass in between them where a few children played. He remembered being told: 'At the time of Tsar Nicolas II in Russia, the children of the poor had no toys of any kind. They invented games with knuckle bones.' And now, thought Hector, the parents of these children will save on food and light to buy their kids sophisticated toys from the West. He felt glad he had no children, nor would ever have any because his sperm count was too low. At least he wouldn't have to choose between absolute needs and infantile ones. He was a man who had always known what was important in life and what was not.

He turned away from the window and picked up his knapsack. He looked at the room he was in, the room where the family ate and played cards and watched TV, and wondered if, when he arrived at his destination, he would think about this room and feel homesick for the black plastic chairs and the painted sideboard and the wall-mounted electric fire. He knew that memory was as uncertain in its behaviour as the sea; it could wash you ashore on any old forgotten beach; it could try to drown you in remorse. But he decided, no, it wouldn't be the apartment he would miss, only certain moments in it, certain moments at dawn, just after Erich had left for work at the cement works on the Landwehr Kanal, when he walked from his own room into Ute's and got into her bed.

It is best to leave now, Hector told himself. Don't dwell on Ute.

So he walked out of the apartment without looking at anything more and went down the six flights of concrete stairs to the lobby where the post boxes had been installed. These he stared at. Neighbours passed him and said, 'Good morning, Hector,' and still he contemplated the metal post boxes, imagining news of his future life arriving one day inside them.

He took small roads out of Prenzlauer Berg and the streets were mainly deserted. These days, East Berliners trekked into the West to see what their few D-Marks would buy. He saw what they came back with: coloured shoelaces and luminous condoms. A lot of what they chose seemed to be a bright fearful pink or a harsh lime green, and these objects reminded Hector of the day when he'd been stopped by a group of Wessies, dressed in pink and green shell suits, who had asked him the way to Alexanderplatz. 'What have you come to see?' he'd asked them, more out of habit than out of interest, and they had laughed and swigged expensive beer and said: 'Oh, we've come to the East German closing-down sale! Many bargains. Everything must go.' And it had been at this moment and not at any other that Hector S had decided to leave his country and leave Ute and cycle to Russia. He said to himself, I'm not going because I'm afraid. I'm going because these people make me feel sick.

He joined the Leninallee and pedalled towards Lichtenberg. His back ached with the heaviness of the knapsack and the awkwardness of his rifle. Elvira was buried in the Socialists' Cemetery at Lichtenberg and it now occurred to Hector to make a small detour to look one last time at his mother's grave. He thought that he would confide to her his passion for Ute and in this way try to leave it behind. In her life, Elvira had relished confidences, licking her sensual lips . . . 'oh so delicious, Hecti! Tell me more!'

When he reached the cemetery, he couldn't remember where Elvira's grave was. There were so many hundreds of people buried here and he hadn't visited the place in five years. He knew he could spend hours looking for Elvira and then it would get dark and he'd still only be on the outskirts of Berlin. This would be a stupid way to waste the first day of his long journey.

Then he found her: *Elvira S 1931–1980*. A small polished stone. Hector parked his bicycle and took off his knapsack and rifle, flexing his shoulders. He removed his hat and stood, measuring the stone in his mind. The stone looked smaller than she had been. Did the state stone-cutters cheat on everyone by a few centimetres? And if they did, was this a thing of importance? Probably not. There were so many hundreds of millions of dead under the earth, it was amazing there was any earth left on which to grow cabbages or build kindergarten schools.

Before he could form any thoughts or words on the subject of Ute, Hector was disturbed by movement quite near him. He turned and looked and saw that a young man, poorly dressed, was going from grave to grave with a trowel, brazenly digging up the bulbs planted on them and putting them into a plastic carrier bag. The youth didn't seem to have noticed Hector – a figure of authority in a winter uniform – or else he *had* noticed him and was now deliberately taunting him with his distasteful little crime.

'Hey!' called Hector. 'Don't do that!'

The youth looked up. A white face, blank, without expression. No fear in the eyes.

'Who are you?' he said.

'Border Police,' announced Hector.

'*Border* Police?'

'Yes.'

The youth stood up straight and laughed. 'Border Police! The border is down, or didn't anyone tell you? You mean they didn't tell you?'

'Please leave,' said Hector, 'before I have you arrested.'

The youth didn't move. He made an obscene gesture with his hand. '*You* leave!' he said. 'You fuck off out of my world!'

Hector was used to insults. Insults had been part of his life for six years and now they troubled him no more than a few flakes of snow, say, or a shower of leaves blown across his path by the wind. Except that, under normal circumstances, he had his rifle with him and at this moment his rifle was a few feet away, leaning against a tree.

'You are stealing flowers from the dead,' said Hector.

The youth had a high-pitched laugh, the laugh of a girl. 'Ah, you think the dead planted them, do you, Border Guard? You think they stuck their bones up into the soil to make little holes for these bulbs?'

'This is a graveyard . . .' began Hector.

'Is it?' said the youth. 'Oh, I thought it was a communist rubbish dump. It contains the scum who made our lives a misery and a farce for forty years. But it's changing now, right? Every fucker in here was *wrong*! And I tell you what they're going to do with this place. They're going to bring in the bulldozers and dig up these stiffs and use them to put out Russian reactor fires and then when they've vacated it, they're going to – '

Hector walked three paces to his right and picked up his rifle. The click the youth heard was the release of the safety catch. The click stopped the flow of words and the pale face looked blank once again.

'Leave,' said Hector. 'Leave now.'

'OK, OK,' said the youth and put up his hands, one of which still held the bulb bag. The putting up of hands was a gesture which Hector had been trained to ignore when necessary. He aimed the rifle at the youth's groin.

'Hey,' said the youth, 'don't kill me! I know you bastards. Don't kill me!'

'Go, then,' said Hector. 'Go.'

The youth tried to walk away backwards, keeping his eyes on Hector's gun. He stumbled over a grave and fell down and the bag of bulbs dropped out of the hand with which he tried to save himself. Then he got to his feet and ran.

So there were no confidences shared with Elvira, nothing to make her lick her lips, or bring on one of her storms of weeping. And Ute wasn't left behind, but was carried onwards in Hector's heart.

Hector was sitting now in a café in Marzahn, the last housing estate in East Berlin, built to accommodate 160,000 people in 60,000 apartments, 2.6 humans to a unit. Beyond Marzahn were the Brandenburg Marshes and the wide open sky.

Hector had come to the café because after what happened at the cemetery, he'd started to feel chilly. He sat at a plastic table with his hands round a cup of coffee and the life of the café went on as if he wasn't there. He hoped that, in Russia, people would talk to him more, in whatever language they could muster. He really didn't want these familiar small sufferings – feeling cold inside, being ignored by people in public – to go on for the rest of his life. But nor would he ever pretend to be something other than what he was. It wasn't his fault if ideologies had a finite life span, if his world was falling away like flesh from bone, a little more each day. He'd been a communist and a patriot. He wanted to stand up in this cheap Marzahn café and say: 'My name is Hector S and, to me, the word "patriot" is not a dirty one.'

He sat in the café for a long time. He smoked four Karos. He went to the toilet and pissed and washed his face and hands in warm water. He stole a wedge of paper towels and put them into his overcoat pocket. He'd been told by a colleague that one of the marvels coming to East Germany in the near future would be toilet rolls printed with crossword puzzles.

Then he went out into the early afternoon and saw that it was later than he'd imagined and that a few lights were coming on in the tower blocks. Brought up to abhor waste, Hector admired the way East Germans used electricity. Light looked normal here. Across the Wall, he'd seen it become more and more startling and chaotic. On the long night shifts, he used to stare at all the rippling and blinking neon and wonder if it could, in the end, by reason of its absolute pointlessness, create blank spots in the human brain.

Now, he was leaving all the city light behind. It would hang in the sky at his back for a while and he'd be able to turn round and see its faint glow and say, 'That's Berlin.' And then it wouldn't even be a glow and the flicker of his cycle lamp would be all that he had to see by.

He pedalled hard. The only weapon he would have against the cold was his own blood. He grew more and more hungry and, on any ordinary trip, he would have stopped after two hours or so and opened one of the tins of Spam. But he'd set a rule for this journey – one meal a day and only one – and he was determined not to break it. So he just cycled on and the moon came up and then the stars, and he began to hear herons calling and see a second moon fallen into a wide and beautiful lake. To banish thoughts about Ute and her swan, he started to whistle some old tunes he'd picked up from Elvira who liked to sing to herself while she did the ironing.

Before night, Hector stopped at a village and bought bread. By torchlight, by the side of the road, he made a meal of tinned meat, bread and pickles. He wished he'd remembered to bring a plate to eat off as well as the plastic cutlery. Certain things, he thought, we take for granted so absolutely that they become invisible to us – and a dinner plate is one such thing.

He smoked a Karo and lay back on the frosty grass and looked at the stars. The exhaustion he now felt was suddenly intense. He knew he should repack the opened food, wrapping the bread carefully in its paper to keep it fresh for tomorrow. He knew also that he should search for some shelter, a shack or barn in which to sleep. But he couldn't move. He could barely lift his arm to stub out his cigarette.

So he closed his eyes. Some voice in him said, sleep, Hector. Sleep itself has warming properties. You'll be safe and everything will be safe till morning.

Hector was woken when the cold air of the night turned to mild but steady rain. There was enough light in the sky for him to see that a black slug was hanging off his tin of meat. He knew he ought to remove the slug and return what was left of the meat to his knapsack and that his ability to survive this journey depended upon such small acts of determination, but he felt incapable of eating meat that had been sucked at by a slug.

He saw now that he'd been lying by the side of a road and that at his back was a wood. Going into the wood to piss, he noticed that a narrow path ran between the trees, more or less parallel with the road. A red and yellow sign, nailed to an oak tree, said *Fitness Path* and depicted a man in the attitude of a runner. Hector decided to follow the Fitness Path. Here, he would be protected from the rain and, for as long as the track ran roughly level with the road, he wouldn't get lost. Also, he liked the idea of coming across athletes. They were a category of people he admired, patriotic, stoical and sane. He couldn't imagine an athlete stealing bulbs from graves or doing crossword puzzles on toilet paper.

By his calculations, he had about a hundred kilometres to cycle before he reached the Polish border, and if his pace was steady, he expected to do this in three days. He hoped the beautiful forest would go on and on, right to the edge of his country. He took a long drink of water. Despite his short sleep, he felt revived, almost happy. Why, he thought, was I the only one of all my friends in the Border Police to go east? He imagined his old colleagues now, trying to sleep through this wet dawn, but most of them awake in fact, listening to the traffic beginning, listening to their blood beating, and none of them knowing which to worry about more – the past or the future.

Hector met no athletes, not even any amateur ones. And, to his disappointment, the Fitness Path quite soon veered north and he was forced to rejoin the road or risk becoming lost. But by this time, the sun was starting to glimmer through the rain clouds, making the road shine, and Hector's contentment didn't really diminish. It stemmed, he decided, from an acknowledgement of his own bravery. Bravery was the word. Most people in East Germany had their eyes turned towards the West, as if they were kids in a cinema queue and the West were the last show on earth. Only he, Hector S, had the courage and the vision to ride east towards the Russian winter, towards the wilderness.

He stopped at a public wash-house to shave and shower. Keeping clean was something he intended to do. He loved showers. He habitually masturbated under the shower, as did his father since the death of Elvira, and didn't care if anyone saw him do it. But here, the streams of hot water only soothed the ache in his back and in his calves and he had no erection. The most significant thing that he had to deny himself on this journey was Ute. He knew that his sanity and his ability to keep to his resolve depended upon this. Only when he arrived at his destination, wherever that turned out to be, would he get out the photograph of Ute leaning on the stool and take her from behind, as often as he felt inclined. And if his yearning for her then – for the real Ute, with her soft hair and her cunt that tasted of the sea – became serious like an illness, he would send for her.

He left the wash house with bright pink skin and wearing clean underwear. He went to a village café for coffee and a sweet cake and, although it was still early in the morning, there were old people dancing here, on the wooden café floor. The band consisted of an accordionist and a double bass player and these two were also old. Hector stared round him. On they danced, partner with partner, men with women, women whose men had died or been mislaid dancing together, all smiling and proud of the way they could still move their feet. Hector now realised that he was the only young person in the café and he wondered whether he was in some old persons' club and had only been served out of deference to his uniform. He closed his eyes. The music was jaunty and light. A country where old people can dance in the morning must be a good country. And Hector imagined how this music could beckon people from their beds and that instead of lying under their feather quilts waiting to die, they would examine their dancing shoes for signs of wear, comb what remained of their hair, put on a shawl or a coat and walk down to the café, humming or whistling. Yet soon this scene would be annihilated by history. Hector opened his eyes and said quite loudly to an old woman who had sat down at the next table: 'This dance café will be closed.'

She hesitated. Had Hector just uttered an order? You could never predict what extraordinary orders were going to come out of the mouths of uniformed men. Once, she had been stopped on her way to the butcher's and told to remove her wig.

'I beg your pardon?' she said.

'Yes,' said Hector. 'It will be closed. In less than a year. This place will become a discotheque. They will play Western music here, pop and rock and rap, and nobody in this village will sleep, ever again. And nor will you old people dance.'

Hector had finished his coffee and cake. He didn't want or expect a reply. He'd said what he wanted to say and now he would just leave. The old woman stared at him as he got up and shouldered his knapsack and his rifle. The musicians watched him and the dancing couples watched him, but nobody spoke out. When Hector emerged into the street, it was raining again, a light but steady rain.

Living in this way, off his meat and dill pickles, spending a little money on hot coffee and bread and sleeping on the good German earth, Hector S reached the Polish border.

He was perhaps forty kilometres inside Poland when he fell ill.

He fell ill from cold and exhaustion and from something

else he couldn't name. The illness came over him just outside the town of G, when he found himself in a landscape of striped hills, strip-farmed plough and fescue grass. And coming towards him on the quaint ribbon of road was a funeral procession, led by a priest holding a mighty cross. And it was as if he – with his bicycle and his rifle – was the only living thing in a terrible old painting and the low sunlight was the varnish on that painting, yellow and sickly. His legs, so strong when his journey had begun, felt suddenly hollow, the weight of the knapsack and rifle on his back unbearable.

And he could hear singing. It was the priest and all the mourners wailing in Polish for the dead person, and to Hector this human music was more disagreeable, even, than one of Elvira's attacks of weeping in the apartment in Prenzlauer Berg. It made his stomach heave.

He got off his bicycle and leaned his weight over the handlebars and the saddle. He wanted to get right away from the road, so that he wouldn't have to come near the mourners or smell their fusty clothes or hear them breathing as they sang, but the striped hills on either side of the road were quite steep – too steep in fact for a man who has been stricken with sickness.

It occurred to Hector in the next second that he would have to shoot the mourners down. He would start with the priest. But he felt a little confused by numbers: how many mourners and how many bullets? And confused by distance: optimum range for this calibre of rifle was . . . what? He once knew it by heart, just as a man knows his own name by heart. And then, he was confused by currencies and their terminology. Was 'dollar' a universal word, or was there a Polish word for 'dollar' that was not 'dollar' differently pronounced? Was a zloty a coin or was it a note? Was it a letterbox? How many zlotys in a golden cross? How many letterboxes in a striped field . . .?

Of course, Hector felt himself begin to fall, but a person falling may not reach the ground to his certain knowledge, but instead arrive somewhere else. Hector fell on to the grey tarmac of the ribbon road and the priest and the mourners, seeing a man in a foreign uniform lying in their pathway, came on steadfastly towards him. Hector, however, is entering a different moment of time. He is reporting for duty. It is summer, perfect summer. It is dawn in East Berlin. Hector is entering the door at the base of a watchtower and he begins to climb up the concrete steps. Above him is the perfect octagonal of the tower itself, with its eight viewing windows. And through these windows will be falling . . . at the very moment Hector enters the octagon . . . at this very moment of short duration but of long residence in the mind of Hector S . . . will be falling the extraordinary beauty of the dawn light, arriving from the East.

When Hector woke, it was dark. He was lying in bed in a small room, painted brown and lit by an oil lamp. The flicker and fumes from the oil lamp eddied round on the brown ceiling. He could remember nothing.

Something cold touched his face. A dampness lay on his forehead. There was the smell of roses.

Then a voice, very near, said in broken German: 'Are you waking, Sir?'

Hector didn't recall making any reply, but the same voice decided to say next: 'I am a train driver.'

Then the lamplit room and the train driver and the smell of roses are removed from Hector's consciousness and he is submerged again in sleep, while the man who was a driver of freight trains between Poznan and Warsaw got up quietly and went to talk to his wife, Katarzyna, telling her reassuringly that the German soldier had woken up and that his fever was passing.

'Good,' said Katarzyna, 'so I hope he can leave tomorrow.'

'Well,' said the train driver, 'we shall see.'

'I don't want to "see",' said Katarzyna, who was old and afraid and had a long memory. 'I want him out of our house tomorrow. I don't know why I had to marry a man with such a stupidly kind heart.'

'He was lying in the road, Katarzyna.'

'I don't care where he was lying.'

He is lying in Ute's bed. He knows he shouldn't be here, not yet. He'd forbidden himself to come here, but here he is all the same. Outside the apartment building, in the first light of morning, Ute's swan, Karl, is screeching in his cage. Ute is lying on top of Hector, kissing his eyes. He isn't inside her, but he can feel his erection begin against her flat stomach, and with his encircling arms he presses her closer to him, moving her body so that her breasts rub against his chest. He whispers to her that he wants her, that he will want her for ever, that he can't help himself, that his passion for her will have no end, and she says to him sweetly, giggling, licking his ear: 'Hecti, it will end when you die . . .'

The dark room returned. A nightlight on a saucer had replaced the oil lamp and Hector could just make out the shape of a small window, shuttered with louvres, beyond which it was possible to imagine an icy, moonlit sky. Hector turned his head, looking for the train driver sitting beside him, but no one was there.

He lay very still. There was a wet patch in the bed and Hector supposed that he had pissed in it in his sleep, but wasn't very disconcerted because this was a thing that had gone on happening to him long after boyhood and two doctors had told him that there was nothing to be done about it.

Then, hearing a train's mournful whistle, Hector remembered that he was in Poland. He remembered the striped fields and the procession of mourners. He sat up and looked around the room for his knapsack and rifle and, not finding them, was overcome with anguish. Weeping was for the weak, for people like Elvira, not for him. But in this Polish night, Hector wept and he didn't seem able to stop, however hard he tried.

After a while, he heard someone get up in the room next door and an old woman came and stood by him, wrapped in a shawl, with her hair in a grey plait. She stared at him for a few moments, then shook his shoulder quite roughly. 'German soldier,' she said, 'stop crying, please.'

*

Hector S lay in the little room for another day and a night. Katarzyna swore at her husband and prayed on her Bible. The train driver changed Hector's sheets and fed him beetroot soup.

Katarzyna went through Hector's knapsack and removed the lemon and made herself a beautiful jug of lemon tea. She said to the train driver: 'This is the first gift I've ever had from a German. And the last.'

Then Hector and his bicycle and his knapsack were helped into a truck and driven to Poznan station and put into a freight car full of cauliflowers. 'I am sorry,' said the train driver, 'to put you with vegetables, Sir.'

After this, there was just the dark of the freight car and the sound of all the miles and miles of the Polish heartland moving under the train. Hector lay down and covered himself with his overcoat and was as still as a man can be on a bed of cauliflowers. His head and body ached and it seemed to him that this ache was right in the substance of his skull and in the marrow of his bones.

His future was going wrong. Every thought that came to him, instead of being clear and precise, was clouded and difficult. It was as though thoughts were harmful chemicals, setting off explosions in his brain. The train was taking him nearer to his destination, but he began to see, with embarrassment, that it was towards the old eternal Russia of his imagination that he was travelling and that although he'd prepared quite well for his journey, he hadn't prepared at all for his arrival. When his D-Marks ran out, where and how was he to live? For a start, he spoke only a few words of the language. He knew the Russian word for 'tomorrow', but not the Russian word for 'now'. What kind of work could he find which allowed him to be totally silent?

Then a new thought came. The colour of its chemical felt white. It was a thought about silence and the new world, the world of the West, creeping east. Westerners were thieves of silence. They stole the quiet in a place and in the mind of a man and replaced it with longing, just as they stole the mystery from a city by lighting it orange. Darkness and quiet were leaving the world. It was only a matter of time before the dawn wouldn't be the dawn any more, but some other computer-adjusted piece of time, with colours other than its own.

Hector felt pleased with this thought, not because it was an optimistic one, but because it seemed rational and not blighted by confusion, and so he said to himself that perhaps he was going all this way in search of the perfect silence. He'd imagined a wilderness, a birch grove, a lake, or at least, he'd imagined cycling or walking through this kind of landscape on his way to his future in Russia. But the truth was that the future had no location. He'd never got further with his own story than the lake. Now, he understood that he might never get further – ever. In all probability, the lake was his destination.

Hector sat up and tried to eat a pickled cucumber. He had no appetite for what remained of the tinned meat. He lay down again, liking the train now, soothed a bit by the train, as if the train were Elvira and Hector a child falling asleep on her lap, wrapped in her apron.

He didn't want to show his face in Warsaw. He knew he would be stared at and he couldn't abide the thought of meeting the stare of Polish women and girls.

He dreamed the place smelled of spun sugar, that there was dry rot in the old houses, that church bells kept ringing and ringing the hours, that pigeons continuously ruffled the air. He would fall ill again in such a place.

So he resorted to bribery. He offered DM10 to the train driver and asked him to put him in another freight going east to the border with Belorus or beyond.

The train driver took the money and looked at it and shook his head. 'Now from here in a freight going east, you will die of cold, Sir.'

'I'm used to the cold' said Hector.

'Not this one. This is more cold.'

'Please,' said Hector.

So the money was paid and a second driver was found

who agreed to take him in a night train carrying medical supplies to Minsk. Katarzyna's husband then performed his last act of generosity: he gave Hector the blanket he kept in his cab. 'In the cold night,' he said, 'cover your body, German man.'

Hector missed the cauliflowers. In this second freight car, piled with boxes, every surface was hard and in whatever way he lay down, Hector's bones hurt. He tried folding the blanket in three and lying on top of it. This was more comfortable and Hector was beginning to drift towards sleep when he opened his eyes and saw in the darkness the freezing cloud of his own breath lying over him like a ghost. In time, he would have breathed all the air in the box car and the ghost would be very large and attempt to make more room for itself by entering the cavities of his body and taking away his life.

The blanket smelled of oil and it was old and worn, but there was still a little warmth in it. Hector stood up and wrapped himself round and round in it and lay down again on the boxes of pharmaceuticals. He imagined he was lying on glass syringes, as clear as ice.

The night would be so long. Poland, thought Hector, is a place where the nights have subdued the days and stolen half their territory. The bit of space left to the light is so pitiful, you just have time to cycle a few kilometres, buy some hard bread, pass a church where women kneel at open-air confessionals, hear a village band wearing hats with emperor's plumes play an ancient march, and then the dusk comes down, and it's futile to look forward to morning, because morning is so far away. It wasn't so mad, so completely foolish to imagine that here, on certain days, you could go into a post office, say, to buy a stamp, and that when you came out again with the stamp in your wallet, the day had given up hope and the words 'post office' had faded into the wall.

These thoughts made Hector remember the line of post boxes in the lobby of the apartment building in Prenzlauer Berg and how he'd imagined letters from Russia arriving here, letters which described an epic journey, an honourable arrival, a life built in a place where the structures of the old familiar world were still standing.

Now, in his freight car, wrapped in the train driver's blanket, as heavy snow starts to fall, Hector begins to compose in his mind a letter to Ute, to the sister he's desired since the day, at the age of five, when she licked his penis in the bath. It may be, he thinks, the only letter he will have time to think up and so he wants it to describe a place that will seduce Ute, a place in which she will recognise that she could be happy, a place he has made safe for her in advance:

Dear Ute,

I have arrived at the loneliest, most beautiful place in the world. Let me describe it to you. It is a great forest that has been growing silently for more time than anything else on this part of the earth. Bears inhabit it. And reindeer and wolves. Snow lies over it for seven months of the year. Sometimes, I fall into conversation with a solitary hunter and we discuss weapons and the individual characteristics of flight of certain difficult targets and how, in one's aim, one may compensate for these and so kill after all and not starve. Bears are protected and may not be shot.

And this brings me to swans. At the feet of the forest is a lake. The north side of it is frozen, but a little water still laps the snow on this southern side and here I have discovered a fine family of your favourite birds. They whoop like cranes in the early morning. They're plump and sleek from the quantity of fish they find in the lake. They are as tame as Karl and will come if I call them and feed from my hand. When you join me here, this is the first thing we will do: go down to the lake and visit the swans.

I expect you're wondering where we're going to live and how we're to find shelter. 'Hecti,' I hear you say, 'are you asking me to make love to you in the snow?' No, Ute. No, I'm not. Unless you want to do that.

I have found, at the lakeside, an old grey dacha, built of wood, with a stone chimney and a steep shingled roof. I walked into it like that girl in the fairy story and sat down in the largest of the chairs. I found a smoked ham hanging inside the chimney. I found a larder full of apples. I found folded sheets for the bed.

It's as if this dacha was designed with me in mind, with everything necessary for my survival: an axe to chop wood, a fire to cook on, even a featherbed quilt for the nights, which are as cold as nights on the moon. So now, I'm able to say to you, don't waste any more time, sell whatever you have to sell – Elvira's hairbrushes, Father's cache of cigarettes – and take the next train out of Berlin going east . . .

It was at this point in his imaginary letter that Hector was jolted forwards and almost fell off the ledge of boxes on which he was lying. The train had stopped.

Hector listened. He hadn't seen the thick snow falling, but by the temperature in the car and by the absence of any sound, he was able to judge that it was the deep middle of the night. The train would still be a long way from Minsk, a long way even from the border, so he supposed that it must have stopped at a signal and that in a few minutes it would get going again.

Somehow, the immobilisation of the train made the cold inside the freight car more intense and the ghost of breath that filled the space around and above Hector became agitated and began a strange kind of wailing.

The train moved. But it was going backwards, Hector could tell by the way his body rolled. And then it stopped again. Hector raised his head off his knapsack, to hear better, to see better, but he could hear and see nothing except the ghost in the air.

What Hector couldn't know was that the train had been re-routed into a siding because the line further east was temporarily closed by snow. What he couldn't know either was that the driver of the second freight had forgotten all about him and, once the train was safe in its siding, got down from his cab and walked away across the white fields towards a village, in search of a warm fire and a bed for the rest of the night. So Hector lay there, waiting for the train to resume its journey, while the soft snow piled up on the roof of the box car.

After an hour had passed, he tried to move himself towards the edge of the car, so that he could bang on the doors with his feet, but he found that his body was unwilling to move. It asked him to let it rest. He attempted, then, to call out. He knew that a human voice inside a freight car would probably make the kind of sound that disturbed no one's peace and altered nothing in the world, but he tried to call nevertheless. 'Train driver!' he said. 'Help me!' It was a whisper, not a shout. Hector believed that he was shouting, but he was only murmuring. And anyway, the driver of the second freight was a mile away. He was sitting by a fire with a schoolteacher and his wife, drinking vodka and eating poppyseed cakes.

After his efforts at calling, Hector's throat felt sore and he was afflicted suddenly by a desperate thirst. He had no memory of where his water bottle was or when he had last seen it, but what he did remember was the solitary lemon he had put into his knapsack on the morning of his departure. And his longing, now, to suck the juice from this lemon became so great that he succeeded in extracting one hand from the blanket and with this one hand reached behind his head to try to undo the fastenings of his knapsack.

He could picture with absolute precision the colour, shape and texture of the lemon as it had been when he packed it and his mind refused to imagine it any other way.

It is difficult to say how long Hector S struggled to locate this perfect yellow fruit, but into his search for it he put every last ounce of his strength.

The snow stopped falling an hour before sunrise and the sky cleared and the dawn was bright.

Woken by the winter sunlight, the driver of the freight to

Minsk remembered at this instant the German soldier he'd agreed to hide in one of his box cars in return for DM5.

He dressed hurriedly, tugging on his overcoat and his hat, and let himself out of the schoolteacher's house.

The snow was thick on the fields. The man wasn't young. Trying to make his way through this deep snow was exhausting for him and it took him the best part of half an hour to reach the train.

He opened the door of Hector's box car and stared in. The light on the snow had blinded him and, for a moment, he could see nothing. 'Hello!' he called. 'Hello! It is morning.'

Hector was lying face up, one arm behind his head that rested on his knapsack. His face had the pallor of bone, but there was a smile on it, as if, in his last moments, Hector had glimpsed something of great beauty.

The train driver walked a few paces from the car and fumbled to light a cigarette.

He stood in the snow, thinking.

It didn't take him long to decide what he was going to do. He was going to leave Hector exactly where he was. He wasn't even going to touch him or cover his face. Even if the day remained fine, the cold in the box car would preserve the body and, with a bit of luck, the train would get to Minsk before nightfall.

At the depot, the freight would be unloaded by rail workers from Belorus, and so it would be they who would find the stowaway. In this way, provided he remembered to get rid of the DM5, the driver would have shifted the burden of responsibility. The dead German, wearing some kind of military uniform, would become a Russian problem.

# Kathy Page

## It Is July, Now

I RIDE THE bus to the airport so as to keep the expenses. It takes an hour and a half and then the plane is forty-five minutes late. Well naturally, I do not take kindly to extra work at weekends and for two weeks the Director has been plaguing me to inspect the flat and before that he rejected one I had found myself, which was with someone I know: one room only and landlady *in situ* would not be suitable – they are used to having personal space, he said. A flat is a flat, I think, four walls: if one of us has lived in it, it will do for her. I did not make the inspection, but told the Director that I had. Some of the people in our Academy, I told the Director when he suggested I have a visitor in my department, are the foremost experts in their fields; it is a joy to hear them talk. But many of the foreigners who come do not even speak their own languages correctly, let alone have a proper pedagogical method or good manners. They all say that they are very interested in us and would rather be here than at home, but it is my view that some of them come here because there is unemployment in their own countries and they are inadequate to secure positions: so I am against it.

'Even so,' he said, clicking his pen in and out, as he does, 'there is nothing to be lost.' So it was decided.

Just as I am convinced that she has missed the plane I turn around and the person sitting on the bench behind me, wearing a dark red coat and no hat, can only be her. The coat is far too long: it will trail in the mud; the shoes will be soaked through. And her hair is cut short about her face, so that she looks like a child, but with very shiny lipstick on: the fashion, perhaps, where she comes from, but to my mind not a good one. Fashion is an odd thing. There, where they have freedom, they follow it. Here, where there has been none, we are all individuals.

'Good afternoon,' I say.

'Hello.' she stands up, her gloves fall on the ground, she bends straight down to pick them up, forgetting to offer her hand.

The Director also said that I should invite her to my home. A glass of wine with cheese was the done thing, he told me.

I have a whole house, in fact, only a minute from the city centre but built in the country style. Three floors, four rooms, a garden, gables: I had it painted ice-cream pink last summer. It is large enough for my daughter Katrin and me not to get in each other's skirts. She has a job at the City Hall but they won't allocate her a flat because there is enough space here. Still, I have my own study in the attic, with waxed floors, fresh curtains, a good rug, a proper office chair and a telephone extension. The house is mine – nationalised, of course, but I have the proofs and it is just a matter of time – and even you, I thought at the Director, cannot compel me to have someone in it if I do not want. He is young, very clever. Before, he was a scholar in a garret; now, he has been given a laptop computer, whereas I am paid nothing extra for being Head of Department, though it looks good on my CV, which we all have to make these days – and eventually, when the country is sorted out, it may lead to something.

The visitor's flat is in an anonymous district on the outskirts of town, big blocks with numbers and no names and because I haven't been there before I can't give good directions. The taxi driver is Russian and loses patience so I decide it is better to walk. She has some boots, she says, but they are right at the bottom of her bag, should she get them out? I tell her no.

'This isn't what I imagined,' she says. 'What sort of place is it?'

'It is typical,' I tell her. Finally we arrive. The stairs to it smell terrible: still, I think, it will probably be all right inside.

'I have never seen so many cats,' she exclaims.

'Actually, I have a cat myself,' I say, as I try to let us in – the lock is stiff – 'it is on penicillin at the moment,' I tell her, 'extremely expensive, an import. People can look after themselves. But pets are helpless, they can't manage: we must take care of them!'

Finally the door opens on a narrow corridor with a room either side and the bathroom at the end. The place is extremely hot and dusty – I go straight over to open a window, but when I get it to open I see there is an old cupboard and some rotting rugs on the balcony, and the remains of a seagull in the middle of it all. I remember also that I told the visiting lecturer on the phone that I had inspected the accommodation and that it was comfortable. I want to escape. But she walks around, trying everything, even opening cupboards and flushing the toilet. She says the television does not work.

'In any case, it would be incomprehensible,' I tell her.

'Well, not the pictures,' she points out.

'The programmes are of poor quality. It wouldn't interest you. Here are your fees for the three weeks.' I give her the envelope. She looks at the money, puts it back in the envelope without counting it, undoes her coat. She has on a pair of close-fitting black trousers and a soft brown jumper that clings to her shape. She stretches her arms and rolls her head around.

'What next?' she asks. It is dark by now. I take her straight out to look at the shop and the bus stop and tell her that I will meet her at Kaarmanni Olletuba at eight for supper; the Academy will pay. Just then my bus comes. Anyone will know where it is, I tell her as I get on.

She wants me to write some phrases down for her.

'Really, there is no point in language lessons,' I say. I have put on my suit and a brooch; she too has changed and it is a cream knitted dress now, with flecks of grey and red in it and a roll neck. 'You will learn nothing in such a short time, it is extremely complex grammatically.'

'I'm not talking grammar – ' she says, 'I just want to be able to point at a sandwich and say please. Or, for instance, to say "Can you give me directions to" rather than just barking the name of a café at some poor woman in a bus, do you see what I mean, Piret?' She has a habit of using one's name all the time.

'You are here for just three weeks,' I say. 'Everyone can see that you are a stranger; they won't expect it of you.'

'That's not the point.' I am not used to being argued with.

'We have a great deal to do,' I say, firmly. We push on and cover the necessary arrangements. I am ready to go then but she is drinking her soup like a snail.

'Well, Piret,' she says, 'tell me about yourself.'

'Here,' I tell her, 'we do not have small talk. We get to know each other slowly.'

'I see.' She plays with her bread and looks around her as if she was trying to commit the place to memory. 'Could we have more wine?' That uses up the money I saved by coming on the bus.

Life is hard, I tell her while we drink it. It cannot be legislated against as you are always trying to do in the West. You have a deal – good parents, bad parents, dead parents, a good country, a bad country or in-between. However it is, you use your talents to carve a way for yourself, you just make the best of it. Some people go under. Some people complain too much. Others are too kind . . . Drink makes me talk. When we at last emerge there is a strong wind blowing from the sea; the thermometer in the square shows minus fifteen. 'What is your word for snow?' she asks.

At home, Katrin is still up, eating milk pudding and watching the Finnish television channel, very loud, and reading magazines at the same time. The magazines are dreadful. What is your wildest dream? they ask. Do you get enough? How do you rate on the passion scale? She is not an intellectual, though she could have been, perhaps it is to spite me. She is particularly difficult these days. You resent me, she often accuses. It's not my fault there's an accommodation shortage . . . At least, I tell her when she complains, you have a mother, which I did not have for very long – all I remember is her brushing my hair, and coming to me in the night. I dream of that still once in a while; it's only natural. My father of course was away in the war, then died in it. Mainly I grew up in the orphanage – it was harsh, but invaluable in teaching self-reliance.

I didn't ask to be born, Katrin is always saying. You think you've done such a lot for me, but you haven't. I want nothing from you. You've never really loved me, it's only duty . . . She becomes impassioned. You think he would have stayed with you, happy ever after, if not for me, she says. Don't you? We make our meals separately now. After all, she is twenty-five. Some of what she says is true, but not all.

The visiting lecturer comes to the Academy on Monday morning. Apparently she left the bus at the wrong stop the night before and had to walk several kilometres through the snow and there was some problem with the toilet in her flat, which flooded; also drunken men banged on the door – but this is normal, I tell her, in the district where you are. She has on jeans and a silk blouse and the boots she wears are very odd. She spends the morning photocopying and uses most of the paper for the term.

I do not normally go out with subordinates, but a visitor has ambiguous status so I accept her invitation to attend a concert. 'Let me treat you,' she says. 'Treat?' 'To treat is to pay for, but really a matter of taking turns,' she explains, 'of showing you'd like to provide even if you can't. It works out the same in the end.'

'Here, each of us must keep to her own economy,' I say. 'It is simply too stressful otherwise. It is almost rude to suggest such a thing. You will embarrass people; they will feel that they have to return the favour when they simply cannot afford it.'

'I'm sorry,' she says and her face turns red.

The National Symphony Orchestra puts no one to shame, though the auditorium is unexpectedly full of children. I

don't know why this is, I tell her in the interval. I expect
they have offered the tickets free – for so-called educational
purposes – and because there are so many choices these days
that they cannot fill the hall. To my mind it is far too young;
I did not introduce Katrin to classical music until she was
seventeen, and not to jazz, which is more sophisticated, until
a year after that. This accounts for these people who clap at
the wrong time: they are the parents of these children; they
have been forced to come, and have never before attended
such an event in their lives; they simply don't know how to
behave.

'Did you enjoy the music?' she asks suddenly.

As we leave she says, 'May I ask you a favour? I need to
call home, and none of the boxes does international calls, or
am I missing something? But the phones at the Academy
would do it, I think. Do you possibly have a key? Or maybe
you have the right kind of telephone yourself, at home?'

'It is urgent?'

'Very,' she says. I do not feel I can reasonably refuse so we
go to the Academy, which seems eerie without students and
colleagues being there. It is hard to find the light switches; I
give up and wait in the dark on a bench in the corridor while
she uses the departmental phone. I can hear her voice but
not the words; perhaps she is whispering. It rises and falls
and there are long silences, exclamations, laughter once or
twice. It is not business, and not very urgent either. It is
twenty-five minutes before she emerges, a half smile on her
lips, eyes shining. When Katrin wears that kind of face, she
always avoids questions, and goes straight to her room. I am
angry.

'You have dealt with the matter?'

'Oh yes, thanks, Piret,' she says, smiling.

I cannot sleep at all that night. I keep thinking of Karel, who
was Katrin's father. We were both students. It was the last
year when we grew close. In summer we were both sent to
do compulsory training in medical studies, so that we could
fulfil our obligations if war broke out. It was in the forest,

lectures all day, anatomy and so forth, but the nights were mainly our own and they were long, warm nights. We swam in the lake together, while others drank and sang patriotic songs; we despised them. Out there, beyond the reach of their voices, the water was smooth and cool as glass and afterwards our bodies were like silk. At this point I remember thinking that so long as you knew someone else who thought like you, anything was tolerable. Across whatever horrors you could hold to that connection. When we got back he came every night to my flat. It was not deliberately that I became pregnant but I do not believe in interfering with what is meant.

'But I do not believe in being trapped if there is something that can be done to prevent it,' Karel said. He took up a post in the north before she was born and I never heard from him again; I don't even think of him often now.

The cat climbs on to my bed. It is wheezing when it purrs, but otherwise it seems all right. I smooth down its fur and it stretches out flat with its ears back; it is very comforting. I can hear Katrin snoring at the other side of the house. She has done so since a child. To start with I tried to cure her of it by waking her, but gave up.

Next it is the Post Office. I have told her the directions, but she insists on being taken. She insists also on having her letters weighed: they cost four times what they would have. Just put the stamp on, I tell her, are they going to sit at the airport weighing each one? 'Maybe that's why your last to me never arrived,' she says, but the fact is I did not get around to writing it. I excuse myself from lunch. There are some cheese pies at home and I want to check the cat: the vet said that since it was a virus the medicine might strengthen him but the cure was down to his natural resistance. Katrin often says I care more about that cat than I do about her, that I never made a fuss over her, though of course that is not true. It is an instinct to be tender with children, it happens whether you will it or not. She simply does not remember. Children who have their parents take things for granted. She says that I love that cat in a way I never loved her. She says that the money I spend on the cat, added up, would get her a plane ticket anywhere in Europe. She means Paris: a Frenchman came with a trade delegation. She has many boyfriends. However, I do not allow them to stay in the house.

'This country is supposed to be *liberated*,' she tells me. 'There is nowhere for us to go. You are greedy,' she says, 'a greedy, jealous old woman . . .' Sometimes, when I get in, I have a sense that someone else has been in the house, though there is never any proof. I feel the cat knows too.

Towards the end of her last week, the visiting lecturer waits outside in the corridor for me to finish my Level One class and asks for the fourth time now to go to lunch together.

'Somewhere cheap,' she says, 'we'll go Dutch of course.'

'But actually, I am going home today,' I say. 'Dutch?'

'Well I can't,' she says, 'it takes an hour each way on the bus — you could stretch a point.'

'Is there a reason?' I say. 'Is there some particular academic matter you wish to discuss?'

'No,' she says — her voice very even — 'there isn't. Just some food and a chat. For the sake of itself.' None of my regular lecturers would suggest such a thing.

'Perhaps,' I say, 'I can organise it so that we go out for a drink on your last night, along with the Director, who would be interested to hear what you think about our students and their progress; I can ring him this afternoon and make arrangements.'

'No,' she stares at me, 'I was asking you, Piret, whether you wanted lunch, with me, now.'

'I have told you.'

'You,' she said, 'take the biscuit.'

'The biscuit?'

'This is a one-way street,' she says. Again I query the idiom. 'There is no point in language lessons,' she says then, and her voice turns hard: 'seeing as we are never going to communicate.' She turns and walks off.

*

179

It is very upsetting. Then, when I get home I walk straight up to the cat's basket to pick him up. Katrin has fed him in the morning and the wrapper from the medicine is still on the table. But he is lying there dead, his body stiff and his fur cold. My whole skin shrinks and I run back to work. I have a meeting arranged with the Director. He tells me he is going to Stockholm at Easter, for a month, paid for by the Ministry for Education; would I please take over his administration while he is away?

I tell him that the visiting lecturer is going well. I ask him for more money for books, and whether we could set the exam later in the year – after all, I say, we can make up the rules how we want them now. He says that he will note my ideas. But he has already closed his notepad and started putting things away in drawers while I am still talking. I stay in my chair. He stands up. So everything is fine? I try to stand up too but my legs will not do it. And I try to say in a brisk, businesslike voice – oh yes, absolutely – but I cannot do that either. I say nothing at all for a few seconds, and then the words blurt out of my mouth:

'Actually, I have bad news. My cat is dead, I am just going home to bury it.' But I do not want to. I do not know how to go about it, I do not want to touch it. I have had that cat for six years. He turned up on my doorstep, very thin, and I took him in. He has slept on my bed and sometimes I used to talk to him. The vet cost more than my food for a month, just for one injection, but I did not begrudge it at all. Not at all! This is how I feel. It was of course the wrong thing to say to the Director; his brother died in a labour camp, two thirds of the way through twenty-five plus five.

He puts his hat on. 'There are plenty of cats,' he says. 'You can get another one.'

I pull myself together and think how there is a chance Katrin will get home before me, and perhaps she will wrap it up and deal with it: she's a practical sort and it would be easier for her since she didn't love it.

I decide to have the afternoon off. I need some groceries

and am walking up the main street when I see the visiting lecturer on the other side. She has her hands stuck deep in her pockets and that, I think, is because she will keep leaving her gloves on the desk by the copier. One of the brass buttons is missing from her coat. I stop walking. I want to turn and go away, but instead I just freeze, watching her peer into the shops as if she had never seen things before. And it seems to me that she looks sad. And suddenly I know what it must be like to be unable to speak or understand a word of the language, not even guess at it, to get everything half right or wrong. It must be like walking around with a shell around you which no one could get through, hard outside but very, very tender beneath.

At that moment she sees me, crosses the street, shouting 'Piret! How are you!' even though it is only hours since she asked the same thing in the corridor, and even though we parted on a bad note. I do not understand, and again I find myself saying something unintended:

'You?' I ask. 'How are you? You have not been lonely on your visit here, I hope?' She laughs. I burst into tears. It is very embarrassing.

She takes hold of my arm. 'We'll go in here,' she says. I am crying so much that I can't see where she means. It turns out to be the new place, Palace Café, with a pink marble floor. It is very warm inside. All the crockery has a broad gold rim. The coffee is strong, and they serve it with chocolate truffles on a saucer. In the middle of the ceiling hangs a huge chandelier, a strange thing made from liqueur glasses and bits of welded kitchen implements, and the chains from sink plugs: post-modernist, perhaps. I find I quite like it.

'This is a very expensive place,' I say, 'for tourists only.'

'Let's have something else,' she insists, 'brandy, pastries, whatever. Look,' she says, opening her purse. 'This is worth nothing at home, I'll only have to put it in the airport charity box.'

When everything is there on the table and the waitress has gone, she asks: 'Are you going to say what was the matter out there?'

'No. There is a great space,' I explain to her, 'where nothing can be said. It is not personal.' There is silence and she bites into a pastry, filling her mouth. She dusts her fingers, swallows, looks up.

'These,' she says, 'are the best thing I've eaten since I came here. They remind me a bit of something I had in Greece but those had mint in them too.' She smiles lightly, as if none of the things that have taken place between us had ever been.

'We have mint ones,' I find myself saying. 'At Easter.' Again, it is not intended, but the feeling is of it slipping out, rather than jumping.

'Do you? Does it grow here?' She pats her lips with a serviette. I wonder how old she is. Anywhere between thirty and forty, it is hard to tell. Like me, she has no wedding ring.

'I have two types in my garden,' I tell her. 'It dies and then comes up again, very reliable. Of course, you can dry it for winter . . .' She takes a lemon cake, I a cinnamon biscuit.

'The biscuit,' I say, and we laugh. I tell her more about my garden, how I prepare the soil for carrots, and how I store them. I tell her about the different kinds of daffodil bulb. Every now and then, between mouthfuls, she asks me to clarify: you have to put those under glass I suppose? What time of year would that be? And I think: how easy these things are to say! The content, I sense, is not the point at all. Yet at any minute, I think also, she could ask me something I don't want to answer. At the same time the feeling of waiting for this to happen is almost a pleasure and I am somehow disappointed when finally the bill comes and it has not occurred. They bring our coats.

'Can we go back to your house?' she says.

She does not at all mind burying the cat for me, though the ground is still frozen, so it has to be a shallow hole. I watch from the kitchen window as she stamps the earth flat. Afterwards we drink some wine and she goes home in a taxi. I pay for it because she has spent all her money in the café, but I don't mind.

Two days later, I see her to her plane.

'Life goes on, Piret,' she says. We embrace. I watch her through the passport control. 'I'll write,' she calls at the last minute.

But no letter has come and it is July now. The peonies were particularly good this year, the lettuce was early. I have not replaced the cat, but I planted a new lilac close to where it is, yet not so close as to disturb it. Death is always such a shocking thing: it makes one reconsider Life. Once, here, that seemed endless; now it feels shorter all the time. I would like someone from outside to tell these things to.

# Paul Magrs

## ANEMONES, MY LABRADOR, HIS PUPPY

WE ALL LIVED, working on our separate, idle little projects, in a slate grey town that had a history rank with witch burnings and a one-way system of irate traffic as futilely intricate as the patterns inside your ear.

It rained all the time and especially during that last third of the year when they held there, in our nascent Cultural Studies department, a ten-week course of papers on Witches. Papers were given by a variety of visitors in a duskily lit common room which always looked to me like an airport lounge, although I've never flown. An hour of turgid historicism at teatime, Wednesdays; letting somebody's god-awful academic prose wash heedlessly over you, an hour of questions, drinks, then a meal in town, in the same, cramped, crimson room hung with horse brasses and a single, long table, reserved for a set who disturbed other diners with raucous, entirely theoretical talk of sadomasochism, incest, female circumcision.

Julian was beginning his MA on father/son incest in Renaissance drama. He sat at one end of the table, his first night at one of these do's, in a home-made linen shirt, cuffs trailing heart-breakingly in his silver platter of garlic mushrooms. The regulation glossy dark hair flopped over this face arrogant with its own half-apprehension of its beauty; lips quite pink and curling now, with a clumsy wit, as he tried to winkle something noticeable into the conversation between his supervisor, Stephen, and the visiting academic, Ivy.

When Julian laughed it was to draw attention to the post-

184

vocalic 'r' completing each 'ha'; he was making a feature of a rather cultured dippiness. He was all flannels and affected stammer, groping towards the correct critic's name, a distracted hand through hair stylishly awry with three days' grease.

'Yes, my shirt was made for me by my wife,' he told me when I'd said he had oil up the cuffs but that it was a nice shirt anyway. He added, 'She makes all of our clothes; mine and my son's.'

I was making a point of smoking particularly heavily at the meal's end, and working through the last cafetière, defying the puritanical looks I was getting; the modern critic does not abuse his own body. And I pictured Julian and a whole family togged up in clothes too large for them; the thin and young family, cultured and enunciating properly. Dressing up as grown-ups.

Ivy was the American visiting professor; researching the length and breadth of Britain on instruments of torture used to quieten women. Asked her area of expertise she would square up her padded shoulders, toss an immaculate Golden Girl perm and declare: 'Scolds.' She talked and talked that evening and took a group of us for coffee to the house she had borrowed for a month by the castle.

It was the oldest house I had ever been in, I think, and oddly proportioned; I felt it creak about me as she showed us to a darling little sitting-room, and proceeded to slosh coffee on to a milky coloured carpet. Stephen leapt up to stamp out the stain with J-cloths; all a-sweat now (whereas, minutes earlier, he had been replete with a good meal's strain and an evening of intellectual chitchat). The old house by the castle belonged to a dear friend of his; he was the agent of its rental and blame for the carpet was something he could see reverting straight to him as the patch widened, darkened, and Ivy flapped about, helpless, pissed, and Julian and I sank deep into a plum sofa and chatted, making up a friendship from bits of shared bibliographies and very coy eye contacts.

All this while, past midnight, fog came up over, around

the squat castle from the marshes. Ivy hadn't closed her chintz curtains; we were high over the town, quite comfortable, with no need to hide from aggressive passers-by. So the night punched its opacity into the room and I watched Julian's profile; as the Renaissance people chatted, occasionally jotting down names, references, on the backs of their hands.

So this was networking. I could feel Julian thrill with the thought of that beside me on the sofa. On nights like these are important contacts made. Before he had to leave – earlier than the rest of us, for his family – Ivy was dropping big hints his way; interest in his as yet unbegun work, for an anthology she was preparing in Texas on Shakespeare's abusive fathers.

I am not a Renaissance person, but I've read all sorts of things. We came into the early hours talking about the Sitwells. Ivy staggered off to fetch a copy of her last book from her still packed luggage, to show me the cover painting. A young Edith as a captivatingly scarlet woman beside her father.

Stephen began to make noises that it was time to leave. Already Ivy had dropped off once or twice, but she was narcoleptic and we'd been sure – as she'd exhorted us earlier, over coffee – not to mistake her lapses for heavy-handed hints. Still, Stephen felt we oughtn't overstay.

On the pavement outside, beneath the castle still full of condemned men, Ivy told us about the new season at Stratford. Stephen pointed out a hotel's single yellow light; told us that in that very room Dickens and Wilkie Collins had written a ghost story together; some fevered, fond collaboration, on just such a night.

It took some doing to shut Ivy up, get her back indoors and the door locked, to get ourselves free. Stephen was still of a mind to be gentle with her; not so when she returned to Texas a month later, having let the shower run a full week in the empty, ancient house, while she trotted about Scotland peering at gravestones. The house was wrecked.

It was that kind of term; friendships struck up, spectacular as the last fag I lit for my long walk home across town, and damped suddenly down; all trust and bravado lost.

It was a cloying mist that night, coming through bone cold, blue. I said to Stephen, before he turned off towards his swish little place down on the quay, that I thought Julian was very pretty.

The following Sunday evening we were drinking gin in Stephen's flat, shouting between rooms as he braised various things for dinner – I could hear the carrots screaming and spitting in a dish of boiling honey – and I was reading Susan Sontag by his french windows, way above the river.

Once I called him out to watch a woman sitting on a bench by the river, spiting the cold and taking off her socks and shoes very methodically, putting them in her shopping bag. I had to smoke out on the balcony; the flat's distinctly mini-malist lines were also supremely health-conscious ones. I took an ashtray decorated with scribbles by Cocteau outside and so missed the young family's arrival. Julian came in with heaps of brightly coloured bedding; cheerful and scarlet he deposited his son on Stephen's bed for the evening and ushered me in so he could explain to us all that they had spent the day walking, out in the hills.

His wife was even younger; some four years younger than me, she was called Elsa and was small, brown, beaming. Yes, she added, they'd been to their church in the country, had lunch with the vicar, and went for a good hard walk afterwards.

Elsa wrote novels; managing three each year, even though she was a full-time mother and wife. We boys looked shame-faced over our starters. She explained that she handwrote several drafts in neat exercise books. Her works were often autobiographical. Playfully Stephen muttered something about intentionality, textuality; at least something ending in -ality, as most comments *did* in those heady months of high theory and its intrigues.

I helped dish up dessert. 'I think Elsa's a decadent, really,' Stephen hissed. 'Don't be put off by all the talk of church.'

'They're whiter than white!'

'She's a decadent eager to burst out; just listen to her!'

'What does that mean?'

He'd made a kind of plum pudding thing; cloying and spiced.

'I think she's just dying for our Julian to have a man on the side. I think she finds it quite an exciting idea.'

'Oh, right. Yeah.'

I picked up dishes to carry, desultorily. But I was piqued.

When I was doing literary theory research, as I was then, I could never quite get into it. My work was on my contemporaries; other theorists and what they say about other theorists. I was writing about the Subject; subjectivity's awful wrangle with itself in the context of postmodernity. I would treat the library as a shopping mall; I took a trolley now and then between its shelves and my cavalier research consisted of grabbing books whose covers, titles, reputations preceded them or made me fancy them on the spot. My work was chancy and promiscuous and I spent my time picking up choice cuts of quotation; various notable names writing on the subject of the subject, of the body, of identity; all jeopardised now, all their integrity gone. An exciting time to be writing about such things, as my colleagues – their work more absorbing, hierarchised, historical – commented to me. I often worked at home. Sat on the 1940s settee in a rented house by the canal. There I was shanghaied into watching morning television, smoking too many cigarettes.

I bumped into Julian in the corridor and he invited me to dinner, suggesting also that I might like to work with him, in our department, in the small room kept quiet for postgraduates, to be company in these darkening afternoons on the slope down to Christmas. Because of course, one could go mad reading tersely academic discourse in complete solitude. Couldn't we hold each other's hands?

He did a full day, nine to five, since he couldn't work at home, where the Child absorbed hours and love like a doughnut dunked in half-finished coffee. The Postgraduate Room

188

was soundproofed with polystyrene and so he played Stravinsky on an old school-type record player. There was a combination lock on the door; from the jabbing noises made from outside you knew of someone's arrival well in advance. Sometimes we talked about having oak panelling, a fireplace, smart prints; living our most excessive Brideshead fantasies. Those were the fantasies welling head to head across the desk in the middle of the room as we flipped through books, scribbling notes, glancing up now and then. We could relish the indulgences of the other; play opera and flounce about so long as we kept our heads down at work; him on incest, myself on transvestism as a metaphor for postmodern subjectivity.

He took to wearing full linen suits, stripy sailor tops and I – God help me – knotted my paisley scarves as the weather took a colder turn and I bought a long dark coat.

Our department was in a building cobbled together in 1966 but it had a grassy quad criss-crossed by paving stones and here we could meet in the lowering gloom and hold conversations about nothing, before saying ta-ra till tomorrow morning.

Well, if not nothing, at least about homoeroticism in *Henry V.* Remember: 'A little touch of Harry in the night?' Harry's erotic largesse, dispensing himself, his body, about the sleeping troops the night before battle. Oh, that was the kind of thing to be made a meal of, here in Cult Stud. We were Cult Studs all right. I lent him my video of *My Own Private Idaho*; he was extremely keen on the homoerotic motif. It was the mortar which held Western culture's tenets in place; even in a fractured modernity. Rome was built solely from men rubbing each other up the wrong way. He evinced a keen, theoretical interest; steam blowing out over his coat collar as we stood in the quad. Gave me a kind of mock punch before running off to fetch the Child from the crèche. He carried a daft little suitcase about with him. Once, giving me a lift back one frozen night, he went to a car that looked only a little like his and, mistaking it, tried to force the lock. For hapless things like these I can feel a quirk of fondness;

other times ineptness in someone with whom I've had odd, difficult scenes just makes me impatient and sick.

Another American woman! At the meal with Julian and Elsa. She was another writer, who lived near Washington in an entirely green farmhouse with a mother who thought she was Miss Lavish from *A Room with a View* and who, upon reading one of my letters to her daughter, Teri, had declared: 'He is one of us.' Things had looked promising for me and Teri, then; almost coaxed into a full-time heterosexuality by the promise of being one of the people who live in a green house in Washington and who *understand each other*. At weak moments the promise of being understood is enough to tempt me to anything.

So we'd fucked and had a few nice talks, meals, awkward scenes. The marrieds invited us to coo over their house in the terrace by the park. A piano of blond wood dominated their dining-room. There were shelves of bright new hardbacks; Elsa talked of A. S. Byatt, Alan Hollinghurst, how she loved gay fiction and thought she might really adore being a gay man. The Child woke once upstairs as wine was mulling on the open fire and was brought down in a blanket, fierce, warm as cheese on toast, to be inspected. My heart went out, as it always does, to kids, babies, anyone without an ounce of guile.

I sat across from Teri. She was chewing on fat and bones; we ate pheasant, plucked fresh from the market. Her eyes wide with disgust at its gaminess. 'It was,' she told me, the following week, 'the worst thing I have tasted in all my life.' To me it looked a little raw; those pink, streaming ends of bones. But what did I know? At least one and a half class distinctions away from an understanding of poultry, our birds were always banged in the slammer for four hours a time; we were terrified of salmonella. With knowledge and class comes an insouciant carelessness. That night we sucked slivers of steamed courgette dipped in sour cream and Teri had fallen quiet, grimacing.

*

I stood in the road with Julian, right up on the hill above the town. A fag outside since they, too, were conscious of health. We looked at the real smoke coming from his chimney; that inscrutable, solid blue. 'Signifying everything I protect,' he said, with a rare flash of earnestness. The arc lamps of the cathedral distorted the plumes' shapes weirdly; they made an umbrella. He gave me his scarf and leather driving gloves since it had begun to snow and I had a fair way to walk home. And he told me he never drank much because of his mother's problems with it. His father owned a company in America and lived there now. I heard Julian phone him for free from the room where we worked. He often phoned his wife, too, while she wrote her novels in exercise books at home. And they talked baby talk for minutes on end. The first time I heard it I went scarlet; a problem I never had with eavesdropping usually. Hearing him babytalk was worse than nudging his foot under the desk, with my own, accidentally, as we worked; breaking the braced weight of our tension clean across and patching it with an embarrassed smile. We watched the smoke go up a bit longer and then I had to get home. We didn't hug goodnight; we never did. I walked down the middle of the road, as advised, to the bottom of the hill.

We had a friendship developing which wasn't bluff, hearty, cruel, as two straight men might seem to us. It wasn't implicit with use and suspicion like two openly gay men. We were romantic friends.

'We have a very romantic friendship,' he told me on the phone the following tea-time. He'd rung to say Teri was about to become engaged to some Irish bloke and get her dual citizenship.

'We do?' I was sitting on the top stair at home.

'You're a very romantic figure in our department,' he said. 'Rupert Brooke.'

'Fucking great.' Then I delivered a short lecture on flirtatiousness. How I thought people ought to take responsibility for the signals they give off. Watch how you signify; it's all a language. He thanked me, a little warily, 'You're a wise man!' was how he ended the phone call; hearty, bluff, casual. I put the phone down wondering why I'd lectured him on messing about with things he couldn't carry through. It was a warning in advance, I thought; just in case he got ideas. Bless him; had he an idea in his head? Oh, it was all high theory and his work seemed prohibitively complex, but he had as much sense as a Labrador I'd kept when I was seven who'd been called, incidentally, Julian. The same brown lucidity in his eyes; a careless and distracted fidelity.

To take my mind off research which had a disturbing knack of creeping up on me every minute of the day and waking me at night with its implications, its references, its myriad, swimming footnotes, I had taken up drawing again. I filled a thick sketchpad each month with scratchy sub-Hockney line drawings. Rooms quivering with poignancy and cluttered everyday use, figures observed from afar in the very act of the humdrum and, more recently, figures and faces of those about me. My fascination with getting their expressions down for all time as if they might suddenly be lost to me in their most ordinary, usual aspects, is apparent now, when I flick through the books, in the way each drawing is labelled and dated. My sketchpads of the time have their own in-dexed, academic coherence; as if I'd set about cataloguing my friends. I was alert; an old hand at having friends in a town where people do research and come to talk about books; they pass you by. It's a relay race and the baton is something you can't afford not to fling away from you, heartlessly, when need be.

I needed to draw, to have days off, to do things other than read and write in the locked Postgraduate Room. Its windows steamed up with claustrophobia, it seemed. The white board was smeared with words as though they flew about the room like Hitchcock's birds when we weren't looking, then flat-tened themselves to the board when we were. Julian's desper-ate concentration wore me out, too; sometimes he was too panicked to break up a morning for coffee. When we did have coffee, in a campus bar with red gingham tablecloths, his conversation was weak and repetitious and you could tell he was just worried about his note-taking on the Renaissance. I'd forgotten, in a year, how intensive MAs can be. I was out to pasture in the grassless hinterlands of a Ph.D.

So I relished my days at home; breakfast watching the frozen canal and its swans turned clumsy, skidding their way about. The canal went dusty with layers of snow; it was like *Orlando*. I had the cat twisting about beside me, and I drew some anemones we had on the mantelpiece until half nine that morning, until Julian arrived, fresh from dropping the Child at the crèche. I'd persuaded Julian he needed the odd day away from our soundproofed room, too, and, given the circumstances we'd settled on, he agreed.

'Ready?' he asked breezily when I opened the front door. He had his flat cap on, jauntily; wrapped up for winter. He looked determined and businesslike, as he always did when going for piles of research texts in the library. Today's activity was something he was equally set on doing right. Meanwhile I was quivering inwardly, having expected him to have run a mile by now, all resolution, curiosity gone. While I made us a pot of tea I found I couldn't swallow and just nodded as he fussed about with conversation.

'I ehm . . .' he stumbled, and I passed him his tea. He struggled to take off his coat and hat, still holding it. Perhaps he'd gone as nervous as I by now. 'I told Elsa about this. Asked her, really, if she thought it was all right.'

I took a scalding sip of Earl Grey. Earl Grey was something else we concurred on; alongside Michael Nyman's music, Chagall's circus paintings. 'And?'

'She didn't see why I even mentioned it. She says it's up to us. But she'd like to see what we come up with. If you don't mind . . .'

I shrugged.

A week ago there'd been a coffee break over scarlet gingham. We'd been joined by Teri and Elsa and Teri's talk of marriage. She wanted to piss me off, did so, and left. Elsa went after her, a little later; they were doing a writing course together.

Left alone again, Julian started asking me about my drawing. He showed me some contact prints of his he'd done in a rented dark room the previous night. He had whole films of statues from Italy. Pearly white men stretched out and, in these mismatched, tiny contacts, interlocking in a bizarre panoply. Then there was a film of Stephen, dressed in his usual crumpled cords and jacket, in a dusty room, lying, standing or sitting in a glass cabinet. Julian explained that these were all his father figures; their poses paralleling one another. Oh boy. I said I thought they were very nice and that I'd like to see them finished.

'And,' I added, pouring more tea, 'if you ever have film left over, I'd love some nice, proper photos taken of me. I've never had any done, really.'

'Of course, of course,' he said in that rushed, cajoling tone, one eye on the clock and the other on the next topic of interest, as though wary of being caught out.

We talked about Roland Barthes or something or other for a bit, before Julian said, 'Of course, what I'd like to do is photograph a bloke naked. That's what I really need.'

I coloured again but couldn't let the conversation drop. 'I don't know about that . . .'

'Oh! I wasn't asking you . . . I just meant . . .' He floundered and my heart went out to him again, as it was tending to do. 'Would you, though?'

I felt I had a dire body and, in my excited indecision, felt it sliding, like molten butter, into slabs about my feet.

'We'd draw up a bargain,' I said.

'What for?'

'I've got the same problem drawing. The next thing I need is a nude model, and I want a man. But who do you ask? How can you ask?'

We giggled in complicity.

'But we understand each other . . . where we're at . . . and our romantic friendship. It needn't be a problem. Why don't we pose for each other? Make it mutual?'

'A mutual appreciation society,' he smiled.

Held every Wednesday and Friday morning, we decided.

And I would put the central heating on full blast, pull down the blinds in my tiny bedroom, switch on the lamps, get the Nyman CDs ready. We needed an atmosphere redolent with trust and artifice to see us through.

Into this warmth and conspiracy, Julian actually turned up that first Wednesday morning. He walked into my room ahead of me as we came up carrying our cups of tea. He wore the expression of a potential house buyer and looked down at my drawing book and pens, pencils slung as if nonchalantly on the bed. He turned to smile at this and carefully put his posh camera to one side. I switched the music on and sat on a chair, finding I couldn't actually say anything now we were here.

He produced a very old hardback. 'I'm afraid I'm sticking to the other condition. That I'm allowed to read while you draw, since it could go on some time.'

'Fine,' I nodded, and he tossed it on to my duvet and then shrugged his heavy jumper off over his head, fluffing up his hair as he emerged. His home-made shirt was rucked up; he tugged it and revealed a sparrow-thin torso which goose-fleshed over at first, its delicate nipples startled, on end. He was braced like a bird's skeleton on the bed as he prepared to pose; milk-bottle white, fragile, a mass of shifting, fluent shades of cream and blue-grey. I judged and altered trap-ezoids, rhombuses of bones and shallow muscle and he car-ried his old book through all of these negotiations, keeping his eyes on the small print. He wrenched off shoes and socks, slinging them, followed by his trousers and, suddenly, he stood beside my bed in cotton undershorts and I had a moment of ontological doubt; as to how he could be revealed so beautifully explicit to me by means other than an idealising imagination or the fervid mutual decision that we were about to fuck. Yet it was neither of these things and terribly, frus-tratingly realistic as he took down his pants and sprawled almost hairless and wan across the bed, the thick hooded nub of his cock slapping against his stomach and lolling under my nose.

There were so very few poses, it turned out. Sprawling

contextless provides the average body with a limited amount of things to do. I interrupted his reading each quarter hour for something new.

He flipped about. 'It's cock or arsehole,' he said, showing a streak of vulgarity I'd not heard before and more shocking, strangely, than his actions of that moment; belly down on the now-rumpled bed, raising his arse to display his pendulous prick, neat little balls.

My part of the bargain was to be naked too as I drew him; ready for the photos he wanted to take in the bathroom. We lay side by side and I scratched away at the page; each drawing had its lavish crest of pubic hair and his prick looking different each time. It seemed natural to both of us that what we really wanted representing was his face, his cock, the smooth chest and stomach between. When he looked at the progress made he was fascinated by what I'd made of his cock. 'It looks like a little face!' he said.

I undressed fearing that I'd get an erection, but I figured that, that being inevitable for both of us, we'd deal with it all right. I didn't however; hung limp and small alongside him. Julian appeared to cast the most cursory of glances.

But I stood against our half-plastered, dramatic bathroom walls and he closed in on my skin, the shadings of muscle, the sullen defiance of my cock and murmured lovingly at it all through his viewfinder. He shot his pictures still naked and when he leaned in to show me how things focused, how light was squeezed out, nonchalantly brought us into contact and I felt my dick slide wetly along his thigh with a trail of precum.

When I flipped through the drawings for Elsa over our next meal together – at my house this time – I noticed a shocking continuity for the first time. She had expressly asked to see them and, embarrassed, Julian and I said she could. She picked up on this certain feature immediately. Julian's cock was bigger, more alert in each drawing. By the last, warmest, most faithful version, he was sprawled entirely safe and sleepy and drawn from waist level. So safe and guileless he lay, giving a thoughtlessly rude view of a vulnerable, puckered arsehole and his thick cock arched up his belly as if to drink from the well of his navel. It hadn't struck me before but in this drawing his foreskin was drawn back of its own accord, to reveal a tender, blushing dome; the urethra's needle eye. He had a negligent, luxurious erection. The pose was so calm and accustomed, I hadn't noticed. And how do you test hardness, readiness, with the circumspection we basked in?

At the front of the Halifax there was one of those little tables for the kiddies, cluttered with Lego. The Child and I played there while Julian queued up, cap literally in hand, for the counter. We were making a tower sort of thing, putting a kind of conversation together. The Child was stuffed into a blue and yellow romper suit; when we walked through town Julian slung him carelessly arm to arm and it was as if the Child bounced, resilient, squalling, and attracting the attention of each shopkeeper we met.

Especially in the indoor market they were known and watched out for; primped and petted, the young father and son exhibiting this astonishing precocity at buying their own groceries. Friday afternoons were when Julian had the Child to himself. This one in November was my birthday and we were having lunch together; at a table strewn with red, white and blue napkins in *Café Monet*.

We spent all afternoon round town and it was dark before the shops shut. We were a family. A gay couple and child. And we basked in the fondness of shopkeepers. How nice it was for them to see how we were coming on. Nice to see the young ones managing. We were laden down with shopping. We bought Earl Grey in a speciality shop where everything came in redolent wooden kegs and barrels. I was learning that Julian and family liked to buy things which were, if not expensive, at least authentic. Handwrapped parcels of moist, fresh loose tea, authentically dead and dripping birds hung outside butchers' windows. I got caught up in it and it made me feel more bogus than ever; me with my penchant for snooping round Just What You Need and Superdrug.

That night, the night of my twenty-fourth, I had a lovely time with a friend of mine in a cocktail bar done up exactly like the studio set for *The Scarlet Empress*. My friend was a sternly phlegmatic, one-handed fencing instructor. He took me to task.

'You're fucking with the bourgeoisie,' he warned, adjusting his glasses and sucking on his cocktail straw. He'd recently done a counselling course and, while he kept the tone of voice they'd given him, he threw out their ideas of objectivity. 'Or rather, the bourgeoisie are fucking you. They always do. You never win. Don't bother with it. Don't be daft.'

I frowned, sunk into myself. 'It's just a laugh. I need a laugh. There's no risk. Nothing's happened. I can lap up a morning or two of mutual glorification with no strings attached and not get hurt.'

'I dunno,' he said. I wasn't sure if that cast doubt on me or the situation. He added, 'It's a complex one. Because you reckon that he's really a queer, don't you?'

'Oh God, I can't tell anything any more.'

Nowadays I just thought all sex was pretty androgynous. This caused problems for me in Cult Stud; where centuries' worth of accumulated theoretical discourse told me that there were all sorts of differences to be problematised.

Yet . . . regardless of the biological accoutrements of the bodies I had encountered, their lovemaking always occurred to me as an androgynous affair. Sleek, lightly haired limbs folded about one another or reserved in a charged proximity. Their very vulnerability in the act or the presence of love helped them transcend gender. Surely.

'Bollocks,' said my fencing friend. 'You're queer or you're straight and anything else is just fucking around. Tell him to get himself sorted.'

We wandered home that night and he got me to promise to stop fucking about. He took the radical position. It wasn't fair to expect people – me, since he was being supportive here – to stand in the background, in their own marginal position and let others – straights, he spat – get away without commitment.

'Bourgeois fucking straights,' he sneered as we walked along the slimy towpath. We went to mine for coffee, and watched Ken Russell's *Women in Love* off video.

On the mantelpiece – and the fencer commented on them – in my gorgeous blue Habitat vase: a squashed bouquet of shocking pink and midnight anemones. Their stalks bent beneath the dull black weight of their hearts, and their vellum petals sodden and bruised.

Walking back at tea-time, Julian made me wait outside Interflora with the Child. I had a feeling what he was up to. A nice gesture. A kiss-off. A promise. The Child flapped his arms to be picked up as it came on to freezing rain and I did so and received for my pains a swift, grateful hug. Julian came out with his shoulders hunched; brandishing his prize. He had two separate parcels of dark, glamorous flowers.

'One for Mummy and one . . .' he gave me mine, 'for you.'

# Sarah J. Evans
## A POWDERED FLY

I WATCHED THEM dance on the beach under the disbelieving eyes of my father. I watched them, their patterned skirts dragging in the water, their hair damp with the joy of it, their faces shiny with youth and with relief. The three of us watched for a while, my father shaking his balding head, my brother whining to go down after them, but only I watched after them, feeling suddenly old, feeling strange, feeling sad.

'What's Mummy doing, Dad?'

'Ralph, come away from the edge,' I said to him, his mouth a sulky pout.

'Daddy? What's Mummy doing?'

He came to look. He came to stare – and he did, for a short while, his cold gaze on their buoyant forms.

'Good grief. You wouldn't believe one of them was dying.'

I looked at him; his head shook from side to side, his mouth was slack with surprise, with distaste, or something.

'I wanna go down,' Ralph sang, the strings of his kite forgotten and tangled, skimming the tops of the grass, strummed by the wind.

I can smell that day, you know. I can smell the sea, and the gorse. I can even smell my father, his aftershave, masked by the sweat, the washing powder my mother used. I can smell the food I ate, the tomato soup, the grainy bread, the strawberry jelly. If I concentrate, I can taste it too, and the air: its salt, its warmth.

Their voices carried up to us, in our make-believe castle, as if they were enemies. Their laughter flew on the wings of

the screeching gulls and fell upon our spines like mourning
does. When they occasionally fell quiet, we breathed a sigh
of relief; that maybe they had returned to being normal –
that they weren't really middle-aged women with hormone
imbalances. And I, hoping I would not turn out like them,
travelled forward in time and hated what I would undoubtedly become.

They splashed about and that water must have been cold.
Even though it looked blue and little white chef's hats rode
the waves – that water must have been cold. I remember
feeling the spray sometimes on the wind, landing on my face,
making me shiver. And when they splashed, they squealed
with joy, with shock, and I, concerned and bewildered, understood nothing. Nothing real anyway.

'Maddie, don't watch them any more, love. Come and
have some of Aunt Vera's special cake.'

'Don't call me Maddie please. My name is Madeline.'

And I did not want anything Aunt Vera had prepared. Her
illness might have contaminated its fibres. The creatures of
disease might have jumped like lice, or fleas, on to the bread,
or the meat, and I would devour it. And die. Maybe before
she herself did.

I remember that Ralph ran past me then, right in front of
me, along the edge of the cliffs. He trod on my foot with
one of his own juvenile feet, trailing his limp kite behind
him, and I had a strange feeling. It took a corkscrew to my
heart and popped a cork. I couldn't believe what I was seeing.
I still can't. I never shall.

I remember my little brother being born. It had to be a boy,
it had to be: how could I possibly go through life with a
sister? Please, I prayed to God every night, please make it
a boy.

It was a hot summer's day, but I wasn't outside, because
Aunt Vera was. Every now and then, I heard her scissors go
snip as she filled every vase in the house with buds and
blooms to welcome my mother and the new baby home. I
went into my parents' room. There, draped on the chair,

were some of her dresses discarded by my father in his hurry, or indecision. He had perhaps taken half a dozen anyway – just in case – and flung the floral flimsiness of the rest over the back of the chair.

She would have known where I had been had I sprayed her perfume on me, so I opened the top of her face powder and dropped in a stunned fly. I thought of my mother's disgusted face, and smiled to myself.

I played with her glass animals. I took them from the shelf in twos, lining them up on the patterned bed cover, calling them by their names, smearing them with greasy fingerprints. When I put them back, I lined them up carefully, so that their shapes matched the dusty outlines on the shiny wood.

Sitting there, in that room, I looked at my face in the mirror. I saw my mother's in it, I saw Aunt Vera's, I saw Aunt Helen's. Outside, the scissors went snip. Mother's dress didn't suit me – the colour was all wrong. I held my head this way and that, marvelling at the stunning curve of my cheekbones. One by one, I polished the glass animals, watching the way the sunlight cascaded through its stuff.

The gravel was a warning. The wheels of father's car ran over their brown backs. Lethargically, I took off Mother's dress and screwed it into a ball, it lay in the corner of the room, discarded and bereft. As I passed the powdered fly, I smiled, then sauntered out to greet the three of them.

My mother's elegance was astounding – I could never take that away from her. She had chosen the lilac dress that Father had taken her, perhaps because it made roses of her complexion, perhaps because it is the colour of hope.

Father brought the baby in, a grin from ear to ear, his hands giants against Ralph's tiny body. They had wrapped him in white, a snowflake fluttering between the adults. Aunt Vera held him then. Already old, her skin sagged drily under her make-up, a smell about her like the air of decay, like something inside her was dying. (Did she know something was wrong with her even then?) Ralph came to me. He was asleep, I remember, as if he were still in the womb, like a little angel in a cloud. Far too innocent, I thought, and far too clean for this house.

'How's Maddie been?' Mother asked.

'A good girl,' said Aunt Vera. 'Mostly.'

But it went unnoticed. I stuck my tongue out at Vera, she half-closed her blue-lidded eyes, bristling like the fly, I thought. The fly even now, covered in my mother's face powder, buzzing around in that sickly scented little box, desperate to get out.

'I want a lolly,' Ralph whined. His father ignored him. 'Dad?'

'Ralph, later. We'll get one later.'

So he ran off with his ball, so small against the trees, so fragile.

'Maddie, come and have some cake, love. It used to be your favourite.'

I looked towards him. He had taken his socks off, his bare feet were bony and ugly, the remains of some prehistoric creature. He was holding out some cake as if it would make me love him. The doily beneath looked limp and soggy.

'My name is not Maddie, and Aunt Vera's cake is certainly not my favourite.' I turned back to watching the distant stony beach where my mother and her sisters frolicked like teenagers.

Their squeals continued as if they had something important to say; something of relevance to the whole world. Their legs splashed in the cool dip of the sea, their skirts clung darkly to their calves. The three of them waved occasionally, yoo-hooing or whooping to get our attention.

But they had my attention. I mean, couldn't they see what had happened, what was happening?

Seawards, on the horizon, a cloud was coming, tinged lilac like mother's dress. It hung at sea-level, like some huge misty mountain, like an island where everyone's dreams would come true – where you could live and forget the world; forget parents and dying aunts, and mother's sandwiches and tiny brothers.

Forget Island. Island Forget.

I turned to look at the rock on the beach where they all had lain, holding hands like a row of little men cut out of paper. All joined up they were, like a row of erratic t's. I watched Aunt Vera who was still there, a gentle t shape, but she was quiet now, gently eroding away, it seemed, with the rock – into pebbles and sand.

Ralph was barely walking when Aunt Vera came to stay.

'Your Auntie Vera's poorly,' Mother said, handing me a stiff ham sandwich. The plate beneath its pale crust was as blue as the sky. 'So she's coming to stay, just for a while, just until she feels better.'

I stared at her, she stared down at the sandwich.

'Does she have to?' I asked. 'Can't she stay with Auntie Helen?'

'She is my sister, Maddie. She's poorly. Helen couldn't cope on her own.'

I started to walk away from her. Anger had made my mouth both big and small.

'You don't want your sandwich, Maddie?'

'She's dying, isn't she?' I said. My mother just looked at me, the plate trembling in her hand. 'Isn't she? And you want her to die here.'

I felt sorry then, sorry that I had reduced my mother to tears. I can hear that plate drop, even now, in moments of terror, in moments of shame. It torments me, travelling at great speed through the past, through the fog, through the everyday, and grips my stomach with its fingers of stone. I remember looking down at the sandwich, but I can't tell you my feelings as my mother ran past me. As she ran, a tear from her eye fell on my cheek, and ran down towards my mouth as if it were my own sadness.

My father came in then, and scooped up the remains of the sandwich. 'I'll make you another one,' he said.

But I just walked away.

The day she did come, I hid away in my bedroom. They pleaded with me, they brought food up to my room, but in the end they left me, each in turn knocking on my door to say goodnight. Behind my door, tears whispered down my cheeks, as if snow was melting behind my eyes. I smelled her disease. It sickened me. Under her made-up face, she seemed to crumble, to sink in upon herself. She became a husk, like a very old person left out in the sun. Her face became compressed, concave almost, as if every night someone pressed on her face as she slept, painting deep purple lines under her eyes.

I often crept into her room, sometimes even when she was in the house. Mother had given her the pot of face powder. It was empty now but for a few trinkets. I took its top off from time to time and wondered where the fly had gone. I never tried her dresses on, I could have caught her disease, in fact I scrubbed myself every time I went in there. I looked through her drawers at all her secrets, I read her soppy letters from men, I fingered her jewellery, I sniffed her make-up, and sampled her scent.

She had glass animals too. But she never cared for hers like my mother did. Hers had fingerprints on even before I touched them. Their ears were thick with dust, as was the shelf they lived on, as was the mirror that reflected them. The longer she infected us with her presence, the thicker the dust became.

One day, she brought those furred creatures to me. My mother sat knitting, one eye on the television.

'These are yours,' she said to me. 'I have no daughter. They are yours now.' I looked at my mother, her face was full of tears. Blinking suddenly, she left the room, her hand to her salted face. Some time later I heard her blowing her nose.

They looked up at me, all those tiny, blind eyes, beseeching, they were, as if they had suddenly met their fate. They stayed in the box for some time, still wearing Aunt Vera's dust, her powder, her disease.

But I had taken them with me that day at the coast, hidden in my belongings, wrapped up in newspaper. I stood on the cliff some way from the picnic. My mother and her sisters were still there then. Ralph's babyish cries grated even from that distance, echoing eerily through my roaring thoughts.

I sat on the grass and unwrapped them. Even my father's newspaper had failed to dislodge the dust, as if it were her ashes. They lay on the grass while the shredded paper blew away, scrap by scrap – an antelope, an otter, and one by one, with all my might, I threw them into the sea. I didn't want them. It was enough that I had her blood in my veins, enough that I had her eyes, or her hair. In they went, a bear, a pig. Let the sea wash you for ever, I thought, let the waves rub away your features so that when I find you again, you are just a pebble, a round, smooth shiny stone.

And when I walked back, they were already down on the beach. Auntie Helen, my mother and Aunt Vera. Everyone knew she was dying. They stopped us in shops and on buses to ask after her. They pressed their good wishes upon us, as if we would pass them on to her. They shook their heads and pursed their lips as if that would encourage us not to cry, to sob, to shudder when the time came.

The three of them were stretched out on a rock, a bright wind playing with the flowery patterns of their skirts, lifting their hair in little flags. I watched them, thinking of what I had just done, knowing it was bad. They stood up, took off their shoes and ran, waving to me, into the cold wavelets, up to their ankles, up to their knees.

'Good grief,' my father said then, 'you wouldn't believe one of them was dying.'

I looked at him, I looked back down. Couldn't he see? Couldn't anyone see? That Aunt Vera was already dead, that her disease, her illness had finally claimed her, and we were finally free from our duty.

It was then that Ralph ran past me, his kite fluttering across my vision, and something caught my eye. The Aunt Vera that lay on the rock looked at me and waved, and her eyes, already pale, already cool, shone like glass, like little glass stones under the afternoon sun.

I shivered. Droplets of spray caught me on the cheek as I watched the ghost, or the spirit, or whatever it was, glide between my mother and her sister Helen, dancing and singing like they were still little girls. Didn't they know she was dead? Didn't they know, when they rose from the rock and took off their shoes, that it was only a part of their sister: that the corpse, the hollow, deceased body, was left on the rock behind them.

Or could it have been the other way around?

Because nobody else saw it. No one else saw the body on the rock. Not my father; he was too busy disbelieving their antics, too busy to notice what was going on about him; not my little brother; not my mother or Auntie Helen.

The dancing girls eventually tired of the cold, lapping sea, and made their way slowly back to the rock, where they lay, once more, joined at the hand. I watched them, still animated for a while, still vital, but then they calmed, their chatter ceased, their limbs were like quenched candles: at once still and quiet.

I sensed the panic before it came. I knew that they would find her dead, limp and cold – her eyes staring, like marbles into clouding sky. I knew mother and Helen would stand up, tugging at Vera, trying to bring her back to life, to stem the flow of her voracious disease, like a tourniquet. But it was much too late.

I knew they would shout up to us, to my father, and find me already staring down at them, struggling to come to terms with the shame and regret that had been uncorked in my heart. And when my mother did look up, our eyes met and struggled – hers wet and huge with fear and loss. I watched her lilac dress billow in the wind that came from Forget Island, I watched Aunt Helen shaking Aunt Vera as if to pull her from a nightmare, I watched my father's portly figure sprint across the pebbles and into my mother's arms as if he would be of some help. I watched my little brother wring his hands, tears sprouting from his cold blue eyes. I took hold of his shoulders and ushered him towards the car.

It was then I felt the first spot of rain. At last, I shuddered, at last it was over.

*

Some time later, we went through her things. Here was the hairbrush I had inspected so very carefully, feathered with Aunt Vera's greying hair, here were her shoes, thankfully too big for me, here was her make-up – for which I was too young. But here, of course, was her box, the powder box which I had handled so often, with the tips of my fingers. I plucked the contents from it with disdain, with reverence, and here inside, I found something I had never seen before. I turned it over in my hand, appalled and amazed. It was covered in the cream face powder that had lived in the little box.

'What have you found, Maddie?' Mother asked me; there was a sweet smile on her lined face.

'A fly,' I told her. 'A glass fly.' I turned it over in my hand, watching the light cascade through its fibres. I looked up at my mother. Glassy tears had sprung from her emerald eyes, autumn's sun sang from the little globes as they ran down her cheeks.

'That was always her favourite,' she said. 'Always.'

# Simon Brittan

## FEMININE ENDINGS

One adolescent memory: a market
Whose fascination lay for me in staring
Sidelong at the seafood-bar frequenters,
Grey men with *Ansells* breath who dipped and hovered
Above white plates of peppered whelks and mussels,
And ogling the vinegary dragon
Straight out of *Amarcord*. After each visit
She heaved her way with devastating hunger
Through stifling nights of gastropodous giants.
Her ruinous smile left me unprepared for
The Real World of non-submarine women –
Though her trail still can send me sliding
At moments of incaution, find me scuttling
At first faint whiff of salt, a true crustacean.

## AMOR VULGARIS

They were right, Ficino and the rest,
In seeing it as a temporary hold
On reason, a huge blotting-out
Of everything they stood for. History
Had been so easy: Arts and Remedies
Had all the answers pat for those who read,
And those who didn't, didn't – down towards
The bottom rungs of nature's ladder, where

God's ways were rather more mysterious,
Pimp and charcoal-burner could at once
Bring *dies irae* on themselves, and claim
Hereditary rights in His Grand Scheme.

But *choose* disorder as a fate? – How sly
To give the inescapable a name
So exculpatory; kind to endow
The most patently transparent lech
With medical respectability.
Spleen and humour of their own accord
Could still enact their havoc preordained,
New sciences set the spheres flying off
At tangents to each other – all of this
Could be accommodated, but to nail
That last embarrassment was easily
The loveliest feather in their velvet caps.

So where does that leave those of us who love
Their lyric doubts but less their cock-sure prose
And have no taste for Systems? Way out here
Towards a universe's rushing edge,
No longer in such awe of gravity,
The comfort definitions brought grows cold
And we make do with what we always knew:
It happens; it can hurt; it sometimes lasts;
If sometimes it can lead to greater things
It usually peters out. It leaves behind
A memory of the power to allow
Rather than to cause things to occur.

# FAMILIAR LANDSCAPE

Encountered first at second or third glance
When middle-distance suddenly becomes
A window-frame or archway on to scenes
Of which the subject's eyes, fixed on the space
Behind our own, will never be aware,
It is where things happen: horses prance
In wooden unison as someone prays
Or dies; elaborate dishes are prepared
While children crawl among the broken eggs;
A dog sleeps in a corner – most of us
Can feel at ease in landscapes such as this.
Familiar, habitable, more than a mere trick
To beautify with chiaroscuro tones
A contour otherwise unbeautiful,
It counteracts all foreground vanities –
The book, the globe, the hand laid on a scroll,
Or worst of all the frightened half-wit son:
*This is my achievement, my bequest*
*To a hapless city. He will no doubt*
*Allow the French to overrun our lands*
*And occupy dependent territories;*
*Get used to the idea.*
                  It takes the edge
Off being sneered at by this *arrivé*
In far-too-heavy clothes, to know that one
So used to power that power itself becomes
Portrayable in curve of mouth or eye,
Should have none over what we choose to see:
A scenery hospitable to those
Who find an option in the ordinary,
Acknowledging the province of the past,
Distinguishing it from the merely dead.

# Alan Brownjohn

## A Defence of Reading

O in the spring the legs were out,
   And they were smooth and trim,
And every eye that saw them felt
   They must be out for him.

O in the spring the legs were out,
   And they were cold and pure,
And chastised the ambitions of
   The eyes that felt so sure

– But they declined to play the game
   The proud legs had begun,
And they could stare down anything
   Faster than legs could run.

Therefore the summer saw the legs
   Give up their cold disguise,
And sun themselves to frazzles for
   The catching of the eyes;

And thus it was the bolder eyes
   Could stare down easily
The flimsy ramparts of the legs,
   And have their victory,

Have it, have it and tire of it
   Much sooner than they thought,

And spend the autumn brooding on
   The truth the legs had taught:

That love is not as hard-won or
   As worthwhile as it looks,
And those who tell you differently
   Have only stared at books.

# Ian Duhig

## A Cnoc Souvenir

The last real fight he had with his brother
their equal grips locked: like a stricken crab
or a beast with two backs they fell, and broke
the cabinet of gifts for their mother,
a Celtic cross in Connemara stone
and her calendar with the Sacred Heart.

They've all died – I couldn't give you death-dates
any more than mine, although I turn it
every year with its prayer and saint
on my calendar, a Cnoc Souvenir
for their mother, her anniversary.

# THE FOLKLORIST

*for Katherine Grant*

She pulled its fur up to the rabbit's ears
past the red torc left by her snare,

and said some bodysnatcher fell
hoisting kin of hers over yon church wall;

how the slipknot slipped to his neck
as he slipped forward and the corpse slipped back

all cradled from sight by their yew-thicket,
and would I like a lucky foot?

# Gavin Ewart

## AUDEN'S JUVENILIA REVISITED

### 1  CRUSH

I sedulously imitate
Edward Thomas, Hardy –
I wouldn't use a word like 'late' –
The 'Hardy' word is 'tardy'.

I wouldn't want to write like Pope
Or Rochester or Sedley –
To lie in bed's my dearest hope
With lovely Robert Medley.

### 2  RURAL

All I want's the pianissimo roll on a bugger's gong
And the soaring of the soul in a blackbird's song
And the darkness of the mole when the words go wrong
As Solomon grew wise while talking with his Queens as they
    walked along.

I want the old dry-eyed dreams of the empty barn,
not the blood-sucking streams, the Somme and the Marne,
where Kindness scarcely redeems, or the deep unlettered tarn.
And I want some Wordsworthian Inversion to fiddle with,
    cobble and darn.

216

I want to lean on a gate, just biting a straw,
A genius soon or late – with Frost I'll thaw –
I've got a lot on my plate, though it's still quite crude and
　　raw,
Including Edith Sitwell and the rustic rooks that so crabbily
　　caw.


## 3　ANTHROPO

　　　Tits, sharpening their saws, taunt Mars
　　　With the Venuses' pert bras.
　　　There's something priapic and odd
　　　In the stone-smiling garden god.

　　　Crocuses are always phallic,
　　　Old Kings, dolichocephalic,
　　　Give an Easter Island nod
　　　To the stiff erotic rod.

　　　Everywhere the lovers' moan is
　　　Hot for lingams, yings, yangs, yonis.
　　　Edith and Tom make quite a row,
　　　The smart ones with the Golden Bough.

W. H. Auden, *Juvenilia: Poems 1922–28* (Faber & Faber, 1994).
'All I want's the pianissimo roll', etc., see p. 203. 'Tits sharpening
their saws', see p. 183.

# David Harsent

## THE BLACK MUSEUM

'You'll see the garotte is a noose of cord
with a single knot that sits
under the gullet. You give a twist
to bring your man up short, then give a twist

to straighten his back and fetch a wet to his eyes,
the iris plain
like a roundel in the white, and give a twist
to start a crack through the larynx. Another twist

will open that hairline up to more of a fissure
you might call it, about which time
his face gets that red-cum-black
of a summer damson, and all the breath you've trapped

is unpicking the stuff of his lungs, *tik-tik*,
and soon enough you'd see,
were you cleric or medic or some such scrutineer
a great, fat laugh

jump up to his face, and then how his teeth
were grouted pink and how the tip of his tongue
could fall as far as – ' while all the time
the waxwork man was looking me straight in the eye

backed-up to the strangling-post
but set on a plinth with his executioner
handy to take up the slack – yes, looked me full in the eye
as if to say, 'I can vouch for that,

or some of it, but what I remember best
is three-steps-up-four-down
with a passageway in between that brought me out
from my lockup to a yard cleggy with moss,

then a short, steep tunnel, a bull-run,
down to this bunker. All the way he laid
a hand to the back of my neck
like a parent bringing home a wayward child . . .

Which doesn't mean I was special to him, not at all,
one of, oh, a dozen or more
that week, a dozen the next,
all tested for truth, helped with the truth, though it's true

I couldn't give a shred of it back
nor drum up a lie
except you would laugh out loud, like him, to hear it
then bring me in disappointment to the post.'

At about that moment, someone pulled the plugs
on the hubbub of dungeony
SFX, leaving just
the stereophonic *clop* of a clepsydra

and a dusty light
that fell straight between amber and umber
to give him a liverish look, apart from the touch
of rouge to his cheek, apart

DAVID HARSENT

from the dark of his eye, which even now held mine
as a door slammed somewhere
back towards the street. 'Hear that? That's how it was,
    that's how
it always started. If it starts

again, don't watch.' Just then that other man
who stood at the first man's back was measuring off
a good arm's length
when he seemed to notice me, and might have moved

a step closer, a step or two, wanting to say
'Is it cleric or medic or some such? Or else
what in Christ's name,
tell me, what in all hell could you ever want with us?'

# THE CURATOR

Everything under glass and still as stone. Where an item was
    out on loan, a photograph gave its likeness: at a glance
    you'd own they were little but horn and bone. 'I'm busy
    just now,' he said, 'why not go on alone? You can't get
    easily lost. Those arrows will bring you home.'

> *This is the razor that turned on its owner,*
> *this is the finger that fired the first shot,*
> *this is the flower that poisoned its wearer,*
> *this is the riddle that started the rot.*

But when I turned the corner, he was there; of course he was.
    'Aren't we a pair?' he laughed, as if climbing the stair
    in step, as if breathing that mouldy air, might make
    us sudden partners in Truth or Dare. He thumbed the
    catalogue; the sheer size of it made me stare: the weight
    of loss. 'Is it something particular?' As if he didn't know.
    'Is it something awry or unfair?'

220

> *This is the poodle that bit Aristotle,*
> *this is the tongue with the strawberry wart,*
> *this is the rattle they found in the shtetl,*
> *this is the cutie who wouldn't abort.*

He stood at the door to see me off, and wore the cloths of
frailty like the Godless poor: which fooled me not one
bit. 'You've seen damn-all, you know, but if you're
sure – ' He snicked the ID off my coat and tore the lapel
a token inch. 'A souvenir . . .' Now I no longer wore my
face and name. 'It's queer,' he shook my hand, 'this way
or that, they all come back for more.'

> *This is the tumour that grew like a rumour,*
> *this is the rafter and this is the rope,*
> *this is the drama that buried the dreamer,*
> *this is the hope beyond hope beyond hope.*

# Douglas Houston

## SUNDAY ON THE CUILLIN

*for Alan Isherwood*

I am becoming wild up here
Among the lichened gabbro,
With my minor infections
And unruly appetites.
I have shed the customary,
Lived on the like of dried fruit and oatcakes,
Gulped at the pale turquoise water
That spills in sunlight from the high pools.

Now I am up on that black ridge
Flanked with ageing snowfields,
Whose prospect had me desolate
On arrival.

As the sky's engines haul on worse weather,
I'm about to meet Mr Isherwood,
Who knows the way,
Who forgets it undaunted,
Who is neither too reserved nor too friendly,
And is the gift of my place in a pair.

We proceed in sleet
Down the long rock wedge
Of Sgurr nan Gillean's west ridge
To halt at a gap with lethal drops;

I lead through in about five moves,
Acquiring half way the knowledge
That panic is the option not to be chosen
And am glad to see you not choose it.

Well matched, indeed, Mr Isherwood,
Our bits of talk, small swops of food,
Three summits plus the sodden miles
Across the moor back to your car,
Where names at last occur to us
And your whisky flask softens weariness
To ease adrift in the blood's warm stream.
Goodbye, Mr Isherwood, driving to mass
Twelve miles away and in a hurry.
The solitude you civilised resumes,
Better for knowing you, poised on the sense
That we'll probably never meet again,
Though tracks and chances might allow we will,
Some other day, some other hill.

# Maggie Gee

## THE KEEPER OF THE GATE
*Extract from a novel in progress*

### PROLOGUE

**THOMAS IS AFRAID OF THE TWENTY-FIRST CENTURY**

THERE'S TOO MUCH noise, everywhere. It gets into your head. It drives out the voices. I like my voices. I need my voices.

Sometimes they come from far away. Sometimes they come from long ago.

I have tried ear-plugs. They're a disappointment. The foam ones rustle like the sea, and the wax ones feel like a cold in the head and sit on the desk like overchewed gum or tiny pink organs removed from mice, not the impression I want to give if Selina suddenly knocks on the door. If only she would. But she's still at work.

I wonder if the shouting woke her last night? Boys in the street, or that Scottish couple . . . Too young to be married. But everyone's young. And they'll all still be young when the next century starts. So maybe they aren't afraid of it. I am afraid of it. Yes, I am.

It's coming. It's coming. It's been coming for ages, but this time it means it. And I'm scared. I was born in the middle of the last one. A century that's sliding into the past. It seemed so new once, 'the twentieth century'. With everything modern; world wars, machines (and infertility, and chewing-gum, and teenagers, films, supermarkets, walking on the moon . . . will all those things look, well, *nineteenth-*

*century?*) Will my century go dark like a spoon? Will it all be . . .

*like something from the last century?*

And is the next one really for me?

I'm not that old, you see. I have all my hair and Selina – a sensational-looking girl in the flat downstairs, I mean woman, you're not allowed to call them girls, well really she's a babe, they call them *babes* these days, which I think is vaguely disgusting – a *very beautiful* young woman down-stairs considers me her friend, not too old to talk to, not too old to hang out with, not boring, not finished, not antique. I'm not, you see. Not old. I wear jeans and overshirts and swear a lot and don't have a straight job (though sometimes I think I might like a straight job – but I mustn't say that; glad to be free). I could pass for thirty-five, Selina tells me, and yet . . .

Selina. The first Selina I've known. The name is cat-like and sweet, like her. Honey-tongued, delicate, purring, golden . . . very groomed, is Selina, in the mornings, when I'm lucky enough to meet her on the stairs, when I'm feeling good enough to wake before eight-thirty (not often), but meeting her is . . . *memorable*. Stumbling back upwards with my milk and my *Guardian* and my pyjamas under my clothes, I sometimes hear her come tip-tipping down in her brisk little booties with their neat gold eyelets . . .

A dozen gold eyelets, slim pale ankles. I gaze on her feet before I meet her eyes. She smells of cinnamon, apples, musk, and soap and cornflakes and cleanliness. I probably smell of old beer and bad breath but she still blesses me with her celestial smile, always slightly surprised, as if she thought she was on the moon and has just discovered that someone else lives there. 'Oh,' she says, breathless, pleased, I really believe that she's pleased to see me – 'Oh, hallo. *You're* up early.' As if she wasn't always up early. She has a real job, of course she's up. A job so hard I shudder to think of it, teaching hordes of savage young children. How can they ever appreci-ate her? I smile at her, her Man on the Moon, and imagine them trampling her sensitive feet. I could protect her. I could look after her.

Actually of course I have nothing to offer. A bad track record with relationships, a three-bed flat in a seedy part of London, a high-ish income that I still overspend, a guilty slither of credit cards, a reputation among a few thousand people she doesn't know or care about, a second-hand car, a gift with words, my amazing penis, currently unused, needing tenderness, loving, licking . . .

I never think like that when she's with me. It makes me ashamed to think like that. Sweetie. Selina. Her . . . sweetness. Yes.

I wonder if she heard the shouting last night. I wonder if she lay in the dark afraid. I thought about her. I wished she were with me. Then neither of us would have been afraid. Noise in the day is merely annoying (or hugely, murderously annoying) but noise at night, when you don't know who's there, shouting, screaming, running feet or a door that keeps banging and isn't a door but the sound of a soft body thumping on walls – at night those noises are outriders of a fearful future. A new dark ages.

(Or perhaps she isn't frightened; perhaps the young *aren't*. She seems to shine with confidence. As if anyone on earth would be pleased to see her, which I think is a pretty sound assessment, any male person on earth, at least, I and my heterosexual brothers, great horny ranks of us, bursting with hormones . . .

One shabby man in a room alone. I wish I had brothers, I wish I had friends. Darren's my brother, and my friend . . . my friend, my enemy. Half a world away. If he saw Selina, he'd be jealous.)

Because she does like me. It isn't an illusion. She nearly always asks me for something, or offers me something, not just 'Hallo'. 'I'm not back till eight and I'm out of coffee, if I pop round could you lend us some?'

I say 'yes' to everything, of course, although visits from Selina disturb my work, disturb my sleep, disturb my . . .

safety. The safety of being unobserved. So I can slowly moulder without anyone noticing.

Her eyes are large, unkindly young, the whites unreasonably white, dazzling me in my fug of greyness, my morning moleskins, hangovers, headaches. She looks at me, and it cuts like a knife. She looks so kindly, but the damage is done. I'm caught in the light, exposed, unmasked, and all of a sudden I'm out on the runway.

It's freezing cold. I have lost my pyjamas, which she probably noticed were stuffed under my jumper. I've lost my voice. I can't call for help, or explain the past, and why I wasted it. I'm here and now. There is no escape. She's no longer with me. Of course she isn't. Already boarded. Seat-belt on.

The year 2000 has me in its sights, a vast jet plane, electronic eyes blazing, getting up speed, beginning to scream, screaming, blaring, bearing down on me, and everyone's aboard, Selina's aboard, I can see her small heart-shaped face at a window, but I'm trapped outside, on the rainy tarmac, frozen in the light, seen for what I am.

Small. Naked. Thickened. Scruffy. A matchstick man, wadded with flesh. Dated. Outdated. I no longer register. The instrument panel denies I'm there, and it's suddenly upon me, blinding, deafening . . .

And after it's gone, nothing left on the runway.

I've disappeared as if I'd never been.

Melodramatic, of course. But what do you expect, I'm forty this year. Forty years old; no wife, no kids, no house, no salary, no pension scheme. I'm self-employed, which is actually quite *cutting-edge*, if you believe what the papers say. All I can say is, it feels very chilly, when I'm not sure the future will buy what I do.

I have my freedom, though. I am free to sit here in my sun-yellow flat on a brilliant winter morning, dazzled by the view, its clarity, its razor brightness, the rust-red roofs, such gleam, such detail, the sharp green of the Park beyond – and wonder, what will become of me. Am I any use? Any good to anyone?

I write. That is the point of me. But writing isn't what it

was. The literacy figures are going down. More and more notices don't have words. Airports, stations, guidebooks, computers . . . Pictures are easier, and more fun.

I think so too. I don't deny it. Pictures let you make up your own mind – an illusion, of course, since someone chose the picture – but words can be very, well, *controlling*. Ants on pages, marching in lines, from the Boss Intelligence towards the poor reader.

And will my column ever get there, I wonder?

Because if it won't, then what's the point?

Sometimes that line between the centuries, that intake of breath before we get to the next, seems to me like a giant chasm between cliffs, and everything will tumble down the gap, word after word, my little black lemmings . . .

And I shall come bumbling after, poor author, poor preposterous lemming-farmer, trying to leap across the gap but taking off badly, flailing, plunging . . .

Thank God for that window of green. That well of green in my urban view. I bought this flat because of the Park. And even human beings, when you catch a flash of them, walking their dogs, trampling the flowers . . . human beings look all right, in the Park. Like animals, in a living world. You can't predict what they'll do, in there, like you can when they're queuing at the bus-stop.

That boy running up the hill like a sprinter . . . Yellow hair, catching the sun. Running across the green. I sit so long I'm forgetting how to run . . .

Green, green, a wetness, thirsty. Blades of grass, creeping across . . . Something bright, young, cutting. What does it remind me of, that yellow hair . . .?

Just dozing, of course. Eyes losing focus.

Darren's too busy to look out of the window. I don't suppose he ever dreams or dozes or doubts himself or feels afraid. But he must be forty too, if I am. Darren's forty. The golden boy.

He's a journalist. They'll get over the chasm. Effortlessly, as of right. There are bridges with five lanes of traffic for them. The twenty-first century will belong to them, the instant experts, the four-a.m.-faxers. The bloody world belongs to them. He inhabits the world. LA, Hong Kong, wherever he files his copy from . . .

He lives in the world. I live in Hillesden.

But he'll have to come back, now his father's ill. And we'll meet again. And compete again. At least it won't be for women this time. Darren's just married for the third time. To someone younger, glossier . . . but I don't know that. I just assume that Darren can only move on and up . . . His Mum didn't seem to know much about it. May Brittain, my surrogate mother.

– I wish she were mine. I'm jealous of him.

Ridiculous really. Two turkey cocks. And we're both aware it's ridiculous. Just because we were at school together. Just because we were the two bright boys. I shall never stop wanting to show him I'm best. Even if he's richer, with more children, more wives . . . Even if everybody knows his name. Which is *not* his name, the name he uses, *Dale Brittain*, the Voice of the Left . . .

The bloody left. Left us high and dry. Left itself behind in the twentieth century. Give Darren his due, he hasn't changed sides, even now when the old side's been disbanded.

But *Dale* . . . he'll always be Darren to me. We fought together against Sawyer's gang when they were stealing the little kids' dinner-money . . . really we were fighting to see who was best. Who could do best at fighting the baddies. Darren will always be the one to beat. Nothing will change.

*No, something will change.*

A voice as clear as the piercing note of the Park Keeper's whistle blowing time.

*Something will happen. Someone will die.*

I'm alone too much. It can drive you crazy.

Pull myself together. Get on with my day. Do two more pages, then go to the hospital. Buy some grapes and go to the hospital.

It doesn't seem believable that Alfred's in hospital, Alfred

Brittain who's never been ill. He used to say he'd never had a day off work. Up every morning at half-past five to open the Park, outside all day whatever the weather. A man of iron, Darren's Dad. Darren's Dad, the Park Keeper. Round here, Alfred's more famous than Darren. Everyone in Hillesden knows him.

The Brittains doted on Darren, of course, but he often treated them like dirt. Even his mum, who was nice to all of us hungry boys, awkward and ravenous, piling in for tea after a football match . . . Alfred could be a cross old bastard, but she was a darling. Still is a darling. May Brittain, with her slow sweet smile and her dry sense of humour and passion for books. I always thought she did Darren's English homework, but I was probably wrong. And yet, we have so much in common . . . We both love words, in our different way.

How curious, to live for words, ghostly things, marks on paper.

I suppose that's what I've done. If I died tomorrow, that's all I would leave. Maybe I thought they would make me safe, because they'd remain, they're bigger than us. Tiny symbols, but bigger than us. Because they go outside this room. Because they're not . . . personal. Not when you're writing for thousands of people.

Selina knows about Egyptian writing. She's teaching her kids to write hieroglyphics, though quite a few of them still can't write English. But Egypt's on the National Curriculum.

She's lent me the Egyptian *Book of the Dead*. I think I'd have been happier in ancient Egypt . . . especially if I could have lived with Selina. Almost nothing changed in three thousand years, and the scribes lorded it over everyone. Five thousand years later, I can sit here and read them. The spells they wrote to place in the mummy, to carry the dead back into the day . . .

Five thousand years! Such tiny symbols!

Crossing the bar from century to century effortlessly, in their ship of gold . . .

*

So two fat fingers, Millennium! Thoth, God of Writing, be with me now. Ibis-headed god, as the flat gets dark, as the darkness pools around my desk, bless my pages, keep them safe, bend your long elegant beak above me. On your strong back bear us away, five thousand years into the future . . .

   – Oh, I'm so glad we can take Selina.

## MAY

*Where do we come from? Where do we go? Why are they here, these waves of words . . .?*

May read, as usual, before she went out.

First she got herself completely ready. Alfred's pyjamas, freshly laundered, neatly folded in a plastic bag inside another, larger plastic bag that held today's *Daily Mirror* and a quarter of extra strong mints, just in case he should be feeling a bit better, just in case he should fancy something. It was comforting, getting the bag together. It meant she could still look after Alfred, though she also experienced the usual sense of boredom; women spent their lives looking after men. And even that tiny skin-tag of irritation was comforting, because entirely familiar. Not the new blankness, the thin wind of freedom. The house was so much colder since he had gone.

She was completely ready, hat on, coat fastened, twenty minutes too early to leave for the hospital, even if she walked slowly, even if she dawdled, not that she would dawdle on a day like this, even if she stepped into the Park to have a quick look at the café and the flower-beds so she could report to Alfred later. Each day she had half-meant to do it; each day she had found herself unable to, because she couldn't bear to see the Park without Alfred. Without the hope of seeing Alfred . . .

Without the hope of seeing Alfred come hurrying down one of the distant paths, trim, narrow-shouldered in his old brown coat and the new check cap she had bought him for

Christmas, eyes turned away from where he was going to follow the deeds of some child or dog. Then she might hear him shout or whistle to recall the wrongdoer to order. Not today. That piercing whistle. The Park Keeper's whistle which had sometimes pained her like the sound of chalk pulled the wrong way across a blackboard now seemed in its absence an arrow of light, a clear white line shooting out across the darkness.

Twenty minutes early. So she sat in her chair as she had done every day this week and began to read, clumsy in her coat, catching its heavy woollen sleeves on the pages.

And again she noticed a difference. It was normally evening when she read and Alfred would be there, rustling his newspaper or clicking the cards as he laid out a game of patience, and he always said 'What are you reading?' in a grumpy, almost affronted way, as if he had failed to entertain her, as if she was rejecting him, and she always made herself answer cheerfully, she always ignored his tone of voice and said 'Auden, dear,' or 'Catherine Cookson, dear,' as if he might really want to know; and it always annoyed her, always, always, though he had been doing it for nearly half a century. And now he had stopped, and May found she missed it. 'Tennyson, dear,' she whispered in the silence, slipping inside the entirely familiar Victorian patterns in their long cool scrolls, the beloved rhythms of her other Alfred:

> He watches from his mountain walls
> And like a thunderbolt he falls.

But she couldn't concentrate; *Alfred, Alfred.*

It was still too early, but she picked up her bag, checked its contents and the angle of her hat (for she wanted him to be proud of her; appearances mattered a lot to Alfred), slipped in her book as an afterthought although she knew she'd have no chance to read it, and let herself out into the January wind.

She always liked to have a book in her bag. In case she got stuck. In case she got lost. Or did she feel lost without her books? There wasn't any point, but she liked to have one with her, a gentle weight nudging her shoulder, keeping her company through the wind, making her more solid, more substantial, less likely to be blown away, less alone. More – a person.

Perhaps it was a little piece of the past, since her books all seemed to belong to the past, a far distant past when she was thin and romantic and in love with – what had she been in love with? Hope. Dreams. The world before her, when everything was still before her. Life, which seemed to mean happiness then, a word for the future, not the past. Not 'Life gets you down,' or 'That's life, I'm afraid,' but *life, life, hope, poetry* . . . Maybe it was words she had been in love with.

The harsh wind battered her hands and face, pummelling her ears with great noisy blows, and she felt she would never get in through the high red gate-posts of the hospital with their ugly array of cardboard notices, temporary things with clumsy writing . . . What was she but another piece of scrap, blown willy-nilly across the forecourt? Would the main entrance be closed again because of the endless building works? (They were building new bits all the time, but it never got finished, and the rest was falling down.) She tried to ask a nurse on her way home but the light was already beginning to fade and the wind blew hard between her teeth and turned her voice to a soundless whisper, so the woman passed by oblivious.

I don't exist. I no longer exist. When Alfred dies, I'll be nothing, nothing . . . I couldn't even read, today. The words were there, but they didn't help.

I love them still . . . *idyll, ambergris* . . . but where do they come from? Where do they go? Maybe they're no more solid than us. Dirk only reads his computer magazines, Darren never liked poetry, Shirley reads mostly catalogues, so who'll have my books, after I'm gone . . .?

> *Twilight and evening bell,*
> *And after that the dark!*

*And may there be no sadness of farewell,*
*When I embark . . .*

Onward, onward. Over the threshold. Into the frightening new place which was suddenly part of their life together . . .

Part of their new life apart. As essential to their life as the Park had been. A place where he must go alone, a place where she could only visit . . .

But she shouldn't be frightened of this place. It must be one of the last good places. May told herself, *this is here for us. We fought the last war for places like this. Hospitals and parks and schools. Not concentration camps, like the other lot had.*

A hospital was a place to share. Where all could come in their hour of trouble. The light was harsh, but it shone for all . . . (though some of the bulbs were dead, she had noticed. Broken glass was replaced with hardboard . . .)

She stood for a moment, blinking, breathing.

She would get there first, because she loved him. Proud always to be the first. She stood by herself in the fluorescent sweep of the hospital foyer, patting her hair, slipping off her coat to show the blue dress, for blue was always his favourite colour . . . She saw herself reflected in the glass of the doors, astonishingly tiny, a little old lady, *but I'm not old, nor particularly small . . .*

Soon other figures would come out of the shadows, out of the dark with their bags and bundles, their flowers and sighs and shruggings-off of coats and scarves and hats and gloves, their nervous smiles, their frowns, their whispers, biting their lips, blind in the light. Newcomers. Latecomers.

May set off briskly, ahead of them.

# William Trevor

## TIMOTHY'S BIRTHDAY

THEY MADE THE usual preparations. Charlotte bought a small leg of lamb, picked purple broccoli and sprigs of mint. All were Timothy's favourites, purchased every year for April 23rd, which this year was a Thursday. Odo ensured that the gin had not gone too low: a gin and tonic, and then another one, was what Timothy liked. Odo did not object to that, did not in fact object to obtaining the gin specially, since it was not otherwise drunk in the house.

They were a couple in their sixties who had scarcely parted from each other in the forty-two years of their marriage. Odo was tall, thin as a straw, his bony features receding into a freckled dome on which little hair remained. Charlotte was small and still pretty, her grey hair drawn back and tidy, her eyes an arresting shade of blue. Timothy was their only child.

Deciding on a fire, Odo chopped up an old seed-box for kindling and filled a basket with logs and turf. The rooks were cawing and chattering in the high trees, their nests already in place – more of them this year, Odo noticed, than last. The cobbles of the yard were still damp from a shower. Grass, occasionally ragwort or a dock, greened them in patches. Later perhaps, when Timothy had gone, he'd go over them with weed-killer, as he did every year in April. The outhouses that bounded the yard required attention also, their wooden doors rotted away at the bottom, the white-wash of their stucco gone grey, brambles growing through their windows. Odo resolved that this year he would rectify matters, but knew, even as the thought occurred, that he would not.

'Cold?' Charlotte asked him as he passed through the kitchen and he said yes, a little chilly outside. The kitchen was never cold because of the range. A long time ago they had been going to replace it with a secondhand Aga Charlotte had heard about, but when it came to the point Odo hadn't wanted to and anyway there hadn't been the funds.

In the drawing-room Odo set the fire, crumpling up the pages of old account books because no newspaper was delivered to the house and one was rarely bought: they had the wireless and the television, which kept them up with things. The account books were of no use to anyone, belonging entirely to the past, to the time of Odo's grandfather and generations earlier. Kept for the purpose in a wall-cupboard by the fireplace, their dry pages never failed to burn well. *Slating: £2 15s.*, Odo read as he arranged the kindling over the slanted calligraphy. He struck a match and stacked on logs and turf. Rain spattered against the long-paned windows; a sudden gust of wind tumbled something over in the garden.

Charlotte pressed rosemary into the slits she'd incised in the lamb. She worked swiftly, from long experience knowing just what she was doing. She washed the grease from her fingertips under a running tap and set aside what remained of the rosemary, even though it was unlikely that she would have a use for it: she hated throwing things away.

The oven was slow; although it was still early, the meat would have to go in within half an hour, and potatoes to roast – another Timothy favourite – at eleven. The trifle, gooey with custard and raspberry jam and jelly – a nursery pudding – Charlotte had made the night before. When Timothy came he chopped the mint for the mint sauce, one of the first of his childhood tasks. He'd been a plump little boy then.

'I can't go,' Timothy said in the flat that had recently been left to him by Mr Kinnally.

Eddie didn't respond. He turned the pages of the *Irish Times*, wishing it were something livelier, the *Star* or the *Express*. With little interest he noticed that schools' entrance tests were to be abolished and that there was to be a canine clean-up, whatever that was, in Limerick.

'I'll drive you down,' he offered then. His own plans were being shattered by this change of heart on the part of Timothy, but he kept the annoyance out of his voice. He had intended to gather his belongings together and leave as soon as he had the house to himself: a bus out to the N4, the long hitch-hike, then start all over again. 'No problem to drive you down,' he said. 'No problem.'

The suggestion wasn't worth a reply, Timothy considered. It wasn't even worth acknowledgement. No longer plump at thirty-three, Timothy wore his smooth fair hair in a ponytail. When he smiled, a dimple appeared in his left cheek, a characteristic he cultivated. He was dressed, this morning, as he often was, in flannel trousers and a navy-blue blazer, with a plain blue tie in the buttoned-down collar of his plain blue shirt.

'I'd get out before we got there,' Eddie offered. 'I'd go for a walk while you was inside.'

'What I'm saying is I can't face it.'

There was another silence then, during which Eddie sighed without making a sound. He knew about the birthday tradition because as the day approached there had been a lot of talk about it. The house called Coolattin had been described to him: four miles from the village of Baltinglass, a short avenue from which the entrance gates had been removed, a faded green hall-door, the high grass in the garden, the abandoned conservatory. And Timothy's people – as Timothy always called them – had been as graphically presented: Charlotte's smile and Odo's solemnity, their fondness for one another evident in how they spoke and acted, their fondness for Coolattin. Charlotte cut what remained of Odo's hair, and Timothy said you could tell. And you could tell, even when they were not in their own surroundings, that they weren't well-to-do: all they wore was old. Hearing it described, Eddie had visualised in the drawing-room the bagatelle table between the windows and Odo's ancestor in oils over the fire-place, the buttoned green sofa, the rugs that someone had once brought back from India or Egypt. Such shreds of grace and vigour from a family's past took similar form in the dining-room that was these days used only once a year, on April 23rd, and in the hall and on the staircase wall, where further portraits hung. Except for the one occupied by Odo and Charlotte, the bedrooms were musty, with patches of grey damp on the ceilings, and plaster fallen away. Timothy's, in which he had not slept for fifteen years, was as he'd left it, but in one corner the wallpaper had billowed out and now was curling away from the surface. The kitchen, where the television and the wireless were, where Odo and Charlotte ate all their meals except for lunch on Timothy's birthday, was easily large enough for this general purpose: a dresser crowded with crockery and a lifetime's odds and ends, a long, scrubbed table on the flagged floor, with upright kitchen chairs around it. As well, there were the two armchairs Odo had brought in from the drawing-room, a washing-machine Timothy had given his mother, wooden draining-boards on either side of the sink, ham hooks in the panelled ceiling, and a row of bells on springs above the door to the scullery. A cheerful place, that kitchen, Eddie estimated, but Timothy said it was part and parcel, whatever he meant by that.

'Would you go, Eddie? Would you go down and explain, say I'm feeling unwell?'

Eddie hesitated. Then he said:

'Did Mr Kinnally ever go down there?'

'No, of course he didn't. It's not the same.'

Eddie walked away when he heard that reply. Mr Kinnally had been far too grand to act as a messenger in that way. Mr Kinnally had given Timothy birthday presents: the chain he wore on his wrist, shoes and pullovers. 'Now, I don't want you spending your money on me,' Timothy had said a day or two ago. Eddie, who hadn't been intending to, didn't even buy a card.

In the kitchen he made coffee, real coffee from Bewley's, measured into the percolator, as Timothy had shown him. Instant gave you cancer, Timothy maintained. Eddie was a burly youth of nineteen, with curly black hair to which he daily applied gel. His eyes, set on a slant, gave him a furtive air, accurately reflecting his nature, which was a watchful one, the main chance being never far out of his sights. When he got away from the flat in Mountjoy Street he intended to go steady for a bit, maybe settle down with some decent girl, maybe have a kid. Being in the flat had suited him for the five months he'd been here, even if – privately – he didn't much care for certain aspects of the arrangement. Once, briefly, Eddie had been apprenticed to a plumber, but he hadn't much cared for that either.

He arranged cups and saucers on a tray and carried them to the sitting-room, with the coffee and milk, and a plate of croissants. Timothy had put a CD on, the kind of music Eddie didn't care for but never said so, sonorous and grandiose. The hi-fi was Bang and Olufsen, the property of Mr Kinnally in his lifetime, as everything in the flat had been.

'Why not?' Timothy asked, using the telecommander on the arm of his chair to turn the volume down. 'Why not, Eddie?'

'I couldn't do a thing like that. I'll drive you – '

'I'm not going down.'

Timothy reduced the volume further. As he took the cup of coffee Eddie offered him, his two long eye-teeth glistened the way they sometimes did, and the dimple formed in his cheek.

'All I'm asking you to do is pass a message on. I'd take it as a favour.'

'The phone – '

'There's no phone in that place. Just say I couldn't make it due to not feeling much today.'

Timothy broke in half a croissant that had specks of bacon in it, the kind he liked, that Eddie bought in Fitz's. A special favour, he softly repeated, and Eddie sensed more pressure in the words. Timothy paid, Timothy called the tune. Well, two can play at that game, Eddie said to himself, and calculated his gains over the past five months.

The faded green hall-door, green also on the inside, was sealed up because of draughts. You entered the house at the back, crossing the cobbled yard, to the door that led to the scullery.

'He's here,' Charlotte called out when there was the sound of a car, and a few minutes later, as Odo arrived in the kitchen from the hall, there were footsteps in the scullery passage and then a hesitant knock on the kitchen door. Since Timothy never knocked, both thought this odd, and odder still when a youth they did not know appeared.

'Oh,' Charlotte said.

'He's off colour,' the youth said. 'A bit naff today. He asked me would I come down and tell you.' The youth paused, and added then: 'On account you don't have no phone.'

Colour crept into Charlotte's face, her cheeks becoming pink. Illness worried her.

'Thank you for letting us know,' Odo said stiffly, the dismissive note in his tone willing this youth to go away again.

'It's nothing much, is it?' Charlotte asked, and the youth said seedy, all morning in the toilet, the kind of thing you wouldn't trust yourself with on a car journey. His name was Eddie, he explained, a friend of Timothy's. Or more, he added, a servant really, depending how you looked at it.

Odo tried not to think about this youth. He didn't want Charlotte to think about him, just as for so long he hadn't wanted her to think about Mr Kinnally. 'Mr Kinnally died,' Timothy said on this day last year, standing not far from where the youth was standing now, his second gin and tonic on the go. 'He left me everything, the flat, the Rover, the lot.' Odo had experienced relief that this elderly man was no longer alive, but had been unable to prevent himself from considering the inheritance ill-gotten. The flat in Mountjoy Street, well placed in Dublin, had had its Georgian plasterwork meticulously restored, for Mr Kinnally had been that

240

kind of person. They'd heard about the flat, its contents too, just as Eddie had heard about Coolattin. Timothy enjoyed describing things.

'His tummy played up a bit once,' Charlotte was saying with a mother's recall. 'We had a scare. We thought appendicitis. But it wasn't in the end.'

'He'll rest himself, he'll be all right.' The youth was mumbling, not meeting the eye of either of them. Shifty, Odo considered, and dirty-looking. The shoes he wore, once white, the kind of sports shoes you saw about these days, were filthy now. His black trousers hung shapelessly; his neck was bare, no sign of a shirt beneath the red sweater that had some kind of animal depicted on it.

'Thank you,' Odo said again.

'A drink?' Charlotte suggested. 'Cup of coffee? Tea?'

Odo had known that would come. No matter what the circumstances, Charlotte could never help being hospitable. She hated being thought otherwise.

'Well . . .' the youth began, and Charlotte said:

'Sit down for a minute.' Then she changed her mind and suggested the drawing-room because it was a pity to waste the fire.

Odo didn't feel angry. He rarely did with Charlotte. 'I'm afraid we haven't any beer,' he said as they passed through the hall, both coffee and tea having been rejected on the grounds that they would be troublesome to provide, although Charlotte had denied that. In the drawing-room what there was was the sherry that stood near the bagatelle, never touched by either of them, and Timothy's Cork gin, and two bottles of tonic.

'I'd fancy a drop of Cork,' the youth said. 'If that's OK.'

Would Timothy come down another day? Charlotte wanted to know. Had he said anything about that? It was the first time his birthday had been missed. It was the one occasion they spent together, she explained.

'Cheers!' the youth exclaimed, not answering the questions, appearing to Odo to be simulating denseness. 'Great,' he complimented when he'd sipped the gin.

241

'Poor Timothy!' Charlotte settled into the chair she always occupied in the drawing-room, to the left of the fire. The light from the long-paned windows fell on her neat grey hair and the side of her face. One of them would die first, Odo had thought again in the night, as often he did now. He wanted it to be her; he wanted to be the one to suffer the loneliness and the distress. It would be the same for either of them, and he wanted to be the one who had to bear the painful burden.

Sitting forward, on the edge of the sofa, Eddie felt better when the gin began to glow.

'Refreshing,' he said. 'A drop of Cork.'

The day Mr Kinnally died there were a number of them in the flat. Timothy put the word out and they came that night, with Mr Kinnally still stretched out on his bed. In those days Eddie used to come in the mornings to do the washing-up, after Mr Kinnally had taken a fancy to him in O'Connell Street. An hour or so in the mornings, last night's dishes, paid by the hour; nothing of the other, he didn't even know about it then. On the day of the death Timothy shaved the dead face himself and got Mr Kinnally into his tweeds. He sprayed a little *Krizia Uomo*, and changed the slippers for lace-ups. He made him as he had been, except of course for the closed eyes, you couldn't do anything about that. 'Come back in the evening, could you?' Timothy had asked Eddie, the first time there'd been such a summons. 'There'll be a few here.' There were more than a few, paying their respects in the bedroom, and afterwards in the sitting-room Timothy put on the music and they just sat there. From the scraps of conversation that were exchanged Eddie learned that Timothy had inherited, that Timothy was in the dead man's shoes, the new Mr Kinnally. 'You'd never think of moving in, Eddie?' Timothy suggested a while later, and afterwards Eddie guessed that that was how Timothy himself had been invited to Mountjoy Street, when he was working in the newsagent's in Ballsbridge, on his uppers as he used to say.

'As a matter of fact,' Eddie said in the drawing-room, 'I never touch a beer.'

Timothy's father – so thin and bony in Eddie's view that when he sat down you'd imagine it would cause him pain – gave a nod that was hardly a nod at all. And the mother said she couldn't drink beer in any shape or form. Neither of them was drinking now.

'Nothing in the gassy line suits me,' Eddie confided. It wasn't easy to know what to say. Timothy had said they'd ask him to stop for a bite of grub when they realised he'd come down specially; before he knew where he was they'd have turned him into the birthday boy. Odo his father's name was, Timothy had passed on, extraordinary really.

'Nice home you got here,' Eddie said. 'Nice place.'

A kind of curiosity had brought him to the house. Once Timothy had handed him the keys of the Rover, he could as easily have driven straight to Galway, which was the city he had decided to make for, having heard a few times that it was lively. But instead he'd driven as directed, to Baltinglass, and then by minor roads to Coolattin. He'd head for Galway later: the N80 to Portlaoise was what the map in the car indicated, then on to Mountmellick and Tullamore, then Athlone. Eddie didn't know any of those towns. Dublin was his place.

'Excuse me,' he said, addressing Timothy's father, lowering his voice. 'D'you have a toilet?'

Charlotte had years ago accepted her son's way of life. She had never fussed about it, and saw no reason to. Yet she sympathised with Odo, and was a little infected by the disappointment he felt. 'This is how Timothy wishes to live,' she used, once, gently to argue, but Odo would look away, saying he didn't understand it, saying – to Timothy too – that he didn't want to know. Odo was like that; nothing was going to change him. Coolattin had defeated him, and he had always hoped, during Timothy's childhood, that Timothy would somehow make a go of it where he himself had failed. In those days they had taken in overnight guests but more recently too much went wrong in the house, and the upkeep was too burdensome, to allow that to continue without financial loss. Timothy, as a child, had been both imaginative and practical: Odo had seen a time in the future when there would be a family at Coolattin again, when in some clever way both house and gardens would be restored. Timothy had even talked about it, describing it, as he liked to: a flowery hotel, the kitchen filled with modern utensils and machines, the bedrooms fresh with paint, new wallpapers and fabrics. Odo could recall a time in his own childhood when visitors came and went, not paying of course for their sojourn, but visitors who paid would at least be something.

'You'll have to ask him if he wants to stay to lunch,' Charlotte said when Timothy's friend had been shown where the downstairs lavatory was.

'Yes, I know.'

'I'd fix that toilet for you,' Eddie offered, explaining that the flow to the bowl was poor. Nothing complicated, corrosion in the pipe. He explained that he'd started out as a plumber once, which was why he knew a thing or two. 'No sweat,' he said.

When lunch was mentioned he said he wouldn't want to trouble anyone, but they said no trouble. He picked up a knife from the drinks table and set off with his gin and tonic to the downstairs lavatory to effect the repair.

'It's very kind of you, Eddie.' Timothy's mother thanked him and he said honestly, no sweat.

When he returned to the drawing-room, having poked about in the cistern with the knife, the room was empty. Rain was beating against the windows. The fire had burnt low. He poured another dollop of gin into his glass, not bothering with the tonic since that would have meant opening the second bottle. Then the old fellow appeared out of nowhere with a basket of logs, causing Eddie to jump.

'I done it best I could,' Eddie said, wondering if he'd been seen with the bottle actually in his hand and thinking he probably had. 'It's better than it was anyway.'

'Yes,' Timothy's father said, putting a couple of the logs on to the fire and a piece of turf at the back. 'Thanks very much.'

'Shocking rain,' Eddie said.

Yes, it was heavy now, the answer came, and nothing more was said until they moved into the dining-room. 'You sit there, Eddie,' Timothy's mother directed, and he sat as she indicated, between the two of them. A plate was passed to him with slices of meat on it, then vegetable dishes, with potatoes and broccoli in them.

'It was a Thursday, too, the day Timothy was born,' Timothy's mother said. 'In the newspaper they brought me it said something about a royal audience with the Pope.'

1959, Eddie calculated, fourteen years before he saw the light of day himself. He thought of mentioning that, but decided they wouldn't want to know. The drop of Cork had settled in nicely, the only pity was they hadn't brought the bottle in to the table.

'Nice bit of meat,' he said instead, and she said it was Timothy's favourite, always had been. The old fellow was silent again. The old fellow hadn't believed him when he'd said Timothy was off colour. The old fellow knew exactly what was going on, you could tell that straight away.

'Pardon me a sec.' Eddie rose, prompted by the fact that he knew where both of them were. In the drawing-room he poured himself more gin, and grimaced as he swallowed it. He poured a smaller measure and didn't, this time, gulp it. In the hall he picked up a little ornament that might be silver: two entwined fish he had noticed earlier. In the lavatory he didn't close the door in the hope that they would hear the flush and assume he'd been there all the time.

'Great,' he said in the dining-room as he sat down again.

The mother asked about his family. He mentioned Tallaght, no reason not to since it was what she was after. He referred to the tinker encampment, and said it was a bloody disgrace, tinkers allowed like that. 'Pardon my French,' he apologised when the swearword slipped out.

'More, Eddie?' she was saying, glancing at the old fellow since it was he who was in charge of cutting the meat.

'Yeah, great.' He took his knife and fork off his plate, and after it was handed back to him there was a bit of a silence so he added:

'A new valve would be your only answer in the toilet department. No problem with your pressure.'

'We must get it done,' she said.

It was then -- when another silence gathered and continued for a couple of minutes -- that Eddie knew the mother had guessed also: suddenly it came into her face that Timothy was as fit as a fiddle. Eddie saw her glance once across the table, but the old fellow was intent on his food. On other birthday occasions Timothy would have talked about Mr Kinnally, about his 'circle', which was how the friends who came to the flat were always described. Blearily, through a fog of Cork gin, Eddie knew all that, even heard the echo of Timothy's rather high-pitched voice at this same table. But talk about Mr Kinnally had never been enough.

''Course it could go on the way it is for years,' Eddie said, the silence having now become dense. 'As long as there's a drop coming through at all you're in business with a toilet cistern.'

He continued about the faulty valve, stumbling over some of the words, his speech thickened by the gin. From time to time the old man nodded, but no sign came from the mother. Her features were bleak now, quite unlike they'd been a moment ago, when she'd kept the conversation going. They had met when she walked up the avenue of Coolattin one day, looking for petrol for her car: Timothy had reported that too. The car was broken down a mile away; she came to the first house there was, which happened to be Coolattin. They walked back to the car together and they fell in love. A Morris-8, Timothy said; 1950 it was. 'A lifetime's celebration of love,' he'd said that morning, in the toneless voice he sometimes adopted. 'That's what you'll find down there.'

It wouldn't have been enough, either, to have had Kinnally here in person. Kinnally they could have taken; Kinnally would have oozed about the place, remarking on the furniture and the pictures on the walls. Judicious, as he would have said himself, a favourite word. Kinnally could be judicious. Rough trade was different.

'There's trifle,' Eddie heard the old woman say before she rose to get it.

The rain came in, heavier now, from the west. A signpost indicated Athlone ahead, and Eddie remembered being informed in a classroom that this town was more or less the centre of Ireland. He drove slowly. If for any reason a police car signalled him to stop he would be found to have more than the permitted quantity of alcohol in his bloodstream; if for any reason his clothing was searched he would be found to be in possession of stolen property; if he was questioned about the car he was driving he would not be believed when he said it had been earlier lent to him for a purpose.

The Rover's windscreen wipers softly swayed, the glass of the windscreen perfectly clear in their wake. Then a lorry went by, and threw up surface water from the road. On the radio Chris de Burgh sang.

The sooner he disposed of the bit of silver the better, Athlone maybe. In Galway he would dump the car in a car park somewhere. The single effect remaining after his intake of gin was the thirst he experienced, as dry as paper his mouth was.

He turned Chris de Burgh off, not trying another channel. It was one thing to scarper off, as Timothy had from that house: he'd scarpered himself from Tallaght. To turn the knife was different. Fifteen years later to make your point with rough trade and transparent lies, to lash out venomously: how had they cocked him up, how had they hurt him, to deserve it? All the time when there had been that silence they had gone on eating, as if leaving the food on their plates would be too dramatic a gesture. The old man nodded once or twice about the valve, but she had given no sign that she even heard. Very slightly, as he drove, Eddie's head began to ache.

'Pot of tea,' he ordered in Athlone, and said no, nothing else when the woman waited. The birthday presents had remained on the sideboard, not given to him to deliver, as Timothy had said they probably would be. The two figures stood, hardly moving, at the back door while he hurried across the puddles in the cobbled yard to the car. When he looked back they were no longer there.

'Great,' Eddie said when the woman brought the tea, in a metal pot, cup and saucer and a teaspoon. Milk and sugar were already on the pink patterned oilcloth that covered the table top. 'Thanks,' Eddie said, and when he had finished and had paid he walked through the rain, his headache clearing in the chilly air. In the first jeweller's shop the man said he didn't buy stuff. In the second Eddie was questioned so he said he came from Fardrum, a village he'd driven through. His mother had given him the thing to sell, he explained, the reason being she was sick in bed and needed a dose of medicine. But the jeweller frowned, and the trinket was handed back to him without a further exchange. In a shop that had ornaments and old books in the window Eddie was offered a pound and said he thought the entwined fish were worth more. 'One fifty,' came the offer then, and he accepted it.

It didn't cease to rain. As he drove on through it, Eddie felt better because he'd sold the fish. He felt like stopping in Ballinasloe for another pot of tea but changed his mind. In Galway he dropped the car off in the first car park he came to.

Together they cleared away the dishes. Odo found that the gin in the drawing-room had been mostly drunk. Charlotte washed up at the sink. Then Odo discovered that the little ornament was gone from the hall and slowly went to break this news, the first communication between them since their visitor had left.

'These things happen,' Charlotte said, after another silence.

*

The rain was easing when Eddie emerged from a public house in Galway, having been slaking his thirst with Seven Up and watching *Glenroe*. It dribbled away to nothing as he walked into the city. Watery sunshine slipped through the unsettled clouds, brightening the façades in Eyre Square. He sat on a damp seat there, wondering about picking up a girl, but none passed by so he moved away. He didn't want to think. He wasn't meant to understand, being only what he was. Being able to read Timothy like a book was just a way of putting it, talking big when nobody could hear.

Yet the day still nagged, its images stumbling about, persisting in Eddie's bewilderment. Timothy smiled when he said all he was asking was that a message should be passed on. Eddie's own hand closed over the silver fish. In the dining-room the life drained out of her eyes. Rain splashed the puddles in the cobbled yard and they stood, not moving, in the doorway.

On the quays the breeze from the Atlantic dried the pale stone of the houses and cooled the skin of Eddie's face, freshening it also. People had come out to stroll, an old man with a smooth-haired terrier, a couple speaking a foreign language. Seagulls screeched, swooping and bickering in the air. It had been the natural thing to lift the ornament in the hall since it was there and no one was around: in fairness you could call it payment for scraping the rust off the ball-cock valve, easily ten quid that would have cost them. 'A lifetime's celebration,' Timothy said again.

'It has actually cleared up,' Odo said at the window and Charlotte rose from the armchair by the fire and stood there with him, looking out at the drenched garden. They walked in it together when the last drops had fallen.

'Fairly battered the delphiniums,' Odo said.

'Hasn't it just.'

She smiled a little. You had to accept what there was; no point in brooding. They had been hurt, as was intended, punished because one of them continued to be disappointed and repelled. There never is fairness when vengeance is evoked: that had occurred to Charlotte when she was washing up the lunchtime dishes, and to Odo when he tidied the dining-room. 'I'm sorry,' he had said, returning to the kitchen with forks and spoons that had not been used. Not turning round, Charlotte had shaken her head.

They were not bewildered, as their birthday visitor was: they easily understood. Their own way of life was so much debris all around them, but since they were no longer in their prime that hardly mattered. Once it would have, Odo reflected now; Charlotte had known that years ago. Their love of each other had survived the vicissitudes and the struggle there had been; not even the bleakness of the day that had passed could affect it.

They didn't mention their son as they made their rounds of the garden that was now too much for them and was derelict in places. They didn't mention the jealousy their love of each other had bred in him, that had flourished into deviousness and cruelty. The pain the day had brought would not easily pass, both were aware of that. And yet it had to be, since it was part of what there was.

# C. K. Stead

## CLASS, RACE, GENDER –
## A POST-COLONIAL YARN

IT WILL PERHAPS serve a disarming purpose and make what
I have to record seem less serious than it is, or than it ought
to be, if I begin by explaining that this is a story told by
Bertie to Billy, who told it to me. More recently Bertie told
me the story himself, so I've heard it twice and have had the
chance to ask questions and fill gaps that remained after
the first hearing.

I got to know Bertie and Billy a long time ago when we
were all students in England. Bertie was, and indeed is and
will always be even when he's dead, an Englishman. His
fuller, though not entire (there are several intermediate ones)
name is Herbert Lawson-Grieve. Friends and family called
him Bertie, and so, although we, Billy and I, found it absurd,
adding to the general feeling that he was less a real person
than a character out of P. G. Wodehouse, Bertie is what we
called him.

Billy is South African. His full name is Villiers de Groot
Graaf which among our group became Billy Goat Gruff –
Billy for short. Billy and Bertie were friends before I knew
them. They were at Oxford together, at the same college,
Merton, Billy studying ('reading', as they say in England)
engineering, Bertie law. Like Bertie, Billy had money, lots of
it, which came from what he called 'a family in diamonds'.

I was a graduate student on a scholarship from New Zealand, writing a thesis which I hoped might be published as a
book. But it was our passion for sport that brought us
together – that, and a particular kind of boyish temperament.

('Chappish', I think it would be called these days, with, of course, deep disapproval.) There was a lot of beer-drinking, a lot of horsing about, a lot of talk about 'girls'. We loved Western movies and practised shoot-outs in the parks. I think we were quite serious students, but we were having a good time.

There was another student of that time I should mention because he has provided my title – or the first half of it: Peter Mapplethwaite from Scunthorpe. I've once or twice glanced at a map looking for Scunthorpe and not succeeded in finding it, but the way Pete pronounced it, and the word itself, suggested slums, coal mines, sunless skies and rickets – the part of England which those of us who were (shallow and ignorant, no doubt) visitors skirted around on our way to the lakes or the moors, to North Wales or to Scotland.

Mapplethwaite was a Marxist and a man of the people. Peoplethwaite, Bertie called him; and then Marplethorpe, Pepperpot, Maxiwank, Whistlestop, Cuttlefish – anything at all but his real name. Pete could be good company. Billy and I imitated his accent and he imitated ours. He knew me as the New Zillander who liked igg sendwiches; and Billy as the Seth Ufrican who didn't want to talk about Bleck prytest.

Pete had absolutely no sense of tune, but he sang dialect songs – I suppose they were from his region – in a flat ugly-funny voice. Some of these took the form of dialogues, one of which went, as I remember,

> 'Where's tha bin, lud?'
> "awkeen paypers.'
> "o for?'
> 'Meyuncle Benjamin.'
> 'Wha's 'e gin thee?'
> 'Skinny ole 'et'ny.'
> 'Silly ole blawk
> 'e ought ta dee.'

I tried to make Pete part of the group but it was no use. It didn't matter too much that he sometimes wanted to lecture

Billy about the situation of the 'Blecks'. There were a few occasions when Billy hung his head in helpless shame, and then flared up in angry Boer pride; but mostly he could cope with it. But it was the two Englishmen, Pete and Bertie, who couldn't mix. It wasn't even that there was great animosity between them. It seemed more like embarrassment.

Once I asked Bertie was it a problem for him that Mapplethwaite was a Marxist. Lord no, he said; that was no problem at all. Lots of chaps from school (he always spoke of 'school' as if the word meant to me exactly what it meant to him) had been Lefties. I waited for him to go on and for a moment he seemed flummoxed. Then he lowered his voice and said that for him, personally, the problem was Mapplethwaite's feet.

I thought at first that this was some kind of joke, but it wasn't. We'd all been at a party in north Oxford when Pete had vomited and passed out cold – so 'cold' we thought he was dead. We'd got him on to a bed and someone had taken off his shoes and socks.

'He had such nasty long white monkey-feet,' Bertie said, almost in awe; 'and the soles – did you notice? – they were *black*.'

Those feet, and Bertie's reaction to them, belonged to something peculiarly and impenetrably English, and I gave up my efforts towards an accommodation. I didn't want to seem a busybody on someone else's turf. But I've gone on seeing Pete on my visits to England, calling on him at the North London Polytechnic where he lectures on what's called Culture and Gender Studies, and going for a drink with him at his local.

Over the years Pete has been a Moscow communist, then a Peking communist, his faith coming to rest finally, when Mao died and the Gang of Four were arrested, on the régime in Albania. Later again, when the Berlin Wall came down and piece by piece the whole communist empire fell apart, I expected to find him depressed and defeated, but he wasn't. On my last visit he seemed more relaxed and confident than he'd been for years. Communism was pure now, pure theory;

it hadn't yet, he explained, been put into practice – not anywhere. All those attempts at it had been corrupt and imperfect. Communism lay somewhere up ahead, the great future which all the world's peoples would enjoy when at last they came to their senses and realised the evils of capitalism. Meanwhile all serious 'analysis' (his favourite word) of anything and everything came down to three words: class, race and gender.

That's why Peter Mapplethwaite figures in my account: because if I told him this story (something I can't imagine I would want to do) he would say that it illustrates perfectly the justness of the intellectual framework which has ruled his life; whereas to me it illustrates (if it illustrates anything) just the opposite – that life is subtler and more complex than the theories men construct to explain it.

I've also continued to see Bertie – much more of him than of Pete – and so has Billy. But Billy's visits to England and mine have never coincided; and it wasn't until he came to New Zealand, accompanying the Springboks on their first post-Apartheid tour, that we were able to get together again. Our talk was of Rugby, of the new South Africa (which made him proud, but nervous too), and of the old days when we'd been students in England. Bertie's name came up often, and we were sorry he wasn't there – but we knew he would be watching the test matches on television; and I had an amusing and, as Pete would have said, culturally insensitive fax from him when a South African forward bit the All Blacks captain's ear and was caught by the cameras.

'Anent ear-eating,' Bertie's message ran. 'Why the fuss? When in Rome, n'est-ce pas?'

What did he mean? What could he have meant except that cannibalism was a local tradition, wasn't it – so why not?

From time to time Billy and I have each tried to persuade Bertie to visit us at home. His answer to Billy has always been that he would come 'when South Africa has a Black President'. Since none of us believed this would happen in our lifetime, it was his way of saying he would never come. To my invitations he always replied (adopting what he thought was my accent), 'Tow far, moite. Thenks – oi'd love tow. But tow far.'

Bertie, of course, speaks that tortured, alternately clipped, squeezed, swallowed and diphthongised English which signals, even (and perhaps especially) to those who mock it, impeccable social credentials; and it is one of the jokes we share, and revert to often, that his second mother-in-law, who was French, could always understand my outlander's English but had the greatest difficulty making sense of his.

Bertie has lived most of his adult life in a beautiful house with a beautiful walled garden in the town of Marlow on the Thames. He inherited the place from a maiden great-aunt when he was still a young man; and for many years he commuted all the way in to London where he worked as a solicitor specialising in marine insurance which he liked to tell us was properly called 'bottomry'. After his third marriage Bertie gave up the City firm in which he'd risen to become a partner, and opened a small office of his own in his home town. He's still there, prosperous and apparently content, with a wife so young he sometimes jokingly introduces her as 'My wife and child'.

Bertie's house is full of sporting prints and cricketing photographs. Along the hallways and up the stairs you can see the rugby and cricket teams – school, university, business and local – he has played for. There's a cabinet of sporting trophies, and pictures of two or three racehorses. I've noticed too that he's something of a Narcissus. There are several painted portraits of him around the house; and a rather grand gold-framed mirror in his dining-room, placed where, when conversation around the table begins to run into the sand, he can pass the time staring at himself.

In the 1970s Bertie let his hair grow rather long, with sideburns, and that's the look he has tended to stick with; and as the hair has thinned and gone grey-streaked, and fashions have changed, it has left him looking less than the dashing and fashionable fellow he once was. But he's tall (six foot two or three), strongly built, still handsome, still full of charm and energy and generosity. Bertie does things in style; and to be met by him at the station with flowers and champagne, as if you were a visiting foreign dignitary, is to experience a sort of expansiveness which none of us where I come from would be capable of, even if the wish and the impulse towards it should happen to stir.

It was when Billy was on one of his visits to England that Bertie told him the story about his involvement with the cockney woman whose name was Thelma Button, but who was known to her workmates as Thelly, or sometimes Shell. During Billy's Springbok-accompanying visit to New Zealand he passed the story on to me. ('You're a writer, Carlo,' he said; 'you can disguise it, can't you?') And so, on my most recent visit to England, when I recognised during a late-night drinking session with Bertie that we were on the borders, so to speak, of this same narrative territory, I prompted, listened, questioned, remembered, reconstructed. Here is what I learned.

Bertie was, as he put it, 'between marriages at the time' – depressed, bored, restless. This was in the last of his years working for the big impersonal City firm he'd been with for almost twenty years. His second wife, Françoise, had left him, not for another man, nor for any reason except that she'd grown to hate living in England. One day, with the help of the mother-in-law who couldn't understand Bertie's conversation, she packed her things, and with their child returned to Paris.

'It was a fearsome blow to the pride,' Bertie said. 'Nothing like that had ever happened to me before. So of course the old mind went blank for a time and I came to consciousness a few months later, realising I was drinking too much, eating fast fodder, not getting any exercise, becoming fat, ratty and inefficient. It was bad. All bad. That was when I started thinking about Shell.'

She served lunches in a popular place where lawyers often went for a quick bite when they weren't entertaining clients. She was small, well-shaped, bright-eyed, pretty, good-humoured, with the broadest of London accents, and she and Bertie had hit it off right from their first encounter. She teased him; he responded. Their exchanges were always (as he put it) 'remorselessly jokey', but with an undertone of flirtation. But what really attracted him was her hair. It was shiny brown, wiry and curly, and despite her best efforts to keep it neat it sprang out from her head as if it had a life of its own. It was the kind of hair, he said, that you want desperately to touch.

Bertie never thought about this woman except when she was there in front of him, serving him salad or cottage pie. She was a very minor character in his life, one of thousands with walk-on parts. The idea that she might be more, or other, never occurred to him. When she disappeared from the lunch place and went to work somewhere else he didn't notice that she was gone.

Then one day he met her in the street. He was used to seeing her in a white smock and apron, and if it hadn't been for that head of hair he might not have recognised her. She told him she had a new job, with hours that suited her better because she started early and was finished in time to pick up the kids (she had two, Jack and Jill) from school. Also she had every Wednesday afternoon free.

And then, taking him by surprise, she said if he was ever passing on a Wednesday afternoon he ought to drop in for a cuppa.

'It was the boldness of the thing,' Bertie said. 'You couldn't be mistaken about it. She just looked me in the eye, grinned wickedly, and said it. And then she wrote her address on a piece of paper and pushed it into my hand. I must have looked flabbergasted, but that only made her laugh. She said, "Come on, Mister, don't look so frightened. Hasn't a pretty girl ever invited you to tea before?" And she walked off and left me there.'

Shortly after that Françoise, his lovely French wife, left him. There were those months of dereliction, and the realisation that he must take himself in hand, re-order his life, discipline himself. But it shouldn't, he told himself, be all hard work. There must be some fun, some entertainments, some good times. Clearing the pockets of a jacket and trousers one day, readying things for the dry cleaner, he found the slip of paper with Thelma Button's address, and remembered that invitation with its suggestion of a good deal more than tea.

So an affair (if that's the word for such an arrangement) started. Thelma, or Shelley as he was soon calling her, lived in a block of flats just off Clerkenwell Road near to Gray's Inn, only twenty minutes' walk, or five by taxi, from Bertie's office which was close to the Barbican. His secretary learned to keep the hours from one to three-thirty clear on a Wednesday and he spent them in bed with Shelley; and even many years after what was to be their last dreadful encounter, Bertie couldn't speak of the first weeks and months of that association without a certain brightening of the eye and a lift in the voice.

The flat, on the second floor of a dingy red-brick apartment block, was drab and cramped, but it had a balcony looking inward to a shady courtyard with a single tree. They used to make love, then lie in bed looking out into the upper branches of the tree, talking, exchanging stories, dozing, until they'd recovered sufficiently to do it again, after which they would shower together and return to their separate lives.

Their talk was full of teasing and banter, but with a rich undertone of affection. He told her about the people in his office; she talked about Jack and Jill, family, neighbours. Because he called her Shelley he told her about the poet who had once lived in his town of Marlow, writing revolutionary poems while his wife Mary wrote *Frankenstein*. A week or so later she had *Frankenstein* beside her bed. She'd found it in a bookshop, bought it and read it. He asked what she thought of it.

''orrible,' she said. 'Did you like it, Bertie?'

He had to admit he'd never read it.

Once he bought her a gold chain, knowing – or thinking – that she would have to hide it from her husband. But she made him help her put it on, saying she would never take it off.

'What about Arthur?' he asked. She said she would say she'd found it in the street.

Bertie seldom asked about Arthur, preferred not to hear or think about him; but now and then she would speak of him. He was a guard at the British Museum; and though she always said he was 'harmless', that was the best she could say of him. All day he sat in a chair watching over ancient vases and statues, and in the evening he sat watching television, especially football which didn't interest her in the least. His back was bad. He never had anything to say. Sometimes Shelley would tell him about something she'd read or seen and he would say, 'That's very interesteen, Thel.' That's what he'd said when she told him the story of Frankenstein. 'Interesteen.' She seemed to find Arthur's pronunciation of that word unforgivable. It drove her mad. It excused her infidelity.

As Bertie explained it to me, it was some time before he began to understand what kind of a woman Thelma Button was and why she'd made him this, as it had seemed, outrageously frank offer of herself. She was not at all what he'd supposed – either 'wild', desperate, a beaten wife, or even attracted to him by his patrician looks and manner. Shelley was not inexperienced; but her life had been on the whole sober and orderly, constrained by modest beginnings, low income, early marriage, and two children born within a year of one another.

As for Bertie's attractions: she knew perfectly well that he was of a certain 'class'; but to her such men had always seemed faintly comic – not to be taken seriously. It was almost an obstacle to her liking him; just as her 'class' – the fact that she referred to her husband as 'Arfur', complained that her children came home 'filfy' from school, talked about someone having 'nuffing in 'is 'ead', or said she'd heard this or that 'on good aufori'y', had made her seem to Bertie quite beyond the pale. No. Bertie's attractiveness to her had been something else, something she herself found mysterious and inexplicable. All she could say about it was that it had something to do with his voice and his eyes and his laugh. And also, once she got to know him better, his smell. But almost from the first exchange between them she'd felt she was falling in love with him.

This was a fact which only slowly became clear to Bertie. He found it flattering, disconcerting, unintelligible, reassuring – both welcome and unwelcome; for while it made for great sex, and helped restore the confidence which a much-loved wife's departure had undermined, it also added a burden of responsibility and of guilt. Increasingly as he got to know Thelma Button, Bertie felt affection and gratitude. Her talk was lively and witty. Her generosity was boundless. Her body was lovely and her hair magical. He began to think of her as his secret garden. But to fall in love, even a little, with someone who had things 'on good aufori'y' was quite beyond him.

'Not possible,' he said when I asked him. 'Simply out of the question. Sometimes, you know, I'd try to imagine taking her to things – to dinner parties, Lords, Wimbledon, Covent Garden. I'd try, Carlo. It was . . .' He looked at me with an expression that appealed for understanding, for absolution. 'It was unthinkable.'

So he decided he must stop seeing her. If she'd been able to take their affair as he did, as an adventure, a diversion, an unlooked-for luxury, a secret bonus Life had handed out with no strings or complications, there would have been no problem. But he could see that every visit made the love she felt for him, and which he couldn't think of matching, more powerful, more all-consuming.

She, of course, soon recognised that the depth of her feeling troubled him, and she tried to conceal it or make light of it. But there were moments when she would say, 'I'd die for you, Bertie,' or even (and much worse), 'I'd let you kill me if you wanted to. I'd love you for it.' He would be struck with a sense of awe and helplessness then, and with the wish to escape. To have evoked great love could only be good for his wounded ego; on the other hand, to find himself unable to return it inevitably reduced the beneficial effect. Herbert

Lawson-Grieve's secret garden had begun to have about it the feel of a cage.

But still the decision that he must end their affair wasn't translated into action. He would think of it as he left her flat, resolving that this visit would be the last. By the following Monday the resolve would be gone. By Wednesday he would hardly be able to complete his morning's work for thinking of what the afternoon was to bring. But now, because he was in two minds about Shelley, a sort of ambiguity had begun to creep into his feelings about what he did with her in bed. He enjoyed – enjoyed enormously – and yet did not enjoy. He marvelled, and was half-repelled. Sometimes he felt like a circus animal required to do ever more remarkable tricks. Shelley was the trainer and her whip was true love.

The break didn't come until he was sent to New York on business for the firm. It wasn't a city he enjoyed and he would normally have asked them to send someone else. This time he accepted the task willingly, and even made it last longer than was necessary. By the time he got back to London he felt the Shelley habit had been broken.

But now came phone calls from her; and when these were blocked off by his secretary, there was a postcard. It was of a large pink breast painted to look like a winking pig, the nipple its snout. On the back she had written, 'Here's my knocker, Bertie luv. Where's yours?'

This, coming to him in the office, giggled over by the secretaries, was outrageous – but of course she meant it to be. Bertie was angry, but he was also ashamed. He had tried to end the affair because she loved him too much, and that seemed to him the honourable thing to do; but it had not been honourable – it had been cowardly and wrong – to try to end it by simply absenting himself without a word. He must go and (as he put it) 'face the music'.

The 'music', however, when it came on the following Wednesday was not a simple and catchy tune. At first, when he tried to tell her they must call it off, she reproached him – something she hadn't done before; then she wept, shouted, told him she would always love him, threatened suicide, insulted him. He found it painful, and the pain focused especially on one fact – that she appeared to have dressed herself up for the encounter, and that the clothes seemed to him in the worst possible taste.

As Bertie explained it to me, he has no exact memory for women's clothes, often doesn't remember colours, or remembers them incorrectly – yet at the same time he always takes away a generalised, and in some ways quite precise, impression. Shelley, as he remembered her that day, was wearing a yellow dress of some kind of stiff material, with a short skirt, and around her head, over that rebellious but briefly tamed hair, a band of the same colour.

'There seemed to be little bows and frills everywhere,' he said. 'I may be exaggerating, but it seemed to me she only needed a tray of sweets and ices and she could have gone to a fancy dress ball as an old-fashioned cinema usherette.'

He had never, he told me, felt so fond of her, nor so self-reproachful and so determined to protect her. He couldn't give her what she wanted – he could not; and so the only thing for it was to remove himself. That's what he tried to explain, while she argued, wept, threatened, pleaded.

At last, however, when he was on the point of exhaustion, despair and rage, she changed tack – seemed to accept that he was going, and that he wouldn't be back. Before he went, however, she would like, she said, to show him her 'new friend'. She went to the drawer beside her bed and took something out. He thought it must be a photograph, but what she held up to him was a plastic vibrator. Bertie knew what it was, but only because there had once been an Ann Summers sex shop in Tottenham Court Road and from time to time he'd looked in as he went by and had seen such things, all manner of phallic shapes and sizes, on shelves in long rows.

She held it out for him to touch, but he drew back from it. She pressed a little switch and it began to buzz. She put one foot on the bed and he saw that she was wearing no underclothes. She ran the plastic head of the buzzing phallus

262

through her pubic hair, which grew as coarse and curly as the hair on her head. And then, while he watched, slowly, very slowly, she pushed it into herself.

'My mouth went suddenly dry,' Bertie said, 'and I knew it – I was done for. I said, "I'm going, Shelley" and she said – putting her head back, you know, as though she was really enjoying it – "You're not going nowhere, my Ber'ie." She was right of course. I felt as if I was going towards the door but I wasn't. She was like a magnet. It was like being dragged bodily, against your will.'

He'd been looking down into his drink as he told me this, and I remember how he looked up now, appealing for a friend's compassion. 'You have to understand, Carlo, I was hungry for it. I'd been all those weeks in New York, and there'd been nothing. Nothing but the occasional hand-job.'

'So,' I said, when he fell silent. 'What did you do?'

It was a silly question. 'What do you think I did?' he replied. 'I took *it* out and put *mine* in. We did it dressed, half-dressed, undressed. We did it up against the wall, on the floor, in the bed. We did it standing, sitting, lying. I didn't care any more. Fuck it, I thought. Life's too difficult. Let's just enjoy ourselves. And that's what we did. Three o'clock came around, three-thirty – I didn't care. I was busy. I was fucking. I was happy. I was being myself for a change and I was enjoying it.'

So the afternoon passed. And it occurred to him afterwards that she must all along have been confident of success, because she'd arranged for Jack and Jill to go to a friend's place for supper. They fucked and they talked, and talked and fucked, and finally they slept . . .

Bertie was woken by her shaking him, staring down at him. 'Wake up,' she was saying. 'Jesus Christ, Ber'ie, wake fucking *up*. It's 'im! It's *Arfur!*'

Then she was out of bed and across the room to the hallway. He heard her snib the Yale lock. There was a conversation going on in the corridor – Arthur talking to a neighbour. In a moment he would try to open his own door with the key, and find he couldn't.

263

Back in the bedroom Shelley was gathering up her things. She hissed at Bertie to get dressed. ''E'll go downstairs to the caretaker to report there's something wrong with the lock. Then you scarpa. Go down the other stairs. I'll pretend I snibbed it by mistake.'

She vanished into the bathroom. And now from the front door came the scraping of Arthur's key as he tried to turn it in the lock. Bertie dragged on his underpants and trousers, wrestled with his shirt which he found had lost a button in the earlier, equally violent, struggle to get it off.

Arthur's voice came through the door. 'Thel? You in there, Thelma?' He rattled the door handle. 'Thel?'

And then the key was withdrawn, the voice muttered to itself, footsteps receded down the corridor.

Now, Bertie thought – now was his chance to escape. He would get out and would never come back. He thought of setting off, running, carrying his shoes. But no, the idea was ridiculous. Some sort of dignity had to be preserved.

He was sitting on the bed's edge dragging on his socks when he heard a new sound, a scraping and scrambling. The balcony out there was shared with the flat next door. Arthur had gone through the flat of the neighbour he'd been talking to in the corridor. Now, from the balcony, he was scrambling up over a closed window to an open fanlight.

From where Bertie sat he could see, across the hallway and through another door, a pair of long black-trousered legs pushing, sliding, hanging, dropping.

There was a thump as two feet hit the sitting-room floor. Shelley's voice quavered from the bathroom. 'That you, Arfur?'

Bertie put his head down and dragged at his shoes. He tugged at the laces. Footsteps approached. At that moment, he told me, he felt a desperate calm. The blow would come down on the back of his head, on his neck – he had no doubt of that. He wouldn't defend himself; couldn't. He would die; but it wasn't fear he felt – it was embarrassment. It was shame.

Two large black shiny guard's shoes arrived and planted

themselves opposite the two brown shoes into which Bertie's feet were still refusing to fit. He persisted, dragging the laces wide apart.

'One has to do something while waiting to die,' Bertie said. 'I remember wondering would the blow hurt, or would I pass instantly and painlessly into another world of floating shapes saying things like "Hullo, dear. I'm your mother." '

But there was no blow. Nothing was said. There was only the heavy breathing of a wronged husband who had just climbed through a fanlight.

'I raised my eyes slowly.' (Bertie was acting it out for me now – bending forward, twisting his head around to look up at the occupant of those shiny shoes.) 'There was the line of the trousers. When I got to the thighs I saw the hands, hanging at his sides. They were coffee-coloured, with sickly palms. I raised my eyes further and there was a coffee face to match. My first thought was, "Why the fuck did she never tell me he was black?" '

The dark mask looking down at him showed no violence. That ought to have been a relief; but violence would have been simpler. It would have given him something to do.

He tried to read Arthur's face. There was anxiety in the eyes; and around the mouth something like contempt.

'This is a dreadful business,' Bertie managed to say. 'I'm really most frightfully sorry.'

He stood, picking his jacket up from the floor. That uncovered the vibrator. They both, he and black Arthur, looked down at it lying there like a severed penis.

Bertie said he'd better go.

Shelley had been right – Arthur wasn't a talker; but his silence at this moment seemed strangely powerful and impressive.

Bertie moved out into the hall. His walk was unsteady. At the bathroom door he stopped and called to Shelley that he was going.

The bolt slid back and she appeared in a dressing-gown. Behind her he could see the yellow dress trampled on the wet tiled floor. She nodded to him, glanced at Arthur.

Bertie moved to the front door – only a step or two in those cramped quarters. He unsnibbed the lock, opened the door, and felt a moment of relief.

But was it right to leave without another word? He turned. Shelley had come out of the bathroom, Arthur out of the bedroom, and they were standing side by side, 'like two piano keys,' Bertie said, 'the ebony and the ivory. They made a handsome couple.'

To Arthur Bertie said, 'You won't hurt her.' He meant it to be something midway between a question and an instruction.

Arthur said, 'Out.' That was the beginning and the end of his talk.

Shelley looked at Bertie reassuringly. She was quite safe, seemed to be the message. So he went, closing the door gently behind him.

Out in the street he was assailed all over again by embarrassment. He turned west, away from his office, crossed Gray's Inn Road, walked along to Southampton Row. In Kingsway there was a men's clothes shop that had always, as long as he could remember, announced that it was having a Closing Down Sale. He went in and chose himself an unpleasant business shirt that had a faint green tinge to it. It would replace the one with the tear and the hanging button. He also thought of it as a penance. Handing over his credit card he asked the young woman did she have any with hair linings.

'So-rree?' she quacked at him. He didn't repeat it.

It was raining now. He took a taxi back to the office. The secretaries had gone. He sat at his desk looking out at the rain drifting past the ugly looming towers of the Barbican. He thought of Françoise and a few tears sprang into his eyes – a mixture of anger and regret. He thought of Arthur's shiny black shoes and winced. He heard the partner in the next office getting ready to leave. He went to her door. Her name was Coral Strand. They'd worked together for years, knew one another well.

'That's a nasty shirt, Herbert,' she said at once. 'It's not the one you had on this morning.'

He never got used to the fact that women noticed clothing so precisely. 'The other one,' he said, 'got torn off my back by a woman desperate to have me.'

Coral smiled wearily. 'Of course.' It was a tired old joke. How odd, Bertie thought, that it should be true.

'Do I seem to you an absurd person?' he asked.

'No,' she said, 'not especially.' She snapped her case shut. It was a signal that she had little time for talk, and certainly none for what he had once overheard her call 'a therapy session with our Bert'. Deluded by her name, which still suggested to him a tropical paradise, Bertie had long ago, and very briefly, imagined he and Coral Strand might become lovers. Inwardly he now thought of her as the Head Girl.

'Not especially,' he repeated. It was hardly reassuring.

'About average,' she said, easing him into the corridor and closing her door. 'We're all a bit absurd sometimes, aren't we? See you tomorrow, Bertie.'

He didn't go back to Marlow that night but spent it at his club. He has taken me there sometimes for lunch or dinner and I can report that it seemed a dreadful place where faded lackeys served tasteless food to dead men in suits. Bertie, however, finds some kind of ancient comfort in brown leather and panelled walls, and comfort was what he needed.

Next morning he went first, not to his office, but to the British Museum. After a lot of aimless wandering through the halls and galleries he found Arthur dozing on a chair in a corner among ancient clay burial urns. Bertie roused him with a sharp cough and said his piece: that he was very disturbed at what had happened. That it had not been as bad as it must have seemed (this in an attempt to allow for any story Shelley might have concocted) but that he wanted to apologise sincerely. That it had been his fault entirely, not Thelma's. That she should not be blamed – he took full responsibility. That it would never happen again.

Arthur didn't get up. He listened, staring with blood-shot eyes at a large broken urn. When the little speech was over he asked, 'You got fifty quid?'

Bertie was taken by surprise. For just a moment it seemed

a wonderful relief, the possibility of doing something, paying something, by way of recompense, of absolution.

Yes, he said, he had fifty, certainly. He had more . . .

All the while scrabbling to get his wallet out, to get it open . . .

He held out a fistful of notes. There were at least fifty pounds, probably seventy. He didn't count, and there hadn't been a moment to reflect on what Arthur's request might signify.

Arthur beckoned him closer. Bertie leaned down over him, holding the money.

'Now stick it up your arse,' Arthur said, 'and fuck off outa here.'

Out in the street he seemed to have lost control of his legs. He ambled uncertainly in the direction of the City, still holding the fistful of notes, looking for a passing taxi showing a light and then, when one came along, not hailing it. He saw a florist's shop, went in and put the money down on the counter. What he wanted, he explained, was as many flowers as this would buy sent at once, this morning, to . . . And he gave her name and address.

'And for the card, Sir,' the florist said.

Ah yes, the card. He took it and after a moment wrote on it, 'To Shelley from Keats. Love you for ever.'

For the duration of the brief moment it took to write it, Bertie said, and for perhaps thirty seconds afterwards, he felt it was true.

I didn't quite believe – or was it just that I didn't want to believe? – that that was the end of the story.

'Just for thirty seconds?' I said. 'No more?'

He met my eye for a moment, shrugged, and looked down at the table between our comfortable chairs. 'Let's refill these glasses,' he said.

# Peter Porter

## PUBLIC AND PRIVATE IN CONTEMPORARY BRITISH POETRY

POETS ARE USED to being told that they would enjoy a
wider audience if they wrote about matters which interested
the public more. Such advice is accompanied often by a
specific pointing to difficulties of meaning and to what are
seen as obscure references within poems. Two monstrances,
both rather out of date, stand as opposing book-ends – T. S.
Eliot's, that poetry today of necessity will have to be difficult,
and Adrian Mitchell's that most people ignore most poetry
because most poetry ignores most people. Neither is wholly
true: there is a considerable body of opinion which does
concern itself with contemporary verse and which is not
especially worried about poetry's popularity, but is disturbed
by the wilfulness which obscures much work by vigorous
and inventive writers. So stylistics are my subject, not moral
intent or social responsibility.

First, a preliminary observation or two about Modernism.
From the Greeks to Milton and Pope, poetry has been difficult in the sense that its purpose has been serious and the
range of its references fixed to provide examples to help
clarify its argument. You can see this for yourself by looking
at a modern annotated edition of Shakespeare or Pope. References, metaphors, similes, names, quotations and the rest of
an apparatus for conveying and clinching meaning which
would have been absorbed headlong by readers or audiences
during the poet's lifetime are exhaustively annotated in
modern editions. You find them silting up the bottom of the
page or swelling notes and explanations at the back.

Originally, in the swiftness of their absorption, such references were a natural stock-in-trade of writers and were clearly relished by their public. For this to be so, they had to be drawn from a common hoard of myth, history, precedent or proverbial knowledge. 'Hyperion to a satyr', 'Niobe all tears', 'rough-hew them as we will', 'Thy hand, Great Anarch', 'the mighty Stagyrite', 'Lucretia's dagger, Rosamunda's bowl' and so on – the authorial purpose is personal but the references are public ones. The wit and conviction of each poet's writing springs from his or her own experience and acquired wisdom, but personal effects are kept out except where they are part of the public debate. The turmoil of Shakespeare's plays, of Herbert's poems and Pope's satires is intensely felt but its presentation, in the manner of courtroom evidence, comes from elsewhere. The classical style is ideally suited to the dramatic – i.e. to open conflict. Modernism internalises the drama: art becomes its own stage and its characters aspects of the author's personality. The pointers are self-referential.

Of course there has always been a quantity of personal in-put in writing, a willingness to introduce what Blake described as 'minute particulars' to keep verse fresh and to escape the tiredness of referring to a canon fast losing effectiveness through overfamiliarity. It has become a cliché to say that cliché itself is just exhausted metaphor. Examples abound of such particularising: the Elegies and Satires of John Donne, the aphoristic curtness of Thomas Gray and Browning's and Tennyson's hailing of their friends and acquaintances, as in *In Memoriam* and 'What's Become of Waring?' Immediately, though, we notice that however personal such material is, it is not arcane. The circumstances are representative, the mode is Theophrastian: we may not know the protagonists but we understand their predicaments instinctively.

Modernism, a term defined with extraordinary relaxation and exceeded in diffuseness only by Post-Modernism, is a delta of approaches to the recording of life in literature. Few artists, however experimental and original, are without antecedents and fewer still are uninterested in the past and its formal devices. But one channel in that delta has been particularly fertile in modern poetry. This is the confessional or internal historical method. Not surprisingly it coincides with the rise of psychoanalysis, though there is a pleasant irony in Freud's seeking classical myth to offer authoritative precedent for his hypotheses of human behaviour. The patient who tells his/her shrink minute details of personal conflict may still be filed and treated under the labels 'Oedipus or Electra Complex'.

What was considered madness in the eighteenth century (witness Christopher Smart's Bedlam poem *Jubilate Agno*) becomes by the middle of the nineteenth century an example of tribal or national dementia in Baudelaire and Lautréamont. The general flight from Reason, however, was not immediately accompanied by an indifference to inherited form. Baudelaire adopts quatrains and sonnets with the conviction of an Isaac Watts or a Keats. The initial revolution was of subject or theme. Style has always been seen to evolve over the centuries: sometimes, as in the English Renaissance, it was a process of imitation, of becoming aware that a new language could attempt the achievements of classicism. Indeed, the European Renaissance, in all its departments, was a conservative looking-back to a past which represented restraint and precedent. The fact that its new recruits had such abounding energy that they made brilliant new art under the illusion that they were retreating to classicism is a wonderful bonus but not a helpful example.

Inevitably, an introduction of home references or an insistence on personal choice of illustrative matter, began to change the shape and structure of both poetry and fiction. A comparison of Dickens and James Joyce may offer clearer insight than a direct opposition of two poets, if only because poetry went through a bad patch at the turn of the twentieth century. *David Copperfield* and *Ulysses* both teem with life, and both are heavily autobiographical. Dickens, though, is much more straightforward. He picks his way among a nightmare assortment of people following a line of development parallel to that he took in his own life, and his obscurities are all embellishments, humours and caricatured aspects of humanity. Joyce, on the other hand, employs a realism he inherited from French (Flaubert) and Norwegian (Ibsen) writers as so much material for parody, to be broken down and reassembled in different styles. Autobiography here is equivalent to what used to be called 'a bad trip'. Dickens is as much a distorter as Joyce – the difference arises from their respective attitudes to presentation. Joyce wrote only two long novels and he incorporated in them a lifetime's obsession with art. Dickens had a huge stock from which he constructed in book after book simulacra of the observable world. Joyce's urge to define by systems opposes Dickens's storehouse method. The contrast is not challenged by Joyce's basing *Ulysses* on *The Odyssey*. What Stephen Dedalus and Leopold Bloom do in Dublin would be the same if the Homeric parallel had not been evoked. In general, only academic analysts ever bother with it.

By the time our century's difficult classics were being written, the whole question of what an audience could be expected to recognise had changed radically. It's instructive to look quite simplistically at the editing Ezra Pound performed on *The Waste Land*. We are seldom shown so clearly the origins of a classic. T. S. Eliot was not much younger than the recently dead Rupert Brooke when he wrote *The Waste Land*. The full text of Eliot's original is much less 'modern' than the final version prepared by Pound. In its original state *The Waste Land* is a more consecutive work than the one we know so well. What gave shape to Joyce – namely the parodies in *Ulysses* and *Finnegans Wake* – is otiose in Eliot, and Pound took them out. A plot is visible in the original manuscript, as its proposed cryptic title, *He Do the Police in Different Voices*, suggests. In Pound's treatment, the poem becomes a cinema epillion with missing reels. Eliot appreciated that Pound had turned a rambling and sardonic exercise into a modern showpiece. Strangely, Pound's pruning did not make the poem less personal, though his excisions were of personal material as well as of pastiche and parody. The first readers of the poem could not know how it had started out: they had little idea of how accurate Eliot's tribute 'il miglior fabbro' to his friend was. By leaving out connectives, those modulating passages so relished by the Victorians, Pound replaced public sensibility with private. Generations of readers have felt that *The Waste Land* is a classic of deracination and depression, but each reader has had to work out what the details of this epochal poem signify. As Joyce, Eliot and Pound seem to have understood from the start, fragmentation of material need not – indeed should not – lead to absence of style.

It is perhaps our century's way of reviving Alexandrianism to pursue an anthology method among the inheritance we are faced with. The great geniuses have been able to find styles appropriate to their need. But there is a price to be paid – the personalising of the impersonal. And a further step beyond lies the sacralising of individual experience. Instead of a single mind's view of the known world, we are asked to substitute one special set of experiences. We are forced to understand that what happened to the poet is already, as far as his intention goes, legendary. We must accept the radical importance of chosen emotions and events. Though what comes over may be more appropriate to a magistrate's court, we are expected to find it as authoritative as King Arthur's.

Change seldom occurs on a wide front, and some writers may swim in an opposite direction to the main current. At the beginning of the 1930s the subjective revolution of Eliot and Pound in poetry underwent an unconscious challenge from poets who were drawn to a more objective stance. They seemed modern enough when they appeared, and show how stylistic development may go backwards as well as forwards. In all arts there seems to be alternation between making work more complex and simplifying it. Milton is more congested than Shakespeare; Pope more open than Milton, and the Romantics more single and simple-minded than the Augustans. In such a way, the poets of W. H. Auden's generation, coinciding with a *Zeitgeist* which included Freud's simplifiers, Mass Observation, the Popular Front and the opposition of communism and fascism, were hailed as developers of Modernism, whereas they were reactionary in a non-pejorative sense. Reference went outwards once more, *Gestalt* mattered more than individually endorsed experience, and the audience, at least by intention, was a general one, not the élite addressed by Pound and Eliot.

W. H. Auden's poetry gives us the opportunity to see this public/private juxtaposition starkly. *Poems 1930* introduced a contemporary terseness which Auden worked up from shreds of the saga style, gritted-teeth Hardyisms and scientific terminology. Yet mingled in were copious references to friends and family and a conspiratorial division of sensibility into 'gangs'. This mixture was intensified in his 'English Study' *The Orators* (1932), one of the strangest and most potent assemblies of the public and the private ever composed. 'What do you think of England, this land of ours where no one is well?' he asked. But he also composed an ode to the captain of a public school rugger team; apostrophised his own anal fissure in 'Letter to a Wound'; and in the work's original form named the many friends and colleagues whom he called to the colours to deliver his homeland from its deep-seated psychological sickness. Later he went over it all and removed the detonators, so to speak, declaring that the work seemed to him to have been written by a person on the edge of madness or about to turn into a fascist. What makes *The Orators* (it is a mixture of prose and verse, all of it hieratic) a particularly relevant composition today is Auden's pioneering of the mixed mode – archetypal analysis of a whole society, gaining its special strength from the personal cases presented. It is not too far-fetched to see in it a pattern enlarged in a virtuoso mode by the Northern Irish poet Paul Muldoon in his long sequence 'Yarrow' (*The Annals of Chile*, 1994). This book won Muldoon the T. S. Eliot Prize for 1994 and is certainly one of the most remarkable collections of poems published in the past decade.

Muldoon is more parochial than Auden, whose ambition was Europe-wide, but he creates a similar poetic terrain into which he musters the politics and social contentions of three communities – Ireland, England and the United States. 'Yarrow' is a kind of verse diary, a daisy-chain of lyrical episodes through which Muldoon traces the progress of his life from childhood in rural Ulster to his years as a poet in Belfast and America. What makes 'Yarrow' harder to follow than *The Orators* is Muldoon's unsignposted melding of the private and the public. One might argue that nowhere in the world is the private more public and the public more private than in Ireland of the Troubles. And tipping into the mixing bowl anything which strikes the poet's fancy is a technique practised by Auden as well as by Muldoon. Yet Auden's creation is, for all its forensic detail, 'en plein air' compared with Muldoon's. His is murky and lit by a kind of lyrical hellfire glow: its dramatis personae seem barely to know each other and to have no valency among themselves or in the poet's mind. If Muldoon's poetry were not obviously powerful and his tropes commanding in themselves, the critic would have no reason to worry that a reading of 'Yarrow' evokes such a sense of frustration. Hard work will yield up the pertinence of most of the difficulties of reference and allusion in Auden (and he never wrote anything as mysterious as *The Orators* for the rest of his long literary career, while each book which Muldoon publishes is more arcane than the last). Such hard labour will not be so effective with Muldoon. Yet he doesn't use *non sequitur* as a deliberate technique as John Ashbery does: he is simply unconcerned with any need for emotional logic. The connectives in the course of this long poem are as mysterious as crop circles. There is a great deal left untranslated from the Irish (or if it's translated Pound-fashion the reader may not know), and name and rank are inconsistent and unexplained. Everything is subordinated to the lyrical impulse, the pavane-like procession of heroes and the summoning of numinous ghosts. Authority is assumed, not even claimed. Readers who are not clansmen are expected to recognise the sound of command, though they could not hope to be initiates.

It would take a much longer article than this to go through

'Yarrow' to demonstrate its obscurities and wilfulnesses and, to be fair, its many beauties as well. Here are two consecutive passages from early in the poem where the general direction is slightly easier to make out. Muldoon is summoning images from his childhood – scents and smells are important – as are plants and the bygone heroes of his circle of friends, ranging from the familiar (*Treasure Island*) to some very obscure ones indeed.

> *Would that I might as readily follow*
> *the nosegay of yarrow as Don Junipero Serra*
> *led us all the way back*
>
> *along El Camino Real*
> *by the helter-skelter path*
> *of poppies we'd sown in the sap-sweet April rain*
>
> *I zap the remote-control: that same poor elk eland*
> *dragged down by a bobolink;*
> *a Spanish Lear; the umpteenth Broken Arrow;*
>
> *a boxing-match; Robert Hughes dismantling Dada;*
> *a Michael Jackson video*
> *in which our friends, the Sioux, will peel*
>
> *the face of a white man whose metacarp-*
> *al bones, with those of either talus,*
> *they've already numbered; the atmosphere's so rare*
>
> *that if Michael's moon-suit of aluminium foil*
> *were suddenly to split at the seams*
> *he'd not only buy, but fertilise, the farm.*

It is difficult but not too difficult to gloss these lines. Reminded of childhood by a plant, itself emblematic, the poet looks forward and backward over his life, from the Northern Irish countryside via the heroes of youthful reading to the fare offered by American television. Robert Hughes is the highly articulate TV art critic and Michael Jackson the hero of popular promo videos; presumably Michael is a friend who played Moon Landings with Muldoon when they were children. But there are approximately 150 such stanzas and part-stanzas and as the poem proceeds it thickens up alarmingly. Certainly there is a general drift, one which is affiliated surprisingly with the Nationalist cause in Ulster – surprisingly, since Muldoon is no propagandist and many of his earlier poems, such as 'Why Brownlee Left' acknowledge the complexity of the political situation in the Province. One of the main players in the poem is named only by the capital letter S and a dash. She appears like the ghost of Hamlet's father every time Muldoon is in danger of forgetting his duty to the Nationalist community, as his career moves from success to success.

'Yarrow' follows Muldoon's even longer poem *Madoc*. 'Yarrow' is as abstruse on the surface as *Madoc*, but should be easier to identify with since it is set in the present and has recognisable events mixed in. *Madoc* is an amazing presentation of American Indian history and the westward migration of European settlers, with particular emphasis on that idealist community 'The Pantisocracy' with which Coleridge and Southey were involved as young men. There is even a long stretch which attempts to encapsulate the major Western philosophers from Greek times to the present in one-line cryptic summaries. Yet *Madoc* is no more difficult than 'Yarrow'. It is the private references of 'Yarrow' which elude our understanding, precisely because we expect them to be more open than they are.

Muldoon is not the first and will not be the last poet consciously to mythologise his own experience. Most appreciators of poetry have a taste for the arbitrary, that epiphanic listing of people and places which is at once the most primitive of literary devices and the most oracular. What is disturbing in the way contemporary poets sometimes proceed is an arrogance which rests all too often on the well-subsidised ghettoising of serious writing. An underlying confidence appears to assert that a general readership is dispensable if there is an élite audience which can be topped up with good academic jobs and copious and well-signalled praise in various partisan journals. An atmosphere of immanence is conjured up: stars are followed, and wise men led to freshly established shrines. There is a great deal of wilful self-mythologising. Writers today stand at the end of a long and fruitful pilgrimage. Any way of asserting an individual style, any path to proprietariness, is welcome. Joyce was perhaps the first to insist that a writer's personality be printed right through his work like the lettering in a stick of rock. And Pound's admonishment to 'make it new' has been more generally interpreted as 'make it recognisably you'. The great Modernists were not interested in the reactions of the general public but they had a well-developed sense of fame and rank within the body of connoisseurship and innovation. They personalised to convey superiority, which meant in practice that they believed their personal histories the most significant material they could draw upon.

Nobody would want to pass an Act of Uniformity to restrict poets to references readily understood within the public domain. Nor should critics desire some unnatural return to simplicity or any banal overemphasising. A poet's complexity is always likely to be the most creative thing about him or her. Surveying the enormous quantity of poetry in English which continues to fill the bookshops, one concludes that this most ancient of arts still appeals to some deep-seated response in human nature. The hard question is – what out of the surfeit which confronts the modern reader is truly significant, what moves us and makes us feel that it matters to us? My own belief is that paradoxically we are in a good period of poetry writing – now, at the end of one of the most turbulent centuries in human history. But I am not confident that today's poetry can make much of a mark on the forces which shape our lives. Perhaps it never has. The point of seriousness lies with the practitioners of verse, those who look on it as the most deep-cutting of the literary arts. We must take stylistics seriously since that is where life best reveals itself.

To that end, I shall conclude this short survey by pointing to some poetry which seems to me to embody the mystery of effective creation while stopping short of demanding that its readers pay tribute to a personal mythology. There is another poem of Muldoon's in *The Annals of Chile* which demonstrates his worrying manner more succinctly and which leaves one unsatisfied but nevertheless significantly startled. This is 'Incantata', subtitled 'In Memory of Mary Farl Powers'. It is an extended threnody for a musician friend, and it is as stuffed with private references as 'Yarrow'. The same hagiography, the pervading Irishism as relentless as Atlantic mist, the hinted-at squalors and terrors of love and death and the incantating rhetoric prevail, though in this poem a discipline of grief helps focus our attention on the underlying feeling. We may be miles from knowing what Muldoon knows and almost as far from instinctively sympathising with his particulars, yet there is a public mode which leads us into the entire verbal edifice. The general is seen to prop up the private, as it must in grief:

> . . . *how you simply wouldn't relent*
> *from your vision of a blind*
> *watch-maker, of your fatal belief that fate*
> *governs everything from the honey-rust of your father's*
> *terrier's*
> *eyebrows to the horse that rusts and rears*
> *in the furrow, of the furrows from which we can no*
> *more deviate*
> *than they can from themselves, no more than the map*
> *of Europe*
> *can be redrawn . . .*

A more thoroughgoing apotheosis of the insistently hagiographic published recently is Craig Raine's *History, The Home Movie*. Raine's early style, nicknamed a little misleadingly Martianism, is a simple-minded system of cartouche-writing whereby visual similitudes are hieroglyphed into jokey and startling images. Once the shock of this method wears off, there is not much which poets can do with it. However, it is a refraction of the oldest device in poetry, the metaphor, and Raine develops it in more sophisticated ways in later books. *The Onion, Memory* and *A Martian Sends a Postcard Home* embody the early pleasantries of Martianism, but his next volume *Rich* extends Martianism by a technique which might be called 'a narrative of metaphor'. *History* develops this into a giant personalised photo album in which two families, the English Raines and the Russian Pasternaks, represent the entire century. Raine and his publisher market this long poem as a novel, and it resembles in its progress if not in technique what novelists call 'documentary fiction' or 'faction'. Historical persons of weight and significance are put into action alongside the author's family representatives. Raine's belief that the Raines and the Pasternaks are quite as important as Stalin or Hitler or any of the world's major players gives his poem a hallucinatory dazzle which his heavily embalmed style makes even more intense. You could argue that his poem does no more than the ruminating human mind performs naturally – i.e. we are all bound inexorably into the solipsism of our own existences. Everyone from Jesus to the tax inspector can expect no more than a walk-on part when the ego tells its own story. This may be true, but the result in Raine's case is not an easy read, nor even a very interesting narrative. Like Muldoon, Raine exhibits an egregious confidence. We are taken back to the age of the peacock poet, which Raine, an admirer of John Donne, clearly intends. While the self is indisputably the origin of all feeling, it is only through the generic and the repetitive that such feeling can be conveyed to others. Nobody owns language: it is the property of the tribe. Those who serve the tribe's public duty find moulding their individual personalities into a convincing style easier to achieve than those who look to their egos as oracles. Raine pays the price of turning his verse into a textbook of mannerism. The objective Auden is revealed as more himself than the subjective Raine.

There are poet contemporaries of Muldoon who work in the same vein as he does but less hieratically. I would draw attention particularly to Sean O'Brien, Peter Didsbury and Ian Duhig, all in their late thirties or early forties, who have several stances and gestures in common. These poets are something new in English poetry. In shorthand terms, they are provincial Surrealists, masters of the *paysage moralisé*, sleepwalkers on the shores of naturalism where they record phantasms and nightmares of a brilliant order. Their poetry is a moral Ordnance Survey of modern Britain. Together it forms a study like *The Orators* fifty years on. They certainly believe that something is wrong, that quite as surely as in the 1930s ours is a land where no one is well. O'Brien especially puts together collages of malfunctioning daily life to produce an overall portrait of social disquiet.

> *It's midnight. On schedule, the ghost train*
> *Is failing the bend by the claypits,*
> *And stiff with old service revolvers,*
> *Unsleeping on old wooden chairs –*
> *The price of this unnecessary trip –*
> *We stare at the waiting-room fireplace and know*
> *That the corpse in its bundle of coats*
> *Will awake and the door be flung open*
> *When Hammerpond enters, no longer a tramp,*
> *To deliver the long explanation*
> *Whose end we will miss when the radio coughs*
> *And announces that all roads are flooded,*
> *The sovereign's in Canada, Hitler in Brighton,*
> *And no one will leave here tonight.*

It's as though merely the superficial quirks of Auden's style influenced writers in the 1930s, and it is only now in the last two decades of the century that his powerful landscaping presence is making itself felt. O'Brien, like the Ulster poet Tom Paulin, has mastered the Audenish minatory mutter, but has harnessed it also to an Absurdist violence which surveys with clear-eyed alarm the millennial exaggerations and horrors of right-wing reformism, Third World and Pacific Rim hegemony and the rust belt of communal failure.

Peter Didsbury, another poet of the North-East, is even more estranged from social calm than O'Brien. He brings an anthropological, almost an archaeological skill to everyday life in Hull and its environs. Philip Larkin wrote the Old Testament of these poets, and Douglas Dunn the New. They, in their turn, may be said to be working on their Acts of the Apostles. Their work is certainly not penny plain, but where it differs from Muldoon's is in the absence of personal mythologising, of the devising of holy texts from diary-keeping. Yet it manages to avoid too much archetyping as well, the sort of streetwise instancing which all too readily becomes journalistic cliché. Both the gods and the historians of Greece and Rome sneak up on Didsbury as he goes about his daily urban business. There is nothing facetious in this: rather it is Didsbury's recognition that the past is subsumed in the present, and that the most extravagantly personal perception of events is an outcropping of the universal. He can imagine himself a bee enacting a bee code transposed by human needs, or watch the chariots of the gods invade a furniture store.

> I'm drinking tea in a furniture store,
> idly thinking of Phoebus the sun-god,
> when a sky-blue sofa on which a youth reclines
> glides slowly through the cafeteria,
> pulled by a couple of girls in nylon shop-coats.
>
> I used to enjoy such theological problems
> but now they make me tired, as one is by a child.
>
> I watch in the last few minutes of my lunch-hour
> this tableau as it steers its direct course
>
> towards regions where no customer ever goes,
> through swinging doors equipped with rubber aprons
>
> which gasp behind it as it disappears from view.

Without recourse to Disney Martianisms, Didsbury cleanses

the doors of perception and inseminates the world with the strangeness which is always just below the surface.

Ian Duhig does for history, especially that of the early Christian Church and of nineteenth-century colonialism and *fin-de-siècle* artistic upheaval, what Didsbury does for the ancient gods. Duhig has a wonderfully unbuttoned fancy and a humour which he employs as a door into verbal ecstasy. None of these poets is interested in warring with Oxbridge decorum: they have no chips on their shoulders since they regard the world of learning as their own adventure playground. Duhig sees the poet's place as that of an omnivorous commentator, erudite judgement-passer, who nevertheless recognises that the world is complicated beyond even a saint's reforming programme. Reading Duhig's poems is a liberating experience since his viewpoint is uncoloured by either retrospective indignation or determinist patterning. Many of his exuberant scenes strike the reader at first as parody, but they are usually well supported by history and strangely plausible. Duhig has taken to heart Louis MacNeice's observation that the world is 'incorrigibly plural'. His gamey, camp atmosphere is in fact wholly robust: he can forgive us all since we are so immensely interesting, even if we are also definitively nasty. His funny poems are the best examples of uproarious bad taste since the early works of Lawrence Durrell or James Fenton's *jeux d'esprit* in 'The Kingdom of the Senseless'. In the following passage, an Irish monk in the Dark Ages labours at transcribing a psalter, with Duhig on hand to record the miseries of his labours.

> *Oh Forgiving Christ of scribes and sinners*
> *intercede for me with the jobbing abbot!*
> *Get me re-assigned to something pagan*
> *with sex and perhaps gratuitous violence*
> *which I might deplore with insular majuscule*
> *and illustrate with Mozarabic complexity*
> *Ad maioram gloriam Dei et Hiberniae,*
> *and lest you think I judge the book too harshly*
> *from pride or a precious sensibility*

*I have arranged for a second opinion.*
*Tomorrow our surveyor, Ronan the Barbarian,*
*will read out loud as only he can read out loud*
*selected passages from this which I have scored*
*while marking out his new church in Killarney*
*in earshot of that well-versed man, King Suibhne . . .*

*(Text completely illegible from this point because of lake-*
*water damage and otter dung.)*

There is a muster of good poetry in Britain today which has slipped the halter of gentility (something it had not done according to A. Alvarez a few decades ago) while not entering the domain of High Aestheticism (a Yeatsian temple never vacated in Ireland though often wafted, like a *Casa Santa*, across the Atlantic to the United States). To the names recorded above should be added, as founding fathers, those of Peter Redgrove, Alan Brownjohn, Douglas Dunn and George MacBeth. Farther back still are the exemplary figures of Auden, MacNeice and Empson. Two strains have come in from America – the brilliant conservative technicians who are also imaginative moral landscapers, Anthony Hecht, Howard Nemerov and Richard Wilbur – and the New Model Modernists, John Ashbery and Frank O'Hara, these last drawing the illuminated cart of Wallace Stevens. Troops to be found beside O'Brien, Didsbury and Duhig include Douglas Houston, Don Paterson, W. N. Herbert and Michael Donaghy. With this talent on hand, all the most unsanguine commentator could ask for is a wider audience of readers and a less fashionable set of journalistic reviewers and assessors.

# Matthew Sweeney

## A BLUR

She was a blur when he first saw her.
He was the last into the tent,
his head full of lion growls and the tart
comments of his bank manager.

He stood at the back, scanning the crowd
for his two kids, but his eyes were swiped
by her swinging above him,
over and back and upside down.

She let go and a blond man caught her.
If she'd missed there was no safety net.
He sent his applause round after her
as she bowed in a ring, then ran.

When his kids wouldn't go again
he went alone. He sat in the front
so he could be underneath her
as she went upside down.

That night, he knew he caught her eye
as she swung above him,
but she was moving so quickly,
if she smiled it was a blur.

The minute she left he left.
He ran around the tent
to catch her going into a caravan,
blue-painted, big enough for two.

He stood outside in the shadows
as she took off her gear
but he took off his glasses,
he wanted to keep her a blur.

# George Szirtes

## PALEFACE

Americans get the best of the deal.
No longer colonials, they can be gentlemen
Twice removed. The cabbie at the wheel
Harangues the professor in the demotic *parole*
Of an overcrowded *langue*. All those sudden
Nightmarish dislocations of the soul.
You hardly know where to start. But then
Haply you meet a Lithuanian poet or
Exchange notes with a Venetian grandee.
Come to think of it, it is hard to see
How a European can fail to remember the unfor-
Tunate isles he has escaped from all too recently.

## TINSELTOWN

Nothing but a glittering you can't describe,
nothing but names and smiling at faces: no
jewels but plastic beads, no tiaras but card,
no face but that which fits you, a tall mirror
hung by the magazine rack, some pearls of frost
on the window beyond, dripping elegance,

full of December, and rain starting to dance
on the pavement where a woman has just crossed
this busy road to push through the double door
to where you stand by the counter, working hard,
totting money at the till in a green glow
of figures, servant to that commonplace tribe

queuing for papers though it's nothing to do
with you what the tabloids blaze across the front
page, you simply read it along with the rest
and it's good for a giggle, just like this crown
of tinsel you got wound into your hair, which
catches the lampglow all the way down the aisle

and slips occasionally forward, so while
you are counting you're always having to switch
hands and flick the thing back so it won't fall down,
but sits perky and sparkling, a silver nest
of light, frivolous, and when it falls you don't
stop to pick it up, it means nothing to you.

# Robin Robertson

## ARTICHOKE

The nubbed leaves
come away
in a tease of green, thinning
down to the membrane:
the quick, purpled,
beginnings of the male.

Then the slow hairs of the heart:
the choke that guards its trophy,
its vegetable goblet.
The meat of it lies, displayed,
up-ended, *al dente*;
the stub-root aching in its oil.

# SHEELA-NA-GIG

He has reached her island by stones
pegged in swollen water,
through rain that has fallen for days.

He touches the welling mouth, the split stone;
she shows him the opening folds
where rainwater troubles and turns.

The rain slows, and stops; light deepens
at the lid of the lake, the water creased
by the head of an otter, body of a bird.

# AT DUSK

Walking through the woods
I saw these things:
a cat, lying, looking at me;
a red hut I could not enter;
the white grin of the snared fox;
the spider in a milk bottle,
cradling the swaddled fly,
rocking it to sleep;
a set of car keys, hanging from a tree;
a fire, still warm, and a bone
the length of my arm, my name
carved on it, mis-spelt.
The dog left me there,
and I went on myself.

# Jamie McKendrick

## NAME-TAG

Every sock and collar has a name-tag.
I have a name, a surname, and a tartan rug
with tassels. What else? A zip-up
pigskin letter-writing case that's pitted
where the bristles have been scorched away.
Once a week we write neat letters home with
our marks and team scores which the master reads.
Mornings, we get a tick for shitting
after the prefect has inspected it.
Through the keyhole old MacMillan
is sitting on his single bed
and talking to the service revolver
he uses with blanks to start the races.
Our toes are fat red bulbs from chilblains.
Already one skin has rubbed away, another grown
harder than the first, a kind of pigskin.
We must never 'sneak' or 'blub' or 'suck up'.
We wear steel studs that spark. Scoured lugs
stick out from crew cuts as we learn by heart
the Latin for pitching camp and waging war
and the psalm where I am made
to lie down in green pastures and a table
is prepared for me and my enemies.
The tables are mopped with swab rags,
the dustbins tipped among the ferns
and bamboo of the watergarden
for this was once a Country House

and we are lucky to enjoy the fine grounds
which we see through the barred windows
or on Sunday walks trying to keep up
with the master who ran the marathon.
In the wooden locker by the metal bed
I have a chipped enamel mug,
a toothbrush, a comb, a nailbrush and two shoebrushes
with which, with time, I could scrub away
my shoes, my nails, my hair, my teeth, myself,
given time enough, the buildings, the pitches,
the gate's ironwork with its clawing lion
and all we've learnt till nothing's left
but the Blasted Oak I carved my name on
and perhaps the derelict pavilion.

# Michael Hulse

## SIMLA

They say two senile memsahibs still live here,
colonel's daughters who stayed on into their dotage,
carefully collapsing into British dereliction:
slippage, dementia, smallness.

They say they were wonderful once.
Their bodies were young and fresh and proud.
Their bodies were fragrant of cotton and vanilla.
Willowy. Wily with innocence.

When the colonel's daughters turned in the door
of the Viceroy's lodge, to drop their curtseys
under the portraits of Dufferin and Curzon,
the men were a beat in the air, a held breath.

I think of the colonel's daughters dancing under the deodars,
moonlighting, flirting, wanting it all,
the music heard below, in the hillside bazaars,
by Indians who were banished from the Mall.

What am I doing here?
This café was converted from a British army bandstand.
We're sitting on the terrace, Jagdish Bhatt and me,
the city a litter of history below us,

the mountains a jagged white, far off, a glare.
By Christ Church, near the statue of Indira Gandhi,
three vans are parked, marked AMBULANCE,
and a fourth, lettered in red DEAD BODY VAN.

A correspondent for *The Times of India*.
Behind his Ray Bans, irony writes, and writes afresh,
as he talks of covering Himachal Pradesh,
the state where nothing happens any more.

Not that he'd want it back, the summer capital
of garden parties, balls, and Raj adultery,
Gilbert and Sullivan at the Gaiety,
archery at Annandale.

But still, the British got things done.
The trains. The roads. A vision with a map.
When Delhi was laid out anew, the roadside trees
were planted with such foresight, such precision,

that decades and three or four widenings later
there's been no need to fell them yet.
Clerks and police and government did their work
efficiently, politely, and unbribed.

I've heard the argument before. And Jagdish means it all.
It's not a sop to the visiting Brit. But still,
it puts good engineering where good ethics ought to be.
Like praising Hitler's motorways and Mussolini's trains.

Liberal goody-two-shoes that I am,
I want to say that nothing compensates
for robbing a people of their self-esteem,
stripping them of their independent power

to make their lives in ways to suit themselves.
I'd mean it. But I'd be dissatisfied.
It's not the whole truth either. Something stops my mouth.
Our talk is not of history, but how we know our home.

One night I watched the light die over Simla.
Dusk was stroking the town like a hand on a breast.
Lights were starring the landslide of homes on the hills,
and I ached for something I didn't have a name for:

if the colonel's fragrant daughters had been there
I'd have wanted to make a kind of love to them,
as the night came in like a warm and comforting tide
lapping the starry past in a mantle of black.

# Michael Hofmann

## HOTEL NEW YORK, ROTTERDAM

*for Joachim Sartorius*

Clouds, oil barges and airliners blow down the Maas,
chimneys, cranes and warships stay where they are,
the *Hotel* – you should be so lucky – *New York*
stays where it is, half church, half castle,
on its headland or island, fork or confluence,
where emigrants camped out in the Thirties,

watching the river, the schedules, the post, each other,
the great clock and the smaller one with the cardinal points,
the clipper ship weathervane, the tubby warehouses,
taking it in turn to eat and sleep and talk,
the wind blowing the money out of their pockets,
their morale out of the window, their lives into a flat spin.

# An Education

*for James, again*

At the old Tramontana
on Tottenham Court Road
among the hi-fi shops
I learned to order

what you ordered,
not studenty noodles
but sophisticated things
like the special.

After years of our
playing at lunch,
the faithful waiter shook himself
to death with Parkinson's

practically before our eyes.
(I remember the rattle
and slop of one last
saucerful of coffee.)

One afternoon,
when we no longer went there
like Hem to the War,
I saw Joseph Brodsky

sitting in the window
with paper and a cigarette,
the recording angel,
miles away.

# JUNE

Short forms. Lines, sentences, *bon mots*.
Part of an afternoon, a truncated night,
interstitial evening. Rarely a paragraph
or stanza ('room'), never a day and a day and a day . . .
Half-pints and double-deckers, the river, the cemetery,
always on the *qui vive* (why, ourselves of course!) –
our honeymoon epic in illicit instalments.

# Timothy Mo

## FIGHTING THEIR WRITING:
## THE UNHOLY LINGO OF RLS AND
## KUNG FU TSE

FOLLOWING THE SENSIBLE precept of Dr Goebbels, when I hear the word 'culture' I reach for my *eskrima* staves. From childhood, my association of race, of the clash of inimical civilisations, has been with the seductive beckonings of rival systems of hand-to-hand violence that were as technically ingenious as they were philosophically incompatible.

I was born in Hong Kong in 1950 on Rizal Day to a twenty-eight-year-old Cantonese lawyer and a twenty-two-year-old Yorkshire/Welshwoman with family origins in rural labour and domestic service (my grandmother shining tables for the Marquis of Anglesey at age twelve). The Chinese side could point to a military mandarin in the pedigree and gold ingots stashed in the chimney. In other words, it was a union where the woman had clearly married beneath herself. The Peak Residence Ordinance, restricting the mist-shrouded heights of the Victoria Peak and Mount Austin (resolutely unmetric and imperial at 2,175ft) to Whites, had been re-pealed but four years previously. Pug marks of lost tigers could still be seen in the New Territories on paddy that is now the site of light industrial satellite towns, while Old China Hands spoke of lunch as 'tiffin' and, with a strange affection, of 'Camp' – internment under sadistic Korean and Japanese guards on (Lord) Stanley Peninsula. Sikh guards with shotguns protected the already unassailable 15ft high counters of the traditional South China pawnshops of the Western District (our 'Bazaar'), Sikh Bren-gun teams and Vickers crews having won a reputation for suicidal valour in

December 1941 in contrast to the prejudiced local perception of the resistance offered by the Middlesex Regiment and the Winnipeg Grenadiers. Similarly, Cantonese bank-guards were perceived by their compatriots as being so cowardly they couldn't be trusted even to discharge their firearms in the air before fleeing from Triad attackers, whereas a pair of turbaned, *tulwa*-wielding temple-guards had made mincemeat of a horde of secret-society robbers in pre-war days. Chinese loan-sharks backed these racial hunches with their capital, or it might be the other way round. Of course, the disadvantage of the *mo lo cha* ('no morals people') was that they got your maid pregnant and spat red juice all over the place. Nowadays, Gurkhas from the battalions disbanded under post-imperial defence budgets supply an equally formidable but unarmed private security corps for the car-parks owned by Jardine Matheson, the quondam opium traders.

But it was Billy Tingle and Robert Louis Stevenson, not the *mo lo cha*, who were my first preceptors in the unarcane but noble arts of Western self-defence. This was the heyday of 1950s Man who put Brylcream or Vaseline on his hair at a time when only two brands of cigarette were available in the Crown Colony, Camel and Lucky Strike. My stepfather, ex-Indian Navy, ex-BOAC, ex-Ben Line, thought I ought to know 'how to look after myself'. The word 'manly' was mentioned without contemporary embarrassment but not the likely circumstance that I might have occasion to punch a greater number of noses on my way through an English school than a blue-eyed boy with less ambiguous cheekbones.

Billy Tingle was an Australian but, naturally, more English than the English. Mr Tingle was no mere cricket coach or boxing instructor: he was character-builder extraordinary by appointment to the children of the expatriate gentry. And what a name, with its overtones of the TV school comedy *Whacko!* and that other Billy, Bunter. He didn't look unlike a spry, weight-trained, cross-countried version of the Owl of the Remove, down to his wire-frame spectacles. At the time I was enrolled in Tingle's Athletic Institute at the age of seven I was slightly shorter than him and by the time I left, pushing ten, I could look him straight in the eye, so I deduce he must have been about 4ft 11ins. Mr Tingle had been flyweight champion of the Queensland goldfields in the early years of the century but his values were pure Victoriana. Recently, I came across a yellowing photograph of us Tingle boys in our red and white caps, sitting glumly before a placard emblazoned TRUTH, LOYALTY, DILIGENCE. I can still hear BT's gravelly voice as he led us in the Institute oath: 'I will conduct myself like a sportsman and a gentleman at all times. I will not abuse my knowledge but use it to protect women and the defenceless. I will respect my opponent and not take unfair advantage of him.'

This was the boxing preamble. Cricket vows were unnecessary as enshrined in the game itself ('keeping a straight bat in life', 'not cricket, old boy'). Mr Tingle's cricket I dreaded: both boring and scary, the ball hard and reminiscent of sutured eyebrows.

But right from the start flurries of fists held no terrors for me. I had an affinity for the gloves, dank with the clammy hands of previous users and prickly with horse-hair as they were. It does have to be said that Mr Tingle's method of teaching boxing was hopelessly outmoded even in 1956. We stood up like guardsmen and were drilled by numbers: one, left lead to the head, two left lead to the body, three double left lead to head, four (you guessed it), double left lead to the body, and so on. That was the Tingle offence in all its rectilinear classicism. Defence consisted of: one, block, two, parry, three (distinctly as a last resort), duck. We all ended up with the same Corinthian style as Mr Tingle, probably not dissimilar to that of the great eighteenth-century Jewish champion, Daniel Mendoza. Some three decades previously Gene Tunney and Joe Louis had developed modern boxing but Mr Tingle reserved the same scorn for the up-jab, the left hook, combination punching, and a bob and weave defence as admirals of the battleship era had for the aircraft carrier. In its way it was a splendid disdain.

However, the spirit of Western boxing could not be denied. Unlike classical Asian systems of unarmed combat, from earliest days pugilism was geared for an eventual real confrontation and free sparring was a vital part of the training. No oriental style laid such an emphasis on the individual and the practical. From the days of Mendoza and those other great bareknucklers, the Gas Man and Hen(ry) Pearce (the Game Chicken), from the time of Byron and the Fancy and their dabblings with the 'mufflers' on, during the heyday of the great school of arms at the cavernous Fives Court in St Martin's Lane (boxing, small- and back-sword, single-stick, cudgels, and rackets – with rackets clearly the most dangerous, many a retired champion losing an eye to the evil little ball), the essence of boxing instruction was that the academic lessons should be put to a moment of proof, if not truth.

At the age of eight I had my first fight, or 'contest' as Mr Tingle insisted we call it. This was against one Anthony Maine in a raised ring pitched in the centre of the cricket ground (where at the height of the Cultural Revolution ten years later someone would hit a six straight through the windows of the communist Bank of China). The blue corner was reserved for the usual Tingle boys from those bastions of racial supremacy, the Peak School and Quarry Bay, the red for Chinese foundlings from a less distinguished institution where Mr Tingle coached for free.

To my extreme chagrin, I was handed not a blue but a red sash.

Without exception all twenty-odd Chinese boys who had preceded me from the corner had lost, putting me in Childe Roland's boots on the lonely walk to the ring. English sergeants from the garrison seconded both corners. Jovial fellows in the mould of Kipling's Learoyd, Ortheris, and Mulvaney, they didn't speak to me when I arrived or during the interval between the opening and second rounds, but sponged my face down, held the bottle and spittoon for me, and pulled my shorts away from my abdomen so I could breathe more easily. Recuperating between rounds two and three, I asked, 'How am I doing?'

If a dog or cat had spoken to them in English, they could hardly have looked more flabbergasted. A burst of urgent instructions followed: stick out the left, keep your guard up, all the clichés of the British amateur corner. As Mr Tingle's contemporaries would have put it, I succeeded in 'tapping the claret' from Master Maine's nose in the third, and I think the Sergeants Two were more pleased than I was when after the cards had been collected I had my hand raised by Mr Tingle. The SBO in the Colony, a naval Commodore, presented me with an electro-plated nickel silver cup which the south-west monsoon corroded before the autumn.

Mr Tingle's stern code was underpinned by a romantic literary culture which I embraced with an even greater enthusiasm. All this time I was devouring the work of Robert Louis Stevenson, *Kidnapped* first, and second *Treasure Island*, and, much too early, *Island Nights Entertainments*. Graham Greene, in *A Sort of Life*, rates Stevenson highly as a master of the language of descriptive action. I agree 99 per cent. The scene in the cramped round-house of the brig *Covenant* is still vivid in my mind: that violent tableau where the dandyish little Jacobite Alan Breck, mindful of the disadvantages of a long blade in such a situation, runs through half a dozen men in as many seconds, then with a bad, blazing exultation cries out to the narrator, David Balfour, 'Oh, man, am I no' a bonny fighter!' The tubercular Stevenson's description in *The Beach of Falesá* of the blood from a fatally stabbed man gushing over the hands of his assailant 'hot as tea' is a brilliant entry from the quotidian into the exotic. Earlier, the same assailant, Wiltshire, 'gave him first the one and then the other so that I could hear his head rattle and crack and he went down straight'. (Which I instantly recognised as the only combination in the Tingle repertoire, the left-right or one-two.) And when Wiltshire says to his victim, 'Speak up, and don't be malingering there, or I'll take my feet to you,' I get the authentic whiff of Scottish street violence going abroad – as it still does – in the robes of mandarin irony. Stitch that, Jimmy, says the modern lout as his head-butt goes in. Yet don't we hear in Wiltshire's words a consciousness of the infraction of the Tingle code?

Where I believe Stevenson, and Greene, fall short is as

303

comprehenders of action. Greene states as an axiom for authors that action must be described sparely, e.g. high verb content and low adjectival quotient per mandatorily simple sentence. This is all very well for creating an effect in the untutored reader's mind but is not adequate for *analysing* what actually happened. There is a grammar of combat, a syntax of movement, which the human body has to obey in all fighting systems, just as there are less iron rules governing language and communication.

Unfortunately the literary skill of the writer is not at all related to her or his comprehension of the action they are realising. Hazlitt's *On Going to the Fight*, for instance, is the perfect example of the literary intellectual waffling stylishly about something he has no knowledge of whatsoever. *Cashel Byron's Profession*, GBS's contribution to the genre, is quite feeble and Thackeray, one of my very favourite novelists, is also distinctly unreliable on a fist-fight, whereas the comparatively mediocre R. M. Ballantyne (better known for *Coral Island*) excels in *Martin Rattler* where in the first few pages the eponymous schoolboy narrator jams a rising kick with a counter-kick of his own: this the sophisticated measure only a prince among street-fighters could employ (although it's also part of the approach work of the classic short-range style of Chinese boxing, Wing Chun). 'Where did you learn that?' someone asks young Martin. 'I only ever saw that used at Eton.' No comment.

I would put John Masefield on a par with Hemingway as a first-rate writer who knew what he was watching. I read *Sard Harker*, his only novel, aged ten, so the pastiche Conradian time-jump which begins it was lost on me, but the boxing match which follows struck me as perfect then as it does now: the unpaired cluster of tatty gloves thrown into the ring in some back-of-beyond Latin American port, the lanky young blacks scrambling for them and boxing with great speed and skill before the main event, a clandestinely fixed match between an evil-aspected white man ('the muscle had all gone to brothel with his soul,' says Masefield of the fixer) and a magnificently built Carib. 'He's well-ribbed,'

Harker's captain observes of the white man and then memorably adds, 'If we have to meet, may it be moonlight and may I be first.' What a line!

I don't believe I'm being partisan but I also find Americans, with the exceptions of Hemingway and James Jones, notably poor on fisticuffs. Jack London was hugely overrated in this area.

I disparage the Americans but I embraced Yankee culture wholeheartedly at my English-language school, Quarry Bay. All the more so after my short-lived Chinese classical education at the Convent of the Precious Blood, an institution run by ferocious Cantonese nuns who thought RC meant Rigid Confucianism. I called it Bloody Blood, influenced, I think, by tales of Japanese atrocities in *Camp on Blood Island*.

I was the dunce of the calligraphy class who managed the characters for one, two and three, but baulked at four. I wore the same tall white dunce's cap Cultural Revolution victims would wear to their executions. I got put in the corner with sticking-plaster over my mouth for asking questions. I got hit in the face ten times, very, very lightly, but still ten times.

Unfortunately, Billy Tingle had yet to drill me in his one, two, three defensive routine. (Twenty years later, I was interested to read in the local paper that a teacher had just got the sack for striking one child in the face three hundred times.) The nuns instructed my amahs to feed me just white rice, without soya sauce. In fact, it was fish fingers and chips at home.

With all my heart, I detested these attempts to brainwash me out of such individualism as I already cherished but the real problem, as I reflect on it now, was to find myself, endowed through genes and upbringing with a precocious conceptual intelligence, adrift within an ideographic literary culture. I had no gift at all for Chinese characters, those complex and beautiful constructs of spatial metaphor and pictorial allusion, both external and internal, to the closed universe of the system. Just as I have no musical inclination or mathematical acumen (I was to fail Elementary Mathematics

O-level eight times), so I lack all artistic ability in appreciation of proportion or perspective, or the extension of line.
Virtually all Chinese literate in their own characters have
elegant Western handwriting in the same effortless way the
Dutch speak almost accentless English from lesson one. I
have the handwriting of a child of five, sundered by potent
but ill-understood psychopathic drives. Had I remained
within the Chinese pedagogic system I would never have been
an intellectual, still less one with artistic aspirations. God
knows what I would have been, but certainly a lot richer
than I am.

Once dropped into the alphabetic information flow, I was
the ugly duckling taking to water. I found an immediate
reassurance in the logic and coherence of the system, in the
way the mere twenty-six letters could be taken apart and
bolted together like a Meccano set over and over again into
limitless meanings. Even words utterly alien and perhaps
unsuitable in a childish vocabulary could be stuttered out
phonetically, like summoning a genie from thin air, and their
adult power exploited. 'Zounds, ten thousand curses upon
you,' I said to my new teacher, the New Zealander Mrs
Penman, and got a laugh, rather than the death of a thousand
cuts. One could read a journal and later ascertain the meaning of 'rape', 'heuristic', and 'counter-productive', or often
enough work it out from context – on empirical OED lines,
did one but realise it, in the spirit of Marco Polo's explor-
ations – whereas Chinese children have no notion at all how
an unknown character might be pronounced and once taught
the sound and its pitch have to remember it by parroting it
every time the ideograph is displayed to them. Some time
later, they might be spoon-fed its meaning by the benevolent
teacher.

Some say reading Chinese is like viewing a vast, darkened
plain from a mountain-top through flashes of lightning,
association and allusion piling in fast and thick in a way
alphabetic languages cannot match. This I can accept, and
the Sino-Arabic convention of opening a book from the back
(to the Occidental eye) and reading the lines from right to

left should disconcert no one. What I have never adjusted to is the maddening circular logic of traditional Chinese dialectic (only those who've faced it can understand the full depth of exasperation) and the notion that somehow a middle position between opinions is always the correct one, however absurd it actually is (the centre being crucial to the Chinese intellectual and moral position, even figuring as a compass direction and the name of the country itself, the Middle Kingdom).

By the time I had spent a year at Bloody Blood I'd learned to hate both my teachers and my classmates. Taunting and ostracism were the weapons both young and old employed to break recalcitrant spirits, to make them obedient to instructors and parents and, in due course, government, frightened to be different from all the other sniggering conformists. It was the quintessence of small-mindedness – in its extreme form, the petty spite of solemnly sending an executed man's family the bill of five cents for the bullet which terminated his existence – while both Tingle and RLS with all their ingenuousness, their romanticism, were large-minded spirits.

I've always smiled inwardly when people complain about Western 'racism'. The vilest racists in the world, without guilt or compunction, are drawn from the ranks of the Japanese and the Chinese, those people who can read each other's script with mutual transparency. Ask any African who studied in Peking.

What I learned early was this: those craven souls who like to make life miserable for those who are different, whether blue Mao-suited mob or bovver-booted green jackets, do not have noble instincts to work on. They are best met with an utterly inappropriate degree of retaliatory violence; if you, or yours, lose you are far less likely to be picked on again because you are crazy and dangerous. Let me illustrate: Bangladeshis are easy prey; Sikhs, with the blade their religion enjoins them to carry, are not.

After I was taken to a child psychiatrist for dreaming about the nuns hanging from trees (the shrink thought I meant by executioner's knots), I was removed to the international

Quarry Bay School. I dived into American junk culture with a vengeance. We devoured Blackhawk comics (the black-uniformed Olaf, Heinz, Chop-Chop, and their comrades as cosmopolitan a bunch as we); we played softball, watched the 77th Bengal Lancers on black and white TV, Kipling in the argot of the waggon-train: 'Hey, guys, the adjutant says to go get chow.' We aped the accents of the American boys, couldn't understand why the Brit parents had hysterics at the school play when the Bishop of Hereford asked Robin Hood in the accents of Galveston: 'Say, good my fellow, who is the leader of your rascally bee-aa-nd?'

For me it was a blessed middle-ground between Confucius and Kipling, because I knew I didn't belong within our third-rate Raj (it being on the whole a historical fact that those not blue-blooded or talented enough for the ICS went to Hong Kong). The most harrowing film I saw in those years didn't feature violence or the supernatural; it was *Bhowani Junction* from John Masters' novel, starring Ava Gardner as the young Anglo-Indian, Victoria Jones. Indian friends have subsequently assured me that Masters' portrait of the Eurasians (ran the railways, called the Indians 'wogs') was by and large fair. The film left me with a dread of the aimless confusion of train stations which has never departed my adult psyche, a dismay which connects loss of identity with the darkness of tunnels, flaring torches, and the possibility of missing one's platform change for the express to clarity. The Bhowani Eurasian's hatred of native culture could never have been offensive to the indigene even at the height of empire: it was merely pitiable. How sad, how full of pathos, this self-mutilation.

Unfortunately, it was all too common a phenomenon in the Dutch, British, and French possessions, though far less pronounced with the Portuguese in Macao and Timor. One of the problems was the gender direction of most marriages then. Forty years ago 90 per cent of mixed unions involved a Western male marrying a native female, much like modern marriages between Westerner and Filipina with their huge disparities in age and income. For a Chinese man to have the audacity to take an English wife was virtually unheard of, even for Chinese males coming from those affluent classes where instead of sport a man's recreation was taken in the horizontal plane. So most Eurasians looked white on paper when they wrote their names – Higginbottom, Carruthers – but my surname revealed me: baldly monosyllabic, clearly Chinese.

This didn't suit quite everyone. I was with some sleight of hand registered for school in my stepfather's British surname, though my passport and birth certificate still bore my real name until, aged eighteen, I was able to register myself at Oxford under the correct title.

So, aged ten, I arrived in the UK posing as a little Englishman, with the classical dukes-up style of Corinthian Tom.

Mr Ryan soon sorted me out.

John Ryan had been amateur welterweight champion of Europe at the 1947 Dublin Games; had won the New York Golden Gloves; and held a points win over Randolph Turpin (who as a professional had gone on to beat the greatest ever pound-for-pound fighter, Sugar Ray Robinson, for the world middleweight title in 1951). Mr Ryan was a man marked by disappointment but it took a little while to know it. Turpin had knocked him out in a return match – absolutely no disgrace – but what had broken John Ryan's heart was missing the London Olympic Games of 1948 where he had been favourite to take the gold medal. The team berths had been decided in fight-offs at the ABA finals. Mr Ryan had beaten his opponent several times previously but, not wishing to lose the opportunity, had entered the ring with influenza. Weak and reeling, he was stopped within the distance. After that he hung up the gloves. The war had robbed him of his best years already.

He was short for a 147-pounder, with calves better developed than his thighs, balding, a slightly crooked gait as he swaggered to the Belmont school gym from his Hillman Minx, pork-pie hat jammed over smudged features that were simultaneously those of the stage Irishman and, curiously, the oriental sage, with his flattened nose and deformed eyebrows that were also a warning that boxing exacted an inexorable tribute from even its most talented practitioners.

The Ryan style was as different from the Tingle as could be imagined: an address that was pure America, gloves up by the ears, head weaving like a striking snake's, body swaying rhythmically from the waist, mind alert to any initiative from the opponent, sequences of counter-punches programmed to go before the thought ever crystallised. From Mr Ryan I learned 'punches in bunches'. To this day I can't throw a single shot and stop there; they rattle off in threes, fives, sevens, nines: nearly always an odd number when attacking with these highly schooled punch spreads to head and body, for the front hand (left in the case of an orthodox boxer, right for a southpaw) would usually begin a combination, followed by the rear hand, and however many punches were thrown conventional wisdom had it that the final word in the sentence was a hook with the front hand which 'closed the book', i.e. left you with your guard up and ready to defend or launch another onslaught. Counter-punching spreads would often be evenly numbered as you could begin with the rear hand, say a right cross over the foe's left jab. But whether an opponent is a boxer, a kung fu man, or a wild brawler, he (or she!) can't hurt you unless body weight is transferred to the side they intend to strike you with. So if someone is on the back foot they can't hurt you with a percussion technique off their front hand. Or if the weight is on the right side, there is nothing to fear from the left hook. Or if the opponent is leaning forwards, only the leading hand can hurt with an uppercut, while the rear fist can be regarded as unloaded. Kicks are on the opposing principle: weight is on the supporting leg. These are the unbreakable grammatical principles, though expert practitioners can prevaricate with their bodies. Other cardinal rules: lead with the front hand, never the rear, to unbalance the opponent and find the range; never retreat in a straight line but always sideways, away from the foe's strongest side; keep your hands up; don't try to hit your opponent as hard as you can every time; a straight line is shorter than a hook; don't do the same thing more than twice in a row; relax; never lose your temper.

Of course, some of these rules are less than prescriptive for those with the talent to flout them (just as great novelists can ignore the elementary rules of the novel). I wasn't Sugar Ray Robinson, so I did everything by Fowler rather than Fouler.

We spent long hours practising with our weaker hand – in my case, the left. Mr Ryan made us tuck a book to our body with the right elbow so we couldn't call on that fist at all. That sums up the apprenticeship to Western boxing – honing your weaker weapon until it becomes deadlier than the stronger.

Apprenticeship to Hung gar kung fu, the hard-man southern Chinese school, was quite different: standing stock-still, bow-legged in the 'horse' stance until you collapsed, with a kick in the butt your reward when you wobbled. After that, Chinese 'hard' styles concentrated on your strongest technique and this influenced Korean and Japanese forms, with their emphasis on breaking inanimate objects.

But Mr Ryan informed us that the point of boxing was only secondarily to hit someone very hard; the main objective was not to get hit oneself. This strikes me as more sensible now than it did then. Professional promoters prefer what is called a 'crowd-pleaser', i.e. someone who ploughs forward and gets hit a lot. Pulp always sells best. 'Typical white guy,' is one of boxing's cruel, but truthful, sayings, 'fights with his face.' Mr Ryan taught us to fight like black guys.

He himself was an absolute warlock at avoiding punches. I must make allowances for being young and impressionable but I still believe I have to see his defensive peer. Mr Ryan would plant himself on a chalk mark, then invite one of us to hit him. All he was allowed to do was move his head and trunk. It was like trying to hit a reflection in the mirror, or catching a spectre that lived in a time one second ahead of you. Only once did I strike him a glancing blow when, bored with missing one hundred punches in under a minute, I put my glove where I thought he *wouldn't* be. He knew how I'd done it and was as miffed as a child who has had a vanilla cornet taken from him. Next time he was ready for the cheap ploy and I never connected again. Even two of us attacking at the same time left him unscathed. Yes, we were kids but two mean, well-taught thirteen-year-olds should be a problem for any grown man.

That was the age I scored my first knockout, with a short left hook off the jab that felt like nothing but had John Griffiths out for five scary minutes – scary for the adults, I was cock-a-hoop, especially as they couldn't decently punish me for my indecent glee.

John Ryan didn't push the muscular Christian gentleman bit as overtly as Billy Tingle. (Although I suspect the fee-paying parents of the Tingle Institute merely wanted the kids out of their hair – as an Italian lady once said to me: 'It's not that the English hate children, it's just that they love animals.') But Mr Ryan also had the self-control of the kind of saint who'd done a stint as a centurion. One of the schoolmasters, a strapping white South African, six foot plus and still in his twenties, incautiously observed to us that Mr Ryan was a 'little past it'. We little gossips relayed this to a John Ryan who seemed as old as Methuselah to us but was still in his early forties. Gamely, the younger man put his gloves where his mouth was and the upshot was that John Ryan, who came up to his opponent's chest, handled him like a baby. It was the finest display of skill, and kindness, I will ever see.

Some weeks later, Mr Ryan was late arriving. We saw him hobble from his car. Sheepishly, he told us: he'd stubbed his toe on the tap to his gas-fire.

If my pugilistic skills had improved beyond recognition away from Hong Kong, my reading standards had taken a nose-dive. That Stevenson's work can appeal to the very young is not a knock against him, merely evidence of a great technician's universality of appeal and his directness of sentiment. But I'd taken up Captain W. E. Johns and his Biggles books, G. A. Henty ('the 44th were observed to advance with the utmost coolness into a most galling fire of

grape and musketry', or something on those lines), not to
mention Percy F. Westerman (hardly remembered today but
a respectable craftsman), and the historical novels of bluff
old Henry Treece. In the school holidays I braved the railway
from the cemetery of a suburb my stepfather had buried us
in to Woking – already site of a mosque – to buy the Saint
novels of Leslie Charteris at W. H. Smith's on platform two.
The double irony of the Bhowani ride was that Mr Charteris
was a Chinese Eurasian from Singapore, a destiny quite
uncelebrated in the blurbs of Simon Templar's creator.

At fifteen I embraced the chance to take up fencing, mainly
because I'd enjoyed Anthony Hope's novels *The Prisoner of
Zenda* and *Rupert of Hentzau*. Once again I got a brilliant
exponent, David Martin, French teacher, in 1964 a recent
graduate of St Andrew's University, and a member of the
England sabre team. David didn't look unlike an Alan Breck-
ish Scots hero, with his pale face, neat, blue-veined hands,
faint five o'clock shadow, and voice that was at its most even
when most provoked. I was a better boxer than a fencer but
attained reasonable proficiency with the sabre, a weapon
characterised by broad movements, while foil and epée are
most effective when manipulated in feints less than half an
inch to either side. Too much like pettifogging ideograph
drills for me.

Of all combat sports, Olympic fencing lends itself most
readily to a deconstruction, with the most ostentatiously
articulated grammar of movement. The President at the
centre of the piste 'analyses' the events leading to a hit for
the benefit of the four judges, two behind each protagonist.
I can see and hear David Martin in my mind's eye, with his
fur-collared car-coat thrown over his shoulders, in our freezing gym, for all the world parsing a piece of Voltaire or
Racine for us. 'Left took his opponent's blade and initiated
a balestra attack, which Right parried tierce, and riposted
with a lunge to head. Left parried quinte, launched a *flèche*
attack to head, which Right made to parry quinte, but Left
changed the plane and cut to chest, which was . . .?'

'Good,' we juvenile judges chorused.

In those days sabre was not yet electric so the re-phrasing of events was more detailed than with the point weapons, foil and epée, which had the benefit of lights and buzzers on a scoring machine. Sabre champions were older, less pure reflex-dependent, and some considered epée, where you could hit any part of the body, to be crude and violent.

Epée was John Stanbury's weapon, and he was neither crude nor violent.

When I meet sadistic karate sensei, sub-neanderthal bantamweights, in short all the emotionally arrested icebergs and assorted tantrum-throwers and racket-chuckers who've reached the top of their sport, I console myself by thinking of John Stanbury. Then I reflect that it's perfectly possible to be a champion *and* a nice guy.

John and I, exactly the same age, picked up a foil on the same afternoon under the indulgent eye of David Martin. Thereafter our paths diverged. John became a world junior finalist, double Olympic and multiple England representative. I forgot all about fencing after I was eighteen, until two years ago the publisher Richard Cohen (himself an Olympic sabreur whom I fenced in the 1968 London championships, though Richard affects not to remember this epochal moment in his career) mentioned John as one of Britain's most successful fencers. It's a little difficult for me to adjust my picture of the sunny Stanbury from schoolboy fellow-dabbler to maestro. For in those early days he lost about as many times as he won and his modesty and affability were tested over and over again (fencing being even more adrenalin-laden and tense than other combat sports while lacking the emotional release of hard physical activity). I remember John's dark skin, his straight hair, and his unassuming smile as if it was yesterday and not a quarter of a century ago. Interestingly, John's coaches could all see the potential in him, and the late Steve Boston, 'Professor' Boston as fencing coaches are entitled, himself a former professional boxer, once observed, 'That boy stands like a world champion.' Little did he know.

In my last year at school, aged seventeen, I went back to foil and exchanged a few hits with Stanbury, the click of blades on guards no more threatening than the tinkling of a defective telephone of that day. I scored a few times, then John did something so simple but so elegant that all I could do was boggle at the blade bending against the plastron on my chest. He did it again.

'God, John, that was fantastic. How can anyone beat you?' He laughed. 'Well, they do.'

Then he skewered me again. I've never forgotten his next words. 'You're not bad actually. But that just makes you easier to read, Tim.'

If I had to pick an ability common to John Ryan and John Stanbury it would be just that: the ability to read the grammar of movement so instinctively and so swiftly that the rest of us became stumbling illiterates.

Oriental weapons systems which I was to study in my twenties were philosophically more flatulent than Olympic fencing and a good deal less effective. I'd now say a real duel with bladed weapons would be over in under half a minute, as opposed to Hope's confrontation between Rudolf Rassendyll and Rupert Hentzau which Rassendyll wins on stamina and a history of clean living. I do have a slightly higher opinion of kendo than I do of karate, mainly because the protective body armour and cane swords, with the occasional competition, promote a realistic understanding of the concept of critical distance (the point at which an attack must be launched because defence will be impossible). On the other hand I now believe the ancient Book of Five Rings by the duellist Musao Musashi ('Strike slowly, strike with the whole body') to be a Nipponese disinformation exercise.

Of the Asians the Filipino *eskrimadors* (rattan and dagger fighters) and the Gujerati sabre and buckler exponents impress me the most. In particular, the Doce Pares school of the central Philippines incorporates some highly original, fluid strokes in which one technique melts into the next in a way unknown to the more severe, more discrete phrasing of French and Hungarian-originated fencing. As with boxing, fencing is more creative and pragmatic than the non-occidental forms but I have to say nothing ever matched the terse definitions of the short-lived Turkish knife-fighting school in Stoke Newington. Did they teach deceptions, fancy footwork, blocks, dodges? Assuredly not. One was somewhat taken aback by – how can one put it? – their fidelity to circumstance. The essences of the knife, the instructor said, were concealment and a quick draw. You didn't display a knife to control or intimidate, like a pistol. The blade came out, preferably while the opponent's attention was somewhere else, went into his body, and back to the place of concealment before you could say Kemal Atatürk. This is an unimpeachably logical, unrhetorical analysis of the knife in the era of the repeating hand-gun but I am still too much the Tingle boy to care to be too glib in such an unholy lingo.

During my twenties, no longer a reader but a writer, I found myself completing the circle. Oriental fighting systems, the more arcane the better, became suddenly fashionable in the wake of the late Bruce Lee's films. Lee (whose mother was a Dutch Eurasian) would have found this ironic as he had learned to reject the precepts of traditional kung fu and karate, referring to their stiff, programmed practitioners as being in a state of 'vertical death'. Unlike the current Hollywood oafs, Lee was a real fighter and brilliant instructor who incorporated boxing and fencing (learned from his brother Robert, a foilist) into Jeet Kuen Do: a system which stressed all-out attack and individual creativity.

Unfortunately, I was re-inventing the wheel, doing the rounds of self-styled masters in Hong Kong, London and Taiwan. This is not the place for a detailed technical examination of the inadequacies of Asian martial arts. Suffice to say, I was reversing the pattern of my literary experience, going now from the occidental system to the oriental and finding the anatomical contortions and shadow-boxing patterns as inimical as I had the ideographs. The philosophy of unreflective reverence for style and master was uncannily similar to Bloody Blood, right down to repeated blows in the face. With my stumpy legs and narrow hips, my deep chest and brawny arms I was built to throw multiple left hooks, not kick. From being the star of Tingle's, Mr Ryan's pride and joy, his thirteen-year-old with the anaesthetic left hand, I became the *kwoon* and *dojo* Bumble, the idiot everyone took liberties with in three-step sparring. One day I broke a Ryan precept, lost my temper, and threw a flurry of left hooks.

In general karateka have failed the test of the kick-boxing ring and have had to go back to the drawing-board. My current opinion is that fighting systems are effective in inverse proportion to their sense of self-dramatisation and spectator appeal. Muai Thai, with its grappling, knee-butts, and five-minute rounds, is abominably scrappy but its champions have swept the board with everyone. Judo and Olympic wrestling are unspectacular but their exponents are truly formidable. The Brazilian form, Capoeregem – or a dilute form of it – is currently sweeping the all-comers tournaments: again, it's scrappy, involving – it seems – little other than throwing a foe on the ground and bashing him in the face, but it is undeniably effective. One art that does look good, and also works, with its graceful *fouetté* and *chassé* kicks is French savate, which had its heyday under Charleroi and Baron Coubertin in the nineteenth century ('fencing with the limbs,' according to the Baron) but has made a vigorous comeback under modern greats such as Christian Guillaume, a lightweight who held his own in Thailand.

Unarmed or alternative fighting forms are the last recourse of the oppressed, those denied access to firearms: Okinawan farmers with their rice-flails, Filipinos with their canes and bolos. In the Confederate States there was a resurgent interest in archery in the 1860s and 1870s, while Napoleonic adventurists took to savate after 1815, euphemistically calling it 'l'adresse française'. And, of course, the Boxer rebels of 1900 thought they were invulnerable to bullets.

So did I. On only one occasion in my adult life have I had to fight for my life. This was not in Mexico City, Davao, or Detroit, but the Balls Pond Road, London N. against nine little cowards armed with milk bottles (which were non-felonious until smashed and held by the neck). What saved me stitches was still being able to run three miles in under eighteen minutes, a modest enough feat of which my legs and cardio-vascular system are no longer capable. I would rather draw a veil over this chastening experience but it began with overweening physical conceit when I walked straight through the 'rascally band' on the assumption that I could make a continental breakfast of them. I was hit on the head from behind with a bar, and that was just the start. Had I never learned jab, cross, and hook or a *coup de pied bas*, what would I have done? I'd have crept quietly away before they saw me. And it would never have happened.

Perhaps there's something to Buddhism after all.

# Louis de Bernières

## LIVER

OF ALL DOMESTIC jobs it was the fortnightly drag to the launderette that I hated the most. It was our misfortune to live in a small flat where there was no room for a washing machine, and it had long been our habit to use up all our underwear before deciding that I really must go and do a wash. It was therefore always an emergency when I went to the launderette, because otherwise we would have been reduced to rummaging through the laundry basket for the least unsavoury items. It wouldn't have been too bad for me, because I went to private schools where we were expected to change our underpants just once a fortnight, and I became scrupulous about avoiding accidents and leaks, but my wife went to a state school and lived at home, so for her it would have been a true and terrible deprivation if she could not have changed all her clothes every day, sometimes twice.

When I went to the launderette I used to be burdened by four bulging canvas bags containing all her clothes, and one small and half-empty one containing mine. I felt like my wife's slave under such circumstances, and my bitterness was mitigated only by the thought that she was a conscientious victim of the notion that everything must be ironed. Naturally, I discovered long ago that most garments will iron themselves if folded or hung correctly, but I never was able to persuade my wife of this, so my three hours of exemplary tedium in the launderette were usually followed by dreadful episodes in which she spent an entire weekend dripping with perspiration, delirious with boredom, anger, and dehydration while she ironed everything in an upper room. She would emerge in a state that I would describe as psychotic and vengeful, and for some hours afterwards I would have the trepidatious sensation of walking upon glass. I would be afflicted with awful hurricanes of baseless guilt, which were probably only an exaggeration of the normal feelings of culpability which every wife likes to nourish in her husband's psyche, so that when she was ironing I would feel obliged to do something just as tedious. I did the hoovering, washed the cat's bowl and feeding mat, and cleaned the grime off the light switches.

On non-ironing days I got into the habit of deliberately not doing something that desperately needed to be done, just so that I could do it conspicuously when she was at the ironing board. I was no doubt pathetic and risible, but I am sure that every other husband is similarly the victim of the tyranny of wifely bitterness. I realise of course that one is no longer permitted to generalise about anything, but it none the less seems to me that women are inclined to make the rods with which they beat their own backs, and do not perceive the irony of their subsequent complaints. I once proved this to my own satisfaction by offering to pay someone to come in and do the ironing. Her ladyship was outraged by the suggestion, either because she believed that I was casting nasturtiums upon the quality of her ironing, or because she would only have had to find some other way to make me feel like a dog.

We had a launderette very close by, almost close enough for me to be able to stagger there, festooned with my bulging cargo of mutinous bags. However, it did not supply change, and neither did Patel's sweetshop and newsagent's next door. The floor was always awash, and the machines leapt about in a noisy and even perilous fashion. It was also full of elderly black ladies in disconcerting and unrealistic curly wigs who sat immobile on the benches, clutching their handbags to their laps. But as soon as I entered their female domain they would patronise me in a manner that was most humiliating. They would advise me about separating the whites from the coloureds, about the correct temperature of the wash, and, worst of all, they used to kiss their teeth and make chirring sounds because they disapproved of my particular way of folding sheets. Many was the time that one of them leapt to her feet with a considerable creaking of matronly stays and corsets, and snatched a sheet from my hands. They had smiles that clearly indicated their compassion for my masculine cretinism, and their wonderment at the thought of my attempting a task that only an experienced and full-time black woman could possibly perform correctly. They could be diverted solely by adroit questions about Barbados or Trinidad, in which case they would wax nostalgic and begin to lament that the quality of immigrants was not as high as it had been in their day, and they shouldn't let in any more Jamaicans unless they were literate, and so on. With any luck a mild dispute would arise between them as to the relative merits of their various islands, and I would be left to fold my sheets in peace.

The launderette that I more usually frequented was mainly used by Turks, even though its owner was a charming Iranian intellectual who had fled from the ayatollahs with his family after it had become lamentably clear that even the much-despised Shah had been preferable to the new regime of rustic lunatics and religious terrorists. This man, who called himself Derek because the British cannot pronounce 'Ali', was an electronic engineer by training, and felt that his life had become one appalling penance. We had a natural sympathy for each other because he hated his launderette as much as I hated having to do my laundry. 'I have been doing the service wash since seven o'clock this morning,' he would tell me dolefully.

'I hate having to do this,' I would say, and he would respond, 'At least you only have to be coming once a fortnight.'

'I have fourteen pairs of underwear,' I would say.

'I know, I know always how many pair everyone have.'

Ali's advice was never patronising, and he smiled with delight if he was able to be helpful, quite unlike the black women in the other launderette who only smiled out of pity. He also took an interest in the books that I brought with me to read while my washing churned and flopped drunkenly about in the machines, and it was he who first induced me to read the works of Yashar Kemal, Ahdaf Soueif, and Mario Vargas Llosa. It was Ali who told me to button up the bottom of my duvet covers in order to prevent them from being filled up with socks and shirts that would later refuse to dry in the drying machine, and he had some fecund ideas in the area of folding clothes so that you could get twice as many into one bag. He demonstrated that you need only half the quantity of powder stipulated by the manufacturers, and he helped to fold the sheets only when asked. I found that the male ambience of his launderette left me feeling less crushed than that of the one with the elderly black women in implausible wigs, and it was good to have someone there with whom one could discuss literature and deplore the excruciating ennui of launderettes in general.

Habitually I went to the launderette at about lunch-time, so that I would have a legitimate excuse to go to the Turkish greasy. This establishment was run by a family of Turks who had mastered the dying art of producing meals that appealed to genuine working-class scaffolders and navvies, and to middle-class folk like me who occasionally felt sentimental about the abysmal standard of fried British catering in the distant days of our first acne. In the Turkish greasy you could get properly congealed baked beans, fried bread so impregnated with lard that you felt sick even as you savoured its aroma from a distance of twenty feet, scrambled eggs that bounced and quivered like blubber in an earthquake, and meat-and-two-veg standards all swimming in a very thin gravy that tasted unmistakably of stock cubes. They also had a very marvellous manner of making coffee. The mug would be half-filled with milk and then held under a spout that injected it with piping hot steam. There would be a most edifying hissing, burbling, frothing and fuss, and the milk would emerge looking like a sinister chemical in a gothic experiment. Then a spoonful of the lowest possible quality instant coffee would be thrown on top. This was a very fine dark powder that resembled cinnamon but smelt of nothing whatsoever. Finally the mug would be filled to the brim with tepid water from a jug, and one was presented with something that resembled a cappucino, except that the rich dark flecks floating on the surface were not chocolate, but indissoluble coffee. This latter coagulated upon one's teeth and created the most alarming sensation of overwhelming bitterness in the mouth. It could make the eyes roll and a chill of pleasurable horror trip along the spine.

It was the meat-and-two-veg that I went for, or, to be more honest, it was the meat.

Unfortunately my wife had became a rampant and fanatical vegetarian some years after we married, having watched on television a very sanguinary programme about transplant surgery. Eventually I even had to wear plastic shoes, and she removed the leather straps from my rucksack, and the carrying handles from my suitcases, without replacing them with anything else and without informing me. Imagine how I felt when I had to turn up at the Ramblers' Association South Downs hike with my rucksack actually stapled to my jacket. I would have divorced her long ago, but the fact was that she would have got custody of the children, she would have got the flat, and she would have got most of my income in perpetuity. Worst of all, we would have quarrelled about custody of the dog and the cat, and I knew perfectly well that she would have won them too. I couldn't have borne to be parted from the animals, and that is why I continued to live with someone who had hated and despised me for nearly a decade but would not leave me because she was terrified of her own mother's inevitably acid remarks and reproaches. In my opinion, and I have realised this too late, marriage is a form of theft in which women conspire to appropriate everything that a man has, including his happiness, and in the process their own happiness is lost as well.

Anyway, I had to go to the Turkish greasy to satisfy my occasional craving for meat. In the old days I would have asked for a double egg and chips, and this would have left me feeling pleasurably sinful, but latterly I found that I dreamed of liver. Not ox liver – it is rather overpowering, and they tend to slice it so thin that cooking transforms it into a kind of rank cardboard – but pig or lamb or chicken liver.

I don't really know what the liver does. It cleans the blood or something, and it is supposed to be good for anaemia. Anyway, it was what I longed for when I was making yet another nutroast for my implacable wife, or when I was arranging rocket in another salad fit only for rabbits and guinea pigs, so it was for liver, bacon, and mash that I asked when I ventured to the Turkish greasy on laundry days. I ate it with such desperate relish that afterwards I usually found that I had splashed the gravy and the thin yellow mustard on to my cardigan and my Royal Artillery tie.

It was this desperate relish that got me into hospital. I had a small morsel of liver in my mouth (a mere sliver of liver, so to speak) when I felt the need to sneeze. I made that sharp intake of breath that is the prelude to a good sneeze, and suddenly and horrifyingly I had the sensation of having been switched off. I had breathed in a lump of liver that might have been designed and manufactured by a cork specialist with the specific intention of sealing my windpipe.

I believe that there is some handy technique for unbunging the terminally choked – the Munich Manoeuvre or something – but none of the horrified Turks or round-oathed navvies had a clue what to do.

I had risen abruptly to my feet, and the table had overturned. My liver had slithered away in a pitiable stream of gravy, and my soggy peas, alas too soggy to roll, clung tenaciously to the now vertical surface of the table. I could feel my eyes popping in my head, and I had the ghastly experience of sucking in my breath and realising that with every attempt to breathe I was merely inhaling the liver more and more irretrievably.

It is not possible to think clearly in such desperate circumstances. I probably should have thumped myself in the sternum, or made dialling motions with my right forefinger so that the greasy's habitués would know to call for assistance. Instead I flailed my arms about, clutched at my throat with my hands, and finally fell to the floor and writhed. I felt my head beginning to explode, as though someone had pumped it full of water, and then the world turned red. It turned blue, and then black. I heard someone say, 'Flippin' 'eck, 'e's brown bread,' in a strongly Turkish London accent, and that was that.

I did not regain consciousness in the medical sense of that expression. I didn't wake up and say, 'Where am I?' or look at the nurse all in white and say, 'If this is heaven then you must be an angel.' No, I merely became aware that I was lying in bed and that I could not even close my eyes or move my arms. It was as though I had ceased to be my body, but was temporarily visiting it. I heard the bleeps of the monitors, and all I saw was a buff-coloured ceiling with a crack in it that looked very like the route of the A12 through Chelmsford and Colchester to Ipswich. I heard the voice of my wife, speaking very calmly.

'He's dead then, is he?'

'He is certainly brain-dead, I am sorry to say. Without this machinery he could certainly not sustain life. It's cerebral anoxia, you see. I am terribly sorry. I'm afraid that the ambulance took ten minutes to get to him because of roadworks in Tooting, and then took another twenty minutes to get here because of a demonstration. There was really very little that could be done . . .'

'There's no hope at all?'

'None.'

I wanted to shout at the doctor, 'I'm not dead, I'm not dead, I'm not dead,' but of course nothing happened. I do not know which was stronger in me, frustration or horror. It was akin to that nightmare one sometimes has when one has become entangled in the sheets, or when an arm has gone to sleep from being slept upon, and the dream is that one is paralysed and in dire jeopardy. I tried to shout, 'Help!' I tried over and over again, and nothing happened except that I felt a would-be tear fail to well up in my eyes and fail to course down my cheeks.

'Are you going to switch him off?' enquired my spouse. I noted that this question was asked with a clear note of eagerness in that prim little voice, eagerness coupled with hope and scientific curiosity.

'With your consent, of course. I really think that there's no alternative.'

'He would have liked you to use his organs,' said my wife, and if I could have leapt with anguish and panic, believe me, I would have done so. I had always wanted to be buried entire. Call me superstitious, but I'd read too many stories about Ancient Egyptians or Chinese or whoever, who would not be able to get into paradise if bits of them were missing. If you were castrated you had to keep your testicles in a box, so that they could be buried with you. I did not want my body to be pillaged for parts as if it were some Ford Cortina on a rusty heap in Stepney.

'There are some forms to sign,' continued the doctor, 'I'll just go and get them. Perhaps you'd like to spend some moments with him alone.'

'Oh yes, yes I would,' came my wife's voice. 'Thank you so much, doctor.'

A face, blurred, but unmistakably hers, moved above mine. For one fantastically misguided moment I thought, perhaps I even hoped, that she was going to kiss me. Instead she brought her face very close and spat out, 'You bastard.'

'Charming,' I thought, 'here am I all but dead, and she's still calling me a bastard.'

'A bit of liver was it? A bit of liver? You know what you are? A bloody murderer, that's what. And there's me thinking you were vegetarian too. I suppose you think you're very clever, don't you, sneaking out for meat like some nasty jackal, or whatever it is. Well, you're a murderer, and I'm glad you're dead, and I hope you can hear me, and at least there's one pig that didn't die in vain 'cause at least you choked on its liver. That pig ought to be made a saint, that's what. St Porky the Deliverer, St Porky the Bloody Marvellous.

You know what? I'm going to ask for that bit of liver, and I'm going to give it a decent burial with full military honours, or I might have it set in a lump of glass or resin or whatever it is, so I can kiss it first thing in the morning and last thing at night, and burn candles in front of it on Sundays, and do salaams and genuflectionwotsits and say "Thank you thank you thank you".'

I always knew that my wife loathed me, but I reflected that these remarks and observations were a little extreme. Perhaps if I had choked on a portion of veggieburger she might have been more moderate in her exultation.

I half-listened to her ranting and raving, and the other half of my mind dwelt contentedly upon the happier recollections of my life. The children. The cat pulling down the Christmas tree so that the dog could eat the chocolates, including the silver foil wrappers. My father teaching me how to make small bombs out of weedkiller and sugar. My deaf great-aunt obliviously farting at table in the false belief that none of us could hear her. Our honeymoon, when we did it so much that I actually developed a raw patch. My mother, giving me permission to give up the violin.

I emerged from these happy memories to hear my wife concluding triumphantly, '. . . and, you bastard, I am so bloody glad you're dead.'

I suppose that I should have felt bitter or sad to hear it, but as a matter of fact I began to feel a warm glow of twilight satisfaction. You see, I didn't suppose that they told her which café I was in when I choked, and I certainly had never told her that I was in the habit of going there while doing our laundry. I realised that she didn't even know which laundry I used to go to, and that even if she found out, Ali (alias Derek) would not know that she was my wife, and would faithfully guard our laundry until I arrived to collect it. Which I never would, now that I was officially dead and about to be used for carpentry. Which meant that my dear sweet wife would eventually go home and in the morning discover that she had no clothes whatsoever for daily wear. I had a delicious mental image of her disgustedly putting on yesterday's knickers and bra and skirt and blouse, and searching frantically through the house for the rest of her clothes. She would find none, she would realise that I must have been at the laundry. She would realise that she didn't know which laundry, she would telephone around all the local establishments, she would eventually speak to Ali (alias Derek), who would probably think she was mad, and then at last she would give up and realise that she was just going to have to handwash the same things every night until she had time to go to Marks and Sparks and begin the acquisition of an entirely new wardrobe. As I slipped away I had a most delicious prevision of her fury and frustration.

I may be perverse, but in my opinion that was something almost worth dying for.

# Romesh Gunesekera

## The Lover

HE LOVED PORK. He couldn't get enough of it. Whenever he had the chance he'd go to the Rossiya to eat pork. He was a small man, but looked like someone who always got his way; he handled his silver like a knife-thrower.

One Saturday, late in 1989, he found himself at a table with two tourists: two women, an aunt and her niece, snuggled inside thick foreign herringbone jumpers. The aunt had short grey hair; the niece, who looked darker, had straight blackish hair. They were staring at their plates, silently.

'You like pork?' he asked, pointing at the plate of sliced smoked meat laid out in a fan of fallen dominoes.

'Pardon?' The older woman looked alarmed.

'Pork. That is smoked pork. You like it?'

'Yes,' she replied cautiously, examining the meat.

The other woman nodded in agreement.

'You eat this in England?'

The older woman smiled. 'England?'

Her niece leaned forward. 'How did you know?'

'I knew at once. *Intuition.*' He helped himself to a few slices of pork and some brown bread. He began to hum an old Beatles song.

'And you? Where are you from?'

'Now I am a Muscovite!'

'Oh really!' The young woman's eyes widened. 'But in *this* hotel . . .'

'These days anything is possible.' He smiled.

'Oh yes, we know. *Glasnost.*'

'*Perestroika*,' her aunt added knowingly. Her eyes gleamed as though she was remembering all the articles she had cut out of the Sunday paper in preparation for this trip.

The man had disproportionately large hands; he only had to swivel his wrist to flick the food from the plate to his mouth. A fork flashed. His jaws shifted. Nothing else moved.

'First time in Moscow, huh?'

'Yes. It's wonderful.' The young woman glanced around the tall dining-room and shuddered, almost overcome by emotion. 'Just so wonderful.'

Her aunt stared at her, fastening her, as it were, to her chair in case she fell, swooning. 'Mandy is here to see the Pushkin.'

'And the Kremlin. The cathedrals.' Mandy shut her eyes and shook a cordon of dark hair around her. 'Beautiful. I could spend my whole life in Russia . . .'

'Good. Good. Have some pork. It is excellent.' The man wiped his mouth and leaned back. He had deep eyes and oddly pale cheeks, as though he had recently shaved off a thick courtier's beard. Every few minutes he would scrape his face with his fingers as if to seek comfort in the rasp of his re-emerging bristles.

Mandy put her fork down and a passing waitress immediately whipped all their plates off the table. The two women sipped Crimean wine as though nothing had happened. A little later another waitress wandered by, slightly adrift, and dumped a hot meal of minced pork and cabbage in front of each of them. 'Eat, please eat,' their companion urged and dug in.

The two women picked at their food.

'We were trying to find Pushkin's house,' the aunt said speaking slowly and deliberately with great effort.

'The museum? Very easy. Anyone can tell you.'

'No, not the museum. I mean his *house*. Where he lived.'

'His house! Why, you'd think he lived everywhere. All over, in every street, someone will claim a house where Pushkin slept. He was a great lover of . . .' the man paused, as if searching for the right word in English. Deep in thought he put a thick bundle of meat and cabbage into his mouth. 'Excellent, hm, yes?' he murmured.

Mandy shook her head impatiently. 'But there is one. A special house. We couldn't find it.'

'This house of his is only a house. Moscow has many other things to offer.' The man waved his hand towards the huge plate-glass window.

The three of them looked out at the fancy painted turbans of St Basil's which, magnified by the glass, seemed to eclipse Red Square and the monumental modern tomb that squatted behind it. Yesterday's snow on the wide boulevards had turned brown. Black limousines making the turn in front of the hotel slewed like boats, racing, revving their engines, churning the muddy snow and making a mess of the city's historic grid.

As they watched, fresh snow began to fall. 'If only the winter was not so cold,' Mandy said.

'Nonsense. This is not winter. Just a bit of snow. It is not even time for our hats.'

'Hats?'

'The sign of winter is when my grandmother puts out our fur hats. The day your ears begin to freeze.'

'Your grandmother?'

The man leaned forward. 'She is ninety-seven. Do you know what that means?'

Both women nodded, impressed but bewildered by the intensity of his voice.

'It means she is from the last century. You cannot imagine what she *knows*.'

'My goodness!'

'Is she in Moscow?' Mandy asked.

'She will be for the winter. But at the moment she is dead.'

'Dead?'

'In the summer she had a *vision*.' He rubbed his cheeks vigorously. 'You know this is a very significant time . . . she saw something coming this winter. It was too much. Her heart failed her. But she must tell us. What lies ahead is unimaginable for anyone born in the twentieth century. Only she can tell.'

Aunt and niece looked at each other, their lips sealed in grim purplish lines.

'What you have to understand is today *anything* is possible. You know this country is now full of healers. There is one woman in Moscow – she comes from the east – who is really in touch with the dead. I met her. She is amazing. Metal buckles at her breath. And when she looks at you, you feel feathers on your skin. She wants to fill the world with angels. Love. She is a kind of goddess.' The man moved his eyes from one woman to the other. They both shifted uneasily. 'Our scientists are so excited. She promised me my grandmother will be back in time for the hats. Babushka will not miss this winter. She has too much to say. The world is on the brink, you know . . .' The table seemed to tremble as if about to rise. He seemed to have come closer to them. His eyes were swollen, brimming. 'We are on the brink. *Eat!*'

He scooped the last of his meat up. Mandy watched his mouth work at it. His protruding lips and raised cheeks seemed remarkably familiar to her, although the face as a whole was blurred by a sense of urgency. She too believed something had to be done soon. Time was moving fast. In two days she would be back home, and this moment in Moscow would fade like a dream. It would melt away and be forgotten, even though right now it seemed to promise to her a whole new world of excited poets and fledgeling angels. She looked hard at him, wanting him to talk some more. But after his sudden fervour he had withdrawn and now seemed completely self-absorbed. He was staring at his cutlery. His close-set eyes narrowed even further, his forehead puckered. She followed his gaze and thought she saw the polished knife curl like a feather in his fingers. He looked up and caught her eye. He immediately turned away as if searching the room for someone else. He stood up. 'I must go.' He spoke fast. 'Goodbye.' A few seconds later he had disappeared. Mandy was startled at the speed of his departure. She looked for a reaction from her aunt. The older woman was nibbling

a piece of meat wrapped in grey cabbage. The man's plate
had been wiped clean. It glistened. Mandy realised that she
couldn't even be sure of ever recognising his face again. She
didn't even know his name. She quickly swallowed the rest
of her wine. She had learned one summer, by heart, Pushkin's
small poem on the *wantonness of fatigueful fancy*. She'd
recite it to herself waiting for the bus home from the Picton
library in Liverpool. Outside the snow was falling steadily,
heavier by the minute, silently turning this new Russia white.

# Abdulrazak Gurnah

## ESCORT

I THINK HE saw me approaching, but for his own reasons made no sign. I stood by the open rear door of the car and waited for him to look up. He folded his newspaper and slid out of the door, glancing at me for a second with intense dislike. I stood still, my body emptying in tremors of surprise. Perhaps it was not dislike, merely irritation at the unavoidable, frustration with the inescapable tedium of existence, a disaffection. But it felt like dislike. He tilted his chin forward slightly, inviting me to state my business. When I told him the name of the hotel, he nodded, as if this was the lesser imposition, as if he had expected me to name an impossible destination. I sat beside him in the front, daring the beast, but also conceding to the angry possibilities my appearance seemed to suggest to him – sitting beside him so he could see I was not as deserving of dislike as he had first thought. I did not see how I could avoid finding out about his anger.

The car seat was lumpy and hard (and green), its vinyl upholstery cracked with age. Sharp-edged corners of it curled up like raw hide and pricked me through my shirt as the car swerved out of the taxi-stand. On the dashboard, there were empty recesses and tangled wires where the lighter, or the radio or the glove-compartment might have been. Or rather they were not quite empty, as rolled-up pieces of paper were stuffed into their corners, and a rag which was grey with use hung to dry through one of the holes.

As we slowed in the lunch-time traffic, he glanced at the briefcase I held in my lap. Then he raised his eyes to look at my face while I pretended to be unaware of his gaze. 'Where have you come from?' he asked, modulating his voice to make the question less abrupt, but still managing to sound as if he was snarling with resentment. None the less, he asked his question as if he expected that I would defer to his right to ask it. *Unatoka wapi?* He lurched us into motion again, then leaned back and rested his cocked elbow on the car window. He was lean and tense, his face hollowed with an expectation of disregard. Or so I thought as I turned to give his question my attention. Something grim and tormented in his mobile face made me think of him as someone who had lived a life of danger, and made him seem capable of deliberate cruelty to ease his own pain. I felt fear and distaste for my curiosity and wanted the journey to end as soon as possible. I should have walked away at once after that first bitter look. He glanced again at the case and a shadow of a smile passed over his face, mocking what he took to be my self-importance. It was only a cheap plastic thing with hard sharp handles and a clumsy zip, which I expected to last no more than a few months and which did not deserve such caustic scrutiny.

'Where?' he asked, this time nodding towards the case to include it in his regard.

'Uingereza,' I said. *England*. I spoke gently, distractedly, to show how uninterested I was in the conversation.

He snorted softly. 'Student?'

He meant was I one of those who had gone out to make good in the world and returned with only stories and a cheap briefcase. Was I one of those failures who worked as something shamefully menial and sent back tales of endless studies and clever arrangements that were bound to yield a little fortune in good time? His face was cheerful with malice as he waited to see how I would squirm out a reply. When he got going I expected he would tell me that he had to stay behind and look after an ailing family while everybody ran off, and this despite the expectations his teachers and mentors had of him when he was young. I told him I was a teacher and he snorted again, this time unambiguously. Is that all?

The lunch-time crowds were in their eternal haste, streaming across the road at the slenderest hesitation by a motorist.
The taxi-driver was affronted by these liberties and leaned
on his horn whenever a car ahead of him allowed pedestrians
to get the better of the driver. A group of Indian schoolboys
in their early teens, strolling between the cars and chatting
spiritedly, drew a long blast of the horn and mean words
from him. *Filthy shit-scrapers. What are they playing at?* The
traffic was heaviest by the Post Office. Crowds of people
walked the pavements, some men in shirts and ties hurrying,
busy-busy-busy, while others were more deliberate, stopping
now and then to look at the shoddy wares of the pavement-
traders.

'Uingereza,' he said, singing the name as he turned left
towards the docks, where my hotel was. 'Uingereza,' he
repeated. 'A land of luxury.'

'Have you visited there?' I asked, and could hear the tone
of surprised disbelief in my voice. You? After all the struggle
to make headway against that brazen and self-besotted culture, to find such casual reference made to the wretched
place. A land of luxury.

The taxi-driver leaned savagely on the horn to clear a
water-cart off the road ahead of him. For a minute or so he
seemed lost in bitter affront at the water-seller's existence,
shouting and waving his right arm out of the window as if
any second he would leap out of the car and overturn the
whole cartful of cans. The dock-workers who were buying
their lunch at the road-side kiosks, and who were the water-
seller's customers, waved cheerfully at the taxi-driver. He
swung his car out around the cart and gave a long blast on
his horn.

'Do you have relatives in England?' I asked. I could not
imagine that someone who made a living, with such ill-
humour, driving the dilapidated taxi we were travelling in,
could make the money to afford staying even one night in a
stinking bed and breakfast in that land of luxury.

'I used to live there,' he said, then turned to look at me
quickly and grinned. We had now come off the main road

and were weaving behind the docks, past warehouses and the loco-yard, on the last stretch before the hotel. He had to concentrate on the heaving road, with its gorge-like pot-holes and steep embankments for the railway lines. He started to speak but the crises on the roads came too fast one after another, and he shook his head, not wanting to spoil his story. It seemed the work of madness to put the hotel where it was, the other side of yards littered with derelict machinery and workers' garbage, but the hotel was there before the docks and the railways had turned into a sprawling shambles, and before the road had died.

'I had a malaya, one of these European whores. She took me there, and France, and even Australia. We went everywhere. She paid for everything. You hear these stories from people and you think they're telling lies, dreaming about European whores with money and no sense. I thought so, until I picked up my malaya.' He had stopped outside the hotel by this time, his car shuddering idly in neutral. 'Slim. She used to call me Slim,' he said as he took his fare, his face covered in smiles at the memory. 'The name is Salim. I'm always there by the Post Office taxi-rank. Come by any time.'

I had found the hotel by chance. The Immigration Officer had explained that he could not give me an entry permit unless I gave an address in the country on my form. He said this apologetically, because after seeing the place of birth on my passport he had spoken enthusiastically about Zanzibar, where he too had relatives. He showed me a list of hotels – *Whichever you like*, he said. *You don't have to stay there. Just for the form.* So I picked one, and when I found a cab outside the airport it was the only name I could remember. Its inaccessibility, and the intimidating silence of the loco-yard and warehouses outside working hours, suited me as it meant that no one came to visit me, as they might have done if I had been staying in one of the glittery palaces on the other side of town with their casinos and pool-side combos.

So it was a surprise to have the receptionist ring the following evening to announce a visitor. It was Salim, of course. It never occurred to me that he would come, but now that he was here, it seemed as if I had known all along that he would turn up. He was dressed in a silky green shirt with a pattern of white flowers and blue outrigger canoes – short-sleeved with one handle of his sunglasses visible in his chest-pocket. His corduroy jeans were loose round the waist, and were gathered into folds by the wide, buckled belt he wore. He insisted on buying me a drink, and bought the barman one as well. The bar was almost empty; the Belgian couple who owned the hotel and who were entertaining a friend were the only other people there. *Ces gens sont impossibles*, their guest said in exasperation, raising her voice with untroubled assurance. These people are impossible. She was a slim, well-groomed woman in her forties, sleek with self-regard. Salim glanced at the three Europeans for a moment, as if he had understood what they had said, but they seemed unaware of him.

'She bought me this, my malaya,' Salim said, picking delicately at his shiny shirt and then taking a fuller pinch of the blue corduroy jeans. He was smiling, not mocking this time, and didn't mind including the barman in his circle. 'Do you want to know how she found me?' He waited until both the barman and I nodded. 'OK, I'll tell you. She was a fare outside the Tumbili Hotel, out on the northern coast. Do you know that one? I saw her standing under a tree near the entrance, as if she was waiting for someone. Usually they don't come out until the hotel servants come to fetch us into the drive. Have you seen what they make those baboons wear? They bring them down from the hills back there and dress them in yellow bibs and black bow-ties, and then make them pay for their costumes. I know this.' The barman was dressed in a white shirt, a black bow-tie and a yellow apron around his middle – and he probably had to pay for his costume as well, but he managed not to look uncomfortable.

'Anyway,' Salim continued, 'I guessed she was waiting there for someone to collect her but I thought I'd try anyway. She wasn't young, but she wasn't that old either. She listened to me for a moment, you know, as I gave her the usual chatter about a tour at government-fixed tariffs, and then she got in the car. I drove her around all day, as far as Malindi, Wiatamu, Takaungu. I told her all about those places, making things up when I felt like it or when she asked difficult things. In the evening, as I was driving her back to her hotel, she made me pull up by a beach, and we did it there. On the sand, in the open, like a couple of dogs. It was like that every day. I picked her up in the morning, drove her places, told her stories, then took her to the beach after it got dark. After a few days of this, she told me to go to Ulaya with her. She fixed everything. The tickets, the passport. She paid for it all.'

'You must have been very good on that beach,' I said, unwillingly, for something to say, because I did not believe that any woman so casually approached would look at Salim and not see danger, and anyway I did not want to listen to another story of frenzied European lust for the African cock. The barman laughed soundlessly, and Salim glanced at the two of us one by one, looking a little wounded.

'Call me Slim,' he said, then emptied his glass and pushed it slightly towards me. 'It isn't such a lot of money if you're changing from foreign. You know that. And anyway, she had plenty.'

I paid for his drink and sat listening to some more of the story of his malaya. Her marriage had ended, and she had taken her share of the money and decided to travel. She took him to Liverpool, where she was born and from where her parents had emigrated to Australia when she was a baby. Was it difficult for him? With her? He shrugged. She took care of everything, showed him things, and the bitch wanted sex every day, sometimes two or three times in a day. It wasn't difficult. They stayed for several weeks. He made a couple of friends who lived nearby, both Muslims, one Somali and the other from Mauritius, and they taught him how to get dole. Then he and his malaya lived a life of luxury. The English government is very stupid. Liverpool is full of blacks, rough bastards who do what they like, and the government just gives them money. English women were always touching him, stroking his hair, squeezing up to him and buying him drinks. After a few minutes of this I said goodbye and left. I had some letters to write, I said.

He was back the next evening, with another flowery shirt. I had asked the receptionist to say I was not in but perhaps he was bound to other loyalties I did not understand. I thought I might throw a word over my shoulder as I walked past the desk, but I saw that a different young man was on duty. 'I bought this in Australia,' Salim said, picking at his shirt. 'We went there after a few days in France. Betty. Her name was Betty. Bethany, some kind of religious name, but she called herself Betty. Do you want to go to a club tomorrow night? You still have another night here, don't you? There is a nice place on the other side of Majengo. None of this tourist trash. We'll go there tomorrow. Australian women want it all the time, but their men have no nyege. So the women are always on fire. Blazing with heat. And my malaya didn't mind if I went with them.' There was a great deal more of this, with some details of the arrangements the women made to see him and their shameless abandon afterwards.

'What brought you back to this place?' I asked in the end, trying to force the tale to its conclusion.

'You have to stop playing some time,' he said disdainfully, 'and return to be with your people. Anywhere else, you only end up being a clown.'

That seemed a good moment to say goodbye, but Salim was quite businesslike in refusing to let me go. He took hold of my wrist and held on while he ordered another round of drinks on my bill. The barman served us, made me sign the chit and retreated, carefully keeping his eyes away from Salim's hand on my wrist. We were the only people in the bar. Once the drinks were in front of us, he let go of me with a grin, leaving a cold circle of flesh where his hand had gripped me. I stood up to leave, and I saw him consider saying something and then change his mind. 'What about your drink? Never mind, I'll have it. See you tomorrow, then,' he said. 'You haven't forgotten about the club, have you?'

All day I tried not to think of what I would do when he turned up. I had put the day aside to write up the notes of some of the visits and interviews that I had accumulated over the previous week, and it was the worst kind of thing to be doing while Salim's visit loomed. There was neither virtue nor pain in writing up notes, nothing to distract or excite, just a wearing attention to events whose impact had already passed. By evening, I had persuaded myself that it was silly of me to be so squeamish. I had come to find out what I could about a little-known poet called Pandu Kasim, who had lived here at the turn of the century, to see if I could work up anything about him, and a night-club on the other side of Majengo was nothing to do with that. But it couldn't do any harm, and might even help. My enquiries had not revealed anything interesting about Pandu Kasim, and per-haps a night-club which had Salim as a patron might. I would never choose to see such sights, and would be content to say that I knew the town well without any acquaintance with its greasy under-belly, but what harm could it do apart from making me queasy. I was not looking forward to being brought into Salim's circle of friends, whom I expected to be of the same hair-raising ilk as Salim himself, but I only had just under two more days left before returning to England. I could not imagine that much harm would befall me in that time. The notes would have to wait, and I might have to spend a tedious evening listening to stories of sexual triumph over laughably gullible women, but was that not better than trying to chase Salim away and finding myself the subject of his malice and rage?

So by the time Salim arrived I was ready for him. I was even beginning to think that he would not turn up just to punish me for my scepticism about his stories. He was sitting gloomily in his car when I came down, and started up after a mumbled greeting. That charming welcome made me tremble with foreboding. Why had I not simply told him to go away? I stared ahead of me, not attending to where we were going though I had a good idea of where we were. But my attention must have wandered because I suddenly realised that Salim had turned off the road and was driving on a bumpy and unlit track. The bushes pressed in all around us. The horizontal rays of the car-lights made the sensation more oppressive, as if we were underground. It had been a pleasant, breezy evening, but in this tunnel the air was steamy and smelled of wet earth. Salim turned to glance at me, and I saw him grinning. 'Not much longer now,' he said and began to hum. A dog yelped in the night and a moment later the dark bushes were agitated by the sounds of passage. In another moment, Salim forced the car over a little mound and entered a clearing surrounded by huge dark trees. There was another car parked outside one of the houses. There must have been three or four other houses, but it was impossible to tell in that light. He parked his car alongside the other and we got out.

The club turned out to be the front room of a mud and wattle house, ill-lit by one kerosene lamp. Two other men were already there, and they rose to greet us as if they were expecting us. 'This is our guest from Uingereza,' Salim said, grinning.

One of the men looked about Salim's age, and had a similar aggravated appearance. The other was younger and bigger, and when he glanced at me I saw an involuntary smirk cross his mouth. His name was Majid. I did not catch the name of the older man at first. (It turned out to be Buda.) Even before we sat down around the rough old table, Majid was shouting for beer. From the back room appeared a woman of uncertain middle age, in a tight dress worn with use and stained black under the arm-pits. Her head was covered with a scarf of the same material, and around her middle she wore a faded kanga. After a few moments of frenzied banter and some forced hilarity, she went away again to prepare the food my jolly companions had asked for.

There were empty beer bottles on the table, and these would remain there as trophies of the drinkers' exploits. Majid and the other man had half-full ones each, from which they drank now and then, tipping the bottles swaggeringly to their lips while the beer frothed. They were big bottles.

And not a glass in sight. I had imagined something different when Salim said we should go to the club, not a dark house in a wood where men gathered for a secretive drink.

'They'll be bringing some more,' Buda said reassuringly. His expression was that cross between barely suppressed temper and a moping, sulking malice that I had seen in Salim. Maybe it was the drink. You had to be serious, even obsessive, about the stuff to be a drinker in a Muslim town like this, where discretion was impossible and discovery inevitable. Perhaps the guilt of transgression generated an angry self-contempt, or the necessity to consume whatever destructive poison was available in a culture of scarcity produced those looks of pain. Or maybe it was an unassuaged resentment that drove men such as these to drink despite everything. How could I know?

'I can see you people did not bother going to the maghreb prayer today,' Salim said with rasping ill-humour, nodding at the empties on the table. The two men laughed at his sarcasm and Salim reluctantly smiled, his clenched face creasing briefly. He looked as if he was burning.

Buda was short and plump, even fat, but his body looked hard and tight, as if his plumpness was not to do with indulgence but with something more calculating than mere pleasure. He scowled at me before he spoke, playfully, playing at being monsters. 'Tell us the news from Uingereza. Is it true they have trains that travel under water there?'

'Listen to this savage,' Salim cried. 'Have you never heard of the Underground?'

'You're going to make this Englishman think we're all as ignorant as you,' Majid said, without a hint of pleasantry in his voice.

A girl in a torn and soiled shift came from the inner room, carrying two bottles of beer. Her eyes were intensely blank, looking through what they encountered with some concentration. She put one of the beer bottles in front of me. As she leaned forward I saw through a tear in the shift under her armpit that her body was young and full. She put the other bottle in front of Salim, who stroked her buttocks and made her wince.

'Aziza, our friend from Ulaya wants you,' Majid said abruptly, laughing with two loud barks.

She turned her eyes towards me with a look of mild interest. Then she stood waiting, as if to see what would happen next.

'Go with her,' Salim said, grinning at me like a cadaver. I saw her wince again.

I looked at the girl, at her small pointed face and her slim young body, and I saw no resistance there. I shook my head and her eyes fell. Majid laughed and stood up. The girl turned back towards the inner room, her hands already pulling up folds of her shift as Majid swaggered at her heels. Buda smiled gently and began to ask me questions about England. Salim answered most of them, calling me in now and then to say a confirming word or two. I thought I heard a sharp voice at one point which made the flame of the kerosene lamp flicker. Majid was in there for what seemed a long time, and when he came out he was beaming, his glossy face sleek with health.

'Thirsty work,' he said, reaching for what remained in his bottle. He drained it off and put the bottle down with a conquering smile. 'It's the Englishman's round, I think.'

They called for Aziza and she came in a moment later, her eyes as vacant as before, the corners of her mouth turned down. I ordered beers for them and said to Salim that I would like to go when he had finished his drink. What about the food we had ordered, Buda asked. I had work to do, I said. Buda rose and followed softly behind the girl after she had brought the beer.

'What work?' Majid asked, unsmiling. 'Don't you like women? Go and work in there. Or don't you like women? She won't have anything to do with him,' he said, pointing a chin at Salim. 'What did you do to her?'

Salim took a long pull at his bottle. 'We have to go to a wedding,' he said when he had finished. 'So we'll leave you to your filthy games.'

344

'What did you do to her, you pervert?' Majid asked, grinning for the sheer joy of his life.

We arrived at the wedding just in time to see the procession of family and friends escorting the groom to the door of the bride's house. Two drummers, skinny young men who looked alike, played with tense impassive faces, their eyes turned inwards in all that noise. Palm-frond arches decorated the house, and a garland of coloured lights ran across the front wall. From the house's interior came voices of women singing, which were suddenly transformed into a gleeful burst of ululations as the groom reached the door. The crowd milled around, shouting ribald comments at the groom, then breaking into a loud shout as he was admitted inside. Youngsters' eyes began wandering anxiously around, looking for the food they knew was coming. Salim snorted with derision. 'She's one of my wife's relatives,' he said.

I had not thought of a wife. 'Were you married before you went off with Bethany?' I asked him as he drove me back to the hotel. It was a nice name and I had been waiting to use it.

'Yes,' he said. We were driving down the ill-lit road that led to the loco-yard, but even in that light I could see the spite and anger in his face. 'I was married to her a long time ago.'

'Did you come back because of her?' I asked.

He chuckled. Then after a moment, with the car growling over the broken road, he spoke. 'She gave me something in the end. That malaya. When I went with her, blood came out. I went to see the doctor she sent me to. He said it was nothing but she said I couldn't stay. I don't know what it is, but whenever I go with a woman blood comes out.'

We drove in silence until the car stopped outside the hotel. 'Have you seen a doctor since you've been back here?'

'What doctor? There are no doctors here,' he said, staring ahead. Then he turned towards me with a coy, gentle smile. 'Take me with you tomorrow. I'll see a doctor there. Take me. I'll do anything you want.' He leant towards me, his smile now offering itself beseechingly in that grotesquely overwrought face.

He came for me the next day even though I had told him that I would make my own way to the airport. He talked with his usual malice and arrogance, scoffing at everything that crossed his sight. Even though I insisted that he drop me off and leave, he parked the car and strolled beside me with a rolled-up newspaper in his hand. 'How much does a case like that cost? Bring me one next time. Or send one to me and I'll make sure you get your money back. Not that you'll need my money in the land of luxury. You'll soon stop playing and come back home, though,' he said. 'Everybody has to, otherwise they turn into a joke in some foreign place.'

I shook hands with him and gave him all the local money I had. He looked at the fat bundle of notes with surprise. 'I hope you get better,' I said.

'What are you talking about?' he asked, grinning. He put the money in his pocket. 'Next time you must stay,' he said and then walked away, waving without looking back.

# Julia O'Faolain

## MAN OF ARAN

Dublin

DEAR ROSE,

You ask for details. Well, Paul turned up here in a
stew after Phil and her Greens left Paris without telling
him. They were sick of his wanting to protect her from
what he considered 'bad' company, when some would
say it was the company – Paul included – which needed
protecting! Phil, in another age, could have been a great,
bossy, troublemaking saint. Or whore. Did you ever
come across those porny woodcuts labelled 'Phyllis
riding Aristotle'? They show a whore straddling a frail
old man who is down on all fours. Cruel? Well, better
to laugh than cry! Paul must be seventy!

Anyway Phil and Co. were protesting at the pollution
of the Gulf Stream and had got together some small
boats and hemmed in an oil tanker somewhere near the
Aran Islands. There was a stand-off and a few newspapers took notice. Nothing major. The protesters hoped
the oil company would lose its cool, while the oilmen
were counting on storms to disperse the boats.

Enter Paul.

He borrowed a yacht from his rich cousins and
reached Aran at the same time as the forecast storm. He
then had a row with his cousin's skipper, insisted on
taking the helm – in his youth, it seems, he sailed a bit
– and set forth, in bad visibility, to find and persuade
Phil to give up her mad enterprise. This was just as the

tanker was attempting a getaway which the little boats meant to stop. Phil's boat was in the lead and Paul sailed right up to her across the bows of the tanker which, having no time to slow, had to swerve so as not to run him down, and hit a submerged rock which tore a hole in it. This led to the spill.

He has, as you'll have seen, been vilified and will almost certainly be sued. His old record was mentioned. There is unpleasant coverage on the enclosed video. Whoever introduced him to Phil did a bad day's work. Write to him. He needs support.

Love,
Dympna

Rose thinks: how sharp Dympna has become! *She* wouldn't make rash introductions as Rose did last Easter in Paris. Not that Rose meant to either. As she remembers it, the thing happened almost by itself.

The occasion was ill-judged. The city had shut down, but shops in the old ghetto were open and Rose, racing to lunch, was relieved to see that she could get some sort of groceries here later: a stroke of luck since she had none laid in. Tins, though labelled in unreadable scripts, showed pictures of recognisable food and she could buy that flat Arab bread, since the bakers seemed to be closed. No baguettes sprouted from under shoppers' arms, and the restaurant where she was lunching had only matzos. Squeezing between tables, she saw a basketful on each.

Paul, rising to kiss her, exclaimed: '*Ma chérie, ma chérie*, you don't look a day older! After – how long has it been?'

One reproach? Two? He didn't let her answer. Afraid he'd be toppled from some high-wire topic! Today it was global calamity. Warily she listened while he hectored her with shy, expectant eyes. Expecting what? In that lean-bean coat he looked like an old-time pedagogue.

'It is good of you to come! But then,' he coaxed, 'you are good! *Tu es bonne, ma chérie!*'

348

Unfolding her napkin, she shook her head at this. *No!* Not good! 'I remember,' she said, to illustrate this, 'when this street was sooty and smelled like a bazaar. I came here once with a friend who hoped to sell a violin . . .'

'So the universe, darling . . .' Not listening.

She was a touch *distraite* herself. Vintage memories brimmed, starting with the violin on which her lover had played courtly music which mocked their lives. It was curvaceous and reddish and she too had been like that and had needed money for an abortion.

'Which was illegal!' She laid claim to recklessness: 'Not to say scandalous!' And remembered Sephardic women stepping through bead curtains in dim shops to lift the violin from its cradling velvet. Marvelling at its owner's willingness to sell, they warned him in lowered voices against women who could cost him dear. '*Muncho*,' they'd said in their queer Spanish. A non-Jewish woman cost *muncho*!

'Keep your violin, *hijito*,' they advised, recognising him as one of their own. 'A violin will stand to you! Women . . .' They shook monitory heads, not caring that she might understand.

There were women like that here today. Glossy and noisy, they were savouring a taste for North African cooking. *Pieds noirs*. Or had that word passed from use? Prosperity had reached the ghetto and this restaurant was too dear for Paul.

It was her fault he had chosen it. He had rung to say, 'I heard you were back. People avoid me now,' and she, in her fluster, proposed meeting straightaway, forgetting about Easter and that restaurants might be closed. Poor Paul! He must have tried ten places before finding a free table.

'I'm not coming,' had been her husband's ultimatum. 'And I don't want you making rash promises on my behalf. I bet you made some when you thought he'd die in gaol!'

'Yves! You must! If you don't he'll pay. He'll insist.'

'Sorry.' Yves could be ruthless. 'You'll have to work that one out.'

How? What would the clever Sephardic women have done? Slipped off to arrange things with the cashier? No, that would hurt Paul's pride. Claim to be dieting so as to save him money? Oh dear! How sticky this lunch was going to be! As Yves had known. His knowingness could be maddening. 'He,' she had once written in a letter to Paul, who seized on the notion, 'has betrayed us spiritually.' A silly remark! It was touched off by Yves' taking a job with the political party which had pressed to have Paul's appeal quashed. A naïve reaction, as Yves had made her see. He worked for the state and that party had come to power. Were its opponents therefore to strike or starve until the next election? No? Well then?

Across the room, a pale face floated among the dark ones. Red curls reminded Rose of, might even belong to – could they? – Philomena Fogarty.

'Aren't you appalled, *ma chérie*?'

Paul wanted a response to some moan about – what? She teased: 'You bring jeremiads to the ghetto, Paul. That's coals to Newcastle.' Had someone said that Phil had become a Green?

'Newcastle?'

'Just a way of speaking.'

Could he be unaware of the pessimism which he sprayed like a tomcat appropriating territory? Or might he – his fingers had questingly clasped hers – be *too* optimistic? This was her first real meeting with him since his release, though there had been a welcome-out party. Right afterwards, she and Yves had gone abroad for some months. She had, though, continued to write to Paul. How drop him?

While he ordered wine, she took back her hand and slid a glance at those red curls. From the age of four, Phil Fogarty had been the star of Miss Moon's dancing class in South County Dublin. At parties she would toss the ringlets which Rose envied, fluff her skirts, point a toe and sing. Adults adored her. She must be forty now and the hair-colour out of a bottle. Did Greens dye?

'. . . garbled, as I . . .'

She – Phil – was also said to be some sort of healer. With crystals, was it? Or kinesiology?

'. . . no rigour in their . . .'

Like a peg-bag on a shaky clothes-line, Paul's bones jigged. He spoke of chaos theory and randomness. A shoulder jabbed the air. Rose sighed. For years Paul had owned an influential magazine and seen no need to please anyone. Now, like a pet creature released in the wild, he misread signals and reacted to trouble with a martyred spite. The world, he noted, was getting its comeuppance. The Soviet collapse had unbalanced it. And what was worse, thought was dead. A Dark Age of the Mind was upon us.

'*Je t'assure, ma chérie!*' He was balding, transparent, furious and frail. When the waiter came to say there's no more sturgeon, Paul gleamed. Pollution! exulted the gleam. Dying seas! *Après moi le déluge!*

'They can only live in one near-saltless sea in Russia.'

'No,' Rose argued foolishly. 'In the US they raise them in pools. I've seen them.'

He pretended not to hear. The waiter said there was sturgeon for one.

'The lady will have it.'

'No, I'm on a diet!'

His disappointment reproached her. But why had he chosen a place where the guest's menu showed no prices so that, for all she knew, the slimmer's salad was the dearest dish? Meals with him had been jinxed since, in his wealthy days, his cook gave her fish-poisoning. Rose had guessed the food was off but Paul, his mind on some cosmic threat, could not be alerted and, from sheer frustration, she'd found herself nibbling the fish. After that she swore not to see him again and would not have but for the blow which fell, freakishly, out of a clear – no, out of a murky sky.

What had happened was that towards the fag-end of the Cold War some secret-service people, enraged by Paul's even-handed editorials, cooked up a charge that he was a disinformer paid by the KGB, and to back this up got a double agent at the old Soviet embassy to offer royalties for articles of his which had appeared in Russia. The money was handed over in a plain envelope in a public place, the transaction filmed and Paul stitched up.

In retrospect, this justified his contempt for Western paranoia!

'Westerners,' he used to scoff, 'think the Russians engage in industrial espionage, but why would they? The Japanese do it for them! Do you know how many of *them* work in Western labs? They sell what they learn to the Soviets.'

Mocking! Knowing! Like some slick cartoon-figure – Speedy Gonzalez or the Roadrunner – he got so far ahead of himself that, smashing – SPLAT! – into a trap even an innocent could detect, he ended in gaol. Yet Rose knew that his puncturings of pedestrian thinking were performed not for the KGB but for private demons of his own.

Hearing him now expound the notion of randomness, she wondered if he saw it as an absolution. 'On the micro-scale . . .' he said, 'patterns, darling, do not exist!'

So how could Roadrunners foresee a trap?

Or was it the macro-scale? No, Paul did see patterns there. Big. Macro! Those he watched – not the small. Her mind slid back to when she was pregnant by the poor-but-promising violinist who had hoped to keep her, the baby and the violin. A folly. They would – as she had told him, citing Swift – have been reduced to eating the baby. An abortion – legal even then in Switzerland – was the sensible move.

'All right,' he said at last, 'ask your friend Paul for the money. It's peanuts to him.' So she had both men to dinner in her tiny flat. But Paul talked all evening about some macro matter and neither she nor her lover could get through to him about the micro fish inside her which they needed to abort. Selectively deaf, he left early.

'That violinist, What's-his-name,' he told her years later, 'was all wrong for you.'

'I know. We both did. We told you we wanted to separate but couldn't because . . .'

His eye mottled as if reflecting clouds.

'All wrong.'

'We needed money to . . .'

'Such things are never a matter of money.'

She wondered if he thought that still, now that his lawyers had cleaned him out.

'Please see him,' a mutual friend had begged Rose. 'He's convinced people avoid him. The publicity was devastating.'

Remorsefully, she took his hand. It was the colour of the sturgeon.

They had first met when Rose was twenty in Southern California, at the sort of party where distinctions blur. Incense stunned taste-buds; orchids were tumid and guests' names a puzzle until she guessed that they belonged to second-generation Hollywood: sons of movie moguls who had made their mark in Europe in the 1930s, then fled here from the war. Some Slavic surnames slithered like centipedes. Others were haunted by lopped syllables.

Paul told her, 'I don't belong here.'

Indeed he seemed to lack a skin – unless it was the others who had an extra one? Gleaming, as if through clingwrap, they smiled past her.

'They're not interested in us,' he told her.

Perhaps she had been invited for him? To put him at ease? In Paris, where it turned out they both lived, this was often her role. She worked in fashion and was in LA to show a collection. Paul had come to wind up a legacy.

'It's my first visit,' he told her, 'since I was six. Forty years ago!' Later he said, 'These people write memoirs about the parents they loathed. It helps pay their shrinks.'

'What about you?'

His reproving kiss set the tone for a friendship which, in Paris, would flourish in a jokey way. He became her Pygmalion, correcting her French and grooming her mind – when they met, which wasn't often. Her relations with the violinist had grown difficult and she preferred not to talk about them. Besides, Paul was nobody's idea of a confidant. He was a man for whom a kiss would present itself as a metaphor or semiotic bleep. A gag, joke or echo. Or so it seemed to her.

She was impressed by him though. He was an eccentric

mandarin, boiling with revolutionary ire which was stimulating at a time when it was widely held that intelligence, like
the heart, was on the Left. Subversion was the fashion and
Paul was generous, hospitable and rich, read four languages
and had a court of clever young men, one of whom would
eventually marry Rose.

This led to awkwardness when Paul said he had been in
love with her all along, but had refrained, through delicacy,
from pressing his suit.

In fact he had pressed it, but she had taken it for a joke.
He called her his 'wild Irish Rose' and she, playing along,
had, he now claimed, raised his hopes.

Hopes? How? Surely, she asked, he remembered her lover
the violinist? The dinner in her flat? But Paul had interpreted
what he saw in ways to suit himself.

'I thought you were living with him like a sister. To save
on rent. I knew you were both admirable and poor!'

And the abortion they'd needed? Their request for a loan?

He didn't remember any of that. 'I thought you were shy
and Irish. I thought you were a virgin.'

It turned out that, when he was small, his Irish nanny,
shocked by his parents' morals, had consoled him with tales
of pure colleens. 'When you're big we'll find you one,' she'd
promised.

Nanny Brady had had a 'boy' back in Ireland who was
waiting for her to put together a dowry and come home and
marry him.

'He waited years. And both, she somehow made clear to
me, were keeping themselves pure. Why would I think this
odder than the rest of what went on in our canyon off Sunset
Boulevard?'

'When you were six?'

'Earlier. I was ejected at six. Sent to my grandparents in
Paris. Cast out.'

'From Eden?'

'A celluloid Eden.'

It was a sad little tale. Paul's father whose movies charmed
millions also charmed his son who, at four and five, lived for

the few, short minutes each morning when he was allowed in with the breakfast trolley to snuggle up to a dazzling Dad who would then disappear for the rest of the day. Naturally, this radiant absence ignited the child's fancy more than the humdrum presence of his mother and Nanny Brady.

One day, when both were out, he made for his father's room where he hid in the closet. There, amid vacant suits, tie-racks and leathery smells, his father seemed already half present and Paul waited happily to surprise him. The wait was a long one. Paul drowsed off and some time later was awoken in pitch darkness by frightening noises. Failing to find the closet light, he stumbled out and into the bedroom where he beheld his naked father doing something dreadful to a groaning lady. Paul got hysterics. Secretaries rushed in. Scandal sheets got wind of the thing and his parents' marriage came to an acrimonious end.

'And they blamed you?'

'My mother did. I don't know whether he cared. I never saw him again.'

His father had other wives, but no more sons, so Paul remained his heir. Maybe then, suggested Rose, he should be reconciled with his memory?

'Ah, *ma chérie*!' Squeezing her arm. 'You have a good heart. Good! Generous! Just like Nanny Brady!'

This nanny, despite an alarmed disapproval of films – 'trash' – once took him to see one. It featured Irish peasants whose strengths were the opposite of those animating his father's jaunty movies and equally jaunty life. At this time Nanny herself hadn't seen Ireland for years. As the man and woman on screen struggled over barnacled rocks to get seaweed to fertilise their little fields, her tears began to flow and, to hide them, she took Paul in her arms. He had never felt so needed. The feeling quickened his understanding and there and then, he told Rose, he became a man.

'Don't cry, Nanny,' he whispered while she sniffled in shame: 'I'm not really, Paul; it's just . . . Oh, I'm sorry; pay me no mind!' Then she hugged him until he too began to cry, while the pair on screen laboured to fill their creels, and

sea spray spun rainbows which could have come from his
and Nanny's tears.

'She was seeing the life she had exchanged,' Paul explained,
'for a life among our fake Louis XV furniture. Louis XV was
all the rage just then because of one of my father's studio's
successes: a smash hit whizzing with sword-play. Thinking
back,' he said, 'I see that she must have been quite young –
younger than you are now, *chérie*. I lost track of her when
*he* gave us both our walking papers.' Paul's morose smile
conferred a connection with all this on Rose. A bond and
obligation.

His was a name one could see in lights just about anywhere. Like Fox, Pathé, Rank, Warner, Gaumont, Metro-
Goldwyn-Mayer or Disney, its syllables pulsed glamour:
bright dustings which the silver screen had been trickling into
a drab world for the better part of a century. Once, high in
the Andes, Rose saw the name glint in an Indian mud village.

'I'll bet your Nanny had just decided *not* to go back to
her boy in Ireland after all. That's why she was crying.'

For Paul, this, if true, was one more reason to blame his
father's industry's false values. Its pampering dreams.

'*Man of Aran* was the film!' Rose realised. 'Was that the
bit of Ireland you saw? Aran? No wonder she didn't want
to go home.'

'Paul,' Yves liked to explain, 'can't forgive himself for accepting his Dad's dosh – *le pognon de papa*. It explains everything
about him. His politics. The lot!'

He would then point out how, like Zeus descending, the
father had created a seminal scatter. And how the son, as
though dreams were dynamite, had laboured to disable them.
Just as the Nobel family had funded their Peace Prize with
money from explosives, so Paul put his into a magazine
dedicated to defusing the soft illusions of our time.

A fanatic! Just look, Yves invited, at Paul's face furled in
the ruff of his coat collar! See those white lashes and black-
bullet eyes! Black and white as a bag of gobstoppers! 'He
wears pinstripe suits as though wrapping himself in writing

paper. Or news sheets! Why? Because his Dad was a king of the silent cinema! Paul went back to the medium which his old man's medium displaced! Symbolic parricide!'

Yves should know. Paul, a father-figure to the men who had worked on his magazine, still hoped to revive it. Coming out of gaol with his ideas of eight years ago intact, he could not accept that the political scene had changed as much as Yves said it had. The magazine, Yves had had to insist, *even if* Paul could fund it, had no place in the new order. Its staff had dispersed. 'And,' Yves broke it to him, 'we've all taken new jobs.' Symbolic parricide!

'Remember the riddle,' asked Yves cruelly, 'that asks "What's black and white and red all over"? Answer: "Our old mag." Who's going to read it today?' Sometimes, Yves could overstate his case. Uncomfortably. Like a man with a bad conscience.

Paul, fighting back by fax and phone call, would not take no for an answer. He was this way with women too, as Rose knew, for she was one of several whom he courted doggedly. For years he had been urging her to leave Yves for him who was a worthier man. She must, he was confident, see this if she would weigh the facts.

'Do you,' she had marvelled once, 'think women are weathercocks?'

'No, no, my dear. I admire women. And your loyalty does you credit. But Yves is not the right man for you, whereas I . . .' And he proceeded, without shame or pride, to lay out his arguments: his superior understanding of her, his age – Yves was a 'mere boy' – equable temperament, income – until he lost it – idealism and knowledge of the world . . . 'I'm speaking,' he said, 'for your sake.' He was perfectly coherent, believing as he did in the revolt of reason, the end of cant and the coming of a Golden Age.

Amused, she had once copied out the old quote about the heart having reasons which reason cannot comprehend and sent it to him: a mistake, for he took it to mean that her reasons were weak.

'I'll make a bargain with you,' she'd offered then. 'I'll help you find the sweet colleen that your Nanny promised.'

She tried, though Yves made fun of her efforts to procure a Mademoiselle O'Morphy for Paul – who seemed oddly ready to play Louis XV. So perhaps his Dad's taste for bandy-legged furniture had affected him after all? And perhaps some similar lure had dazzled Rose? The shine of Paul's high-mindedness? Of his having perhaps really been an agent loyal to a fading dream of the Left.

'You romanticise each other!' Yves accused.

In the end, though the women she found *liked* Paul, they didn't like him enough – while he, susceptible to them all, kept breaking his heart, an organ she thought of as perennially in splints.

What did he lack? One could only guess that turning his back on the cinema – his father's creation – had disabled him. The rest of us speeded our pulse to its rhythms; it was our lingua franca, a thesaurus of codes and humours which Paul refused to learn. Ironies passed him by. Refusing to use its spyhole, he had no idea how people lived, and got things wrong – with Siobhán, for instance, who shared a tiny flat, every bit of which could be metamorphosed into something else. Part of the kitchen became a shower. Beds slid into walls. Bicycles hung from the ceiling.

Into this one day a florist's delivery boy, acting at Paul's behest – 'Send her flowers,' Rose had coached – attempted to deliver a flower arrangement with an eagle's wing-span: a bouquet such as might be delivered to a prima donna on a first night. Had there *been* a first night? If so, its commemoration was tropical. There were lilies with spotted tongues, reported Siobhán, bird-of-paradise flowers, 'and some willowy thing which caught in the banisters'.

With difficulty this was manoeuvred up her staircase – she lived on the sixth floor. Through her door, however, it would not go. Nor was there room to leave it on the landing, so she – in whose budget this made a sizeable dent – had to tip the boy for bringing the thing up, then tip him again to take it away.

'Too wide for my aperture!' she told Rose with ribald wrath and put an end to the courtship. She was trying to stretch a grant for mature students and her life had no space for complications.

'He's too old-fashioned,' was her verdict on Paul. 'A nineteenth-century man!'

Add to that his stubbornness – over, for instance, paying for today's lunch.

'I wish you'd let me!'

Sad-eyed headshake. 'Darling, you repay me by your mere presence.'

'But I want to pay. Give *me* pleasure. Please?'

'No, no.' His martyred look.

Rose was starving. The 'slimmer's salad' had turned out to consist of rocket leaves plus one sculpted radish. If let pay she could, even now, order a substantial sweet. A Tarte Tatin or – a man nearby was guzzling one – a Grand Marnier soufflé. Its fumes tantalised her. Hypoglaecemic hunger blurred her mind. She felt a migraine coming on. There was a queue waiting for a free table.

'Perhaps we should go then? As neither of us seems to be eating much? I think the waiters . . .'

'Oh never mind them!' He lit a cigarette. His smoking, which gave her nausea, had got out of hand in prison, so how complain? 'I reserved this table,' he stated firmly. 'It's ours.'

If she could get away from him she could buy something in the street to stave off the migraine. Some quick, sugary fix. Nougat. Baclava. But – she glanced covertly at her watch – he was staring at her with a reflection of her own need. He was an old, needy friend who had requests to make. Stoical, she batted away smoke.

She reproached herself. Hunger, the threatening migraine, and their joint obstinacy over the bill were pretexts for refusing him; yet he was a man without self, a last, gallant, monkish struggler for Liberal hopes born here in France and now almost universally dashed. All he asked was support. Friendship. Yes, but how did he define that?

He laughed abruptly, 'Remember the poem: "Just for a handful of silver he left us . . ." and what you wrote to me in gaol? You wrote that Yves had betrayed us spiritually. What's the next line? "Just for a riband to stick in his coat." '

Her head swam. Had her thoughts leaked? She mustn't get into this argument.

'Spiritual,' Paul gloated. 'That nailed him. You know he's refusing to restart the magazine . . .'

The maître d'hôtel was definitely eyeing their table.

'If we're not leaving we'll have to order something. I,' she resolved, 'will have a coffee.' That couldn't cost much, could it? Wolfishly, she chewed the sugar lumps which came with it and, energised, found herself marvelling yet again at Paul's persistence. He seemed to brim with expectancy and she could tell that not only he but she was about to be presented with a bill – an emotional one. 'Irishwomen,' he repeated, 'are good.'

To sidestep this, she told him, laughing, that for her the word had drab associations. Her school nuns had reserved it for girls of whom nothing else could be said: dim or daft girls who were made to sit on a special bench.

'With me,' said Paul humbly, 'you Irish were goodness itself!'

This was true. She and the others – Eithne, Dympna and Siobhán – had revived the serviceable old quality, as you might take out your grandmother's furs during a cold snap, once he went to gaol. Arranging rotas for prison visits, they acknowledged relief as relations with him took on frankly charitable status. 'Poor Paul!' they exclaimed with safe affection. Briskly. Like four nannies.

Rose chewed two more sugar lumps and defied the smile which this evoked. Illogical female, signalled the smile. Chooses the slimmer's salad, then stuffs herself with sugar!

*

Escaping to the loo – let him simmer down a bit – she was
confronted by the gaudy curls of Philomena Fogarty bounc-
ing in three mirrors and sparking in the bristles of her brush.
'Rose!' yelled Phil boisterously. 'It *is* Rose Molloy?' So Rose
said, 'Not Molloy,' and gave her married name. They
embraced.

'I thought it was you across the room. Is that your
husband?'

'No,' said Rose. Then the two, who had a lot to catch up
with, began to tell about themselves, while freshening their
make-up. They agreed that now they'd met they mustn't lose
touch. Phil's luncheon companion had had to rush off, so
why didn't Rose come and see her flat which was close by?
Well, it wasn't hers, but ... Rose, not listening, tried to
remember why she had lost track of Phil and whether there
hadn't been some hushed-up story back in Dublin years ago.
Gossip, scandal? Yes. That reminded her that she'd better
warn Phil about Paul, so she told some of *his* story fast.

'He'll fall for you!' she warned. 'An Irish redhead! He can't
resist them.'

Phil said she kept her hair tinted because fire colours were
propitious. She had studied colours. Studied them? Yes.
Colours had an influence ... But Rose didn't take this in for
they were now heading back to the table where Paul looked
less disappointed than Rose had feared at having their private
talk curtailed. Have a brandy, he offered recklessly, but Phil
said, no, they must come to her flat for some Colomba di
Pasqua which Italian friends had dropped off. 'We'll partake,'
she said, 'of the dove of peace! Don't you think that's a noble
ceremony?' Then, to Rose's shock, she sat down, leaned
towards Paul and said, 'You mustn't feel bad about having
been in gaol. *I* was for two years!'

Rose blushed at this betrayal of her confidence and was
sure that the usual restaurant noises had stopped punitively
so that everyone could hear. But this was an illusion. And
anyway Phil was speaking in a soft Irish voice. A lullaby
voice. She murmured: 'People care less than you think. I was

inside for shoplifting. I was twenty-one at the time and had a record. I wanted to be caught.'

They left the restaurant and stepped, in single file, along a narrow pavement. Phil led the way, followed by Paul and a dizzy Rose whose headache had begun. She thought of leaving, but felt she must monitor what Phil would say next. Besides, the Italian cake drew her. She craved sweetness as her temples drummed.

The flat had a nursery look. Posters in primary colours showed smiles and rainbows. A mirror was criss-crossed with stickers saying 'Refuse to buy ivory!' and 'Elephants are social animals which live in herds led by elder females!'

When Phil went into her kitchen Rose caught Paul's eye, but he wouldn't return her grin. Phil brought back a dove-shaped brioche covered with almonds and smelling of vanilla, and Rose gagged herself with greedy mouthfuls. Phil, she remembered now, had been described to her as 'a nutgreen maid' and dangerous to know. 'Bonkers, a way-out activist,' the man in the embassy had said. 'She's no end of trouble.'

She had an idea that Phil's troubles had begun about a dozen years after Rose and she had stopped seeing each other. This came about when Rose was asked to leave Miss Moon's Irish dancing class after the boys refused to be partnered with her, saying she was clumsy and tripped them up. Her mother was indignant but Rose herself was relieved. At the age of seven she hated having to wear green kilts and falling over her feet. She would not, however, go on being friends with someone who had witnessed her disgrace.

'Death in the eyes and the devil in the heels,' encouraged Miss Moon and tiptapped a jig with her metal-toed shoes so fast that Rose's eyes were dazzled by her devilishness. Phil was the only one who could keep up with her, but it was hard to see the sprightly seven-year-old in the thick-waisted woman who was now perched on a bar stool, wearing odd – propitious? – colours. She returned to her confidences. Prison, she told Paul and Rose, had been a refuge at a time when she could neither stay at home nor go anywhere else. She had planned to be a nun then, at her farewell dance, an uncle had done something – 'well, you could call it attempted rape' – which made her feel sullied and unworthy to enter the convent. But she didn't want to stay at home either. Thence the shoplifting.

Rose began to argue that Phil should not have blamed herself, but Paul said, no, *no*, she had been quite right. Compromises were no good. He'd seen that. 'We in the Left thought we were being practical by accepting them, but in the end we whittled away our principles. An erosion takes place. Hindsight shows that the naïve Silone was right and the subtle Togliatti wrong.'

Phil who, Rose was sure, had no idea who Silone or Togliatti were, nodded vehemently at this and nodded again when Paul said his own life had been a mistake. Rose was horrified and tried to argue but couldn't. It was partly her headache. But also the other two seemed to have entered some dense element where they were at ease and she wasn't. A gravity had descended on them and they kept murmuring 'yes, *yes!*' and approving of each other's most outlandish notions. Phil said she was a healer and Paul said she should cure Rose's headache. But there was some impediment to this – Rose's disbelief perhaps? – so, instead, they put her into a taxi and sent her home. Just before she left, she heard Paul agree to help Phil start up a magazine on Spiritual Ecology, a movement designed to encourage people to think more deeply about the planet.

The video which Dympna sent Rose has news footage of the oil-spill which must have appeared on TV. An RTE anchor man talks. Oil-spattered seabirds and indignant locals are featured and then there are shots of a white-faced Paul wearing oilskins and apparently in shock. He doesn't speak. His mouth forms a small O as if he were about to release an air bubble. Phil, sitting in a studio, denies that he was a member of her group or that violence had ever been part of its plan.

He would understand that, thinks Rose. Strategy. Sacrificing the one to the many. Wouldn't he?

She and Yves have returned from a trip abroad to find Dympna's letter and video waiting. The last time they saw Paul was some months ago when they invited him and Phil to dinner to celebrate the first issue of Phil's magazine. It was a convivial, if odd, occasion when Paul formally thanked Yves for advising him not to revive their old journal, then thanked Rose for introducing him to Phil. He seemed dazed with admiration for *her* and wore a suit of dingy 'green' cotton which had not been treated with chemicals likely to cause environmental damage.

Phil spoke of plans for the magazine, some of which seemed unobjectionable and others demented. She neither discriminated nor made allowance for surprise, and Rose and Yves found themselves being backed into a polite bafflement which grew ticklish when Paul asked Yves to help her get a subsidy.

'Governments have a responsibility,' said Phil. 'We have abused the planet so badly that it may not recover. Some of the abuse was spiritual. This country in particular has poisoned its air with evil. The guillotining of Louis XVI, the crimes committed during the Commune need to be exorcised . . .'

Paul's smile did not waver. Was his pliancy due to senility or love? What damage, Rose wondered, had she wrought by introducing him to this mad woman? Yet now Phil was talking sensibly about pollution. You could neither dismiss nor trust her. Her mind was a gaullimaufry, a promiscuous jumble. Maybe for Paul all untrained minds were? Did he think that of Rose's? He had said that with the collapse of Marxism a Dark Age of the Mind was on us. Perhaps he was merely adapting to a new norm?

Rose, in distress, took comfort from knowing that Yves was as upset as she. Gratefully, she reached for his hand and, over the next hours, felt reassured each time they caught each other marvelling with the wistful pity of adults at the simplicity of the ancient young. Phil, who had given up Catholicism, seemed to believe in every other transcendental promise, and Paul applauded her with meek, nodding beatitude. As they left, she insisted on taking a hair from Yves' head to cure a pain he had complained of in his back.

'I need something with your DNA in it,' she explained.

'An odd couple,' said Rose afterwards.

'You're jealous,' Yves accused jealously. 'You loved it when Paul was romanticising you. Now it's Phil's turn. Irish women appeal to him because they come from a country inured to bondage. He yearns to rescue a needy Irishwoman, an Irish Andromeda.'

'What about asking you for a subsidy? A bit of a nerve, no?'

'Oh *he*'d never mind sacrificing social considerations. He'd sacrifice himself.'

The RTE video has cruder things to say about Paul: Cold-War insults from the coverage of his earlier trouble to which she does not intend to listen. She turns off the sound and watches his blanched face. It has achieved the simplicity of archetype: hero or villain. No nuance. It strikes her that he has come into his true reality. And that this is the reality of his father's hated old medium: the black and white newsreel. Now, however, the image shifts, and the boat on which he inexpertly crossed the tanker's path appears, all sails bellying, proud as a racer, yawing and canting to one side as the wind tugs it forward in a great white cloud of obliterating spray.

At their dinner some months ago he described a trip he and Phil had just taken to the West of Ireland and how Phil, who had to be with her Greens or her family, left him alone in a hotel for a day or two. It was the off-season. The hotel was empty but for him, and the proprietor and his family had to go to a funeral. 'Will you be OK alone?' they asked Paul and gave him the keys. 'There's food in the kitchen and drink in the bar. Just note whatever you drink on the slate.' This easygoing trust enchanted him and he kept repeating the story with astonishment. 'Just put it on the slate,' he quoted again and again as if he thought of the words as a formula initiating him into a tribe.

# Jo Shapcott

## THE MAD COW IS A *VOGUE* MODEL

Giovanni, trained in Paris, has now spent
twenty-three minutes making me up.
Never before have I shown my whole body,
the full length of my combed-out tail, the visible
panty line, the unfurled rump to you,
my public.

        The photographer has planted me
in deep white space with perspective muddled on purpose.

I can't stand up straight. He doesn't understand
that I fall over sometimes and, anyway,
leaning is natural. But this is *Vogue*
where the upright and obedient send out
for anything they like.

        The Statue of Liberty
might do better. She is over three
hundred feet high from torch to foundation.
Made of copper sheets beaten out by hand,
her first name was Liberty Enlightening the World.
She stands up straight without trying, but then
four gigantic steel supports run through her body.

And what will be at stake in this photo?
It's not an explicit language, but look
how I am snarling at the photographer.
I am snarling at his lens and through it a world
in which my teeth, my eyes, my taste – and not
these words, these little deaths, these individual
devils, these visions of the whole damned lot –
become the way I give out to you.

# Stephen Watson

## ANOTHER SPACE

Afterwards they both could hear it, how the wind outside,
full of sunlight, the afternoon, was carrying through their
    street.
The ordinary weather, come November, for this part of the
    world,
for a peninsula, a city, on the south Atlantic's windswept
    edge –
but even while they listened, their room half-darkened,
    draughty,
lay mostly silent, a little dazed, lazy about going back to
    work,
something was including them in all that which was outside
in a street, still more deserted, before the schools came out,
in a suburb long before the holidays, in the work-time of the
    year,
through which there came, once or twice, receding down
the hill, a radio's sound, carried by, playing in full sunlight,
the tones of a child's harmonica, notes bending in the wind.

More and more, something had come over them, something
was including them in a place this afternoon had made,
with its sunlight blowing by, their blind curving, billowing,
with the light outside, like time, waxing, waning in the wind.
It had happened there in silence, while each avoided getting
    up;
and both could feel it as it happened: how they'd been
    absorbed

into an absence each gust had opened, enlarging in its wake;
how, unawares, they'd both been drawn, included in a space
filling, flooded with the traces of things both near and far –
with a street that sloped more steeply in the air's downrush,
the sky above it slipping, down into its northwest quarter,
landscapes, miles beyond the city, vacuumed by the miles of
    air.

It was no more than a mood, mid-afternoon, mid-week,
a while before the summer holidays, the working-year was
    over.
Or something they had heard, had only chanced to hear
while lying there, still listening, the hour for work long past.
It was little more than this: a place brightly lit, bare
as the afternoon, the street outside in its pre-season
    emptiness,
the sunlight blowing by, and that absence in the sunlight
as each gust foundered, emptying it. Yet it was the place they
knew once that love could make – this place that hasn't a
    name,
imaged, a while longer, in altered space, the shape that
light then seemed to make, that stray radio, harmonica,
thinning in the middle distance, somewhere towards the
    freeway.

# THE SEA CLOSE BY

When summer comes into our city, giving to the sky
at dawn that faint dustiness, foretelling the noon heat,
pigeons calling in the stone-pines, throats watery, dusty,
it comes at first in coolness, deepened overnight in stone,
then heat ascetic in its dryness, a heat that's almost lean,
a sky denuded, solid in its blue, unshadowed by mid-morning
down to the rim of cindered hills. It comes, here, each year,
to add a salt to air, a salt to light, the heat street-baked,
headwind smelling of the docks: it brings the sea into our
   city.

It gives back to you the body, and the memory of the body.
Then, beyond the many beaches with their clean-shaven
   grain,
sea deepens over reefs, the shelving rock, into its own blue;
greens deepen to pine-green. The sea close by still closer,
waves lift from their sea-salad, lift clear into a glassiness,
the colours liquid in them, of green olives in clear brine,
draining, sluicing downward as they peak, and arc, and
   drop –
and there is nothing but the body, deepening in the memory,
its one desire – that water broken, light aswirl – to live
unclothed, cooled by sweat, in the salt of its own blood.

It's like the sea, the sight of it, its own salt quenched
by these colours in the sea: in the clarities of turquoise
corrugated, thinned again to glassy blue across sandbars
then quenched in channels, fathoms of ice-cold ultramarine.
It's like the sun that parches, the fire fed, parched doubly
dry by fires of cold seawater, brine almost acid in the heat.
It is your body, given by the summers here, deepening
in the memory of the body, in that shadow of the blood
(shadow of this sun) that darkens in its thirst, its salt,
the way grapes do, baked hills behind, filling black with light.

# Carole Satyamurti

## SPRING OFFENSIVE

May's the month for optimistic acts:
seedlings – pansies, antirrhinums, salvias –
bedded in, gauche first-day-at-schoolers.
Your thumbs have blessed them, inner eye furnishing
dowdy beds with dazzling coverlets.

Through the lengthening dusk, snail battalions
creep on prehensile bellies from their dugouts.
They bivouac around your bright hopes,
slurp sapid juices, vandal lace-makers,
body-building on your would-be colours.

You stumble out at dawn and catch them at it,
scrawling silver sneers on wall and path,
and snatch them from their twigs, impervious to
endearing horns, their perfect picture-bookness.
You crush them, or worse; lay down poisonous snacks.

Yet, aren't their shells as lovely as petunias,
patterned like ceramic works of art
from a more coherent age? And might they not
defend with slow, tenacious argument
their delicate offspring, soon to fizz in salt?

Summer's on their side. Each night, new recruits
will graduate from dark academies.
You lie, plotting extravagant revenges.
Asleep, you dream a world where, very slowly,
children, friends, are running out of air.

# Dannie Abse

## CHILD DRAWING IN A HOSPITAL BED

Any child can open wide
the occult doors of a colour
naïvely to call, 'Who's there?'
For this sick girl drawing
outstep invisible ones
imprisoned everywhere.
Wasp on a windowpane.

Darkest tulip her head bends,
face white as leukaemia,
till the prince in his tower,
on parole from a story,
descends by royal crayon
and, thrilled, stays half an hour.
Wasp on a windowpane.

Birds of Rhiannon, pencilled,
alight to wake the dead –
they do not sing, she rubs them out,
they smudge into vanishings,
they swoop to Nowhere
as if disturbed by a shout.
Wasp on a windowpane.

Omens. Wild astrologies whirl:
sun and moon begin to soar.
Unlikely that maroon sky
green Christmas trees fly through
– doctors know what logic's for.
Tell me, what is magic for?
Wasp on a windowpane.

Now penal-black she profiles
four eerie malformed horses,
nostrils tethered to the ground.
Unperturbed, the child attends
for one to uplift its neck
and turn its death's head round.
Wasp on a windowpane.

## MY NEIGHBOUR, ITZIG

My neighbour, Itzig,
has gone queer with religion.
Yesterday he asked me
who named the angels!

Today his dog is barking and barking.

But like music that's ceased
in an adjoining room
Itzig is not here.
He is nowhere else, either.

Itzig, listen, your dog needs a walk.

But Itzig is droning on and on
– open the window, someone –
a prayer archaic and musty
and full of O.

His sad feet are on this earth,
his happy head is elsewhere
among the configuration
of the seven palaces of light.

Come back, Itzig, your dog needs feeding.

But Itzig quests for the eighth colour.
His soul is cartwheeling, he's far
from the barely manageable
drama of the Present Tense.

Come back, Itzig, your dog needs water.

But Itzig follows, with eyes closed,
the footsteps of the sages
Amora and Rehumai
who never existed.

## NEW GRANDDAUGHTER

You don't know the score, what's you, what's not.
Remote ancestors return you can't disown.
This prelude, this waiting for an encore.

Is that raised hand yours, this wind-pecked morning?
Enigmatic trees, askew, shake above the pram.
All's perplexity, green reverie, shadowland.

But why this grandfatherly spurt of love?
Your skin is silk, your eyes suggest they're blue.
I bend to smell small apricots and milk.

Did I dream that legend of the Angel
who falls to touch each baby's fontanelle
and wipe out racial memory, leaving *déjà vu*?

I'm confessing! Your newness, petite, portends
my mortality – a rattle for you, the bell for me.
Hell, I'm old enough to mutter blessings.

The determinates of the clock increase.
Sometimes you close your eyes noiselessly, turn
your head, listening to music that has ceased.

# Donald Atkinson

## THE ARITHMETICIAN AND HIS MOTHER

In the field that runs by the Roman aqueduct
I trot beside her. Folds of her summer dress
make a bunch of flowers in my fist; and the grass
so deep, it wets my knees with cuckoo-spit.
Little frog-hopper, all of a lather,
I can hop too, and skip, and fall about
in this apocalyptic green; till she laughs,
and I think she likes me, do it all again;
could keep this up until the cows come home.
Until in truth, like something prophesied, they do,
across the bottom of the field lugubriously.
A blotchy one lags far behind the rest.

Suddenly grown finger-wise, we count the cows;
and then we count the blotches on the cow.
Over and over. Each time a different tally.

Have I ever known anything for sure?
Did I live in her eye, her airy pupil,
or was there another? Collapse of the wave-
function at the point of measurement,
sway of the universe. How hold them together:
the blotches and the counting and the cow?
Why is there so much light tonight?
Has she merged with the planet Jupiter?
Who beckons me, who waits for me?
What formulae are written in these stars?

# Alistair Elliot

## A Death Not Quite in the Family

You needn't hate her any more.
There's nothing left of her to fear.
She will never say again
'Cogito' or smile 'ergo sum.'
She has become a minute of bitter rain
somewhere and a little extra jetsam
on the East Anglian coast:
Non cogitat. Non est.

The little equation marks of genealogy
(the valency of the marriageable)
no longer lift their arms toward her:
her name cannot come into them;
the nubile voice is powder
gurgling down a tidal stream.
Everything about her that you hated
has been obliterated.

You can cross her off. But I
cannot forget so easily.
Even my innocent holiday this summer
carries me back to her embrace:
who could foresee a swimmer
or sailor, cutting the dusty surface
of the North Sea, would blunder through
that puff of sibilance, that 'On se fout?'

# Richard Holmes

## THE DANCING MARINER

I ONCE HAD a dream that I was dancing with an Albatross. The Albatross was a woman, but this did not seem strange. She held me in her white feathers, close to her breast, and we danced in the air. We were suspended high above a tilting sea, which glittered to the horizon with no land in sight. The rhythm of our dancing was strong and surging, not at all like flying, but like blood pulsing. The sense of height and rhythm was exciting, but terrifying. In the dream I knew that the Albatross would eventually let me fall into the sea. So I danced like someone condemned to death when the music stops. But the Albatross never let me go, and we were still dancing when I awoke.

This dream occurred while I was in Malta, working on a biography of Coleridge. It was not hard to see where its images came from; though less easy to see what they might mean.

Malta is a yellow, sandstone island set in the Mediterranean between Sicily and North Africa. Beyond the old historic harbour of Valletta, it is a rocky plateau surrounded by high cliffs, caves and seabirds. Coleridge exiled himself here for two years in 1804–5, when it was occupied by the British during the Napoleonic Wars. He was trying to cure himself of opium addiction.

But he was also working with surprising efficiency as the First Secretary to the wartime Governor, Sir Alexander Ball. He drew up emergency legislation, wrote strategic reports, and drafted despatches which were sent to Nelson in the months before Trafalgar. Coleridge also kept extensive private diaries in Malta. In one of these, he noted that the ballad of the 'Ancient Mariner' – written six years before, and based on the shooting of the Albatross – had now become the symbolic story of his own life.

All this was much in my mind. During the day, I was working on Coleridge's papers at the Royal Library, Valletta, in a panelled room overlooking the drowsy fountain in Queen's Square. In the evenings, I walked along the cliffs and swam from the rocks beyond Slima until it got dark. It was November, and though the sea was still warm, there were few visitors and the coast was deserted. Sometimes I met people by chance: an arms dealer from Libya, a sculptress from Catania. On the evening before the dream I had gone dancing at a little run-down bar, with an open terrace strung with coloured lights, on a promontory high above the sea.

In my experience, such dreams are not unusual for a biographer, who spends many solitary hours both waking and sleeping in the company of his subject, often over many years. They are usually connected with the biographer's suppressed feelings about the subject; or with parts of the subject's life that are not fully understood; or with insights into the subject's work which do not fit within the normal terms of criticism. They can rarely be used within the strict confines of the conventional biography; and will probably never reach the final book at all. But the dream material can sometimes be valuable. (I have often thought that it would be interesting to write a biography *entirely* in the form of dreams about the subject, set within the barest skeleton of documentation. It would, I suppose, be a form of Illustrated Life.)

This particular dream of dancing with the Albatross had several repercussions for me, but one immediate outcome. I began to think of Coleridge's great poem, 'The Rime of the Ancient Mariner', in terms of a modern ballet.

It struck me that the Ancient Mariner's whole story could be brilliantly interpreted, not through criticism, but through physical performance. Its powerful rhythms, its haunting music, its mysterious confrontations between human and supernatural forces, are peculiarly suited to the expressionism of ballet. Though metaphysical in its implications, the poem is directly and even violently physical in its action and imagery. This physical immediacy is the essence of ballet, in which the most subtle feeling can be rendered as movement and gesture.

Coleridge also said (in his *Table Talk*) that critics always forgot that the Mariner was *young* at the time of his original voyage. He grew old only in the obsessional retelling of his tale, over many years. So the Mariner is a young sailor when he meets the Albatross, and there is something erotic in their confrontation. Here emerged my central idea: the Mariner dancing with some beautiful but dangerous embodiment of Nature's power, which had first surfaced in my Malta dream. My sketch for the ballet, which of course never got into my biography, was roughly as follows. It can perhaps be imagined more vividly than it could be staged. But one never knows with dreams.

## CONCEPT

An adaptation of Coleridge's 'Ancient Mariner' for modern dance and music. Two basic sets: an eighteenth-century Somersetshire village with church, tavern and green (like Nether Stowey); and a square-rigged galleon on the high sea, with deck and rigging of the type used by Captain Cook to explore the southern Pacific. The choreography and music score adapt traditional English and folklore forms: the country jig, the naval hornpipe, the sea shanty, the wedding and funeral march, the *danse macabre*. Scenery and laser lighting produce haunting visual effects of dawn, sunset, starlight, moon, and sea storms.

The ballet company dance both the villagers on land, and the ship's crew at sea. The leading solo dancers each take more than one part, and this duplication of roles – one identity melting into another – is central to the concept and should be clear to the audience. The main dance roles include:

381

The Mariner: as ancient bearded sea-salt, and as young sailor.

The Albatross: as beautiful bride; as sea-bird; as the terrible Nightmare Life-in-Death; and as the Female Spirit.

The Hermit: who also dances as the village priest, and the Male Spirit of Nature.

The ballet has three movements, which are divided into five acts. It begins in the bucolic morning atmosphere of a country wedding (Act 1); it then moves backwards in time to the Mariner's nightmare voyage (Acts 2, 3, 4); and finally (Act 5) it returns to a solemn evening wedding-feast, where the hope of happiness is tempered by the tragic presence of the haunted Ancient Mariner. The whole ballet reflects Coleridge's original 'vision' of some profound but inexplicable metaphysical crime, leading to a struggle between love and cruelty in Nature.

## SYNOPSIS

Act 1. The villagers dance and celebrate a country wedding outside the church door. They pay homage to the beautiful young Bride in her long white dress. The village band plays a wedding march. The celebrations are abruptly interrupted by the appearance of the bearded Ancient Mariner, who dances across the village green and insists on telling the story of his voyage. Unwillingly at first, the villagers circle round the Mariner and are gradually drawn under his spell. Helplessly, they start to mime the parts of the ship's crew. The Bride confronts the Mariner, but is also spellbound.

Act 2. The village is transformed into the ship. The green becomes the deck, an oak tree becomes the mast and shrouds, the church door becomes the poop. The ship's crew are joyfully dancing the hornpipe. The Mariner – now young – spies a lovely white Albatross (the erstwhile Bride) dancing alluringly across the deck. He dances after her, and the crew join in wildly. But when the Albatross refuses to dance with him, the Mariner is overcome with the desire to possess her, and maddened by her repulses, suddenly turns and shoots her with a cross-bow. A terrible storm immediately descends, and the Act ends in terror and confusion among the sailors.

Act 3. The ship is becalmed under a burning tropical sun. The crew perform a dance of death, as one by one they drop to the deck, stricken by drought. As they die, they curse the Mariner. The Pacific night comes on, and under a huge moon the ghastly taunting figure of the Nightmare Life-in-Death appears. She dances provocatively across the ship, mocking the Mariner. As the moon begins to set, the Mariner is left alone, the sole survivor, exhausted and grief-stricken, dancing over the bodies of his shipmates. The ship slowly fades into twilit unreality, as the Mariner collapses on the deck.

Act 4. In a haunting dream-sequence (one might say a dream-within-a-dream), the Male and Female Spirits of Nature dance over the prone body of the Mariner. They argue and decide his fate, the Female Spirit pleading for mercy. They transform the dead crew into glittering sea-creatures, who weave hypnotically over the Mariner. He wakens, and astonished by their unearthly beauty, joins in the dance and blesses them. The heavens open, rain pours down, and the ship sails on into moonlight and safe harbour as the dream dissolves. The Old Hermit comes aboard, and absolves the Mariner; while the crew form a silent tableau holding the dead Albatross in their arms.

Act 5. In a sudden blaze of light and music, the same tableau bursts back into life, now as the country villagers carrying the Bride to the evening wedding supper outside the tavern. But the Mariner – an old, bearded figure again (as in Act 1) – moves among the revellers like the traditional ghost at the feast. As night comes on, he stands silently watching them, as he had watched the beautiful sea-creatures. Stars come out, candles are lit, a long table is laid (a white cloth billowing like a sail). The Bride and groom are toasted in wine by the villagers, and blessed by the priest. In a final movement of love and forgiveness, the Bride dances round the table and brings the Mariner a cup of wine to drink. She draws him back into the company, and the whole village rises and dances together happily. But at the last moment the music stops, and all the dancers freeze motionless as the sound of a rising wind fills the air. All that is, except the Mariner, who silently dances on by himself as the curtain drops.

# E. A. Markham

## WHATSERNAME AND LA CONTESSA

### I

I WAS STUNNED. I stopped in mid-chew, as if I'd bitten on a hard thing in the middle of the cake; or – for me – on something unpleasantly soft, like a currant or a raisin. And then I forced myself to continue, to chew on what my mother had said, that she hadn't had a holiday in over thirty years.

My first impulse was to deny it, not because it wasn't true, but because it seemed such an odd thing to say; it seemed so much the sentiment of someone at the far edge of privation, the sort of thing that, in another context, would make me want to protest, to defend the victim. And yet it wasn't like that. (Had she been working all these years? – an ungenerous thought.) It was true, yes, that she hadn't been back home, but that was largely of her doing; she had never, to my knowledge, expressed a wish to go back to see what things were like. She hadn't left the country, hadn't left London, even, in all these years: would a view of Manchester, of Milan have eased the sense of . . . being in the wrong place? Of being constrained? The English took their sorrows to the seaside, to Blackpool, to Benidorm: these were, we like to think, the small dreams rejected by the family. Some of our own people from the Caribbean went back to show off – new clothes, new accents, foreign partners – their new status. And why not? But we had decided not to play that game. It had taken decades to recoup our original position, getting back to roughly where we had been when we left the island. Now, we had to prove more before going back. This was obvious; it was one of the reasons my mother never expressed the wish to go back.

I was beginning to be able to cope with the accusation; I praised the cake.

I was on my mother's territory, in her room. I had learnt, over the years, that coming here was to submit myself to a process of cross-examination, at the end of which I would always leave pleading guilty. She had observed earlier in the evening, apropos a news item on television, that the Governor of Hong Kong was only three years older than me, and had children old enough to be at university. I apologised, routinely, for not having children. I apologised, more feelingly, for not having got myself installed as Governor of Hong Kong, and thus restoring to the mother of the Governor a role commensurate with her inner status – that of keeping an eye on the morality and hygiene of the Colony, and spending her afternoons, in summer dresses, opening new supermarkets and banks. This had amused her enough to call me ignorant. Maybe this would be regarded as a large enough input by me so that I wouldn't have to read to her or to write a letter before leaving. (I used to stumble over her Bible, so reading-matter would be from the book I happened to be carrying, and I took care, usually, when I boarded the train for Upton Park to walk with something unsuitable.)

But this imposed a penalty. It was important to demonstrate that I was among the privileged who were informed, to show that my store of random knowledge was as great at least as those people who appeared on television quiz shows, 'for they don't have your education'. The reason I didn't do all that, we would agree, was that I'd passed it up for something better, more dignified.

So there was a good chance that I would end up regaling her with, say, a list of rivers and towns in Yugoslavia – or anything browsed before the journey. I would then talk a bit about the country in question, making something of a joke of it, enough to bring on the dubious look, which made her girlish, and the reprimand for talking nonsense. This would be a successful 'reading'. I could then make an early exit, for nights in London were deemed to be dangerous, and I travelled by train, and lived a long way away. My guilt, on leaving, would be for a niece, who would be left with the chore of writing a letter for her grandmother, who had a touch of rheumatism or arthritis in her fingers.

I had thought, over the years, of taking her abroad somewhere, maybe to those places in Germany and France where I sometimes worked. I had spent many years trying to pacify little patches of territory in this or that country, and friends had sometimes been recruited for these acts of exploration. Pioneering work. That done – so the theory goes – the family would start travelling in style: a version of my mother, summery and gloved, cutting the ribbons to a Manhattan-style structure in Kowloon, declaring it open. More probably, I saw myself picking her up at Nice airport and driving west into the mountains, careful to take it slowly as she didn't like speed, to her new holiday home.

It seems too raw talking this way about your mother, so I tend to draw back sometimes, or to pull a little veil over it to protect us both; that's when I end up calling her La Contessa. I call her La Contessa because over thirty years ago, weeks before we left the Caribbean, someone had painted a portrait of her and had called it 'La Contessa'. We had never seen the finished painting and knew nothing of its whereabouts; but I fancy the image that the painter trapped was close to the image of herself that both La Contessa and I preserved. We now allowed the thirty years to pass only when it suited us. (I had dreamt of her the other night learning to drive the car, and she had reacted in a way which disturbed and embarrassed me – an old memory: it was the memory of her on the horse at home, Ruby. Ruby's docility was legendary; so when the painter, the man who was to dub her La Contessa, suggested that she sit on the horse for the portrait, it seemed fitting. The queens of England and those sorts of people were said to have their portraits painted sitting on a horse. And we'd also have a record of another aspect of the house; for the horse would soon be given away, and without the horse, the 'groom', who had been part of the house, would revert to being a labourer. As we might not be able to re-create the real thing in England, play it safe with the portrait. So my mother was got on to the horse, not without difficulty for Ruby stood high, even against the front steps, and my mother's dress was newly ironed and not to be creased. Also, the groom and the painter had to be careful where they put their hands as they lifted her on. Eventually, she was sitting in the saddle and Ruby, not knowing what this was about, took a leisurely step forward, then another . . . and a third: was the portrait laughing? My mother's screams seemed so out of proportion to the danger that for a moment no one knew what to do. In the end she was hustled down, somewhat indelicately. My punishment was to have witnessed this. Much later, I was to discover that she had regarded such unseemly behaviour on horseback as an acknowledgement of sexuality, as a display, in public, of a wanton nature. I resolved to find a way, one day, to talk to her about this.)

But not yet. Maybe we could collude on something less risky, like joining the Open University and studying something where we wouldn't stand out among the pensioners from Bridlington and the rapists serving life at places like Albany on the Isle of Wight. Or, maybe I'd just take her on holiday.

But the family had priorities. We had, without articulating it, accepted that *holiday* was in some sense the reverse of *work*, a reward for work or relief from work; and we bought the notion that *work* had something to do with paid employment and little to do with whatever it was that La Contessa did – with her being in the house, etc. With such things informing our thinking, it was easy to see how a holiday for her seemed less pressing than other things we hadn't acted on. For holidays, themselves, had been deferred even by those who had 'earned' them, those who endured the attritions of the workplace, an environment which, if not always hostile, was demeaning. It was there where people pretended not to understand your accent, where they expected your face to be stretched into a permanent smile, where they thought any claim to a history before your arrival in this country was a boast. These 'workers' stored up their holidays, like interest in the bank, until it could be drawn on by children – nephews, nieces – who would need to take their bearings outside this strange world, the better to survive it.

I've become a bit obsessed with this matter because of my life-style, because I was the member of the family who travelled, and was therefore associated with 'holidays'. I'd been to four of the five continents, and I *had* taken people with me on some of these expeditions; so why not La Contessa?

Of course, many of my forays abroad weren't, in fact, holidays. Once, in the mid-1970s, I went to Germany to baby-sit a dog. A holiday. I'd taught in Germany, had friends there, so the opportunity to go back to baby-sit the dog – and to look around the Language Schools at the same time for work – was seen as a holiday. Can you imagine La Contessa sauntering down the Hohestrasse in Köln followed by a dog? Then what? Nip into the *Journal* for a drink, a Kolsch – Kolsch for me, hot chocolate for Mutti? Or maybe passing the hour sitting at one of the little tables in the square outside the Dom, the Cathedral, watching tourists snapping the monstrosity, snapping themselves – so many Japanese set in Gothic? She'd be introduced to the Language School crowd, exchanging Inlingua and Unilingua and Berlitz horror stories, speculating on the German sense of humour.

Possible. But I could go one better than that; I had a plan.


## II


Here is La Contessa looking down from that magnificent *palazzo* on the south side of the *Piazza Signoria* – the one with the clock tower. Ah, we are in Florence. There are people of a humble fourteenth-century aspect looking out from the lower floors.

'Cui flavam religas coman?' I pull out from somewhere to put myself in the mood, though I no longer know what it means. From the raked stand, I point out to my companions all the women in our family – grandmother, mother, sister, nieces – up there at the windows of the *palazzo*, in costume, fifth level up at least, looking down on the square, on the event.

'What event?' Whatsername would ask me later. (Whatsername, like La Contessa, needs her anonymity.)

'The Great Match. Not cricket, unfortunately. Football.'

'Football!'

Then I would have to explain the occasion. 'The family are looking down on a sixteenth-century event. Seats erected all round the square. The pitch sanded; sanded in the sense of tons of sand poured on to the square, and raked. A beautiful Tuscan summer evening. Today the two teams are the Greens and the Blues. But we don't know that yet, because the dignitaries are marching out, ruffed and plumed, in formation; hundreds of them filling the piazza. Then comes the acrobatic stuff, all that business with flags and formation. They're never quite professional here: a few of them drop the flag . . .'

'These are the players?'

'The players have to wait their turn. The ceremonial takes a long time; the family upstairs are in no hurry. This part of the ceremony takes about an hour, while the grand folk look down from their windows, tossing the odd flower down. And the players come on . . .'

'Ah!'

'The Referee has a sword and ceremonial hat.'

'Sixteenth century, you say?'

'Sixteenth century. Linesmen dressed like figures out of Piero della Francesca. OK. OK. Sometimes they step back a couple of centuries. La Contessa sniffs at a flower and tosses it down, carelessly . . .'

'I can see her doing that.'

'Tosses a flower down . . . No one kicks the ball, of course. Very rarely, anyway. Each player fixes his opponent in a half-nelson and pins him to the floor . . .'

'Filth. Filth. Are they all men?'

'. . . Men and boys. And the few remaining standing try to get the ball to the opposite goal. Of course, there are five men in each goal.'

'You're making this up.'

'*Five* men in goal. There are about twenty-five players a side. This is sixteenth-century football.'

'Maybe men were terribly small in those days, and not well-fed. That's why you needed five in goal.'

'. . . But the goal is the width of the piazza. When someone scores, the cannon goes off.'

'I knew there would be violence.'

She is mocking my report of Florentine football, Whatsername is; but I vow to take La Contessa to this annual spectacle; next year would be her coming out. I'd witnessed it with friends, it was just right. After the match, rival supporters fought each other with arias from some sixteenth-century opera, and then they fought with tourists like twentieth-century people. There was no way that La Contessa could get out of coming to Florence to attend the Match next year.

## III

Next year she was in hospital and then she had died. How to deal with recriminations that everyone was too polite to make? Who will charge you with complicity? For already things have begun to ravel. One train journey, at least, has lost its shape, the story ended before we've got to the end. Look, you say. *Look*, you scream: how can it end when there are pages and pages to go! Pages and pages. You can't accept it; how good, how lucky that you're not armed. Planning to do this or that seems silly, tasteless. I had come prepared to read to you . . . something unusual, yes – a list of horses running at Epsom (for we both loathe horse-racing; it would have been funny. Or would it have reminded you of Ruby?). The 2 o'clock at Epsom had names like Sno Serenade and

Dr Zeva and Cantus Firmus and All Shook Up: *All Shook Up, I'm In Luv.* Elvis . . . No one to giggle disapprovingly, no one to be girlish, at seventy-six: *All Shook Up, I'm In Luv.* Elvis . . . I'm building a house in Montauroux, north of Cannes. There, you could rest. Forty minutes from Nice airport. There you would rest and tell us where we went wrong. Then the next day, or the day after, whenever . . . a leisurely ride to Tuscany, plenty of time to choose your costume for the *palazzo*, then to your balcony, a flower in your hand, drifting down to the American tourists below. We're in Hong Kong, I'd say: reassure the people. Once, during our talks, she had asked about the bats that had lived in our old house in Coderington. The house had long been abandoned; a ruin: where had the bats taken refuge – with no large houses, no attics left in the village? I didn't know. I had promised her an answer. Now there was no . . . pressure to find out what had become of the bats. I could go through life now, not having to find answers to such questions. But I had prepared myself for this: I would have said that bats were the only mammals with the full power of flight. And then; and then to bring on the frown, the giggle, the charge of ignorance, I would have mouthed *Plectotus Auritus*; I would have clowned *Vespertilion Ide* . . . She knew bats slept upside-down. So it's enough now to think that bats are creatures that sleep upside-down. Something shared. Foolishly, I turn on her television to see if it works. There's someone wearing an arm-band, a whole football team: who are they to wear arm-bands? I turn off the box. I'm growing coarse. Whatsername had tried to prevent this, and I had defied her. Now, I must return and be contrite.

Whatsername had helped, had got me to the point where I could broach a subject of importance with La Contessa, and I had found the opening, and ducked it. It was before the hospital and I'd popped in to say goodbye, I'd be away for a few weeks; and we ended up watching cricket together. It was early in the summer; not warm. The understanding was that we'd watch the cricket till time for the Australian soap opera, and then switch channels. Though I was preparing to leave before then. But it seemed mildly appropriate, turning from one Australian *play* to another. That led me into a joke and then a sort of commentary on Australia, parts of which I'd toured: should I happen to settle there, would she come and visit? We'd call in on the Governor of Hong Kong on the way. Her image of Australia was uncomplimentary, so I tried to disabuse her, to talk of the beauty of the Sydney waterfront, of the Blue Mountains – nothing like that in London. But her objection to Australia was its *distance*. Foiled again – and by someone who hadn't left London in all these years. But at that moment, something occurred on the television which damned Australia.

It was a bowler whose modern haircut had already puzzled La Contessa but she had been persuaded to give him the benefit of the doubt. But the fellow didn't help himself. Walking back to his mark, facing us in close-up, this big man with the strange hair-style brought the shiny, red ball to his lips, looked at it, and then licked it copiously. Even I couldn't defend him after that. I had to agree that he was 'nasty', and volunteered for good measure the information that poisonous chemicals had been sprayed on the ground in its preparation. But this was a detail. The image that stuck was of a man in public, so uncontrollable, so lascivious that he couldn't resist licking the red ball: was this man's country the sort of place I wanted to settle in? Had I taken leave of my senses? Didn't I know there were strange diseases going round?

It was I who changed the subject. I had been accused by Whatsername of avoiding, of invisibilising La Contessa – all the Contessas of this world; in effect, of denying them their holidays. These women had been uprooted, sometimes in early middle-age, separated, divorced; forced in one way or other to exchange the jurisdiction of husbands for that of sons, no better than husbands, but more puritanical. Forced in this way to live out their lives in a denial of sexuality. I was likened to a gaoler pretending to be an ally. I think now of the Australian licking the red ball. I think of La Contessa on Ruby preparing to have her portrait painted. And I think, yes; this room has been lived in.

# Lorna Tracy

## THE PRICK AND THE PENDULUM

*Das Schaudern ist der Menschheit bestes Teil;*
*Wie auch die Welt ihm das Gefühl verteure...*
Goethe, *Faust*, Part Two

A PROOF COPY of her husband's entry in *Who's Who* had
arrived in the post for its annual update. Yes, Torrens was
in *Who's Who* now. Two columns. (Among People of Distinction it is not being in *Who's Who* that matters, but how many
columns you get.) Torrens omitted, as usual, to mention the
existence of a spouse. Nellys credited him with herself and
returned the proof to the publisher.

By the time the new edition appeared Torrens would no
longer have that spouse, of course, but at least Nellys would
finally get her credit line. Maybe the next wife would have a
bit more acknowledgement than Nellys ever got.

It had been a summer of drought. Late in July like a fair
woman's first grey hair the first yellow leaves had appeared
on the garden birch. By the middle of August the streets were
ankle-deep in leaf-drop and the presence of autumn inhabited
the hazy air, although the sun remained fiery. Its oily amber
light in mid-afternoon left rainbows on the white gloss wood-
work – rainbows with thick yolk-yellows and intense,
infected reds. Nellys responded to the disordered climate by
dressing in red and black, or black and yellow, as if to signal
to predators that she had a bitter taste. The nets hung still
in the open windows. Nellys became unusually aware of the
suburban train dashing furiously up and down its trench at

the bottom of the garden, with flashes of blue lightning and a sudden snaky hiss. The exasperated nagging of a collared dove menaced her nerves; the breaking note of outrage, the monotonous note of complaint.

Nellys had begun to think of her often-decamped husband as Professor Pushpull. From time to time Professor Pushpull would come back home, horny as a buffalo, to read his mail and core his wife, taking her on quick little *tours des hanches* and excursions down *le soutien-gorge profond*. Professor Pushpull believed in having it both ways: gone and not gone; here *and* there.

When Torrens was 'here' and not 'there' Nellys would fall into exhaustion and indecision, whereas when he was gone her body sprang with energy into its own rhythms. Whenever Professor Pushpull lived at home Nellys was almost literally unable to dress herself, to solve the enormous problem: what shall I wear? She would lean against the sink waiting for him to tell her what he wanted, thinking: I cannot live any more as if I were nothing but genitalia with a brainstem inconveniently attached. She was wobbling through life the way an egg waddles towards the brink of an imperceptibly sloping counter.

Then, when he had gone away again, she would regain in solitude the blissful enjoyment of her domesticity, free from sexual obligation that had become no more than the struggle to make ends meet.

What enraged Nellys's scientific husband when she described him as 'ruled by your gonads' was how this slur skipped his entire central nervous system, even bypassing the pituitary, going straight to the most primitive phylogenetic response: sexual stimulus. That categorised him as a lower animal and he was a higher animal. One of the very highest, actually.

Torrens's behaviour was a stimulus to anger that Nellys had put on hold in herself for years before releasing it (that is, before behaving at last in accordance with it). The higher animals *can* put stimuli on hold. That's scientific. That's been proved.

At home Torrens had his helpful ways. Exactly once every week, on Tuesday, as his contribution to a tidy house he emptied the kitchen bin 'whether it needs it or not', even though every week by Saturday night the bin was overflowing. At last Nellys said: 'Please empty that bin when it's full, not when it's Tuesday.' He answered that she was a load of rubbish herself and she could pack her bags and go, he wasn't putting up any longer with her constant aggression.

She composed an advertisement for her replacement.

FULL-TIME EMPLOYMENT OFFERED TO
RESPONSIBLE PERSON ABLE TO MEET
BASIC PHYSICAL REQUIREMENTS AND
WORK UNSOCIAL HOURS. NO SALARY,
NO HOLIDAYS, NO PENSION, NO
MATERNITY LEAVE, NO RETIREMENT.
HIGH RISK OF UNCOMPENSATED
REDUNDANCY OFFSET BY THOUSAND-
TO-ONE CHANCE TO MAKE IT *REALLY*
*BIG*

Afterwards she experienced another of those awful deflations of the will that seemed to follow any initiative she took. She could fuel herself with justified rage, make plans to leave the matrimonial home, then suddenly go flat. Purposeless again. Acquiescing.

How many times can this happen before it finishes you?

An infinite number of times, apparently.

Nellys lay prone in the brilliant sunshine, one cheek pressed to the carpet. Tears poured out of her as out of a cracked cistern, soaking her bare arms. She made no sound. She saw rainbows on rainbows, circles upon circles of flecked gold, metallic magentas and emeralds in her lashes. The salt-and-pepper hair across her face bounced with every heartbeat. *My love – my love – my love –*

The sun dried the salt on her arms. It was time to get on with dying.

On the back of an envelope from an Oxfam appeal she

printed the message she would leave on the hall floor outside the bathroom door laid on top of Figure 677 in the twenty-third edition of Gray's *Anatomy*, the chapter on angiology. Fig. 677: a man's head engraved in half profile, the derm peeled away exposing the blood supply to the right side of the cranium, a net of red rivulets branching from the jugular and the powerful carotid that arise in the thoracic cavity (not shown). The carotid: that is where she would cut.

DON'T ATTEMPT TO OPEN THIS DOOR. IT IS LOCKED. I AM NOT LOOKING MY BEST. SPARE YOURSELF. RING THE POLICE.

This was no emotional suicide note. It would be clear to everyone that she had not been drunk or deranged when she wrote it. People must understand that she had done something she'd thought through and chosen. What she'd chosen was banal; that's all she regretted.

The most difficult thing, apart from making a deep, accurate incision in the precise place, would be fighting off the instinct for self-preservation. It was bound to assert itself at the last moment. If she were serious about dying she would have to take this into account.

At least she would finish in the presence of light and warmth. Somehow, as the water became smoky with her blood, she would have to go on calmly lying in it while it cooled, congealed around her, crusted over and turned black. She must close her eyes so that they would not find her staring. And tie up her jaw to prevent it gaping. One of Torrens's best silk ties, passed under her chin and knotted on the top of her head, would be just right.

She was not afraid. No consciousness remains after the death of the body. Extinction is a great comfort. Her molecules would disperse into their individual immortalities, but that would be nothing to do with her. There is no personal immortality, thank God.

She felt proud not to have forgotten anything, not even the steam to cover the mirror so that it could not watch her die, and the high, kind window would allow in the sun, but no other eye.

She put the note on the open anatomy book next to the engraving of the peeled head and laid her kidney donor card beside it.

*You're a living cliché, Nellys,* she said to herself as she straightened up. Then: *No, you're re-defining the form . . .*

She had many healthy organs.

She was giving her life so that others could live. Others who were loved, as she was not loved.

It wasn't for the sake of fidelity. She didn't believe in fidelity – except her own fidelity, and even that was probably just the expression of a temperamental preference. One cannot legislate fidelity. It is a gift.

Yet why should a *woman* not have someone to encourage, to praise, to comfort, to nurture, to make way for *her*?

Who will mother the mothers?

But hadn't her very own mother always said: 'If you think that's how life is, child, you've got it topsy-turvy. Take your head out of the clouds or you're going to have a very unhappy life. Just remember, it's the *man* who has to earn the living.'

Last night a strange new sound after eight unchanging weeks: rain rummaging at the walls, cars sizzling by in the streets. This morning was bright and dry again – a mellow, refreshed, puddled morning. Her house was clean, her ironing done and Professor Pushpull was somewhere far away. It was only gone noon. She had time to take a last walk around the university grounds, out of earshot of the little suburban train, before she died.

She observed the few students still about – mechanically perfect youth. She paused before the full-scale bronze of 'The Thinker' on its high plinth at the entrance to the Hall of Administration. The thinker – male, of course – did not seem to be thinking so much as wondering how the devil he'd got so muscle-bound. Marked over-development of the deltoids and trapezius muscles gave him the jiz of a razorbacked hog. He was streaked with the sweat and salts of verdigris that trickled over him like a miser's blood. In his posture of dejection he looked like a heavyweight champion of the world who has just lost his title.

Nellys noticed how he hunched over his vulnerable groin in such a way as to put it at the very centre of the heaviest fortifications, yet there remained one undefended aspect. Nellys, with her instinct for weaknesses, found it at once. Leaning against the plinth she looked up. Such a modest, retractile cock! But nothing else.

*Poor pig. A penny for your thoughts.*

Not even Professor Pushpull in his bath had ever looked quite so morose, so puzzled.

*Cheer up*, she whispered. *Next year maybe they'll give you the No-balls Prize.*

Smiling to herself, Nellys entered the marble rotunda at the heart of higher education, where a shallow granite circle had been let into the floor like a waterless ornamental pool. Its circumference was marked out with a railing supported on wooden balusters hardly taller than clothes pegs. A Foucault pendulum, attached to the top of the rotunda dome fifty feet above, passed its tarnished brass ball with stately beats of the cable across the great circle's diameter. Nellys watched the silent operation of the huge instrument in the deserted space and felt she'd gone deaf. The pendulum scythed its bob silently, silently, silently just short of the circular floor. Unlike the infamous scimitar pendulum, its motion was neither rapid nor hissing.

The sharpest edge is harmless until pressure pushes flesh, or silk, or anything against it. Time is a pressure. Nellys felt papery slices of her life nicked off with each passage. She sat down on one of the benches placed at intervals around the rotunda wall, glad to put a little distance between herself and Foucault's elegant, eerie proof of the earth's rotation. She leaned forward, fist to mouth, kissing her knuckles, feeling the floor turn beneath her feet.

A mahogany door opened in the rotunda wall. A man in shirt-sleeves with loosened tie and a grizzled crew-cut came out and stood raptly at the circle's edge. As the cable came within reach he bent forward and seized the brass sphere in both hands. He held it to his chest for a moment, possessing it as if it were a football.

Did the earth stop?

He bowled the bob away along a slightly altered course and returned to his office and shut the door with the gilt lettering on it that said VICE-CHANCELLOR.

The rotunda was deserted again. Nothing had broken its silence, except the solid coming to of the brass catch on the Vice-Chancellor's mahogany door. The pendulum continued its implacable wig-wag. The Vice-Chancellor's intimate moment with the fundamental forces of nature might never have happened.

Nellys stood beside the circle. When the cable was within her reach she gripped it, released it immediately, suppressing a shriek. It was alive! It was vibrating, thrilling internally, pulsing as with a huge electric current.

Nellys ran from the rotunda, clattering up echoes behind her. She did not look again at 'The Thinker' as she rushed past him. But surely he was hung like a horse. Surely she'd been mistaken about his lack?

It wasn't sense Nellys made for herself as she lay in the steaming bath – just a life-saving cable of words. One word after another twisting into something that would never fail her. She could hang from it over the abyss; the thread of words would never break. '*Suns set and are able to rise again, but once our brief day is done night is for ever and must be slept through. Suns set and are able to rise again . . . suns set and are able to rise again . . .*'

Not one word is weaker than another. Not one word annihilates another.

Fear the shears; do not fear the thread.

With or without faith of any kind, with or without knowledge, has she not hung on her word-thread over the abyss all her life?

Suns set and are able – *are able* – to rise again . . .

So someone says: You are rubbish.

400

Someone says this? And does your word-thread break because of *that*? Do you fall into the oblivion ha-ha because of that?

No.

Nor ever will.

Did your mother's words mean that you were one of nature's mistakes to be weeded out? *Hang by your thread of words.* Do your husband's words tell you that you are worth nothing? *Hang by your thread of words.*

Why be in such hurry to be gone? Always watching the clock, whose two hands are the scissor-blades of fatality. *Night is for ever.* That is where one should faint with terror! On the silent shores of Time. Not here, safe on the dangle.

Proof?

*Proof is the hundred and thirteen words already between you and that 'fatal' word. You have survived your husband's judgement.*

*Why the hurry? Put the razor back in its place. Drain the tub. Or better, since you and the water are already together and waste is a sin, make the most of the opportunity. Have a bath.*

# Deirdre Shanahan
## A WEDDING IN THE COUNTRY

THE VARIETY OF hats was impressive and most of the women at the front wore one. Great style, her mother would have said and Cassie had to agree, though she would never have believed so many people could manage to look so fashionable. Nobody had when she was young, when it was just a woolly hat that was pulled down over her head for Mass, and a big old coat wrapped round as she hurled herself out against the wind. Nowadays they did not even walk, everyone had cars. Somehow she had not expected the change and wondered if the gift of four thermal vests for her Aunt Ita was not misplaced, but never mind, her mother had advised, so that was what she would give.

Mass passed, the priest droned on through the sermon. 'Marriage is a special thing. Great things are expected of marriage. No one should enter it expecting an easy time. Marriage is a special . . .' How highly did he rate their intelligence, the way he rephrased everything? Despite the passing of the years priests seemed to be as she had remembered, vain, slothful, indulgent to the sound of their own voices. She wondered if her mother's inability to attend, because of a sudden attack of arthritis, was not a way of getting her into a church, but it didn't matter today because the young pip of a priest made her laugh with his pomposity and dominating manner so far undiminished despite the fact that this was a Nuptial Mass. Sheila was coming down the aisle now with her husband Morris who had red hair. Sheila's eyes were bright and wondrous as if she did not know this was happening. Cassie hoped things would work out for this pair, and was sure they would. Sheila was sensible and with Morris not being a Catholic, things were bound to be better. He might bring a bit of sense to the marriage. Only a few days before, Sheila had enthusiastically told her how Morris did not drink. Oh, he had a pint or two like the others but he did not spend evening after evening in the pub. He has a brain in his head, she had said with pleasure, and Cassie had thought, yes, you're lucky, he has. Cassie calculated how much longer they would have to wait until the food. It might be half an hour or maybe less. She could just about manage. She recognised no one in the congregation although many of these people must be related. Ah now, there was her uncle Eddy with his wife Breege and their two sons. And there was Imelda, Breege's sister. She must say hello, maybe even sit with them, but at least it would be better than having to make conversation with some of these fashionable ones from the town.

The congregation filed out for photographs. They all stood around and at the back of the couple, like a windbreak. There were little pools of ladies in pastel-toned suits. Hats bobbed. Everyone smiled and looked pleased. Cassie looked down the slope from the church perched on a slight hill. Mountains fell behind, opening out to fields where hay was gathered in. There were stooks and a lazy scatter of stone walls and she was reminded how all this, the land and the little houses, were still part of her, how before leaving she had been part of this juggled and scattered land.

'Cassie. Welcome.'

'Uncle Eddy.' She moved close to kiss him.

'She's here, come on up.' He motioned towards his sons.

'Hello.'

'Hello yourself. You're looking great. How many years is it?'

'Too many I fear.'

'Ten? Would it be that many?'

'Not quite. Six.'

'Well, no matter. You're here,' Breege added.

'You must have been having a good time over there so? You never thought of coming?'

'I couldn't.'

'The work? I know what it's like. I am the same way meself. It's hard to get away. Now, have you a lift up to the reception?'

'No.'

'How did you get here so? Have you a car with you?'

'I got a taxi.'

'If we'd known where you were we could have picked you up, couldn't we, Breege? And us having the three cars round the place.'

'Shall we be off now, Dad, to the hotel? It's getting late.'

'He's thinking of his beer,' the other brother said, coming up to join the gaggle. They all walked down to the big maroon Grenada, parked like a tank beyond the church gates on the other side of the road.

''Tis a shame your mother could not make it. But she sent you instead.'

'Yes.'

'And how is Maggie anyway?'

'Much better, thanks.'

'Has she the doctor in to see her?'

'He came twice. She's on the mend now, I think.'

'You can give her news. Will you be up to see Aunt Ita?'

'I've got to. I hope she remembers me.'

'She will, of course. Why wouldn't she?'

'I was small when I last saw her.'

'Were you now? It'll be a nice surprise then, cheer her up. If it wasn't that her legs were bad, she'd be here herself, I've no doubt.'

'It'll be nice to visit.'

'You should. I'm thinking she's sinking. Like the rest of us, I suppose, but quicker. Like a bird. She'll soon be with her Maker.'

'Shush,' Breege said. 'She has a few more years left in her.'

'Not many, I'd think. She's ninety-two gone.'

'Is she? I never knew that.'
'She is.'

On the journey, Cassie tried to reconstruct the old lady in black who had lived all her unmarried life in a cottage among the trees and the mountains. When she last saw her, Ita wore a small bun at the back of her head and walked with a stick, so she must be worse now.

'I said you might be up with the photographs. She'll like that.'

'She loves a good picture,' Breege said.

'Who doesn't? I like 'em too.'

'Nothing like keeping an idea of the big days and what they were like.'

'She does very well and all, with someone up from the village to help her, and she eats like a horse.'

'She always had a good appetite. I heard your mother say that, Cassie.'

They parked and made their way into the hotel foyer.

'Nothing much gets past her,' Eddy added. 'She has a great eye and an ear for everything. There isn't a cry from a mouse, but she wouldn't hear it. Very cross she was, that she had to miss this do.'

'Come on, Dad, let's get on here and sit down or we'll miss the meal.'

'You're right. We wouldn't want to be doing that, missing out on the most important part. Let's get a drink. What'll you have?'

They sat at a table spiked with newly pressed napkins folded like wings and fingers of glass. The crispness of white linen sparkled. After the sherry and during the meal Cassie drank wine which was plentiful. Eddy drank mostly beer and the other men were putting back a good few Guinnesses. Despite this, the reception was quite genteel, even elegant with the women on Morris's side in their suits and their hats with veils. Thick slices of beef were piled on her plate with a huge serving of mixed vegetables and potatoes. She ate as if she had not eaten for weeks, it was wonderful. A dessert followed and then cheese and she did not even have to wash up, never mind have Dave moaning about the cooking and how she had underdone the meat.

The Best Man made his speech about brides being a tax loss and he mentioned mothers-in-law even though the bridegroom would not have one as Sheila's mother had died of stomach cancer two years previously. No one laughed but there has to be one hitch at a wedding, Cassie thought.

'Oh no.' Cassie paused mid-sentence.

'What's wrong?'

'I left my gift out in the car and now they're all piled up.'

'Never mind. What is it? A pair of pillowcases?'

'Eddy,' Breege whispered.

'I must get it, or I'll forget completely and Mother would die. She'd be so cross.'

Cassie left the table and went to Eddy's car to collect the big parcel of saucepans wrapped in paper which had fat angels. Her mother had insisted on both, that the saucepans were what every woman wanted and the paper was bright and innocent. Cassie could not be sure if such qualities applied any more to weddings here but she went along with her. Angels were nothing to quarrel over.

Alex, the groom's brother, was just leaving his car, a battered Mini.

'Hello. How's it going?' he asked with a broad smile.

'Fine, thanks. It's a lovely wedding. But I forgot this.' She held out the parcel.

'I'll take it if you want. I've a few more back there to take to the house. They'll have them along with the rest after the honeymoon.'

He had russet hair and glasses and Cassie saw in an instant the similarity between himself and Morris.

'Thanks. I thought I'd end up wandering around with it for ages.'

'No problem. This can go in here.'

He had a thin though open face, quite bony as if it was one-dimensional, and she wondered if he was working and if so at what, or was he a student? It was hard to tell and she was not going to ask. She remembered his mother in the light blue suit and large hat like a saucer. Nothing too showy but composed and tall like Alex. Cassie wondered what it must be like to have two grown sons. Would they be as solicitous as these, showing their mother the way to her seat for the meal, leading her up the aisle of the church, praising her arrangement of flowers publicly? Grown men. That is what they were and it was almost frightening to think so because their mother could not be much older than her. The years had slipped until she was in her mid-forties. What was it like to have children? She would never know. And yet how reassuring it must be to have them gathered around, mindful of what she said, watchful the way adults never were.

He slammed the door.

'There you are, all safe now.'

'Thanks. I'd hate them to get it too late.'

She tried making small talk on the way back to the meal but the words would not come and she kept thinking of him as a son or a brother or a young man separate from her.

Dancing started and she hung around the bar with her uncle and his sons.

'How come, Cassie, you never made it down the aisle?' Eddy asked in a deliberately low tone, as if to indicate discretion, for which he was not particularly renowned.

'I don't know. No one ever asked me. It just never happened.'

'I find that very hard to believe. You must have met a lot of fellas.'

'It's true. I didn't.'

'Well, you could be lucky tonight. Let's hope so.'

'I don't think so, Uncle Eddy.'

Besides, she thought, I have Dave back at the flat, and isn't he the very spit of a husband, cantankerous, difficult when I least need him to be, crotchety about my friends when I want to go out? Why should I buy into that, it was sufficient that she had the use of his flat, the taste of his ready supply of money, the strong pull of trips to restaurants. He was probably cooking eggs and bacon now or making an omelette because he was good at cooking, and had a knack which they both recognised to be lacking in herself, along with a lot of other skills, as he frequently reminded her, and with which she had to agree. She was neglectful, rarely vacuumed the place and never dusted except when people came over. He went on about her untidiness, the pile of magazines she had left in the toilet, and thought she was sluggish in the bathroom in the mornings. So why did she stay with him? Because she was comfortable and he bought her things? Jewellery and perfume from foreign business trips, clothes that otherwise she would only dream of? Because of the years which bound them, wrapped each to the other like a loaf of sliced bread. What was it that kept her? There was not much they had in common. He did not understand why she had to come over, calling it a country with half-baked ideas.

'I know.' She nodded to him. 'It is.' But she could not explain what drew her after so long. Her mother's need that she attend the wedding for her, and the small request that she should visit her aunt Ita. Maybe the simple fact that she had not been back for years, even though she could not make him understand why she had to go.

He would be at home now, involved in paper work, checking accounts. Perhaps she should phone him or he might phone her later, she thought, so she would leave it. She slipped into the passing crowds. Girls danced with each other and mothers with girls. Morris's mother danced with one of her sons. A pregnant woman was dancing, her big belly a heap in front of her. Everyone, it seemed, had children, or was she imagining this? Even the hotel lobby as she walked through had spawned buggies since she had come in and now they were lining the walls. But then children were the future, company, everyone knew that, even she had years ago.

Years ago when she lived at home and there was Jerome not much older than her in the village with his talk of settling down, how his uncle would give him a field for a house and how it was good land that could raise fine cattle. His eyes brightened and his round face lit up as he told her.

He told her at dances, and when they walked in the fields, and he told her one afternoon when they lay in the barn, the day his parents had gone to Ennis. Pulling down his trousers, he lay on her and suckled at her breasts and she let him, loving the warmth and way his hands moved all over her, like a tractor. He told her about the flock of sheep up the mountain, how they had survived the winter and now had lambs. He was pleased and told her about the lamb who had been rejected by its mother. He had brought it into the house, nestling it by the fire in a small box. He had fed it with a baby's bottle his mother got from a neighbour, and the small thing revived hour by hour, until it was stronger.

'They're really tough underneath though you'd never believe it.'

He talked of fields and silage, mowing machines and the number of sons Marty Frank had, which could only be useful. He loved the work on the place and he would stay for ever to do it.

Men like him were hanging around the bar now. Men like him were half her relations, if she thought about it, and were probably at the wedding and she realised how he could be there, even now as she wondered which way to go, to the ladies or back to the table. He could be here now, waiting.

Could she have stayed, given herself up to the life he wanted? The memory of his mouth on her like a child or a lamb wanting its milk came back to her. But the continual pattern of life in the village bored her; at seventeen she could not wait to get out.

A man with a thick flock of curls peered down from his stocky height.

'Are ye over for the wedding?'

'Yes.'

'It's a great show, isn't it? You must be very close, to come all that way.'

'I suppose you could say so. Sheila is my cousin and my mother's god-daughter.'

'Ah, I've got you. What part of England are you from? Is it London?'

She nodded, looking across the dance floor to see Sheila moving like a cloud, and the groom's brother whom she had met in the car park dancing with a girl in blue.

He asked if she knew Hammersmith and her face strained. It was only there that she had met Dave all those Saturday nights ago, when she had nothing better to do than go to a pub. There were songs on the juke box, a kind of solace, as she drank and hung around and had another drink with the girls.

She had to get away so she escaped to the lift whose doors opened and she stepped in. Just in time. She went up leaving him behind and when she got to the fourth floor she went out, into the panelled-wood landing, so plush and silent she could have slept in it. She walked to the end and found a fire exit leading to emergency stairs. At the bottom she was at the back of the hotel, where laundry baskets filled the floor space and trolleys held layer upon layer of freshly laundered towels. The only place to walk was out.

She was in a side street leading to the main one. Out of the smoke and the music she was glad to be able to walk out, up past the shops and cafés to the little square at the top. She looked overdressed but she didn't care. She felt free, a shiver of delight at seeing the town again. It was bursting with craft shops, some selling paintings and pottery, little bakeries and neat little butchers. It hardly looked the same one she had cycled through to dances and the pictures, so long ago, so long, it was as if she saw the water with new eyes, the pretty bridges and the iron-work lamps by the side. Trees bordered it and there were seats with a shy elegance she had not noticed before.

She went into a café in the square and found it empty except for a cluster of girls around a table. They wore short skirts and tight tops. She remembered senses and feelings coming back like a stroke on hair.

'. . . you can do it for twenty quid, or even less, if you walk . . .'

'. . . could take a bike . . .'

'. . . Patrick ended up in Highbury . . .'

The coffee was bitter. They did not know how to make it but did that matter, for when she left, coffee had hardly passed her lips. Once tea would have sufficed, but working in offices had ruined her. She walked back along the river, following its length through the town. She looked across to the Railway Hotel on the far side, and for one moment thought she saw him, or the shape of his head, Jerome on the other side. On the edge of running after him, she stopped. How could it be? It was one of the hanging baskets.

Back at the hotel, she found Eddy and whispered that she was leaving because she had a bad back. She longed to get out of the place.

'When will we see you?'

'I'm not sure. I'll call up.'

'Tomorrow?'

'I hope so.'

'And you're off to Ita some time? It's a difficult road up to the house, watch how you take it.' She nodded.

'I'm hiring a car for the next few days.'

'The best thing. You need your own transport. So we'll be seeing you then? Give us a ring.'

'I will.'

'Don't be forgetting. We might be out. We've such a wild social life, haven't we, Breege?' He laughed.

'We'll say goodbye so.'

''Bye.'

They kissed and hugged and she left him with Breege and his sons to the drinks and the bar.

That night in bed on her own, she felt strange and lost but knew she could never have persuaded Dave to come. And would she have wanted him there anyway? They had argued for days about whether or not he could spare the time but now it did not matter. Being on her own at the wedding had felt entirely natural, as her days once had before she had met him. She fell asleep to the sounds of the couple next door – the bed head as it banged against the wall in rhythm and the girl cried out in a yelp of pain. She turned away and thought of Jerome, who had first made her feel that way and in such unlikely circumstances. They had been lucky his parents had so much to do in Ennis besides the doctor. They had to buy a pair of shoes, and there was visiting a cousin. Where was he now? She saw his face, weather worn with hair that curled and eyes that were so blue they believed in anything, farms, fields, the land, lambs, love.

Next morning when she left the hotel, a man was gathering leaves on the drive, pushing them into a wide shovel while flecks of left-over confetti fluttered up. Setting off early to give herself plenty of time to negotiate the small mountain roads, she drove following directions her mother had given. She took a small road off the main one heading out of town, finding herself tracking a path. The mountains were blue and dusky, like some old paintings, fields running up to them, the delicate traces of farms that had been abandoned, and she wondered how it was that she had not noticed before, and why it should be that this landscape was such a surprise. The road became almost a muddy track and she realised she had not seen a car for miles. The road was the only one: even if she felt from time to time that she must be getting lost because there were no houses in sight, there was nowhere else to go. It was that or go into a field. Eventually she passed four squat houses, the first two run-down and abandoned, the second for sale, and the last one, she guessed, was Aunt Ita's.

She knocked and knocked again and went in without waiting just as her mother had done years before, knowing she was expected.

'Hello, Aunt Ita.'

'You're welcome.'

She kissed her.

'How are you?'

'I'm fine.'

'You were up at the wedding?' Ita said, propped up in bed in the corner by the window. She wore a white nightdress and a pink cardigan on top.

'I was. You look well, Ita.'

'Better than I was. How's your mother? She didn't come with you?'

'Not this time.'

'She said her arthritis was bad.'

'It has been for a while.'

'It's a good few years since I seen you. What was wrong? Is it afraid of us, you were?'

'I meant to come but I suppose I got carried away. Time goes so fast.'

'It does in England, to be sure.'

'You forget things so easily there, even things you've been used to, because there isn't time to think. You get to be too busy to remember.'

'I know the way it is. You can forget if things are not right in front of you. It's the same with the people down the valley from here. You'd think I was in a foreign country, from here.'

Yes, Cassie thought, anyone would, living so far up in the mountains, in a strange place that even Eddy thought was remote.

'Mother wanted me to give you these.'

'All the way from England?'

'She said you liked them the last time.'

'They're grand out. She's a good woman. Will you have a

413

drop of tea so? You can make it yourself with the things there. And tell me now, was it a big wedding?'

'I've never seen so many people packed in one room.'

'They put down a good day here. And was there dancing?'

'Yes. With a live band.'

'That's the thing, same as it was when we were young. You can't beat a bit of the old dancing.'

Cassie was tempted. There was so little time, either for her visit or for Ita.

'Did you ever think of marrying, Aunt Ita?'

'I had a mind to it once but it was not to be and that's long gone. He was a nice lad.' Her voice drifted.

Cassie waited, holding the lid of the teapot and the spoon with which she was going to stir the tea, adrift.

'He was a lovely lad in a white shirt when I first met him, serving customers in his father's shop, with a smile for everyone.'

Cassie held back, too tense to utter a word and wanting to hear more, and then for something to do, brought a cup of tea to Ita's lips and heard her slurp noisily. She gave her a piece of cake that the woman from the village must have left out.

'Who was he?'

'Seamus. Seamus Fadden.'

'Did he go away to England or America?'

'He went away all right, but it was further than that. The Black and Tans shot him and hung him from a tree. Someone had set fire to the Police House and they suspected him but he never had anything to do with that old stuff. He was just a young lad who worked in his father's shop. All his spare time he spent with me.'

'I'm sorry, Aunt Ita.' Cassie spoke into the silence and then because she could not bear it and had to know asked, 'Wasn't there anyone else?'

Ita shook her head.

'Do you regret it?'

'I don't. He was the one for me. That's all that matters. Why do you ask?' An edge coming into her voice.

'I thought it would matter, marriage I mean.'

'Marriage? That's a different thing. I'm sorry to have missed that but I haven't missed love. I didn't let that slip by. I had him then and I still have. That's all I care about.'

'Did you not ever think of leaving, wanting to get away, after that?'

'After what they did to him? No. Why should I? Wasn't it better I stayed? What would I want to be doing over? The jobs for the likes of me would be sweeping floors or working in factories. That wasn't the kind of thing I wanted. I had too much for me here.'

Cassie sat on the edge of the bed but felt miles away. Was this what love did, carry you forward to another place where a person could live? She wanted to hold her aunt and cry into her arms, tell her she had not meant to rake up the past, unsettle it, but it was too late, the past had tumbled down like a load of old clothes from the top of a wardrobe.

'It's all the same now. I had him once. We went dancing at the crossroads, home in a donkey and trap, walks across the fields. That was the top of it, all I wanted.'

Cassie wondered if she ever went to his grave and whether it was nearby in Castletown cemetery. Did she go on his birthday or the anniversary of when he had asked her out, or just any time?

'You had a nice fella once,' Ita declared.

'Did I?'

'I heard tell from your mother. Before you went away.'

'Oh him. Yes.'

'Would you believe he has a big farm with five children and two cars and one of them an estate, big as the house. I heard he's a representative for the machinery, isn't that a great thing to have on the side?'

Cassie agreed, yes.

What would it have been like? But what had the place to offer when she was nineteen, certain herself that if she had found one boy who had fallen for her, she would find another. Now it seemed that if someone did, you were lucky and mostly they did not.

She drank more tea and ate cake and listened to Ita telling her about her schooldays and what her mother was like and how they had argued over dresses and hats because there were never enough to go around. Soon it was five and Cassie made moves to go.

'I hope I haven't tired you.'

'Of course not. It's great to have a chat. And you'll be giving your mother all the news?'

'I will.'

'She'll look forward to that. And now I've me dinner to have. The woman across will come in and do that and she'll wash up.'

'It was great seeing you.'

'Goodbye. Don't be leaving it so long next time.'

'I'll try not to.' She bent to kiss her aunt and thought how remarkably young her skin looked with a faint blush at her cheeks.

'Watch how you go down that road.'

Cassie drove back to the hotel but that evening could face no food. She stood at the front desk and thought of phoning Dave but could not urge herself. Too much had gone on. She could not stop thinking about a young man swinging from a tree, his long legs going down. It seemed a horribly brutal way to end life and yet he had been loved with a searing love that could have reached his heart if it were the bullet, and there was a kind of peace in Ita as if she had made a pact with the place she lived in and accepted it, a long time ago.

Cassie had been so keen to rush away from it all after Jerome, glad to be away in England, thinking that the farms and cottages, barns and henhouses were intrusions upon her sky, but now she could see how they fitted in, nestled, how they were meant to be. She wondered if he still went up the mountains with sheep, whether if he had sons they went with him, and suspected so, as he would be a good and watchful father, wanting them with him.

*

416

She sat in the bar drinking tea and reading a paper. Her nerves jangled. The tea was a milky brown, milkier than Ita's, which was the colour of creosote. She sipped and read, turning a page, and alighted on an article about the effect of a huge storm the week before. The paper said heavy falls of rain had revealed valuable mineral deposits on the mountains. Cassie paused. Could something like that happen here, where nothing ever did? She did not know, could not think or be aware of anything except the barman who hovered near her with his tea-cloth draped over his shoulder.

'I'd say there'll be a few millionaires round here in a fortnight,' he said.

'Will there?'

'The farmers'll make a mint. They'll be off to Paris and beyond every week. Take a look at what it says. A farmer with a claim to land in the mountains could expect thousands. These companies will be bustin' to get their hands on the stuff. You mark my words. It's not gold, but the next best thing. Mineral wealth, because it takes generations to make up.'

Generations. She knew all about them, how she was the last of one and how no one would be coming after her. There was no one behind her now.

The barman served someone. She wondered if Jerome had land up on that mountain and was sure he would have. He had always loved it. How would he react to his new-found wealth? Plenty of ways, she decided if he had that many kids.

Out of the window of the lounge bar, the land dipped and swayed. He was out there with his land, scrubby, rough but now resplendent, possibly going after the sheep, and she felt drawn, like a woman who might have walked into a river, letting the waters touch over her. She thought of Dave. Would it last? Did she want it to? Did she not want to break free? The dangerous scent of the idea swam in her head. There is nothing for me, she thought, except money and his bed. Shall I gather my clothes, even the ones he bought, and leave for another place?

# Lana Citron

## LAPDOG DAYS

THE REVOLUTIONARY STUDENT stood between the arch and the main gates of Trinity College, Dublin, selling his pamphlet entitled *Shadows on the Surface Cast Doubts in My Mind*. There he stood in his black duffle-coat and PLO scarf. I had been watching him for almost six months. I had a stack of his poetry at home, some of which I had learned off by heart.

I was sixteen. I was innocent.

He was beautiful, and I mean very beautiful, with black curly hair, wild blue eyes. There didn't seem to be anyone special, but there was always someone. He went from girl to girl. I liked the idea of an experienced man, knew that once he met me and like really talked to me, that would be it. What the it was I didn't know, it didn't matter. I was never the modest one. I would stare at him for ages. I used to stand at the gates, pretending I was meeting someone else.

I was so pure of intention. I had to get him.

One day he came up to me.

He came up to me.

And he asked me did I smoke.

Did I smoke?

That he had asked everyone else who was waiting alongside of me was of no importance.

'Hey, I've seen you before.'

'Yeah, I've bought eh some of your poetry, I think it's . . .' said I trying to be casual.

'Great, you don't happen to have a spare cigarette?'

'No, I don't smoke.'

'Too bad . . .' and off he went.

Damn, I should have said something else, something witty. Why didn't I smoke? I ran across the road to the tobacconist's and bought a pack of twenty Marlboro's. I was flushed and there was a line of sweat on my brow.

I ran back to him and said,

'Here look, I've bought you some cigarettes . . .' take me take me take me . . .

'Nice one,' he said . . . nice one, I remember his words so clearly.

He opened the box and took one out. Then he offered me one.

He offered me one of his cigarettes.

Heaven . . . I'm in heaven and I took one and that was how I started smoking.

'You must be really talented,' I said, CRINGE, 'I mean writing all your poetry and stuff.'

'Do you like poetry?' he asked.

'I love it,' I lied.

'Which writers do you like?'

'Mmmmm . . .' What do I say? I told him my favourite poem was about those wraggley taggley gypsies O.

'Right,' he said. 'Who wrote that then?'

'Mmm, it's just this poem I used to like when I was a kid. It's about this lady who is married to a lord but she runs off with these gypsies and . . .'

'Yeah, right.'

I've blown it, I know I've blown it. He probably thinks I'm really thick. Why do I say such stupid things?

He threw the butt to the ground.

'Cheers,' he said, putting the box of fags in his black baggy trousers. 'See you round.'

'Yeah,' I said . . . when when when . . .

. . . whenever.

That night I went back into town to meet Niamh. Niamh had changed schools the year before. She used to ring me up whenever she had no one to go out with. She was light years more mature than me. She had gone all the way and used to hang out with students. We met outside McDonald's on Grafton Street.

'God, this is so uncool,' she said, 'the last time I met anyone here was when I was about fifteen.'

I told her I was in love.

'With who? . . . with who?'

'With the most sensitive, most beautiful, most intelligent . . .' I told her about my revolutionary student.

'You're not serious.'

'Deadly,' I said.

She knew who I was talking about.

She said he was rampant and that even she had had him.

So I'm in with a chance.

'What was it like . . . it like?'

She said, 'OK, but he's a bit of a dish-washer.'

He had dribbled all down her face.

God, I would have stood beneath to catch a falling kiss.

'I know where he hangs out.'

She knows where he hangs out.

I was high-pitched and sixteen, screeching . . . 'No, really, REALLY, oh my God.'

'He's probably down in Keogh's.'

Keogh's is a pub on the corner of South Anne's Street.

We went to see if we could get in.

'You should have worn more make-up.' She made me put on some scarlet lipstick and backcombed my fringe.

Tommy the bar man was guarding the door.

'Sorry, girls, youse can't go in. She looks too young,' he said, pointing to me.

'But we're meeting a friend in there.'

He wasn't having any of it.

Niamh rolled her eyes. 'I don't believe this. Look, I was in here last week, sure you served me yourself.'

'I never laid eyes on the pair of youse before.'

'I swear to you . . . I . . . we have a date . . . look, will ya let me in to see if he's there, God the whole evening will be ruined. Sure the place is packed, what would it matter if one more slipped through?'

Tommy relented, and in Niamh went.

I was to wait outside. Wait. Wait.

I tried talking to Tommy but he wasn't having it. He kept saying sorry love you look too young.

And then I saw Him. Oh my GOD.

He was with a student girl, swaggering down the road.

Cringe overdose and I began to shrivel. Bad enough not being let into the pub you had gone to just so you would bump into this guy, worse when he shows up. I've never felt so humiliated. I was chewing my inner lip, fucking hell Niamh where the hell are you!

'Hi,' I said, stepping out of the doorway to let him pass.

'Huh.' His arm hung heavily on the girl's shoulder.

'Yeah I met you today. I bought you some fags.'

'Oh yeah, the cigarette girl.'

'I'm just waiting for my friend,' I apologised, but he wasn't listening and he walked in.

I felt awful, why did I have to say I was waiting for my friend? Why did I have to make it obvious that I was alone and couldn't get into a pub? Why didn't he stop?

His girlfriend, yeah there's no way he would reveal his feelings for me in front of her. He was just being cool.

Cigarette girl. I was his cigarette girl.

'Please let me in, I promise not to drink.'

'You're not much good in a pub if you don't drink,' Tommy said.

I shrugged my shoulders. Jesus, Niamh had been in there for ages and I guessed she wasn't coming out. I had been stood outside for over an hour.

I was so depressed. 'I'm off,' I said to Tommy and he didn't even reply.

I called Niamh the next day.

'Hi, what happened to you last night?' says she to me.

What happened to *me*?

421

'Guess what, remember that guy Sean I told you about? He started talking to me and he bought me a drink and then I saw that guy you fancy and I asked him if he had seen anyone waiting outside and he said no.'

What, what, I'm devastated, Jesus he called me his cigarette girl.

'I was waiting outside. You said you'd come back.'

'God I'm really sorry, when he said he hadn't seen anyone, I assumed you had gone home.'

'Yeah, OK, it doesn't matter,' I said. Niamh can be such a bitch.

'Anyway Sean and I got off with each other.' She told me about the whole thing, she'd gone back to his flat, stayed the night with him.

She had told her mum she was with me, so I was to remember that, OK?

'So are you going to go out with him?'

'I don't know,' she said . . .

'So he didn't ask you then?'

'No, but he's having a party next Friday . . .' She was definitely going and the guy I fancy would probably be there and did I want to come.

Friday, Friday Friday, that's five days, fifteen hours and thirty-four seconds away. What am I going to wear?

I went round to Niamh's early on Friday evening. I poured half a bottle of Martini into an empty glass jar. The plan was to get pissed at hers and then go over to the party after pub closing time.

She spent ages getting ready. Sean hadn't rung her in the week to invite her properly. He must have lost her number. There was no other explanation. We would have to gatecrash. I didn't care, I just wanted to see Him. I just wanted to be there. We drank the Martini and she read me bits out of her diary.

Sean lived in Rathmines, shared a place with five other students. There was a small crowd waiting outside when we arrived, apparently it was open house. One of the guys said, don't bother it's crap. It's full of Freshers.

Wow cool, Freshers.

We went in, the place was buzzing, we walked round and found Sean in the kitchen.

There was a girl sitting on his lap.

'Hi, Sean,' says Niamh.

'Hi . . .?'

'Niamh,' says Niamh, grabbing me by the arm and racing out of the room.

'Wanker, Jesus Christ, I'm not staying here a minute longer . . .'

'But Niamh, what if . . .'

'I don't care, I can't believe he just did that.' We locked ourselves in the toilet and Niamh started crying.

'Open the fucking door . . .' but we wouldn't and eventually Sean came and he says,

'Look, Niamh, open the door right now or I'll have to kick you out.'

So she opens the door and starts shouting and freaking out at him, 'I'm not a bleedin' slut,' she says.

They go off into the corner and I'm left standing like a lemon.

Where are You? and I wander through the rooms on a mission. But I can't see him anywhere. I go looking for Niamh, but she's tongue-tied to Sean. I sit on the bottom stair.

'Cheer up,' says Acne Face and he offers me a beer and I take it 'cos it's better to be talking to someone and anyway I have a good view of the door. He tells me he is studying engineering at UCD, he's in first year and although it's really hard work everything is cool man. He says he has just broken up with his girlfriend and it's cool man. I feel his hand slide around my waist. He asks me if anyone has ever told me what beautiful eyes I have.

'They're beautiful, man,' and he leans into me.

I'm thinking, cool off man, but before I get to sample his

pussy pinnacles, I'm saved. We are split by this guy lurching forward, knocking Acne Face's arm, spilling his drink.

'For fucks sake man, I'm drenched,' and as they pretend to be men I say 'I'm just going to get a cloth.' And I flee to the kitchen.

The door into the garden is open and I take a stroll outside. I've almost had enough. A guy is having a piss against the wall, I pretend I don't notice him, but I do, how could I not notice my man?

'Hey . . .' I say. I'm not going to let him go, this is it girl, this is it.

'What the fuck . . .' I guess I must have surprised him.

'What you up to?' I say.

'I'm having a piss.'

'Right, oh yeah,' and I break into hysteric nervous laughter. He's fumbling with his flies, steady now I don't want to blow it.

'What do you think of the party . . .' Here we go here we go here we go, OK he's a bit pissed . . . He stumbles . . . sits down, mumbles something I don't quite catch.

Yeah, let's sit and nothing could be more romantic, outside, under the stars and the moon and he truly is beautiful although his eyes are bloodshot and I ask him to recite some poetry for me . . .

'What . . .'

'Oh go on,' I say, nudging towards him, and I ask him to recite the one entitled *Spent Youth*, and he tells me he doesn't like to bring his work home with him. He laughs so I laugh too. His head is hung between his legs and he starts talking about grit. He is so clever, his words are like music and I tell him about all my problems, all the shit I have to deal with at home, important stuff.

'Nightmare.'

I've been saving up loads and loads of stuff to tell him and now it's just pouring out of me. I knew he'd understand.

'I'm just going to get a drink,' he says.

'Sure.' I haven't felt this good for ages. I know something

is going to happen. He rises and I look up at him and into him.

I had spent a whole ten minutes with Him.

The music stopped and I went back inside. There was hardly anyone left, a few couples and unconscious bodies.

'Yo, where did you get to?' I spin round and Acne Face is waiting for me. I tell him I'm just about to go, at the same time my eyes are cruising wildly. Damn, damn it, I can see him and he's in the kitchen and this really gross girl is harassing him, like practically assaulting him and he throws me a glance as if to say you've got a right one there. No. No I can't believe it. We had both been cornered.

'Look, I've really got to go,' and I try to push past Acne Face but he won't let me go and he is slurring his words and starts saying how he hates girls like me and we are all just prick teasers and I must be frigid.

'Yeah thanks, but I really have to go,' and out of the corner of my eye I see her and Him and she is pulling Him by the arm out into the garden.

I went home and wrote a poem.

### Now and Forever

If not Today
Tomorrow.
If not Tomorrow
No matter
Time will tell
You
What I know
Already

I day-dreamed the week away. I kissed His lips a thousand times. I fell into his arms and he wrapped himself around me. I LOVE YOU, I LOVE YOU, I LOVE YOU, written all over my folder with hearts and flowers, balloons and kisses.

Saturday came and I was ready.

He was locking his bike to the railings and the Fates were on my side.

It started to rain. It started to pour and I summoned up my courage and I said,

'Hiya, fancy a coffee?'

'I'm skint.'

'I'll pay.'

'OK.'

'OK,' and I was trembling all over and we crossed the road and went to Bewley's and I asked him how he was and he said he wanted a cream bun too, and I knew I could only afford two coffees so I forfeited my bus fare home.

We sat and again I asked him how he was.

Then there was an embarrassing silence.

I giggled and said, 'You don't even know my name.'

'Names don't matter,' he said, 'names are labels that make us conform. I despise conformity.'

'I do too.'

'That was a really crap bun.'

'What do you study?'

'English and Classics.'

'Really? That's exactly what I want to do.'

He asked me what I knew about English and Classics.

'Nothing much,' I said.

'Then how do you know you want to study it?'

'Oh yeah,' and I laughed stupidly.

'Yo, man,' and a guy bounded over to our table.

They were friends. They started to chat and then he said, 'Catch you later,' and he went off with his mate and I walked home and got drenched in the rain.

I wasn't going to play hard to get. I'd turn up every Saturday and ask if he wanted a coffee or something. He was always broke so I'd buy him little presents, drinks or whatever. What we had was really intense, really special. I saw him every weekend, even if it was for just a few minutes, it didn't matter, I knew he told me things he had never told anyone before. Sometimes we would go for coffee or to the Buttery. He would ask me to do little favours for him. I didn't mind, I did it willingly and I even began to sell his poetry for him. He'd usually end up meeting some friends and then I'd go off. He was really popular. He hung around with Frederick, who studied Law. Frederick was funny. I always dreaded when it came to the punch line as to whether I would get it or not.

One time I was sitting opposite both of them and they started whispering to each other. They were always playing games. I remember I was smiling at them. Frederick folded his arms and sat back.

'I want to ask you a serious question,' and he lent forward and touched my hand. And my heart skipped a beat.

'How come you are always waiting at the gates of Trinity and no one ever arrives?'

And my heart stopped.

If you really put your mind to it, something's bound to happen. I was obvious, I was blatant and I was right, we were meant to be together.

It was only a matter of time and then he would fall in love.

I was with my parents, we had just been to see a play at the Abbey. I was all dressed up in my smart wear and we crossed the road and went to the Plough and the Stars for a drink.

He saw me first.

'Hey, cigarette girl,' he says in front of my mother and I blush and say, 'Er, hi.' He was in a good mood, really chatty and he tells me that I'm looking really swish. Then he said,

'Look, this is really embarrassing, you wouldn't . . .'

And I am waiting for him to say . . . like to go out with me . . .

'Would you have any money for a drink?'

I ask my dad if he'll get my friend a drink and my heart sinks to the pit of my stomach. Dad looks at him disapprovingly and I ask him what's he up to and he tells me he is in love with the actress in the play and he takes the proffered pint from my father's hand and she walks through the door and he leaves me.

I say to my parents,

'Why do you always have to go and ruin things for me, why why why?' and I wrote another poem.

### Hurt

My flower of hope is dying
My eyes are wet from crying
And my heart beats
still.

I didn't see him so much and then he went away for the summer, I lost lots of weight and waited.

Niamh had got a couple of tickets for the Freshers' Ball.

'I don't believe it, the Freshers' Ball,' I gasped incredulously.

'Yeah, and don't go fucking up, we've got to look cooler than cool, got it?'

Niamh's really nice to me. She lent me some of her own stuff and put loads of make-up on me.

We had such a laugh that night. We both got plastered and Niamh kept going up to blokes and pinching their bums. It was about two in the morning and we were freaking out on the dance floor. A snake of dancing people had formed and we joined on the end and weaved about the room.

'Hey, hey, over here,' I shouted, waving my arms wildly. He was leaning against a pillar. I think he was smoking a joint! I decided to play cool. He looked amazing, his hair had got really long.

'Huh, what are you doing here?'

'Niamh got tickets, how are you?'

'Fuckin' A1,' then someone pushed me on and I disappeared back into the writhing snake.

*

Just one look and I was back on course. I was far more calculating than before and wherever he went I just happened to turn up. He began to call me his limpet. I didn't mind, I knew it was a term of endearment.

Then one day, and he had been acting really distant with me.

He told me he was going to stop selling his poetry for a while.

He brought me for a coffee and said, 'I don't know how to say this.'

He said he didn't want to see me for a while. He said he had loads of work to do.

'I understand,' I said.

He needed some space. These things happen when you are in a relationship.

So I began to ring him instead.

He asked me where I got his number from. I told him I had looked it up.

'Jesus,' he said, 'there are thousands of Murphys.'

'I know,' I said.

His voice was so lovely. He told me he was working really hard and asked how school was going.

I began to ring him more often. His mum told me he was working in the library.

'Just tell him I rang.' And I'd leave my number.

I went to the arch a good few times, on the off chance of bumping into him and to Bewley's and Keogh's and around Temple Bar and other places that I thought he might be. I knew he wouldn't lie. I knew he was working really hard. I really respect that in a man.

'You should just say fuck off.'

'I have.'

'How long has it been?'

'Eternity.'

'You've got to be cruel to be kind.'
'You could do her for mental assault.'
'A real sad case if you ask me.'
'The only place she doesn't look for me is here.'
I was walking through the bar of Keogh's, for the third
time that day, and I heard his voice. It was coming from the
snug.
The snug. I hadn't even thought of looking in there. I can't
believe I was so stupid.
I opened the door.
'Hiya.'
There were three of them, Him, a girl and Frederick.
'Speak of the devil.'
The girl started laughing.
I started crying.
With all my heart I cried.
I cried my heart away.
And then I felt empty, really empty.

# Nalinaksha Bhattacharya

## RAVI SHASTRI

THEY WERE SHOWING a good film on the TV but Kanta couldn't enjoy it because Anil had just lit another kingsize Classic. The burns and blisters – there were now seventeen of them on her face and neck – gave her excruciating pain and the stomach cramps had become so unbearable that she wanted to gobble grass and earth. Two half-burnt chapatis and a little dal were all she got for lunch. 'Enough for a dowry-shirker's daughter,' her mother-in-law had bawled when she asked for a couple more.

Rishi Kapur, the plump, well-fed hero, was chasing the buxom heroine Neetu Singh around the bushes singing a full-throated Kishore Kumar song.

'The rogue,' said mother-in-law, adjusting Kanta's five-year-old daughter Pinky on her lap. She was licking an Amul fruit and nut chocolate bar brought by Neena, Anil's sister.

'Beats his father and uncles in acrobatics, no?' said Neena and pinched Pinky's cheek. Pinky grinned and held up her bar to show how much of it was still left. The colour TV, the plush sofa-set, the divan, even the marble-top centre table with the cutglass ashtray were dowry items but everyone behaved as if Kanta was an intruder in this house.

'Get ready, Ravi Shastri.' Anil was sitting on the divan, diagonally across from Kanta, separated by a distance of ten feet or less.

'Bhaia,' Neena pleaded. 'Let her enjoy the film.'

'Don't worry. Ravi Shastri is a good batsman.'

'Why don't you two go to your room and practise?'

suggested mother-in-law as if Kanta was really Ravi Shastri and her son Kapil Dev and both were going to play West Indies next week in Barbados.

'A spinner,' informed Anil and bowled the glowing stub with a cursory movement of his arm. Kanta tried her best to defend herself with her palm but missed it and received her eighteenth burn an inch below her right eye.

'Bowled! Ravi Shastri clean bowled!' cried Pinky and waved her bar. Neena frowned but her mother giggled and this sound mingled with Neetu Singh's squeals as Rishi Kapur finally ambushed her by the gurgling stream at the end of the song.

Sweat coursed down Kanta's face as she entered the small, stuffy kitchen to prepare tea during the fifteen minutes' break in the film show. The salt in the sweat stung like needlepricks wherever the skin was raw; the blisters itched and burned and Kanta had to fight constantly to keep her hands off them, for a minor scratch could give her a sleepless night. She put the kettle on the gas ring and moved to the window for a breath of fresh air. Outside, in the shimmering heat of May everything looked dead, parched and crying for the rains. There wasn't a single blade of green grass in the rectangular park down below where Pinky played with her friends in the afternoon. Earlier, Kanta used to accompany her and enjoyed gossiping with the neighbourhood women. But from last week, after she had returned from her parents empty-handed, her movements were restricted, so it was mother-in-law who now took Pinky to the park.

As she spooned sugar into the kettle, she was tempted to put a fistful into her mouth but she checked herself, fearing that she would be caught by her own daughter. Pinky had always slept with her granny and had been tutored to treat her mother as a domestic. Now she was being used as a spy and rewarded with toys and chocolates for her services.

A sudden vicious cramp in her stomach made Kanta bold enough to reach for the tin of cookies on the shelf. She prised open the lid with a spoon and took out a handful. The door behind her creaked. Kanta sighed and turned slowly.

'Want a cookie, Pinky?'

Pinky shook her head. 'Put them back,' she said coldly with a quiet authority, her small buttony eyes fixed on Kanta's palm. I should have aborted this vicious creature before she wiggled into life, thought Kanta. The cookies crumbled in her hand as she clenched her fist before dropping them into the tin. She slapped the lid shut and showed Pinky her empty hand.

'Now you can go back to your granny.'

'No, I'll stay here,' declared Pinky and watched Kanta with contempt. Kanta created unnecessary noise by clattering the cups and saucers on the tray. She poured some milk in the kettle from a saucepan, threw in two spoonfuls of tea granules and stirred the brew with a big spoon. The door creaked again. It was Neena. Kanta couldn't help noticing that her sister-in-law had accumulated considerable fat since she saw her last six months back. She could now pass as a true copy of her mother, except for the latter's grey hair and the mole on her right cheek.

'What are you doing here, sweetie?' Neena ruffled Pinky's hair. 'Go and see your favourite Nirma and Colgate jingles.' Kanta didn't miss the little wink Neena gave to assure Pinky that auntie would now keep a watch on mum.

'Want to have a cookie, Neena?' asked Kanta the moment her daughter vanished behind the screen door.

'Oh, no. I am full.'

'Please have one. For my sake.'

'If you insist . . .'

Kanta opened the tin and brought out a fistful. Neena accepted just one and nibbled it without relish. Kanta gobbled four, two at a time, choked, coughed and gulped a glass of tepid water from the tap to clear her throat.

'Watch out!' cried Neena. Kanta looked at the door but it was the kettle spilling tea. She turned off the gas and removed the kettle.

'I don't like this Ravi Shastri business at all, Kanta, I tell you,' said Neena, plucking the strainer from a hook on the wall. Kanta suspected that Neena had been summoned by her mother to persuade Kanta to go back to her parents and fetch the thirty thousand rupees Anil had been demanding for his new business. Anil had decided to manufacture spurious soft drinks with all the famous labels – Campa Cola, Limca, Double Seven and the rest – but he couldn't get started without a couple of carbonators and some other equipment for his business.

'Your brother is crazy about cricket, you know that,' Kanta said. 'He is a great fan of Ravi Shastri too.'

Neena frowned. 'Don't try to fool me. It's no fun getting burnt like that.' She poured the tea and then removed two cups from the tray. 'I want to have a talk with you here in the kitchen. Since you are so hungry, you may start sipping and have some cookies too.'

She picked up the tray and walked out of the kitchen.

'Go back and get burnt. Or hang yourself.' That was Kanta's father's final answer to his daughter's tearful pleadings for money. Her father had already contributed about seventy-five thousand rupees to his son-in-law's business ventures, none of which proved successful. Anil blamed his fate but Kanta's father believed his son-in-law's weekend gambling bouts with his cronies and his taste for costly clothes and liquor had much to do with his failures. Anil had inherited a small printing press with a hand-driven treadle machine that ensured a modest but steady income. But he wanted to make a fast buck and hated to toil for his bread in a grimy little shop, collecting orders for bill books and greetings cards and pleading with paper merchants of Chowri Bazar for delayed payments. He sold the press and went into real estate, got cheated by his partner and became an exporter of cotton garments, was elbowed out from the market by his competitors and started an unlicensed video parlour showing tits-and-bums films smuggled in from Singapore and Hong Kong. He had started earning good money in his last business when the police, tipped off by a business rival, busted the parlour and seized his films and equipment. Before he started a new business, Anil would force Kanta to go to her parents for money and she had, until now, managed to extort handsome amounts from her father.

The day she returned empty-handed from her parents, she was beaten up by her mother-in-law and starved for the whole day. Anil came in the evening, heard about Kanta's failed mission and kicked and slapped her until she bled from her nose and mouth and passed out. A couple of days later Kanta saw her mother-in-law lugging in a five-litre can of kerosene though they needed no extra fuel as they had double gas cylinders. She did not need any sixth sense to tell her that her days were numbered, that she would soon join the long list – the figure varies from 600 to 700 every year in Delhi alone – of dowry-deaths. The local police could always be bought with a few hundred rupees and a bottle of whisky. Anil would be free to marry again and claim a handsome dowry from his new in-laws.

Three nights back, as she was spreading her bed roll on the floor (for Anil wouldn't share his bed any longer with a dowry-shirker's daughter) Anil blew a gust of smoke at her and clapped. 'Sit up, Ravi Shastri. We shall play cricket.' Kanta was puzzled; she thought he had taken more than the usual quota of whisky before his meal and was just being playful. She had seen him glued to the TV in the cricket season and occasionally playing cricket with Pinky on the balcony. But as she made for the door, Anil called her back.

'Where are you off to?'

Kanta mumbled something about getting the plastic cricket set from Pinky.

'No need of that. Your face will be good enough for my wicket. Use your palm as a bat and this little stub will be our ball. Now move over there, quick.'

It was an order and Kanta obeyed. Like most of the girls of her class, she had been brought up by her parents strictly in the traditional mould of Sita and Savitri to be humble, docile, uncomplaining and subservient to male dominance.

'Medium pace,' informed Anil as he bowled the stub. She

gave a start and a shriek as it stung her in the neck like a wasp, scorching a little of her delicate skin.

'Bad performance, Ravi Shastri.' Anil shook his head. 'But never mind, you'll improve with practice.'

He was right. After one week and eighteen burns she was now able to deflect one out of five stubs shot at her.

Kanta had reached out for the tin a second time when Neena came back.

'Want to have another cookie, Neena?'

'No. You can have a few more if you are still hungry.'

'Thank you.' Kanta took a couple, dipped them in her tea and licked them. 'You aren't going to tell mother-in-law, are you?'

Neena gave her a reassuring pat. 'I have come to help you, Kanta. Trust me. Didn't I too suffer like you?'

Kanta nodded. A year after her marriage, a pregnant Neena had returned from her in-laws with multiple bruises and a demand for a Maruti car. After a lot of haggling with the boy's parents Anil had settled the deal with a Bazar scooter and five thousand cash. Neena later improved her status in her in-laws' family by giving birth to a male child.

'Did you see Shalini's case on the TV?' asked Neena.

Kanta shook her head. In the evenings she slaved in the kitchen to allow others to enjoy prime time serials and other interesting programmes. The Sunday film was her only entertainment during the whole week.

'They gave her so much publicity only because she comes from a rich family and her husband is a millionaire.'

It was no consolation for Kanta to learn that even Shalini, the rich college-educated girl, had been beaten up, starved and burnt with cigarette butts.

'The girl died in style, one has to admit,' said Neena, slurping her tea noisily like her mother. 'Just imagine! Parveen doused her with whisky before he struck the match. For you and me it's always the foul-smelling kerosene.'

Was it mere coincidence, Kanta wondered, that Neena's

eyes dropped for a moment and rested on the kerosene can below the sink?

'If you take my advice, Kanta, you should take a last chance with your father. Everyone knows there's much profit in sanitary wares these days with so many buildings going up all around.'

Kanta sighed deeply, shook her head and repeated what her father had told her.

'I am sure those burn marks on your face will soften him up. Anil too had been adamant but my bruises helped. Your mother will definitely put some pressure on your father.'

Kanta could now clearly see that marking her face with cigarettes was deliberate, well planned; so was Neena's visit. They were allowing her a last chance before setting her ablaze.

'It won't work, Neena,' she said. 'He has already given more than he had agreed to before my marriage and he has to think about my marriageable sister too. And my mother, she is quite helpless, she has no voice. Father still slaps her for not bringing adequate dowry when his business goes slack.'

Neena put down her cup and looked straight into Kanta's eyes. 'Where there is a will, there is a way,' she said like a schoolteacher haranguing her students. 'You know, Anil is getting madder every day and mother has never looked sulkier. Listen, Kanta . . .' She lowered her voice to a conspiratorial whisper. 'Anil is ready to negotiate. I can persuade him to accept twenty, maybe even fifteen . . .'

'Will you please do me one great favour, Neena?' said Kanta, gritting her teeth. 'There's the can of kerosene and I am sure there is a bundle of rope somewhere in the house. Tell your people to tie my hands and feet, douse me with kerosene and set me ablaze rather than torturing me day and night. I . . . I can't bear it any more.'

Kanta broke into a sob, gagging her mouth with a corner of her sari. Neena held her briefly, uttered the usual comforting noises and when Kanta finally wiped her tears and blew her nose, she said, 'It's our karma, Kanta. We can't change it. But as they say, there is hope as long as there is life. Don't you think, being alive, just *alive* is wonderful and full of possibilities? Think it over. Now, come on, we shouldn't miss the latter part of the film.'

While the vamp crooned and wiggled her hips in a seedy night-club and the villain conspired with his men at a corner table, Kanta thought about the joy and the thrill of being alive and kicking. Neena was definitely not on her side but she had spoken the truth. Hadn't she felt it herself two days back when she crawled out of her bed after midnight and slipped into the kitchen to pour out half of the kerosene down the drain and refill the can with water, carefully spreading a little phenyl around to cover up the smell?

'Ravi Shastri.' Anil had just finished another Classic. Neena protested, for Rishi Kapur seemed to be in real danger, the brakes of his red, sleek sports car had been tampered with by the crooks and he was about to drive away to the hills with Neetu Singh.

'A yorker,' said Anil, ignoring his sister's frowns and his mother's gentle suggestion to practise elsewhere. Kanta had already played three overs and knew that whatever ball Anil delivered, be it pace, spin or swinger, for her it was always bodyline bowling. Yet she lifted her arm and watched Anil's hand going through the motion of bowling.

Lucky Kanta. It turned out to be one of those one-in-five occasions when there was contact between the bat and the ball. The stub hit the wall and landed on the carpet. Anil jumped up to stamp it out with his boot.

'Sixer!' cried Pinky and clapped, momentarily forgetting which team she was playing for.

'Shameless bitch!' hissed mother-in-law. Neena shook her head ostentatiously.

'Fine batting, Ravi Shastri,' Anil complimented Kanta to display his sportsmanship and then added, 'I think next time I'll have to bowl a real googly to beat you.'

# Alasdair Gray

## WAITING IN GALWAY

Kneel
pressing brow to floor, elbows to knees,
hands to ears strangely comforted
waiting for blows.
Kneel pressing hands, comforted, waiting for blows.

Stand
looking out with quick eyes, ears,
ready tongue, hands, feet strangely helpless
waiting for blows.
Stand looking ready, helpless, waiting for blows.

Sit
sipping Guinness with Morag in Galway. Dominoes click
being snugly, easily guided,
waiting for blows.
Sit sipping being, guided, waiting for blows.

# Winter Housekeeping, Glasgow

In weather like this the homeless can hardly live
and every year sees more of them, none of them me.
I give to beggars of course, though charity
prolongs their pain. So do market forces.

Strong brains who tackle problems of this kind
need the protection of a cosy house
or several. I manage with only two
and love these freezing slushy Glasgow streets
at home in bed here, holding and held by you.

# April 1994, South Africa

'We are richer, more real than you,'
said many who would not go away.
'Aim as well, push as hard as you can –
we stay deaf, unyielding, tell lies
until we make you make them come true.'
Your chance was that they could not be
always, everywhere, the same.

# Gwyneth Lewis

## COCONUT POSTCARDS:
## A GOAN HONEYMOON

### I

Wrapped in the palm trees' parentheses
the peninsula sighs. The repeated Vs
rustle of rain to come, but not tonight . . .
One tree is everything to us – is food, is light,
shelter and matting, drunkenness and shade,
boat or a ladder. We use it shamelessly –
eating it, plaiting it, as though it were made
solely for us, and still it gives more.
It is rooted in loving and has no fear
of its own exhaustion. Note how its star
is an asterisk: something important is planted here.

### II

'You can have all the one-night stands you want
with me once we're married.' Along the waterfront
bee-eaters squeal as they rob the air
of its writing of insects and seagulls pilfer
wrist-watch crabs from the clock of the sea
which tells us our time. Like a silver boat
the moon has set sail on the light that we
must take as our monument today,
for we married each other's dying. We pay

441

the ferryman's fare as he poles his way
past porpoise rip-tides in the darkening bay.

## III

Back in his Sanskrit childhood, when a pile of stones
was a god, the Contractor was never alone,
was pantheistic. Now his head's a Kali
fixed to the sway of an avenger's body
in a ruined temple – a pose he holds for the wife.
He refuses to swim because of jellyfish,
which disgust him. He has lived a life
of thrust, of direction, he is a man of spine,
despising drift. But he fears the sting
of the floating organ, whose transparent design
can kill him by willing nothing.

## IV

Entombed on their towels, the honeymooners gleam . . .
Alabaster limbs and gothic dreams
keep waiters away, for they lie in state.
Burnished by unguents they concentrate
on just being, now that all their delights
are formal, official. So their smiles are fixed –
eyes closed to the wheeling Brahminy kites
above, to the mess around them, to the dissolute
hibiscus tongues, to the siren's alarms,
as a baby's found buried in a palm tree's roots,
born from the earth into fostering arms.

## V

Palm number eight is a toddy-tapping tree,
is fortunate, owns a family
which tends to its every need. In return
it allows them to place a strategic urn
over its sweetly bleeding stem
so that Polycarp d'Souza's still
is full. All night the palm tree bleeds for them.
But at noon, girls gather in its fertile shade
and are striped like tigers, for their husbandry
is ferocious – best marriage a tree could have made
against its main enemy, gravity.


## VI

By the shack a man wants to clean out my ears
and then massage me. In the end I concur
and settle my shell-like so that he can reach
its whorls. He digs and suddenly the beach
is louder. He picks out detritus, wax and more –
out comes a string of my memories –
leaving me light in the midday roar
of sand grains crashing and singing crabs. I'm
relieved of all the rubbish I've ever heard,
retuned, a transistor that can hear the first time
the call of the heart's hidden weaver-bird.

## VII

On the beach you can practise our history
and crawl, Neanderthal, up from the sea,
then on to umbrellas to be something cool
in shorts and dark glasses, looking quizzical
as the sea's empty metre sighs at the feet
of a palm that carries flowers, acorns, fruit
all the same moment. At dusk we are freed
from shape into colour. On an opal tide
we swim: skin opens into lilacs and far
below the tuna's silver shoots through my side.
I reach out my tongue and lick Africa.

## VIII

This place, like paradise, is better than us,
but accepts us graciously, lets us take our ease
in its love's retribution, for it is so kind
that it only condemns the begrudging mind,
which exiles itself. For the moment, my dear,
simplification is the name of the game.
Set me up slowly like a folding chair
in the sun and, serenely, let's look out together
at the 'sceneries and common life'
which bless us repeatedly in the insect stir
of a palm-frond husband with his sea-breeze wife.

# Pauline Stainer

## MUSIC FOR KSHANTIVADA

### JOSEPH KNECHT TUNES THE CLAVICHORD

It is the pure octave he is after –
he lowers his heartrate
like a marksman,
tunes the beating fourths and fifths
to his own pulse.

As master
of the glass bead game
he sets an equal temperament,
no longer hears
how *hazard has such accuracies.*

Suddenly
a billow of scent
through the open window,
soft-focus uprising
of elder in full flower

his heart outpacing
the fourths and fifths,
their impure intervals
flooding him
like an intoxicant

as if the property
of music

were not perfect tuning
but a disparity
that defines.

## GLOSSOLALIA

In the Japanese temple
the sprung floor
sings when anyone
steps on it

funeral jades
speak through
the nine orifices
of the body

and outside,
the nightingale
rinses the bubble
in its throat.

## MUSIC FOR KSHANTIVADA

*who was dismembered but did not lose his patience*

What engineers the blood
when a severed head sings
of a full moon in March
and the scattered body
remembers music by heart?

Immortality
is the verve of
*all that is made*,
Isis reassembling
the limbs of Osiris

the high tessitura
with which, in the guise
of a hawk,
she flutters
against the phallus.


## CANZONE FOR TADZIO

*after Britten*

It is the measure of desire
that your body completes the music
before I write even a note

the fish scoring the sea
with their own cross-rhythms
as you dance on the sand

the air ribboned like rococo silk,
the horizon a rim
of running bronze.

So many girdles of gravity –
the wide vibrato
between rods of rolled glass

when you walk
*the seven bright gold wires*
into the sea.

# VARÈSE IMPROVISES THE LEVITATION OF THE PYRAMIDS

I require
the most coaxing acoustic –
the quartet
in one movement,
the zither with waxed silk strings.

I introduce
a siren, Chinese blocks,
hawkbells and ocarina,
ghost drum-set,
the roar of the desert lion.

They levitate
to tape alone,
rising *gradazione*
through the haze
by grace of electronics

and as they dream
at altitude,
flexing their photons
against the hot mouth
of the swallow

I build the echo

# THE WOUND-DRESSER'S DREAM

*In May 1819 John Keats considered signing up
as a ship's surgeon*

> *Do you not hear the sea?*

I read *Lear* in the ship's pharmacy;
the crew pray
and clean their weapons,
birds rise like grapeshot
into the Egyptian blue

the ship ghosting
the Sargasso
with only a mizzen raised
above the ambergris
and floating weed

we sleep lightly
as falconers,
our cargo of quicksilver
soughing against
the sun

no dew, no dew
only incidental bleeding –
on the 6th
the large white pig
executed on a curved ocean

the baffled air
full of wild ginger,
the masts dropping
medicinal gums
into the sirocco

such investiture
of salt
*I cough my proper blood*
and digest nothing
but milk.

# Lavinia Greenlaw

## THE SHAPE OF THINGS

There is no eighty-eighth storey from which
to point out three buildings, each the tallest
in its time. I sleep but can't sleep

on the fourth floor of a deluded hotel.
In such an early industrial city,
this is as high, as late as it gets.

I have seen no one, heard only
the sigh of the exoskeletal lift,
the firedoors' groan and cough.

The trill of the Bakelite phone by my bed
I imagine, but not the two ballrooms,
theatrical staircase and slipping lock.

Someone has left a shadow on the carpet
as if, blinded by champagne and erotic waltzes,
they made a grand unsteady staircase exit

and came to rest with their ear to the ground.
I lie, curl into it, hand on their hand,
neither wanting to be there nor to miss a beat.

The street-cleaning truck scrapes past.
Indecisive, I bring it back
again and again to straighten and empty

my dreams. Body heat. Talk of political death.
I grasp the receiver when the alarm call comes,
whisper *thank you, thank you* . . .

## WHAT'S GOING ON

The demolition crew are petulant.
Swinging the ball, they could lay bets and lose.
We cannot help but stand in the street,
smile up at the light where half the roof
has fallen away and the sky comes at us
from all three sides through a couple of windows,
surprisingly large and somehow intact.

## INVENTION

My six-year-old mechanic, you are up half the night
inventing a pipe made from jars, a *skiing car*
*for flat icy roads* and a *timer-catapult*
involving a palm tree, candles and rope.

You could barely stand when I once found you,
having loosened the bars from the cot
and stepped out so simply you shocked yourself.
Today I am tearful, infatuated with bad ideas,

the same song, over and over. You take charge,
up-end chairs, pull cushions under the table,
lay in chewing-gum and juice,
rip newspaper into snow on the roof.

# Paul Henry

## CONDITIONING

Our avant-garde family unit tilted
its buggy into Old Compton Street,
and before you could say '*Boy* . . . *Boy* . . . *Boy* . . .'
I was in the swivelling chair at *Rox*,
male as you like, while your brother's hands,
quicker than words, showed me how it was done,
in the manner of your father's hands,
touched my head with another man's hands

and I wondered who had shaved his hair
so close to the skull, and how often,
and if the stunned, peroxide strands
were his way of holding time in place.

At the other extreme of the motorway,
that night, in your father's butcher's shop,
in the passage way, I watched him scrub
another bloody silence from his hands,
then bless the sleeping baby's locks,
then scrape a finely ribbed curl
of congealed, fat-like coconut-oil
from the sloughy depth of a small jar,

and then, with the same hands,
in front of the same cubit of mirror,
rub the carcass beyond trace,
work the gel invisible.

# Sarah LeFanu

## QUAIL

*The Quail: Coturnix Coturnix Coturnix: In general appearance much like a very small, delicately built Part- ridge, which it also resembles in flight if flushed, but presence is more often detected by characteristic note of male (see 'Voice') than by bird being seen.*

LAST YEAR IT was ducks. This year it is quails. And because I feel anxious about the changes I am about to inflict on my children and grasp at any semblance of continuity, even quailine continuity, I say, yes: don't send them all back to the city farm once they're hatched. I'll have one, with pleasure. My daughter's teacher is delighted.

Nicholas moved out of our house, although not out of my life, a year ago. I forced him to. It was either that, or murder him; and while the flesh was willing and my hand itched to pour weedkiller into his tomato soup on the few occasions when he was home in the evenings in time to eat with me, the spirit baulked. I dreamt about killing him, often, and each time struggled towards consciousness burdened with an immense weight of guilt. Poisoning is, apparently, a peculiarly female mode of murder. It inspires horror in the hearts of judges: they see it as coldly premeditated, not realising that with the alternative, lashing out in rage, women are more likely to get themselves killed than to kill. Or maybe that's our justification, and the truth is women are drawn atav- istically to poisoning by their witchy past. But think of the poor children: a dead father and a murderess (infinitely more sinister than murderer) for a mother.

My daughter is delighted. She is almost as pleased at the prospect of having one of these speckled little brown birds for her very own as she is excited at the prospect of moving house and school. My children seem to love change. The other day I heard them chanting in a kind of nasal sing-song the names of their father's girl-friends of the last year: Michelle, A-nnabel, A-dele, then they creased up and fell about on the floor shrieking. None of my friends have names like that: we're all simple Jo or Viv or Kate. Nicholas prefers the Annabels of this world. Sexy, young, childless.

Nicholas would have liked me to have other lovers. Correction: he would have liked me to have lovers. That side of marriage, as I remember my mother quaintly calling it in reference to my raffish father, hadn't existed for us since the birth of our daughter six years ago. And that was a fluke, if not semi-miraculous. Nicholas thought that my taking a lover (to take a lover: like an examination) would even things up – this was after the discovery that brought it out in the open – but why should I act to satisfy his balance sheet? Nicholas is an accountant.

And as he gets older, his women get younger.

*The family Phasianidae comprises about 170 species of quails, partridges, pheasants, peafowl and jungle fowl. The group is a very mixed one, showing marked variation in size and plumage; e.g. the splendour of the peacock and the dull, drab coloration of the partridge, and it is difficult to find a common denominator. One such attempt at classification has been to divide the birds into polygamous and monogamous, the brightly coloured species belonging to the first group, the duller, drab ones to the second.*

Moving day draws near. The teacher is distraught. One of the baby quails (eight of them hatched out, only one casualty, they heard its beak tap-tapping inside the shell, growing fainter and fainter until it stopped) has had an accident. The roof of the cage slipped out of her hands as she replaced it after feeding them, its leg was trapped and now is dangling in a sickeningly broken fashion. It will wither away, she says: a one-legged quail won't survive unless it has a special home. Could we possibly? She trails off, her eyes are still wet, her vocation is to care for small creatures (my daughter adores her) and look what's happened.

Of course, I say. I mean who can refuse a home to a one-legged quail? She goes on: But you must have your own one too. They all look the same to me (apart from the one with the dangling leg), but I say: Fine. My daughter is further delighted. Two quails are even better than one. I hope there will be no more injuries.

The one I found him with in our bed was in her early twenties. I felt as if I'd been punched in the stomach. I couldn't breathe, it was like falling off a horse, being winded, desperately trying to draw in breath and thinking you'll die of suffocation. Then I was sick, copiously, in the bathroom where I'd locked myself in, and he was knocking on the door and calling my name in his special concerned voice. He must have hustled Rosie, I think her name was, or perhaps Rosalie, out of the house pretty smartly. You think vomiting in the lav is a bit of an overreaction, do you? I mean what's the big fuss? There're probably statistics, like with the birth and death rate: one adulterous fornication is committed every two seconds. Or every one second.

It wasn't so much the shock of finding him there doing it in our bed. It was the instant realisation that he'd been doing just this for years, if not in this bed, then in beds all over the place; and with that realisation the simultaneous admission, and this is what seemed to hit me in the stomach, that I had known it all along. When I opened the bedroom door there was a moment of utter clarity; it was as if I was seeing him for the first time and my vision wasn't fogged by desire, or fear, or habit, and then I was doubled over, wheezing and retching.

I wonder: are all men like Nicholas, but less obvious about it? Did my father have mistresses? Did my mother know? Did she feel powerless, out of control, like Nicholas makes me feel?

Nicholas now wants to buy a house, and although he is, in my view, grossly overpaid, he says he can't afford a new mortgage on top of what he pays for this house. So the children and I are going somewhere smaller, and I'll manage most of the new mortgage although local arts administration is not exactly lucrative. Particularly part-time and so no chance of promotion. Equal opportunities, what a joke.

Bernard, who has been in the office only eighteen months, is about to get some flashy regional job. He's a nice enough bloke, but hardly out to set the world on fire. I suspect his baldness has something to do with it; it seems to give men an air of authority. It's not quite the same if you're a woman, is it? Even grey puts you at a disadvantage, let alone no hair. Nicholas lovingly tends his thick dark curls. How did I ever fall for a man so vain? Maybe his vanity spoke to mine; my narcissism mirrored in his gaze.

*As always, however, there are exceptions to the rule: some quails, even though their plumage is dull, leave the hen immediately after copulation.*

Nicholas has said he'll help me move, but something comes up. Or someone.

It doesn't matter, as my old schoolfriend Kate is coming the day before and will spend the night and help with the final packing-up.

A skip full of rubbish is parked outside the front door; the baby clothes have all gone to the CancerCare shop; summer clothes have been washed and put away, they won't be needed for another year (perhaps I should have got rid of more of them, well, it's too late now). Most of the big pieces of furniture have already gone, and I thought I'd be left with

just beds and kitchen equipment to deal with. But instead I
am afloat in a sea of rubbish. It's as if I've sieved the contents
of the house over and over, catching smaller and smaller
items: this to be chucked, that to be packed, this to be
discreetly lost when the children are safely out of the way,
and what I'm left with is objects old, dusty, worn, but somehow not easily classifiable as rubbish. Such as: that nice old
faded Asian pheasant serving dish my mother gave me which
I broke two years ago and could easily be mended but hasn't
been. A dusty heap of Lego pieces revealed when the large
pieces of furniture went this morning. Six and a half pairs
of shoes, that might or might not fit someone, from the
cupboard under the stairs. I feel incapable of any further
decisions.

*Covey or pack of partridges; brood, eye (obs), nye or
bouquet (when a number cross the guns at once) of
pheasants; bevy of quails.*

The scaffolding at the back of the house should have come
down two months ago, when Viv and the girls finished mend-
ing the roof, but the scaffolder to whom they subcontracted,
a harmless-looking fellow, I thought, when he put it up, has
since been arrested and charged with threatening behaviour.
With a shotgun. He's now out on bail, but can't or won't
remove the scaffolding. It must go by tomorrow, completion
day. I'm not happy being left in possession of something that
belongs to a man rampaging with a shotgun (sawn-off, of
course, aren't they all?), but Viv says not to worry, it was a
family affair. Oh well, that's OK, then, isn't it?

Kate thinks that I am cynical about men. She tells me that
it is hopelessly old-fashioned of me to see men as the enemy,
that that went out with the ark and I am stuck in a time-
warp. Men, too, can be loving and faithful. The trouble is
that while I can believe that Kate's Peter, for example,
is loving, faithful, clean and has all sorts of other sterling
qualities, he's always struck me as a dull dog and I could

never imagine what clever, pretty Kate saw in him. I do not say this.

I ask Kate to put everything into boxes as best she can. Meanwhile I start to empty the filing cabinet, then remember that the removals men said not to bother. I unlock the door of the back room to check on the quails, collected earlier from school and looking rather cramped in their temporary home, a disused gerbil cage. The crippled quail has made a remarkable recovery. In fact I can't tell the two apart. So much for withering away. They've knocked their water bowl over again. Oh well, I expect they'll survive the night without water. I hope. I lock the door behind me, then suddenly think: where's the cat? Have I locked it in with them? I open the door again, and peer under the table. Yes. I drag it out.

Kate is carefully wrapping each piece of the broken serving dish in a separate piece of newspaper. I stifle my irritation. Kate has a close and loving relationship with her mother. They swap recipes.

The doorbell rings. It's the man next door. He's an ex-Hell's Angel, but mellowed since he had a heart attack two years ago. He offers to ring up some of his mates and ask them to come and take down the scaffolding. In a couple of hours' time, he says: when it's dark. No questions asked. I decline the offer politely, but I can see he's annoyed. I explain that it isn't mine to get rid of, that it was hired by Viv the builder, and I don't want to get her into trouble. This doesn't seem to cut much ice with him, but I manage to get him out of the door, while I grovellingly express thanks for his kind offer.

I am now full of fear that he'll do it anyway, that he'll send his mates over the garden wall at midnight. If that's the case I'll just have to let it go: his mates have not suffered heart attacks as far as I know and are far from mellowed.

Half an hour later Viv arrives. She's spent the whole evening ringing round scaffolding firms to find someone to take it down. None of them will touch it. They've all heard he's on an attempted murder charge. What a network these scaffolders must have, says Kate, like the early days of the

women's movement. But on the eighth call Viv found someone who would take it down, first thing tomorrow morning,
but they won't store it. They said it was probably stolen, and
they don't want any trouble. Who does?

I hope that this move will get me out of trouble. Nicholas
trouble and money trouble all at once. I want quiet. I want
to be untouched.

I make us each a bowl of spaghetti, which we eat with some
pesto I find lurking in the fridge. I open a bottle of red wine
and pour out a glass for Kate and myself. Viv doesn't drink.
She only smokes dope.

I look around the kitchen. On the draining board stand a
cluster of old plastic cups, stained and dusty, a jam jar of
paintbrushes, and three children's paintboxes, none of which
has a lid. A pile of paperbacks leans against the fridge,
thrillers mostly. Where on earth did they come from? I
thought I'd packed all the books last week. There is still an
awful lot of crockery on the shelves. The lampshade over the
table is thick with dust. Mustn't forget to take that: it's
the most expensive lampshade Nicholas and I ever bought –
Italian, wide-brimmed, made of thick, heavy, clear glass with
a black border.

Could you hoover the lampshades, Kate, and then pack
them? I ask.

Hoover them? says Kate. She gives me an odd look.

I can't bear the thought of taking all this dust and dirt with
me. I feel like a huge bear just coming out of hibernation, a
six-year-long hibernation; I want to shake off the leaves and
cobwebs, the mould of old attachments, that cling to my fur,
I want to delouse myself and go out clean.

By midnight Kate has hoovered and packed all the lampshades. I notice she is looking a little pale. I check on the
quails one last time. They are huddled in a corner of the cage,
one on top of the other. Keeping themselves warm, I think.
I put the cat out, am struck with fear that it might be so
upset by the emptying of the house that it will run away,
open the door for it to come in again and then decide against

it. I don't want to be clearing up cat crap tomorrow morning.
I check on the children: fast asleep. Then I go to bed. There
are no curtains, and I lie there watching the dance of clouds,
glowing an eerie orange, behind the solid black criss-cross of
the scaffolding poles.

*But-for-but, Cheshire; corncrake, Sussex; deadchick,
Shetland Isles; landrail, Sussex; quailzie, Scotland; quick-
me-Dick, Oxon; rine, Cornwall; sofliar, Wales; throsher;
wandering quail; wet-my-feet, Ireland, Scotland; wet-
my-lips, Norfolk, Sussex; wet weather, Sussex.*

The scaffolders arrive at eight-thirty the next morning. When
the removals men arrive, fifteen minutes later, there is
nowhere for them to park their van, which is as tall, or so it
seems, as the scaffolders' lorry is long. This makes the
removals men rather surly. They attempt to remove the
covered trailer belonging to the man next door, which has
been parked outside ever since Nicholas and I moved in, and
has been moved only once, when some lads dragged it to a
nearby hill in the middle of the night and let it careen to the
bottom. The man next door throws up a window on the first
floor, leans out and lets rip a string of abuse at the removals
men, me and a couple of passers-by. I ask Kate if she will
take the children to school for their last morning. They are
reluctant to go, and stand by the gate goggle-eyed. The man
next door is leaning further out of his window, and obviously
has no clothes on.

He shuts the window with a crash. The removals men
shrug their shoulders, and manage to back their van into the
space now cleared. They are not yet cheerful, and cast dark
looks at the scaffolders, who are being noisy and insouciant.

I lurk unhappily in the kitchen, feeling that I have set in
motion a series of events that I no longer control. Couldn't
I have managed to stay on here somehow? I remember all
the articles I've read recently about the dire necessity of
providing stability for your children, some of them hinting
at the consequences of failure: criminal tendencies, inability

to form lasting relationships, even (God spare us) a marked swing towards fundamentalist religious beliefs. Well, at least I don't parade a series of lovers in front of them like their father does. No, I don't do that.

A bejeaned pair of legs swings down outside the window, followed by an unpromising buttock cleavage, then a face peers in and shouts at me through the glass: put the kettle on, love, would you? I give him the V-sign as his legs disappear upwards, but only as a matter of form – after all, he is removing the scaffolding, and for that I am grateful. I ask the removals men if they too would like tea but, frostily polite, they say they're not yet ready for it.

Viv arrives. She has found somewhere for the scaffolding to be stored, and within half an hour all the poles are down and the men are gone. There are not many boxes left to go, most of the rooms are bare although thick with dust and fluff. I feel as if I've been cleaning for weeks already. I never realised we lived in such a sea of dirt, it must act as excellent insulation. The sloppy housewife as saver of energy, friend of the earth. Viv returns with an industrial hoover and starts at the top of the house, joint hanging from the corner of her mouth. I think I could fall in love with Viv.

The removals men are all smiles now. One of them tells me, primly, that the scaffolders were unsavoury characters. He should have met the original one.

*Voice: Call of male a liquid 'quic, quic-ic' usually repeated several times and very fairly suggested by the popular 'wet-mi-lips'. Ordinary note of female a soft 'peu, peu'. When flushed birds call 'crwee-crwee' or a more croaking 'crucc-crucc'. Naumann describes the alarm-note when flushed as 'trul-reck-reck-reck', which might represent a combination of these notes. He also describes 'callnotes', 'bubibi' and 'brubrub', a soft 'truli-lil, trulil' and a faint 'gurr-gurr-gurr' not unlike purring of cat.*

I'll miss the bathroom in this house. It's on the first floor, and as the house is in a terrace that snakes around the edge of a steep hill, when you lie in the bath you see just sky, the clouds chasing across it, and on summer evenings hot air balloons in bright primary colours, in red and blue and yellow stripes, waft past, giving a sudden roar as the balloon-ists open up the fire. In the new house the bath is tucked into a corner of the room and you can't see out of the window unless you lie with your head at the tap end – not conducive to watery daydreaming. In the early days Nicholas and I used to bath together, uncomfortably but excitingly, skin slipping and sliding over skin. That was before the babies were born. He has other skin to slip and slide over now, and probably did even then. Later, he was never home in the evenings – work, he used to say – and came home smelling of sweat and sex. I ignored it: I couldn't admit the idea of sharing his body, his lips, the soft down on his belly, his tongue, his cock, with other women. Are men naturally poly-gamous? Do women only want babies? I used not to have these heretical thoughts. Kate would be horrified.

*Cheeper: young bird.*

Viv is still hoovering as Kate and I start to pack the car. Three sleeping bags, one ragged sheep that used to bleat when turned upside-down but now only rattles (son's), one raccoon Fluppet (daughter's: she likes to stroke its fat tail against her cheek), one box of food for tonight with a few knives, forks and plates, the pile of books that once again missed being packed, one suitcase containing a change of clothes for all of us, assorted coats (it is an unseasonably hot autumn day), a basket full of dirty clothes, my bulging handbag, cat scratching in cat basket and miaowing in plaint-ive and pitiful fashion, and the quails. The straw in the cage looks damp and filthy, oh Christ, I hope they survive the journey.

It's only half an hour's drive, Kate points out reassuringly. I'm feeling tight and tense, I hear my teeth grinding together.

Mustn't forget the children, says Kate. The children, oh

Christ again, I had forgotten them. All their accoutrements, but no actual children. We're going to collect them from school and go straight on.

The removals men have gone, Viv has finished hoovering, the house is clean, empty, there is nothing of me in it any longer. I rush into each room one last time. Do I want to cry? No, there isn't time. If I start crying now I might never stop. I find the old wooden stepladder leaning in a lonely pose against the kitchen wall. Curses. What on earth am I going to do with it? Viv says she'll take it to her house and bring it round to me in a few days' time. Oh wonderful Viv.

I lock the door for the last time. Good riddance, Nicholas, I hiss as I climb into the car.

About time too, says Kate, sitting beside me with the cat basket on her lap. Kate thinks I should have left him years ago. Well, she's probably right. But I don't feel joyously free. I feel sick. Keys to the estate agent, then to school to pick up the children. They are full of the anticipated pleasure of sleeping bags tonight.

*The Common or Migratory Quail: Northern populations migrate to Africa and southern Asia, many of them perishing on the way either in the sea or at the hands of sportsmen in some countries where they are netted and shot in vast numbers.*

One of the quails has died. I looked in on them earlier and saw them snuggled up in a corner, one on top of the other, and thought they were asleep. Then wandering round the garden just before I went to bed, I went into the shed again and one of them was still in the corner, looking sort of flattish, and the other one was hopping about the cage. I opened the cage and the flattish one didn't move. I picked it up. It seemed to have shrunk.

Deadchick.

For a moment I think this is a bad omen, a death on our first night in the new house. Then I tell myself not to be so silly. Animals die and that's all there is to it. Maybe it was the crippled one, maybe it had suffered some other injury in the accident and its days were numbered anyway. Maybe it wasn't my fault. What shall I do with it? I'd better not get rid of it tonight, maybe the children will want to see it. I must let them express their grief. What about the other one? I hope it won't pine for its companion. Maybe it was trying to resuscitate it when I saw them earlier, keeping its cold body warm.

The next morning I tell the children. Both become tearful.

Would you like to see it? I ask gently.

Yuk. No way, they chorus.

I'm not going in that shed till you've got rid of it, says my son.

Yuk, says my daughter again.

Later I dig a deep hole and bury the quail. I don't want the cat digging it up and bringing it into the house.

At work I mention to Bernard my worries that my children are not normal. They show no affect, I say. Complete inability to grieve over parents' separation, death of beloved pet, etc. I keep on looking out for signs of disturbed behaviour, I complain, but there's not a trace.

Bernard laughs. Hard-hearted like you, he says.

Hard-hearted? Me?

What do you mean? I say, annoyed.

You keep yourself apart, he says. We've worked together for eighteen months and you still treat me like a stranger, with polite tolerance.

I don't like this one bit, and I grab a floating piece of paper from my desk and fall to a concentrated study of it. It's something about a new community theatre.

I don't think it's because you dislike me, he goes on.

He's right. I don't. But I'll start disliking him soon if there's any more of this uncalled for personal comment.

I reach for the telephone.

We avoid each other for the rest of the day. Then, just as I'm about to go home, he says, You do know about quails, don't you?

Know about them?

Bernard smiles. He has a crooked smile that makes him look rather schoolboyish despite his lack of hair.

You have to be careful to provide the male with at least five or six females, he says. Or else . . .

Or else?

Well, the female dies.

Good God, I cry. Of exhaustion, you mean?

How awful. To think that I kept that poor female shut up in a tiny cage with a voracious male and no means of escape. And to think that I thought that he was keeping her warm.

I look at Bernard and I start to laugh.

When I get home I go and cast my beady eye on the beady eye of the remaining quail. I decide it has a rough and vicious look to it. What's more, it has waxed fat and is now strutting round its cage in what can only be described as a self-important fashion. None the less, I throw it some corn. I can hardly let it starve to death. Although being eaten is what it deserves.

> *Quails from the Sea: And there went forth a wind from the Lord, and brought quails from the sea, and let them fall by the camp, as it were a day's journey on this side, and as it were a day's journey on the other side, round about the camp, and as it were two cubits high upon the face of the earth. And the people stood up all that day, and all that night, and all the next day, and they gathered the quails: he that gathered least gathered ten homers; and they spread them all abroad for themselves round about the camp. And while the flesh was yet between their teeth, ere it was chewed, the wrath of the Lord was kindled against the people, and the Lord smote the people with a very great plague.*

Were they not meant to eat them? Are quails unclean, as fowls that creep, going upon all four, that shall be an abomination? Why then pile them as it were two cubits high?

My daughter worries that the quail is lonely and pesters me to get another one. I repress my shudders and put her off by saying we can't get another one until we make a bigger hutch: they need room to flap around in and they'd like to have some branches to fly up to and perch on, I tell her. That means putting it off for a long time, perhaps until this one dies of old age, I secretly hope. What is a quail's lifespan, assuming it is not drowned, netted, shot or eaten?

*It is now illegal to kill wild quail. Japanese quail are bred for the table: they can be browned in butter and braised with a little stock, port wine and orange peel.*

The following weekend Bernard comes round and builds a new quail house. Quite how this has come about I'm not too sure. The children watch delightedly as he saws, planes, hammers, fixes. They are both so busy helping Bernard they barely squabble all day. Hmph, I think. The murderous quail is put into its new house. Yet another example of vice rewarded, I say to Bernard, as I present him with a bottle of wine as thanks. Still, my daughter is very fond of it.

The school holidays come and go, and then Kate comes to stay. It's cold outside, one of those early spring cold spells that seem worse than winter because you've begun to expect, foolishly, a bit of warmth. I give the children an early supper, and once they're in bed Kate and I eat in front of the fire in the sitting-room. Kate asks me about Nicholas.

Worse than ever, I say: he's become a weekend raver, driving around the countryside half the night looking for parties. He doesn't turn up to collect the children when he says he will.

Bit old for that kind of thing, isn't he? says Kate.

You'd think so, I say morosely. And he hasn't paid any maintenance since Christmas.

I ponder the iniquity of men for a bit.

Oh look, says Kate, I brought this for you. I thought you'd be amused.

She takes out of her bag a dictionary of historical slang.

Look up quail, she says. I do, and read out: *A harlot, or a courtesan, ex the bird's supposed amorousness.*

How disgraceful, I say. How typical, blaming women for male depravity. It's like men accusing women of irrationality, when it's men who have invented and sustained all major religions.

I read some of the other entries. Almost every one refers to women's insatiable sexual appetite. Maybe it's only the Qs; but no, it's everything from A to Z.

Even his own name, says Kate.

Partridge: a harlot.

Kind of obsessive, isn't it? says Kate.

A couple of whiskies later, and Kate tells me that she and Peter make love every night, or almost every night. Good God. I can hardly hide my amazement.

It's so long since I've had sex I can't even remember what it's like, I tell her.

She can hardly hide her amazement.

When the children have left home, I say, I shall probably retire to a convent and live the rest of my life serenely among members of my own sex.

Kate looks unconvinced. Would that be rational? she asks.

One Saturday a few weeks later I am in bed with Bernard. It is the middle of the morning. The children are, amazingly and conveniently, with their father. Bernard and I have just made love for the first time, and now he is gently sucking my nipples, first one, then the other. Trulilil, trulil. Gurr, gurr, gurr. I am almost fainting with pleasure. I roll on my side, hook my legs round his back and pull him inside me again.

This is a relationship begun *ab ovo*. I rang him earlier and invited him over for a cup of coffee – I don't think I had anything else in mind – as there was something I wanted to show him. We stood together in the kitchen looking down at the pale yellow egg richly speckled with brown and purple that lies in my hand.

Look what I've just found, I say.

That rather mucks up your theories, he says.

Your theories, I reply.

Suddenly I know what I want to do. I put the egg down gently on the table and move towards him. He smiles his crooked smile and then we are kissing and I run my hand over the back of his balding head, and I think, I like you. I think: I want you. We stop, and we both laugh.

Well? I say.

Yes, he replies.

Sofliar, throsher, wandering quail. I imagine our quailzie, bonneted, in a croft, baking scones for all her little cheepers. She's such a pretty, plump, brown little thing.

# John Saul

## HELLHOUND

I AM CURATE of the Anglican church of St Martin's, Pendle, and a lover of the blues.

Lewis Lewis is my name.

I can hear the doors of the limousines closing in the rain.

> *So won't you come on, into my kitchen*
> *'cause it's going to be rainin' outside*

I hear umbrellas being spanned and I hear him: Robert Johnson, king of the Delta blues singers. Dead sixty years but I hear him. Making the sway of rain over Pendle turn to a howl; shrinking this church of cold pillars, cold pews under its vaulted heights, to a snugness of packing crates against a warm iron stove. Robert Johnson, head down, a glass bottleneck on his finger, guitar across his knee. Or freeing his lap for a lover. Not that I, the fledgeling curate, have experience of a lover, a seduction, passion. I kissed Pauline in private, aged five. I kissed her sister Lucy in demonstration of what I had done with Pauline. Aged eighteen I wanted Linda but she broke down in tears. At twenty-three, while retaining the same Lew Lewis cherub face, that permanent flush to the cheeks, I now have God. He is becoming equally awkward, however, and equally hopeless; and somehow the blues is coming in between. May lightning strike me if I err, but the blues has come to me in the shape of this man who, when it

470

came to the expression of true feelings, outstripped our own Lord Jesus Christ.

I'm waiting. Waiting. My robes would catch fire in an instant. But there is no storm, no singeing; it just drizzles. I might venture further comparisons. Like Christ Jesus, Robert Johnson died young, violently and by treachery. Poisoned to death, he had to be carried down from the Saturday night stage in mid-performance; to lie down and die in a shack in Greenwood, Mississippi, at the age of twenty-seven. Would that I could spread my robes, fly back sixty years and sit by him. This sight is hard to picture. For God will have been his constant letdown; the devil his torment and inspiration; a hellhound on his trail. And yet the same hound trails me too, yapping and barking at our Lord's contradictions. It distracts me from my tasks; has me think poorly of my fellow creatures. No, there is no more getting around it: wherever I am the devil is at work. (He too, curiously, moves in mysterious ways: his daemonic work once done, God and the devil elide into one. For, I ask, whose hand condemned the Jew; and who is it torments the poor with promises of comfort in times to come?) Mr Ainsworth, I shall tell the vicar, I shall have to hang up my robes, seek a different vocation. The white robes I had so looked forward to wearing. At least I have known the strange pleasure of them now. The delight of gathering them in my young arms; flicking away the folds as the congregation settles down, while the organ softly wanders. I take my time in shaking both hands free, enjoying this little ritual to punctuate the proceedings. Next I shall miss the bright voices of Lee and Mona in the choir. Mona Mona, dare I hope to meet her of an evening? I shall miss the altar, the organ, the cups of wine, the robes. The sweet moment when I take up the book, lift the shimmering red or blue bookmark, and through the soft amplification of the microphone announce the hymn, the psalm, the prayer, the sermon. Even to say goodbye to Mr and Mrs Ainsworth will be to leave a world behind.

*

471

I can hear heels tapping on the path. The door being unbolted.

Lord, grant me two things in this life. I, who was not granted Linda, grant me Mona. And let me in this life also trek down a dirt road in the Mississippi Delta. Where this great but humble man might have travelled. Robert Johnson: despite the dust and dirt, the beating of the southern sun, immaculate in his pinstriped suit; his dressy tie, black shiny shoes. I can see him now on his way to San Antonio, the first legendary recordings. A peculiar, enticing odyssey of a journey. He will cross several states; sleep with several women. At his playing, his beautiful hands, women stared and men grew jealous. And I too, Lew Lewis, speaking God's word by day, by darkness long to hear this unbridled slide guitar, loud in a pair of headphones. In truth I crave the sound in its most blasphemous form; as a shock, ice sharp, white hot, ripping through the air.

Here comes the coffin.

A simple coffin, possibly for a simple man. Certainly he was not cut down, like so many singers of the blues, at the will of a jealous hand. His bladder simply burst, his creaking heart gave out. And so we are here today to celebrate and remember him, lately deceased and of this parish. There are his family. Walking raggedly, unsure of their legs, their footing, the protruding edges of the flagstones. They wheel into the nave much bewildered; heads mostly bowed. They close up uncomfortably on the coffin, and halt a while. The church organ meanders, my mind wandering with it. I have always liked the sound of the organ. In contrast to the steel knife of the guitar, its sound is essentially a fluid, filling space. Or I might say: like God, it fills the gaps and holes, and so comforts. Now it helps the family to find itself, again edge forward. They look down and half ahead, no eyes catching mine. One stares at the strange block of mourners with their ash-grey faces: the twenty-three past presidents of the district

472

golf club, bare-headed in suits and raincoats. They stand like a squad of veteran soldiers, making one half of the congregation.

Mr Ainsworth gives me the look. The wise, grey look. He suspects I have gone amiss, and locks me in his gaze to remind me I am still Lewis Lewis, still curate of St Martin's. I cannot dwell on the fate of the king of the Delta blues singers; nor the imagined thrill of meeting Mona on some unholy ground. Duty demands I turn to the deceased, elsewhere though my heart is. I never knew him. Yesterday at tea his widow showed me him in photographs. As golf club president. As an eminence in the dental association. He sat at dinner-tables; stood with silver cups and salvers, before green golf-course fairways. I struggle to have his likeness uppermost in mind; to be prepared to return the look of his widow, now on her knees in prayer.

> *When the train, it left the station*
> *With two lights on behind*
> *The blue light was my baby*
> *And the red light was my mind.*
> *All my love's in vain*

I ask you all to pray in silence for Frank Ross, beloved husband of Marjorie, devoted father of Michael and Graham, affectionate grandfather of James.

I too pray to the Lord. Lord, I have become a rambling man. Rambling: to have led a life sinful in the eyes of the Church. Rambling Lew Lewis, curating over the deaths of decent men and women. Thanks be to heaven it is Mr Ainsworth will address the gathering. As curate it befalls me simply to direct the service, read the prayers and lead the hymns; look this woman in the eye. As I call for the family and friends to stand she looks straight at me. I look at her jowls, her crimped grey hair under her dark hat. Her look is singing the song about the train leaving the station. But at the committal she will be told: happy are the dead.

We sit, the twenty-three past presidents bending at the knee as one. We attend to Mr Ainsworth's account of the departed. His upright ways. Cups and plaques and accolades. A relative of the deceased is staring at my robes. His look doesn't sing the song about the train. It is a look I cannot fathom. But everything means something, I heard Mona say. It would be no accident, for example, if a man were to end his time as curate at a funeral. A funeral would be the appropriate occasion to make his private autopsy. Nor would it be accidental that the dead dry life recumbent next to him had been autopsied, as indeed he had, and sewn back together with something quite different now inside him. I am intrigued at Mona's words, impressed she can think every occurrence arrives with its meaning. But sceptical. Desirous. I want Mona. Mona, right or wrong. I turn back to Mr Ainsworth. Mr Ainsworth's forehead glistens under the light of the pulpit. He speaks of the Latin scholar; the decent citizen; Frank was a name, *frank*, that the deceased truly wore. But within these brief months of curatorial practice I have become weary of the way a funeral only hands out praise. I listen instead for the omissions; and hear little mention of a marriage lasting fifty-seven years. At which the hellhound yowls, and my intuition responds by voicing the suspicion that this married love had long gone cold. But what then is love? What is it, Mona? Mona in the choir, I do care for Mona. I must love some day. Will it be with her; with whom? I wonder where she is, doing what, with whom, this instant. Perhaps with my rival, Alec Smith. Huddling wet but safely sheltered on Pendle Hill. Sipping coffee with him on the square. Drying beside him in the local swimming baths. I wonder what Mr and Mrs Ainsworth do at night, when daily life is done.

Staring at Mr Ainsworth I catch him raise his eyebrows at me, gather in his robes. I shake my arms through my own white folds, not hurrying, and face the congregation. The family seems to be murmuring its appreciation. I bide my time before asking all those present to stand and join with me to sing *Abide with me*. The organ quietly fills the church. I sing, or have my voice perform the motions. I am deciding not to go to the crematorium but to stop here, alone. I shall wait for Mr Ainsworth at the rectory, explain myself at tea before his wife. I gaze upwards for a while, in the direction I believed, in childhood, heaven was to be. I sing loudly and seem to carry the last verse alone upon my shoulders. The organ dims. As the family desired, we say together psalm twenty-three. We come to the brief final hymn, the last chord, to the organ tailing, tailing, without an end. The dark coats bear the coffin. The doors are unbolted; the past presidents turn towards the aisle. Slowly the church empties. I spend final minutes alone with my robes and bookmarks, I go and touch the altar and the choir stalls. I stare round the walls of the vestry. This evening I shall gather up my blues records and the tapes and say goodbye to young Lee, his bright voice and spirit. From there I shall walk to Mona's doorstep. I shall be ringing her bell, taking things as they come. Whatever she may make of it, I shall tell her too I am no longer curate of St Martin's, I am a lover of the blues.

# Candia McWilliam

## A REVOLUTION IN CHINA

IN CHINA, THAT day, all seemed well. The customary moves towards communication were made, none going so far as to be built upon for more than one fragile day. The usual codes of conformity and transparent speech were observed. Hierarchy and the understanding that its imperilment would have certain horrible consequences lay behind each move and every word.

A new batch had arrived, kitchen services for cheerful families fond of animal antics.

Unwrapping an oversized mug from the corrugated-card box that the china had come in, Else held it up to show Miss Montanari, who lifted her chin a very little. This meant that the line would move well, but that Miss Montanari would give a sigh as she sold any item from it, a little sigh of disappointment as she took the money or the cheque or the credit card. She was a woman all shades of rose and grey, and her sighing was part of her colouring, like the sussuration of a copper beech. Miss Montanari was the china buyer; her skill was for locating designs for which she did not care and being sharp enough to know that what she did not like was what people wanted. No one knew of the revolution that had lately taken place within her.

Benedetta Montanari was looking at the new, garish china, as it emerged from the box, with eyes that could no longer look with disdain upon anything.

People had said that she was a woman with taste, that what she had was 'good taste'. There was a short gamut of things that she found acceptable, a boundless flux of things that she did not. All shades of grey and beige suited, and all the many whites, more than in the vocabulary of an Eskimo. Black came into it, but must not be allowed to engulf a room or a body. Black was a white flag of surrender, Miss Montanari had said recently, and no one laughed, any more than they understood.

One morning seven weeks before, on her way to China through the old department store, Miss Montanari had lingered in Hardware. Her hair was a nutmeg red with two wings of pinkish grey, one at either corner of her white, high, forehead. Her skin was thin, her nose proud, and she was held in awe of an old-fashioned sort, meaning that most of the shop's employees recognised her and none had seen where she lived. She dined with the store's directors at Christmas, for it was feared she might put the celebrants off their stride if she were to attend the staff party everyone came to and to which she never alluded. The directors of the store were three cousins and their spouses, none of the six that far above seventy. The cousins would offer a catered meal, usually, in deference to Miss Montanari's supposed foreignness, rather greasy. Once or twice, a visit had been paid to a restaurant where the cost had proved a matter of concern, amid brave play for the bill among the old cousins.

On hooks under a bright display of unbreakable picnic beakers in the hardware department there hung a row of hot-water bottles, some of them already equipped with hot-water-bottle covers. These covers were made of differing materials – plush, fur fabric, a napless velvet like a shaved Angora cat, or a shiny fabric that glistened like cretonne. The covers were made to resemble animals. They were a puppydog, a furry tortoise, a hippo in specs and a russet orang-outang that held a banana you could unpeel and re-enclose, thanks to the miracle of Velcro.

Miss Montanari looked at the outpushed sad lips in the felty face of the ape. She picked up one of its small hairy arms and folded it with the other arm, arranging the banana towards the lips. She gave the raised shaggy knee of the little false animal an encouraging tap and said to the morose face, 'Aren't you a case, just?'

The monkey continued to hang by its neck tab, a security docket clipped through the warnings printed on the clearly printed label about not using unnecessarily hot water when filling a hot-water bottle. Miss Montanari smoothed the stiff whiskers of an adjoining ginger cat bottle-cover, and walked on towards China. Her seniority stayed behind her momentarily as she passed, chilling conversations, interrupting them, turning them over to speculation about her.

Her fault and her interest, in the general opinion of the other buyers and assistants in the store, lay in her quietness. She uttered those sighs, she gave intelligent replies to the questions of customers, but she never told a thing. No one had asked her either, for Miss Montanari was one of those people for whom others invent a story. Her face, which was startling, poised, somewhere off beautiful, equipped her with a character that might not have been the one she possessed. She was polite, or perhaps she did not know the person whom others had made of her.

Benedetta Montanari had come to the department store in order to fold silk scarves and earn enough to feed herself as a young person of twenty in 1954. So she was still young now, four years off the millennium, she thought, hardly sixty at all. No one had dared bring up the question of retirement since no one liked to admit they knew what age she was, or that she had an age.

The day after she'd been amused by the monkey hot-water-bottle cover, Miss Montanari dawdled in Hardware again. She made a purchase; a pink copper jelly mould, brittle with lightness and casting pink shadows. It was large, fluted, domed, with a twist to the fluting that gave it a smart look of near-movement, like the contortions in a cartoon.

'What's its capacity?' asked Miss Montanari.

'It's a jelly mould; for jelly and that,' said Joan, who was a new mother. She was marking down a gross of jam-label sets and already fit to weep, she was that tired.

'It holds three pints,' said Mr Gilbert, who ran Hardware

as a tight ship, but had a soft spot for babies and had known Joan since she had been one.

'Very nice,' said Miss Montanari, ticking her nails inside the glowing copper mould. 'I'll take it. And has it any little ones?'

Joan was sent off by this into thoughts of the needy baby at night. She just looked, calm as a cow, at the older woman, and said, 'Four ninety with your discount'.

Miss Montanari paid.

'Three pints jelly is a rare amount for a woman lives alone,' said Carol Beveridge, who got by alone on sardines and gin and Lactulose.

Mr Gilbert did not react to this, but said to Joan, 'It's good, isn't it, when there's still blossom about and you get a bit of sun? Not that we see much of it down here, but it'll be great out in the old pram, I expect.'

Joan returned to the jam-labelling sets.

'Take a seat,' said Mr Gilbert, and he fetched the kitchen stool they used for reaching the top shelves where the things no one but the aged and country dwellers wanted – peg-mending kits and trivets and onion-bracers and sink tidies.

The next day, Miss Montanari appeared again in Hardware. Joan had stuck up a picture of her baby, Carl, just below the counter, so she could look at it while she counted out change. Carol Beveridge was thinking what she might bring a picture of, tomorrow. She had no photograph, but perhaps you might buy them. She didn't want a poster-type thing. She wanted a photograph that had the messy look as if a moment had been cut with nifty scissors out of a full and busy day. In the photograph of Carl you could see all sorts of things, a shawl, a toy rabbit, a small wool boot, the side of what must be a three-seater sofa. There was a lot of pattern, and the signs of other lives than Carl's, too, a mug with playful animals on it, a scarf, some keys, an elderly hand with a wedding ring. There was even a plant in a pot, with flowers growing out of the plant.

'May I have the family?' asked Miss Montanari.

Mr Gilbert knew what she meant, before either Joan or

Carol Beveridge had to fill the silence with the particular response each might have made to how she had heard the words.

'All the other moulds of that particular pattern? Yes indeed, if we hold them. I may need to fill any gaps by a rummage down in stock. The copper dessert dome, Carol, in the Sandringham pattern; all sizes down from the three-pinter, please.'

The clattering, shiny moulds came one by one out of their tissue to make a procession of pink metal turtles across the counter.

'The lot, please,' said Miss Montanari.

She made the Hardware department nervous, with her air of transforming things into other things, her unliteral deportment – as though she were someone in disguise – and amused look of being disappointed. It wasn't easy to think of her making sequences of milk puddings with her new family of empty moulds.

It was not long after her purchase of all the degrees of jelly dome in the Sandringham style that Miss Montanari began her daily morning visits to other departments of the shop.

She had never before been a person to venture very far out of China, unless it had been to visit her acquaintance the pharmacist, who had a short lunch hour because of the responsibility that went with her calling. The two ladies would meet for an infrequent but pleasant meal. They shook hands at Christmas and exchanged gifts of good soap. Their hands were cool.

In Linens, Miss Montanari's browsing went on for several mornings. Jessie, whose gypsy hair and leaning bust frothed and toppled over the linens counter with its inlaid brass rule for measuring sheets, thought Miss Montanari wanted something, over and above just bedlinens, and said so to Karen, who said through prim cold lips, 'Don't I know what?', and felt the pulse of the love bites under her rollneck blouse.

'It wasn't that I meant,' Jessie said, shaking her dripping pendant golden earrings. Her hair was so thick it caught their chimes and held them so they stayed silent. 'I mean she's hanging about. Like she wanted to talk. Like the ditherers.'

The ditherers were old ladies who came in, like drinkers visiting far-flung off-licences, infrequently but regularly, and discussed for hours very fine points of pillowcase size or duvet pattern or handkerchief-adornment for some much younger relative, usually rarely met or even, Jessie feared, invented. Infant bedlinen attracted the most.

'She's never a ditherer,' said Karen, eyeing Miss Montanari's careful waist and ankles. 'She's got a secret, more like.'

Miss Montanari, though, had wanted to talk, and went, with Jessie, into some detail about the items she eventually did buy, two dense, light, creamy blankets bound with slipper-satin around all four edges and several pillowcases embroidered with strong wild flowers as if off someone's national costume. As an afterthought, Miss Montanari also bought six bags of cedarwood chippings – 'to keep linens wholesome in the old country way' were the words screen-printed on to the sisal bag – and a bright green sleeping bag sewn into segments, screen-printed with the cheerful, if optimistic, features of a holidaying caterpillar at the head end, and all down the segments with a double run of merry caterpillar feet. Jessie tied up these bulky items and asked if they should be delivered.

Miss Montanari said, 'What a blissful idea.' It was what she had heard said.

'Not natural, that woman,' said Karen. 'She behaves like a customer.'

Miss Montanari arrived later at work than usual the following Thursday, delivery day for the department store. She took delivery of the parcel from the place where she worked.

'Come in and have some coffee, Arthur,' she said to the delivery man for the firm. Although she had known his name for over twenty years, she had never used it before. 'I am grateful to you for bringing my parcel. It was rather heavy for me.'

Miss Montanari made some coffee and stood while Arthur drank his, since he seemed not to want to sit down. He saw the line of twisty pink metal helmets all sizes, just cluttered about in the sitting-room. His wife would never do that. The whole flat was dead bare, modern you'd call it, apart from that procession of the things that looked like nothing better than pudding moulds though he'd swear she paid an artistic price for them – and now the parcel. She could hardly wait until he had gone to open her big parcel, invitingly taped and bound with twine.

She thanked Arthur fulsomely. He had left most of his coffee and the almond biscuit she had put on a plate beside it. Miss Montanari realised that she had given him what she would have prepared for herself. She had not adjusted. She felt this slippage of good manners in herself as acutely as a symptom.

Miss Montanari began to open her parcel of purchases from the shop where she had worked since 1954. She enjoyed punching a knife through the brown tape over the joins in the box and drawing it fast along the crevice, feeling the blade tickling tissue within. She flapped open the cardboard lugs of the box, unpeeled the stickers that held the tissue paper furled around their secret innards, and lifted out each weighty, cool folio of pillowcase with its vehement floral edge. She smelt the cedarwood although it was still wrapped, and could almost feel the warmth of the blankets buried within the box. She would leave the giant caterpillar until later. Maybe she would still get to take it on a great trek through the north, or maybe it would just rest until one day it would solidify, harden and crack and a great fabric butterfly emerge.

She sat among her shopping for a time, enjoying the feeling she supposed was no longer noticeable to those who regularly received deliveries, or, indeed, post.

She dressed carefully, rinsed the delivery man's cup, ate his almond biscuit and poured a few of the cedarwood chippings into a handkerchief, which she knotted and slipped into her handbag.

Miss Montanari was losing her touch. She was beginning to cease to know how to define what things it was right or wrong to like. She would have known before to give the delivery man from the store the coffee he would have liked, the biscuit he might have liked. She would have known unerringly, by gauging her own depth of distaste, by asking herself what she would not have liked, to what degree and how, and offering whatever, according to this negative and unerring canon, proved apposite.

But her distaste had fled. She was prey to an uncritical enthusiasm and curiosity. The possible cause struck her, and she dismissed it from her mind. She had not the time.

On the day when the parcel arrived, Miss Montanari was not able until her tea-break – she forwent lunch since she had arrived late that morning – to make her trip to a department of the store. She found herself in Toiletries. She conducted a long and quite friendly conversation with an assistant who did not seem to know who she was and treated her with the indulgence bestowed on customers, even when she asked the girl what soap she recommended for dry knees and elbows, even when she decided not perhaps to go for the soap but instead to buy a petalled bathing hat and some nail extensions for a daughter Miss Montanari was moved to pull out of the air by the sudden materialising at her eye's far corner of her acquaintance and occasional luncheon companion, the pharmacist.

'She's quite like you,' Miss Montanari said to the assistant, who had dark hair on her arms, white skin and strongly apricot black-rooted hair on her head. 'The same colouring.'

'Clever girl then,' said the assistant, whose young green eyes had received four compliments, that's two compliments each, in the club last night, and who was hoping to knock off when this old bird was through.

'Have you tried these temporary tattoos for your daughter?' Clea tugged at her orange hair and sized up Miss Montanari. Not all that weird, wanting to dress young in private. Not when you'd seen what Clea had seen. There was blokes come in here in frocks looking for depilatory bold as brass, a pair of twins at it one week, splendid ladies in tweeds with a dog they'd handed over to the commissionaire and hands like bloody octopussies, all fur and fingers. This old bird was just suffering from being too correct. It was understandable she might want to rush off home and dress a bit nylon. Maybe it was her good man wanted her with the nail extensions. Perhaps Clea should recommend the Eyelure diamante-tip lash extensions fashioned without cruelty to man or beast.

Miss Montanari fumbled with her change and moved swiftly away, having thanked the assistant with the orange hair, more unsettled than she had thought she could be by the presence of the pharmacist.

These forays into territory beyond China persisted for several more weeks, each day bringing with it at least one conversation during which Miss Montanari managed to shed the coolness that had accompanied her throughout her life in the department store. She achieved certain small triumphs, from time to time being almost certain that her interlocutor did not know who she was, that she was causing no ripple by her break with her own habits. She was speaking, whenever she could, only to recent employees, the youngest boys and girls, who had not had time to form an idea of her, perhaps even, mercifully, did not know who she was.

'She's missing having had children,' said Mr Gilbert of Hardware to Mr Stuart of Photographic, who had never once taken a film from the hand of Miss Montanari and who therefore had no idea of her home life, leisure time, or loved ones, which was not the case with the other employees of the department store.

'She's missing, *not* having had children, do you mean?' asked Mr Stuart. 'Oh no, I see what you mean, right enough. She's a mystery woman. But good at her job. And handsome.'

'Somewhere near beautiful,' said Mr Gilbert, who kept Mr Stuart right on these things since Mr Stuart was not, as he put it, in the business of appreciating women in the very flesh. Mr Stuart lived with a friend whose widowerhood had come like balm in reward for forbearance. Mr Stuart and his friend kept quails in their greenhouse and went on watercolour courses around the coast of Great Britain. It was a beautiful life, when the only thing you ever need complain about was rain or cats, Mr Stuart said to his friend. He described Miss Montanari often to his friend, for her air of foreignness, her dislocated elegance, 'like Garbo's,' he said, meaning something about her private life that he could not say aloud. And that could explain her talking to the young girls quite so much lately. There was only so much hiding a body might take.

'It'll be she's Italian,' Mr Stuart's friend said.

'She's born in Inverness even if the blood has garlic in it,' replied Mr Stuart, wanting his own romance of Miss Montanari to be kept intact, as Mr Gilbert wished her to be pining for the bonny babes she never was mother to.

'It's not unusual for a woman of the older sort to take on. Especially if she's sailed through the earlier part,' said Else to Lindsay Kerr in China, one day when they saw Miss Montanari smiling at some night-lights in the shape of mush-rooms and moons, as they were all about to leave.

'See that,' Lindsay shrieked, muffling it at once. But Miss Montanari, putting on her new overcoat of mauve and russet mohair with a swing back, purchased in the Outerwear department two weeks before, did not turn around.

Else and Lindsay Kerr looked with astonishment at the neatly filled-in order form that was inadequately hidden in a pile on the China cashdesk. Miss Montanari had put in an order for mugs with a message on them, a number of such mugs, the very mugs that she had made an infernal fuss about permitting to be sold at all through her precious China outlet.

'I've a good mind . . .'

'Oh, leave it, Lind,' said Else. 'Leave it, leave it. Any road, you've not. Leave it with me. Come away out of it now and we'll go and get blootered at the Deacon.'

'Ech, posh,' said Lindsay Kerr.

In this way Else kept events in China on an even keel until the day when Miss Montanari, having unpacked the last of the oversized kitchen crocks, decorated so gloriously, radiantly, appealingly, with animal antics, slipped upstairs to the staff ladies to check the neatness of the wings of grey in her nutmeg hair and her thin formidable face and to wash her cool hands, before slipping downstairs back to China, which she wanted to leave without fuss, simply handing over to her colleagues in token of farewell the personalised mugs with the name of the recipient and, crammed in rather, the words 'From Benedetta (Montanari)'.

Later, when Miss Montanari had been scattered, the most elderly of all the three cousins spoke at the service of remembrance. He spoke as though the store were a ship or a great school or a regiment. He spoke of all it had given to Miss Montanari, how it had been for her more than a home.

At the stand-up drinks after the service, she was quick in the memory of the youngest people there, who kept saying to each other and to the older employees of the shop, 'She *was* someone, we thought she *was* someone.'

'What,' said Else, loyal now she was in charge of China, and drunk too on the wine Miss Montanari had surprisingly left to be drunk on this occasion, 'and not just a shop assistant?'

'Girls,' intervened Mr Stuart. 'Girls, indeed now, stop a minute, would you? Lend me your expertise. Are these flowers not a surprise in themselves? Bearing in mind like what she was . . . Benedetta?' In death Miss Montanari fitted her long-hidden Christian name.

Tottering-flowered blue delphiniums, bunched silverleafed stocks and heaps of rowdy roses stuffed in containers all anyhow filled the borders of the church hall, ruffled bright coarse flowers embroidered roughly around the edges of the plain white hall in which those who had known Miss Montanari for the longest still slumbered in the illusion that it was they, not the people who had seen her in the last weeks of her life, who knew her best.

'We should perhaps have known it was the end,' said Mr Stuart, who had brought his friend, the widower.

'My word,' said the widower, 'a real party, this is. Wine, and *several* jellies.'

# Hilary Mantel

## TIES THAT BIND

LOUISA SAID, 'I wish something would happen. I wouldn't mind if it were bad.'

Alice, her lunch-date, looked hard at her. A forkful of green pasta was poised in the air. 'Yes, you would,' she said.

Louisa sighed. 'I just need a change, that's all. I feel tied. I need to go to new places, meet new people.' Hopelessly, she pursued a piece of lollo rosso. 'Adjust my . . . my self-perception.'

'I thought you'd already adjusted it,' Alice said. 'You go to acupuncture. Self-defence.'

'It's not enough. Look, it's not as if I'm after a man in my life. I mean, I'm a realist, I know there aren't any.'

'Some,' Alice said cautiously. 'You can get them a couple of hours a week, like cleaning agencies. Tuesday and Thursday, something like that. Or do you remember my Tony? I used to have a share of him, with Corinne Docherty and that ginger-haired girl, I told you about her, the one who left to go and sell photocopiers.'

'Yes, that's all right for you,' Louisa said. She waved to the waiter for another mineral water. When she looked back at Alice, the veiled insult was hardly veiled at all.

She ran her eyes over her friend. Alice was not fat, you couldn't say that, she acted fat, that was all; her clothes lacked cohesion, her shirt always creeping out of her waistband, her jackets creased across her broad back. And look at the way she sat there, slumped in her chair; look at the way she slurped dressing on her salad! 'I want more for myself,' Louisa said. 'I have never thought I was meant for such a constrained existence.'

The waiter – he was a man, of course, but neither of them noticed him – took their plates away. He creaked the sweet trolley in their direction, and stood mute while they had their ritual debate about pudding. He served them, and offered cream, and they waved it away, and him with it.

'I do wish they'd modernise this sweet trolley,' Louisa complained.

'Yugh, but s'place s'awright, round corner, s'easy,' Alice said, through a mouthful of calories.

Louisa wanted to reach across and slap her, as her own mother used to do: don't talk with your mouth full!

'Alice,' she asked, 'why do you think it's wrong to want an exciting life?'

Alice swallowed her mouthful of cake. 'Because the excitement is usually at the expense of someone else.'

'Why is it more reprehensible . . .' Louisa struggled with the word; one Campari and orange did for her, in the vocabulary department. 'Why is it more reprehensible to want a life with a bit of dash and drama in it, than to want a life in a cottage with roses round the door?'

Alice took her last gulp of wine-by-the-glass. She didn't answer.

Louisa leaned forward. 'My basic problem is credibility,' she said. 'Oh, you're an old friend, I can tell you.'

'Sure,' Alice said. 'I'm like an old carpet. Just walk the dog-shit in.'

Louisa ignored her. 'You see these little slags in the office getting all excited when it comes to Friday morning. That tart Shona said, what are you doing this weekend, Miss Howell, are you going to your mother's again?'

'So that's what's worrying you,' Alice said. She sipped her double expresso. 'Not that your life isn't exciting, but that people don't believe it is?'

'If they believed it was, it would be,' said Louisa, with a flash of sense. They paid the bill and went to the Ladies.

*

When she was washing her hands, and Louisa was rummaging in her make-up bag, Alice said, 'I could fix something for you. A bit of drama.'

'What?' Louisa said sceptically. 'A blind date?'

'Oh no. I wouldn't know anyone you'd like.'

'No, I don't think you would.'

'I'd thought . . . well, I don't know exactly . . . but what are friends for?'

'What? What are you going to do?' Louisa's lip pencil quivered in the air.

'You won't enjoy it if you know beforehand,' Alice said. She smiled, and Louisa saw that there was a fragment of spinach lodged between her teeth. She thought, the years go by so fast; I am getting old.

Two days later, Louisa was yawning at her work-station, when her extension buzzed. 'A Miss Mildmay is downstairs in the reception area, she says she has an appointment.'

Louisa's heart skipped: just the once. After all, it couldn't be a very good drama, if it was Alice who had planned it. But frankly, she'd expected it out of office hours.

For security reasons, you had to go down to meet your visitors. Alice had her briefcase with her, and looked as professional as she was ever going to get; her skirt was an inch too long, Louisa noticed, and she still hadn't managed to get her fringe cut. 'Miss Mildmay,' she said dotingly, offering her hand.

'Miss Howell,' Alice simpered, brushing fingertips.

'Do come up,' Louisa beamed.

In the lift she tried to break the pretence, pinching Alice on the arm: 'Well, what's new?'

Alice didn't answer; she just smiled at herself fatly in the mirror glass that lined the lift.

They stepped out on the fifth floor. Louisa said, 'OK, come on then, what's the surprise?'

Alice said, 'This,' and hit her over the head with her briefcase.

*

Fortunately – as Louisa realised later – it was one of the light-weight female executive type, so it didn't knock her out or mark her for life; but it did stun her. She bent double, and peered fuzzily at Alice's big knees, and then gagged as Alice's arm locked itself around her neck. She clawed at the arm, at the thick wool jacket, then her own arm flailed out for support as Alice began to walk.

From the lifts there were only two ways to go; Alice understood the layout of offices, and she chose the right one. Dragging Louisa with her, shouldering open the swing doors, she strode into the main, open-plan area.

Louisa's self-defence classes hadn't done her much good. Instead of twisting her head free, screaming for help while at the same time jabbing at her attacker's eyes, she bleated, 'Alice, Alice, let me go, you bloody idiot.' There had not even been time to activate her rape alarm.

Alice snarled, 'Mrs Bradshaw to you, you whore.'

'Wugh?' Louisa said. 'Wugh Mrs Bradshaw?' Her chin was forced up at a painful angle; it was hard to articulate.

'Who am I? Who am I? You know bloody fine who I am! I'm Gareth's wife, you sad baggage. Didn't you bother to ask him his surname?'

Chairs and heads swivelled. Eyes peeped over partitions. Alice yanked Louisa's hair, hard, and some of it came out . . . not by the roots, but still . . .

'Call Security,' someone suggested. Nobody did it. Desks were deserted, computer screens blinked unattended.

'Get your own man, can't you?' Alice snarled. 'If you can, you miserable runt. Why are you so skinny, are you HIV positive?'

'Get her off,' a voice called, without much urgency. 'She's murdering Miss Howell.'

Alice turned, to face another segment of her audience. Head clamped under her arm, Louisa turned with her, eyes down on the carpet tiles, her body sagging at the knees. Her tunic sweater was riding up over her bottom; she could see feet, a ring of feet. There were boots laced up to the knee, there were sensible low-heeled courts, and the four-inch spikes on which that tart Shona had been tottering around all week; and there were men's feet, shuffling backwards, peeping from under the room dividers. Tears sprang to Louisa's eyes. 'Dugh break my jaw, Alice. Dugh break my jaw, please.'

Then – tightening her grip, one hand in Louisa's hair – Alice began to talk. 'This bitch,' she said, 'has been screwing my husband Gareth twice a week for the last eighteen months. And you lot, I bet you had no idea, had you? Little Miss Butter-wouldn't-melt, that's what you all thought. Little Miss Carpet Slipper. Little Miss Ovaltine. Oh, come on, admit it.' Alice put on a coy, high-pitched voice. 'What are you doing this weekend, Louisa? Oh, I'm going to the vicarage tea-party!' Alice snorted. She reverted to her normal voice. 'I'll tell you what she does, shall I? Gareth said, "I can't live a lie, Alice: we do bondage." Yes, that's what Gareth said. She's got this kind of leather vest, where her tits peep out.'

'Oh, yuk!' said a bright voice above the ring of feet. It was that tart, Shona. 'Then what do they do? Is there whipping and that?'

Louisa said, 'Is nugh Bradshaw. Is Alice Mughmay.' Her mouth was swelling up – the briefcase's combination lock had caught her lip. 'Nugh nugh anyone called Gareth.'

'Oh, nugh nugh,' Alice sneered. 'Shut up, you pox-ridden baggage. Let these people hear the truth about your nasty little double life.'

She began to hit Louisa then: to slap her on the crown of the head, as if she were a tambourine. And all at once she dropped her – Louisa falling on hands and knees to the floor – and walked out unmolested, the way she'd come in.

Some months passed; yet the noise was no less as the waiters pulled out the chairs with a bow and a scrape, and the first sip of wine still numbed the soft palate.

'Just a small scar,' Alice said. 'Interesting really. Men will wonder how you got it.'

'But my tooth!' Louisa waved a breadstick in the air. 'I had to have my tooth capped!'

'I paid for it, didn't I?' Alice dug into her sauté potatoes. 'Come to that, you never compensated me for my briefcase. It got a dent in it.'

'I asked for excitement,' Louisa said. 'I didn't ask for violence.'

'Well, beggars can't be choosers,' Alice said.

Because of the notoriety, Louisa had been forced to leave her job. She had moved into office equipment sales, like the ginger-haired girl who used to share Alice's boyfriend. Her life had changed. 'That's what you wanted, isn't it?' Alice said.

'Suppose so,' Louisa said. She stabbed her fork into a dry chicken breast.

After all, she travelled a lot now. There were businessmen in hotels, who sat in the bar, rattling the ice in their Jack Daniels. She would hesitate in the doorway; their eyes would pass over her. She never looked into their faces, finding it difficult; her smile would focus on their throats, on the knots of their ties. There had been that rep in Glasgow: short, but exceedingly forceful. There had been the man who had taken her business card, and next day sent her an orchid in a box; that had been the high point, to date. One man had got carried away, and given her an order for a gross of suspension files and an ibico® IBIMATIC Kombo Deluxe binding system ('punch and bind in one'). It's state-of-the-art, she'd assured him, as she picked up her price list from his morning pillow and flung her dirty underwear into her case; but his secretary had rung next day and cancelled it, and had been rather sharp about the whole thing.

She glowered at Alice. Alice's eyes were roving in the direction of the sweet trolley; all these months on, it had not been modernised at all, and still creaked towards them with its freight of jellified mousses and cardboard gâteau. One day, she thought, I will meet the ginger-haired girl at some trade exhibition. I will tell her about Alice's true character. You're lucky to have got away unscarred, I'll say. When Tony left her, she was so sick with jealousy, you know, because I'd got this big affair going with a bloke called Gareth . . .

She said to Alice, 'You shouldn't have said that thing about a leather vest. You should have called it a bustier.'

'No, it was a vest,' Alice said. 'I can see it all.'

Louisa closed her eyes. Gareth came fleetingly to view: the drooling lust on his face, his member erect below his harness. Then she saw the ginger-haired girl, sitting opposite, hanging on her every word, licking her pink lips as she, Louisa, shivered a little and leaned forward to confide: 'Gareth, now, that was something special . . .'

Louisa picked up another breadstick, and pointed it at Alice like a witchdoctor pointing the bone. Then delicately, she put it to her lips and began to nibble it: nibble nibble nibble, towards the unamiable future, and towards the confining darkness that will soon embrace us all.

# BIOGRAPHICAL NOTES

**Dannie Abse** was born and educated in Cardiff and studied medicine in London. He published his first book of poems as a student and since then has had nine collections published, the most recent being *On the Evening Road* (1994). His *Selected Poems 1950–90* were brought out by Penguin who also published his autobiographical novel, *Ash on a Young Man's Sleeve*. He is an Hon. D.Lit. (University of Wales 1989) and a Fellow of the Royal Society of Literature.

**Fleur Adcock's** most recent collections of poetry are *Selected Poems, The Incident Book* and *Time Zones*. She is the editor of *The Faber Book of Twentieth-Century Women's Poetry* (1987) and co-editor (with Jacqueline Simms) of *The Oxford Book of Creatures* (1995). She has also published volumes of translations from Romanian and medieval Latin poetry, including *The Virgin and the Nightingale*.

**Moniza Alvi** was born in Lahore and grew up in Hertfordshire. Her first collection of poems, *The Country at My Shoulder*, appeared in 1993; it was selected for the New Generation Poets promotion and shortlisted for the T. S. Eliot and Whitbread poetry prizes. Her second collection, *A Bowl of Warm Air*, appears in 1996. She teaches in a comprehensive school in south London.

**Donald Atkinson** has been a freelance writer since 1986. His narrative sequence, *A Sleep of Drowned Fathers* (1989) won the 1990 Aldeburgh Poetry Festival Prize for best first collection, and he has since published two more, *Graffiti for Hard Hearts* (1992) and *Othello in the Pyramid of Dreams* (1996). In 1995 he won a Writer's Award from the Arts Council of England.

**Murray Bail** was born in 1941 and lives in Sydney. 'Obliqua' is the opening chapter of a work in progress, *Eucalyptus*. His other books of fiction are the novels *Homesickness* and *Holden's Performance*, and a collection of stories, *The Drover's Wife*.

**Paul Bailey** is the author of *At the Jerusalem* (Somerset Maugham Award), *A Distant Likeness*, *Peter Smart's Confessions* and *Gabriel's Lament* (both short-listed for the Booker Prize), *Old Soldiers*, *Trespasses*, *Sugar Cane* and a memoir, *An Immaculate Mistake*. He is researching a biography of the painter Francis Bacon for Hamish Hamilton, and completing *Kitty and Virgil* which will be published in 1996.

**Martin Bax** is a paediatric neurologist at the Charing Cross Westminster Medical School in London. He has published books on normal child development and problems of disabled children and young people. He is editor of the medical journal *Development in Medicine and Child Neurology*. He is also editor of the literary and arts magazine *Ambit* and has published one novel, *The Hospital Ship*.

**Nalinaksha Bhattacharya** was born in Calcutta in 1949 and spent a part of his childhood in a remote village of Bangladesh. He took a degree in science and published some stories and a novel in Bengali before turning to writing in English. His first novel, *Hem and Football*, was published in 1992 and his second, *Hem and Maxine*, came out in 1995. He now lives and writes in New Delhi.

**Alison Brackenbury** was born in Lincolnshire in 1953. She has published five collections of poetry, including *Selected Poems* (1991) and *1829* (1995).

**Simon Brittan** was born in 1957, and teaches English at the University of East Anglia. He has written on poetry and Renaissance comedy, has translated from German and Italian and is currently working on an edition of Ser Giovanni's *Il Pecorone*, a fourteenth-century collection of *novelle*. In 1994 he founded the *New Poetry Quarterly*, which he edits with N. S. Thompson.

**Alan Brownjohn** was born in 1931. Formerly a teacher and lecturer, he has been a full-time writer since 1979. Collected editions of his poetry appeared in 1983 and 1988. His last individual volume was *In the Cruel Arcade* (1994). His novel, *The Way You Tell Them*, won the Authors' Club Prize for the most promising first novel of 1990; a second novel, *The Long Shadows*, appears in 1996 in Romanian translation only.

**Simon Burt** was born in Wiltshire in 1947 and educated at Downside and Trinity College, Dublin. He now lives in London. He has written a collection of short stories, *Floral Street*, and two novels, *The Summer of the White Peacock* and *Just Like Eddie*.

**A. S. Byatt**'s first novel, *The Shadow of the Sun*, appeared in 1964 and was followed by *The Game* (1967), *The Virgin in the Garden* (1978), *Still Life* (1985), *Possession* (1990, winner of the Booker Prize for Fiction) and *Angels and Insects* (1992). She has published three collections of stories, *Sugar and Other Stories* (1987), *The Matisse Stories* (1994) and *The Djinn in the Nightingale's Eye* (1994). A volume of critical essays, *Passions of the Mind*, appeared in 1991 and her new novel, *Babel Tower*, will be published in 1996. Together with Peter Porter, she will be editing *New Writing 6*.

**Carmen Callil** is Australian but has lived in London since

1960. She founded Virago in 1972 and was its publisher and managing director until 1982, and chairman until 1995. From 1982 to 1993 she was managing director of Chatto and Windus and the Hogarth Press. She is now writing a book, with Colm Tóibín, entitled *The Modern Library: Fiction in English 1950–2000*.

**Lana Citron** was born in Dublin in 1969; a history graduate of Trinity College, Dublin, she has been living and working in London for the past two years and has only recently started writing. 'Lapdog Days' is her first published work.

**Louis de Bernières** was born in 1954, and has worked as a landscape gardener, a mechanic and a teacher. He is now a full-time writer. He is the author of *The War of Don Emmanuel's Nether Parts* (Commonwealth Writers' Prize for best first novel 1991), *Señor Vivo and the Coca Lord* (Commonwealth Writers' Prize, best book Eurasia Region 1992), *The Troublesome Offspring of Cardinal Guzman* and *Captain Corelli's Mandolin* (Commonwealth Writers' Prize, best book 1995).

**Michael Donaghy** lives in North London where he plays Irish traditional music with various combinations of musicians. His collections include *Shibboleth*, Oxford University Press, 1988, and *Errata*, Oxford University Press, 1993. He has won the Whitbread Award for Poetry, the Geoffrey Faber Memorial Award, an Arts Council Writer's Award, and a grant from the Ingram Merrill Foundation. He has also published studies on subjects as diverse as Japanese folding screens, ancient Mediterranean agriculture, and Chimpanzee behaviour. He is currently working on a screenplay.

**Maura Dooley's** first collection of poetry, *Explaining Magnetism*, won a Poetry Book Society Recommendation in 1992. Her second collection is due in 1996. She is currently editing the *Bloodaxe Book of Love Poetry* and a collection of essays entitled *How Novelists Work*.

**Ian Duhig** was born in 1954 and lives in Leeds. He worked for fifteen years with homeless people in London, Northern Ireland and Yorkshire. In 1987 he won the National Poetry Competition and in 1991 his first book, *The Bradford Count*, was shortlisted for the Whitbread Prize. His second, *The Mersey Goldfish*, appeared in 1995.

**Alistair Elliot** spent two years in Iran but has since lived in Newcastle, where he now writes and translates full-time. His collected poems, *My Country*, appeared in 1989; he has more recently published *Turning the Stones*, *French Love Poems* and Euripides' *Medea*. His next book will be a translation of Valéry's *La Jeune Parque*.

**Sarah J. Evans** was born in 1966 and lives and works in Northamptonshire. Her work, so far mainly short stories, has been published in magazines and small press anthologies, and she hopes now to embark on a full-length novel.

**Gavin Ewart** was born in 1916 and studied at Christ's College, Cambridge, and served as a Captain in the Royal Artillery in the Second World War. He worked for the British Council from 1946 to 1952. His first poems appeared in Grigson's *New Verse* (1933), and since then he has published many collections; in 1978 he edited the *Penguin Book of Light Verse*. He has also written verse for children and the libretto for an opera, *Tobermory*, with music by John Gardner. He died in October 1995.

**Maggie Gee** has written seven novels, *Dying in Other Words* (1981), *The Burning Book* (1983), *Light Years* (1985), *Grace* (1987), *Where Are the Snows* (1991), *Lost Children* (1994) and *The Keeper of the Gate*. She has been Writing Fellow at the University of East Anglia, and an Honorary Visiting Fellow of Sussex University. She is a Fellow of the Royal Society of Literature.

**Alasdair Gray** was born in Glasgow in 1934, studied at

Glasgow Art School and has since lived by painting and writing. He is currently working on *The Anthology of Prefaces*, a collection of introductions to great books in vernacular English. His latest novel, *Mavis Belfrage*, will appear in 1996.

**Lavinia Greenlaw** was born in 1962 in London where she still lives. She has published two pamphlets of poems (*The Cost of Getting Lost in Space*, 1991, and *Love from a Foreign City*, 1992). Her first full-length collection, *Night Photograph*, was published by Faber in 1993 and was shortlisted for the Whitbread Poetry Prize and the Forward Prize. In 1995 she was Writer-in-Residence at the Science Museum and British Council Fellow in Writing at Amherst College, Massachusetts. She is currently finishing her second collection.

**Romesh Gunesekera** was born in Sri Lanka and now lives in London. His first novel, *Reef*, was shortlisted for the Booker Prize and the Guardian Fiction Prize in 1994. His book of short stories, *Monkfish Moon*, was published in 1992. He was awarded a Yorkshire Post best fiction prize and his books are being translated into Italian, French, Spanish, German, Dutch, Norwegian, Hebrew and other languages.

**Abdulrazak Gurnah** was born in Zanzibar, Tanzania, in 1948. He was educated there and in England, and now teaches literature at the University of Kent at Canterbury. His books include *Memory of Departure*, *Pilgrims Way*, *Dottie* and, most recently, the Booker Prize short-listed *Paradise*. He is currently completing a novel.

**David Harsent's** *Selected Poems* appeared in 1989; his most recent collection, *News from the Front*, was published in 1993. He wrote the libretto for Sir Harrison Birtwhistle's opera, *Gawain*, which had its world première at Covent Garden in 1991. Two other music theatre pieces are in preparation, together with a large cycle of work in different mediums, provisionally titled *The Inspector of Underground Rooms*. He is also working on an English version of *The Sorrow of Sarajevo*, a collection of poems written under siege by the Bosnian poet, Goran Simic.

**Paul Henry** was born in Aberystwyth and works as a careers adviser in Cardiff. He received a Gregory Award in 1989 for a draft of his collection, *Time Pieces* (1991); his songs, in Welsh and English, have been broadcast on television and radio. His second collection, *Captive Audience*, is soon to be published.

**Philip Hensher**'s first novel, *Other Lulus*, is now available in paperback; his second novel, *Kitchen Venom*, appears in April 1996. His short stories have appeared in magazines and anthologies, and have been broadcast on BBC Radio; they will appear in a collection, *Zuleika Dobson in the Great War*. He wrote the libretto to Thomas Ades' opera, *Powder Her Face*, premièred in Cheltenham and at the Almeida Festival in July 1995.

**Michael Hofmann** was born in 1957 in Freiburg and came to England in 1961. He has published three books of poems, most recently *Corona, Corona* (1993), edited *After Ovid: New Metamorphoses* (1994) with James Lasdun and translated a dozen works from the German: his translation of *The Film Explainer* by his late father Gert Hofmann, won the *Independent*'s Foreign Fiction Prize for 1995. A new book of poems and a book of essays will be published next year.

**Richard Holmes** was born in 1945 and educated at Churchill College, Cambridge. He has written *Shelley: The Pursuit* (1974, Somerset Maugham Award); *Footsteps: Adventures of a Romantic Biographer* (1985); *Coleridge: Early Visions* (1989, Whitbread Book of the Year Prize); and *Dr Johnson and Mr Savage* (1993, James Tait Black Memorial Prize). He is a Fellow of the Royal Society of Literature and was appointed an OBE in 1992. He lives in London and Norfolk with the novelist, Rose Tremain, and is working on the second volume of Coleridge's biography, *Darker Reflections*.

**Miroslav Holub** was born in Bohemia in 1923. After the war he studied science and medicine at the Charles University and worked in the department of philosophy and history of science and in a psychiatric ward. He became MD in 1953, joined the immunological section of the Biological Institute of the Czech Academy of Science in 1954 and obtained his Ph.D. the year his first book of poems appeared. Since 1969, he has published almost one book a year, and has been widely translated – fortunately, since between 1970 and 1980 he became a non-person in his own country. He has written sixteen books of poetry and nine collections of essays and other prose.

**Douglas Houston** was born in 1947 and studied at Hull University. He worked in Britain and Germany before returning to Hull in 1978 to study for a Ph.D., a period vital to his development as a poet. Since 1981 he has lived in Dyfed, working as a freelance writer and teaching part-time at the University College of Wales, Aberystwyth. His collections of poetry are *With the Offal Eaters* (1986) and *The Hunters in the Snow* (1994).

**Michael Hulse** grew up in Stoke-on-Trent and Germany and now lives in Cologne, where he works in publishing and television. His collections of poetry include *Knowing and Forgetting* (1981), *Propaganda* (1985), *Eating Strawberries in the Necropolis* (1991) and *Mother of Battles* (1991). He co-edited the anthology *The New Poetry* (1993) and has won the National Poetry Competition and Eric Gregory and Cholmondeley Awards. He has translated German literature and his criticism appears widely in literary journals.

**Sarah LeFanu** has edited five anthologies of new fiction, most recently *How Maxine Learned to Love Her Legs and Other Tales of Growing Up* (Aurora Metro, 1995) and *Obsession*

(Serpent's Tail, 1995, co-edited with Stephen Hayward). Her book on feminism and science fiction, *In the Chinks of the World Machine*, won the Emily Toth award, and she has recently completed her first novel. She has three children, lives near Bristol and is a part-time tutor in women's fiction at the University of Bristol's Department for Continuing Education.

**Gwyneth Lewis** was born in 1959 and studied at Cambridge and Oxford where she did research on literary forgeries. She writes in both Welsh (her first language) and English. Her first Welsh collection, *Sonedau Redsa*, was published in 1990. Her first English volume, *Parables & Faxes*, followed in 1995, was shortlisted for a Forward Prize and won the Aldeburgh Poetry Festival Prize for best first collection. In 1987 she was one of the *Poetry Review*'s New British Poets, and in 1988 she won a major Eric Gregory Award.

**Douglas Livingstone** was born in Kuala Lumpur, Malaya, and was sent to South Africa as an evacuee in 1942 aged ten. As a bacteriologist he worked in various hospital laboratories in the two Rhodesias. Since 1964 he has been employed on the microbial aspects of sea pollution off Durban. He is the author of several poetry collections including *Sjambok*, *Eyes Closed against the Sun*, *Selected Poems* and, most recently, *A Littoral Zone*.

**Jamie McKendrick** was born in Liverpool in 1955. He taught for several years at the University of Salerno and now works as a freelance teacher and writer in Oxford. His first book of poems, *The Sirocco Room*, was published in 1991; his second, *The Kiosk on the Brink*, in 1993.

**Candia McWilliam** was born in Edinburgh in 1955, where she was educated until, at the age of thirteen, she went to school in England. Her first novel, *A Case of Knives*, appeared in 1988 and was followed by *A Little Stranger*

(1989) and *Debatable Land* (1994). Her stories have appeared in *New Writing 3* and *4*.

**Paul Magrs** (the g is silent) was born in Sunderland in 1969 and was brought up in Newton Aycliffe in County Durham. He was educated at Woodham Comprehensive in Aycliffe and at Lancaster University. His story 'Patient Iris' was published in *New Writing 4*. *Marked for Life*, his first novel, was published by Chatto and Windus in 1995, to be followed by *Does it Show?* in 1996 and by *Playing Out*, a collection of stories, in 1997.

**Hilary Mantel** was born in Derbyshire in 1952. She has been a book and film critic and, since 1985, has published seven novels, the settings of which include Saudi Arabia, Southern Africa in the 1950s and Paris during the French Revolution. Her latest book is *An Experiment in Love* (1995). She is working on an eighth novel.

**E. A. Markham**, born in the Caribbean (Montserrat) in 1939, has lived mainly in Britain since the 1950s. He has directed the *Caribbean Theatre Workshop*, edited *Artrage* magazine and, in the past decade, worked in the arts in Papua New Guinea and Ulster; he now heads the creative writing programme at Sheffield Hallam University. He is the editor of *Hinterland* (the Bloodaxe Book of Caribbean poetry) and the *Penguin Book of Caribbean Short Stories*. He has published two books of short stories and six collections of poetry, including *Misapprehensions* (Anvil, 1995). He edits the magazine *Sheffield Thursday*.

**Timothy Mo** is the author of five novels and Chairman, Financial Comptroller and Publisher-in-Chief at Paddleless Press. He studied history at St John's College, Oxford, from 1969 to 1972 and began his first novel in late 1974. He speaks two Asian languages haltingly and is literate in one. At the age of forty-five he has just started learning Spanish.

He is a nationally qualified instructor with the British Sub-Aqua Club.

**Sean O'Brien** is the author of four collections of poems, most recently *Ghost Train*, which won the 1995 Forward Prize. A selection of his work appears in *Penguin Modern Poets 5* (1995). An editor of the *Printer's Devil* magazine, he is also a critic, journalist and broadcaster. He lives in Newcastle-upon-Tyne.

**Julia O'Faolain**'s novels include *The Obedient Wife*, *No Country for Young Men* (nominated for the Booker Prize), *The Judas Cloth*, and several collections or stories. Her recent short stories have been published in the *New Yorker* and past issues of *New Writing*. Her latest novel is *The Factotum*.

**Kathy Page** has published four novels, the latest being *Frankie Styne and the Silver Man* (1992). Her short stories have been widely anthologised and are collected in *As in Music* (1990). She is now completing another collection, *Paradise and Elsewhere*, and a fifth novel, aided by an Arts Council bursary. She lives in London and works as an addiction counsellor.

**Don Paterson** was born in Dundee in 1963. He moved to London in 1984 to pursue a career as a musician. He now divides his time between London and Scotland, where he has recently held the post of Writer-in-Residence at Dundee University. His book *Nil Nil* (Faber) was a Poetry Book Society Choice, winning the Forward Prize for best first collection and a Scottish Arts Council Book Award. He has also won an Eric Gregory Award and the Arvon/Observer International Poetry Competition. He co-leads the jazz/folk group *Lammas*. *Lammas* were recently named BBC's Young Jazz Ensemble of the Year; their most recent recording is *This Morning* (EFZ). His new poetry collection, *God's Gift to Women*, will be published by Faber next year.

**Peter Redgrove**'s most recent books of verses are *Abysso-phone* and *My Father's Trapdoors*. He has recently published a book on dreaming and the female cycle with Penelope Shuttle; this is a practical version of their famous *The Wise Wound*. He has published twenty-three volumes of poetry and nine prose fictions, and fourteen of his plays have been broadcast by the BBC.

**Robin Robertson** is from the north-east coast of Scotland. In Britain, his work has appeared most recently in the *London Review of Books*, the *Observer* and the *Sunday Times*; in America, his poetry has been published in the *New Yorker*.

**Carole Satyamurti** is a poet and sociologist who teaches at the University of East London and at the Tavistock Clinic. She won the National Poetry Competition in 1986 and won an Arts Council of Great Britain writer's award in 1988. She has published three collections of poetry, *Broken Moon* (1987), *Changing the Subject* (1990) and *Striking Distance* (1994), and her poems have been broadcast on BBC Radio and TV.

**John Saul** grew up in Liverpool and lives and works in Hamburg. His stories have been published widely in the UK and in France, Italy and Germany. In anthology form they have appeared in *Best of the Fiction Magazine* and in *Sex and the City*, *Border Lines*, *Cold Comfort* and in *New Writing 4*. His novel, *Heron and Quin*, was published in 1990. He has written about the short fiction form for the *Observer*.

**Deirdre Shanahan** has published a collection of poems, *Legal Tender*, and won a major Eric Gregory Award. Her stories have appeared in a number of magazines and periodicals in Britain and the United States, and she has written drama for radio and the stage. Her story, 'Well Sorted', was published in 1995 in a Serpent's Tail anthology of prizewinning stories about London.

**Jo Shapcott** is the first person to have won the National Poetry competition twice: it was awarded for the second time in 1991 for her widely acclaimed poem, 'Phrase Book'. Her first collection, *Electroplating the Baby* (1988) was awarded a Commonwealth Prize. Her second volume, *Phrase Book* (1992), was a Poetry Book Society Choice.

**Penelope Shuttle** lives in Cornwall with her husband, Peter Redgrove. Her sixth book of poems, *Building a City for Jamie*, appears in June 1996. *Alchemy for Women*, co-authored with Peter Redgrove, their sequel to *The Wise Wound*, was published in 1995.

**Jon Silkin**'s most recent collections of verse are *The Lens-Breakers* (1992) and *Selected Poems* (1994). He has edited *The Penguin Book of First World War Poetry* and, with Jon Glover, *The Penguin Book of First World War Prose*, as well as *Wilfred Owen: The War Poems* (1994). His collection *Nature with Man* was awarded the Geoffrey Faber Memorial Prize in 1966. He is a fellow of the Royal Society of Literature. His most recent publication is *Watersmeet*, a long poem with drafts. He co-edits the literary quarterly, *Stand*.

**Pauline Stainer** has published four collections of poetry: *Little Egypt* (1987), *The Honeycomb* (1989), *Sighting the Slave Ship* (1992) and *The Ice-Pilot Speaks* (1994, winner Skoob Poetry Competition). The last three were all Poetry Book Society Recommendations. In 1994 she was chosen as one of the New Generation Poets.

**C. K. Stead** lives mainly in New Zealand. He has published nine books of poetry, seven of fiction, four of literary criticism (including *The New Poetic, Yeats to Eliot*), and edited a number of others including the Penguin *Letters & Journals of Katherine Mansfield*, and *The Faber Book of South Pacific Stories*. Three of his novels have been reissued by Harvill, most recently *All Visitors Ashore*. *The Death of the Body* has been translated into French, Swedish, German and Portuguese. He was awarded the CBE in 1985 and is a fellow of the Royal Society of Literature.

**Matthew Sweeney** was born in Donegal in 1952 and moved to London in 1973. He has published seven books of poetry, including *Blue Shoes* and *Cacti*, and, for children, *The Flying Spring Onion* and *Fatso in the Red Suit*. He is completing an eighth, *The Bridal Suite*, and co-editing with Jo Shapcott an anthology of contemporary poetry. In 1994/95 he was Writer-in-Residence at the South Bank Centre.

**George Szirtes** was born in Budapest in 1948 and was trained as a painter. His eight books of poetry include *Metro* (1988), *Bridge Passages* (1991), *Blind Field* (1994) and *Selected Poems 1976–1996* (1996). He has translated poetry and fiction, including the selected poems of Zsuzsa Rakovszky (1994) and *The Colonnade of Teeth*, an anthology of twentieth-century Hungarian poetry, co-edited with George Gömöri (1996). He has won the Faber Prize, the Cholmondeley Award and the Dery Prize and is a Fellow of the Royal Society of Literature.

**D. J. Taylor** was born in 1960. His books include three novels, *Great Eastern Land* (1986), *Real Life* (1992) and *English Settlement* (1996), and two critical studies, *A Vain Conceit: British Fiction in the 1980s* (1989) and *After the War: The Novel and England since 1945* (1993). He is currently working on a biography of Thackeray.

**N. S. Thompson** lectures in English at Christ Church, Oxford. He has published a comparative study of Boccaccio's *Decameron* and Chaucer's *Canterbury Tales*. He has translated Sciascia's *Sicilian Uncles* and Giampaolo Rugarli's *The Crux* and is poetry editor of *New Poetry Quarterly*. His poems, translations and reviews have appeared in *Ambit, Encounter, Modern Poetry in Translation, Oxford Poetry, Poetry Review, PN Review*, the *Times Literary Supplement* and elsewhere.

**Charles Tomlinson** was born in 1927. His paperback *Collected Poems* appeared in 1987 and *The Door in the Wall* in 1992. His work has been translated into in Italian, German, Spanish and Portuguese, and has inspired a large number of critical articles and four full-scale studies. In 1989 he received the Cittadella Premio Europeo for the *face-à-face* Italian edition of his poems. In 1993 he was given the *Hudson Review*'s Joseph Bennett Award in New York. Tomlinson is also a painter (*Eden: the Graphics of Charles Tomlinson*) and a literary critic (*Poetry and Metamorphosis*). He has translated widely from Spanish and Italian and edited Penguin's *Selected Poems* by Octavio Paz. His *Selected Poems of Attilio Bertolucci* was published by Bloodaxe in 1993 and *Jubilation* in 1995 (Oxford University Press).

**Lorna Tracy**, an American living in Newcastle upon Tyne, is a co-editor of *Stand Magazine*. In 1981, Virago published her story collection, *Amateur Passions*. Recently her stories have appeared in *Iron, Panurge, Bête Noire* and *The Cuirt Journal*.

**Rose Tremain** has published six novels, including *The Swimming Pool Season, Restoration* (shortlisted for the Booker Prize and winner of the *Sunday Express* Book of the Year Award) and *Sacred Country* (James Tait Black Award and Prix Fémina Etranger), and three collections of short stories, *The Colonel's Daughter, The Garden of the Villa Mollini* and *Evangelista's Fan. Restoration* has recently been filmed by Miramax, starring Robert Downey Jnr, Meg Ryan and Hugh Grant. She lives in Norfolk and London with the biographer Richard Holmes, and is currently working on a new novel, set in Paris.

**William Trevor** was born in Mitchelstown, Co. Cork. Among his books are *The Old Boys* (1964; winner of the Hawthornden Prize), *The Boarding House* (1965), *Mrs Eckdorf in O'Neill's Hotel* (1969), *Elizabeth Alone* (1973), *The Children of Dynmouth* (1976; winner of the Whitbread Fiction

Award), *Fools of Fortune* (1983; winner of the Whitbread Fiction Award), *The Silence in the Garden* (1988; winner of the *Yorkshire Post* Book of the Year Award), and *Felicia's Journey* (1994; winner of the *Sunday Express* Book of the Year and the Whitbread *Book of the Year*). His short stories have been published by Penguin in *Collected Stories*. He edited *The Oxford Book of Irish Short Stories* (1989) and has also written plays for radio and television. In 1977 he was made an honorary CBE in recognition of his services to literature. In 1992 he received the *Sunday Times* award for literary excellence.

**Stephen Watson** was born in Cape Town where he has lived for most of his life, and lectures in England at the University of Cape Town. He has published four collections of poems, among them a book of verse translations from the /Xam (or Cape Bushmen), based on nineteenth-century oral records. He is also known in South Africa for his literary and cultural essays, collected in *Selected Essays 1980–1990*. The two poems in this anthology will be included in his next selection, *Presence of the Earth*, in 1996.